The Bread Baker's Apprentice

The Bread Baker's Apprentice

MASTERING THE ART OF EXTRAORDINARY BREAD

15TH ANNIVERSARY EDITION

by Peter Reinhart

photography by Ron Manville

TEN SPEED PRESS

Berkeley

CONTENTS

Formulas

ACKNOWLEDGMENTS

What follows is a slightly updated version of the Acknowledgments text as it appeared in the 2001 edition. Without this varied and invaluable group, there would be no anniversary edition. At the end, I have included some additional thank yous that recognize the people who made this anniversary edition possible.

Creating a book of this scope takes, it seems, more than a village, and so I have unabashedly drawn upon all of the villages in which I've lived these past twenty years. Let me begin by thanking my wife, Susan, who endured yet another round of marathon writing bursts, supporting me with patience and lots of tea and vitamins.

The Ten Speed team has been fantastic at every level. Thanks begin with Publisher Kirsty Melville and Editorial Director Lorena Jones. Aaron Wehner, my editor, has been an exemplar of enthusiasm and sage guidance, proving again that behind every successful writer is a great (and overworked) editor. Art Director Nancy Austin is not only talented but also great to work with, establishing a warm, collegial atmosphere and encouraging creative ferment. Ten Speed's enormous support for this project has, I believe, evoked from me the fullness of my potential. Thank you also to Andrea Chesman, Sharon Silva, Linda Bouchard, and Ken DellaPenta for expert copyediting, proofreading, and indexing, respectively.

Ron Manville poured his heart and soul into the photography. I was extremely fortunate, upon moving to Providence, to find someone so close to home who could capture in images the vision that was in my head. It was a joy to work with him. Our creative team was completed by Linnea Leeming, who brought us incredible energy and joy, along with her inventive prop styling.

Johnson & Wales University has also supported this project with great enthusiasm. I'm especially indebted to Dean Karl Guggenmos, who allowed me to use the labs and classrooms for testing and photography, and to my department chair, Martha Crawford, who, as a world-class competition pastry chef, truly understood the nature of this undertaking. Thanks also to Pamela Peters, the director of culinary education, for her unflagging support and consistently positive attitude. The university's leadership team, including Dr. John Yena, John Bowen, Dr. Irving Schneider, Tom Wright, and Tom Farrell, sets a tone of inspiration and forward thinking. Assistant Public Relations Director Linda Beaulieu has been fantastic in helping me spread news of the bread revolution. A special thanks to my colleague Steve Kalble, a great teacher and one of the most passionate bread bakers I've ever known. Thanks also to Ciril Hitz, pastry instructor and bread artiste, who taught me many shaping techniques even while he was in training for the 2002 Coupe du Monde competition. The entire faculty at Johnson & Wales inspires me with their commitment to education and their love of the transmission of knowledge. They are, collectively, my current mentors.

My students are also my teachers, but a few must be singled out for their special contributions, helping enormously with the photo shoot and covering for me on their own time when I was on crutches. Fumie Shibazaki (pictured on the cover), Alex Molnar, Jennifer Passarella, and Rina Hosaka make me proud to be a teacher.

Before Johnson & Wales, I was nurtured at the California Culinary Academy, where I first began my exploration of *pain à l'ancienne*. While there, I was privileged to work with chefs Robert Parks, Reg Elgin, Tony Marano, Nick Snell, and many others, including Greg Tompkins, who is now doing great work for Aryzta. Thanks also to my former CCA student Peter DiCroce for his passion for *pane siciliano*, which led to the breakthrough formula in this book.

Thank you to that unique fellowship known as the Bakers Dozen and its founders, Marion Cunningham and Flo Braker, along with my fellow bread chapter editors, Fran Gage and Carol Field, and all the other chapter editors. After seven years of brainstorming and editorial meetings and countless recipe-testing workshops, *The Baker's Dozen Cookbook* came out, amazingly, the same month as this book. I learned so much about baking and the love of baking by being a part of that group.

Three local Providence bakeries contributed their support and their loaves for some of the photos. Providence, like so many cities around the country, is experiencing the bread revolution through both old and new bakeries that are adopting the slow rise fermentation principles that are causing so much excitement. Thanks to Lynn Rammrath of Seven Stars Bakery, Olga Bravo of Olga's Cup and Saucer, and Mike Manni of LaSalle Bakery for making great bread and leading the way in bringing a new level of bread awareness to Providence.

The Bread Bakers Guild of America, as always, is at the heart of the knowledge contained in this book. Didier Rosada, Greg Mistell, Peter Franklin, Amy Scherber, Toy Dupree, and

Craig Ponsford are among the hundreds of bakers who have influenced me and who have changed the bread landscape in America.

Thanks to Tim and Crystal Decker for letting me showcase them in these pages as examples of the next wave of great bakers. And we all owe a huge debt to professor Raymond Calvel, who passed on his wisdom to an entire generation.

Lionel Poilâne, Philippe Gosselin, and my Paris liaison, Stephanie Curtis, are the French trio who, unknowingly to any of us at the time, were the sparks that triggered this book. That trip would not have happened had it not been for Nick Malgieri and the James Beard Foundation, who organized the competition that sent me on my pilgrimage.

There are more than one hundred recipe testers to whom I owe a tremendous debt of gratitude. Most of them are members of the Bread Baker's List, an e-mail fellowship created by Reggie and Jeff Dwork that brings me a never-ending stream of knowledge. The following people voluntarily tested recipes and sent superb feedback that proved essential in fine-tuning the formulas: Dena Allbee, Treece Ames, Burleigh Angle, Claire Banasiak, Lorraine Begley, Kevin Bell, Deborah Bergh, Bill Bowers, Terri Brooks, Bonni Lee Brown, Dawn Burstyn, Frank Cavalier, Taimi Clark, Bev Collins, Margaret Cope, Corky Courtright, Chris Dalrymple, Carolyn Dandalides, Kathy DeStudio, Barbara Edwards, Marilee Evans, Jill Farrimond, Ellen H. G. Fenster, Rosemary Finch, Natalie Fine, Cynthia Frederick, Jo Gould, Jim Gribble, Sharon Hale, Patty Hambelton, Lois Hansen, Dulcey Heller, Jane Helwig, Jenny Hensley, Bernice Hicks, Carolyn Hollenbeck, George Hower, Alan Jackson, Beth Jarvis, Claire Johnson, Keith Johnson, Mary Jo Kingston, Eve Kinney, Rhonda Kirschman, Pat Kleinberg, Jana Koca, Susan Kristof, Jim Lawler, Dorothea Lerman, Cindy Lewellen, Heidi Lisitsky, Les Lloyd, Charlene Magee, Alexandra Mahoney, Lindell Martin, Tuffy Mattox, Justin McAteer, Yvonne McCarthy, Lynne Miles, John Murren, Jill Myers, Erin Nesmith, Lorna Noble, Valerie Norton, Ed Okie, Larronna Payne, Charles D. Perry, Larry Peters, Bill Potere, Anne Ranish, Matt Ream, Heather Reseck, Joni Respasch, Dick and Willis Richards, Maureen Riley, Shauna Roberts, Wendy Robinson, Debbie Rogers, Joanne Sawyer, Barbara Schmitt, Pat Schuster, Dan Schwartz, Jackie Silberg, Philip Silverman, Amy Smereck, Bill Snider, Jennifer Somerville, Sherri Staat, Dawn Swindells, Donal Thacker, Susan Thomas, Maggie Tucker, Terry Vlassack, Rhea M. Vogelhut, Cynthia Ware, Diana Warshay, Jon Westfall, Jo Ann Wiese, Allan Wirth, Joan Wolckenauer, John Wright, Rita Yaezel, Tamera Yoakum, and Michael Zusman.

Finally, I'm indebted to my agent, Pam Bernstein, for all of her support, counsel, and encouragement.

For this fifteenth-anniversary edition, I want to thank the following people for helping to take the original version to even greater heights.

As in the past, I must begin by praising the always dynamic Ten Speed Press team: my original editor and now Ten Speed publisher, Aaron Wehner, who conceived not only the original book but also this anniversary edition; my editor, Kim Laidlaw, along with Kelly Snowden, Ali Slagle, Ashley Matuszak, Jane Chinn, and Kate Bolen, all of whom have helped to bring this to fruition; copy editor supreme Sharon Silva, who once again, after fifteen years, continues to make me look like a better writer than I actually am; designers Debbie Berne and Chloe Rawlins; and publicists Kristin Casemore and Erin Welke.

Johnson & Wales University, my educational home for the past sixteen years, has generously supported and encouraged me in my writing and teaching. Since moving from Providence to our newest campus in Charlotte, North Carolina, I have been privileged to work for and with some wonderful people, including our first campus president, Art Gallagher; our current president, Dr. Robert Mock; Vice President of Education Tarun Malik; Culinary deans Mark Allison and Jerry Lanuzza; Dean of Baking and Pastry Wanda Cropper; department chairs, chefs Amy Felder and Jennifer Gallagher; and bread-baking colleagues, chefs Harry Peemoeller and Armin Gronert. Our entire culinary faculty is a constant source of positive inspiration and can-do attitude, and their support has buoyed me enormously during the past twelve years of book projects. And a special thanks to Laura Benoit, who has been my on-campus proofreader for my last five books, including this one.

PREFACE

I have conflicted feelings about this revised edition of *The Bread Baker's Apprentice* (*BBA*). I am in denial that I am fifteen years older than when I first wrote it. Time isn't supposed to move this quickly, though I'm slowly coming to grips with the perception that everything seems to go faster as we get older. Many incredible bread books by others have been published in the last decade and a half, which means the bread-baking community is larger and far more educated now, and that, at the very least, I must totally update the Resources section in this edition.

I have kept busy in the intervening years. I have managed to write five new books and numerous forewords and various contributions for the books of others, I have spoken and presented at national and international conferences (including an appearance on the TED site), and I have moved from the original Johnson & Wales University (JWU) Providence campus to the newest JWU campus in Charlotte, North Carolina, which I helped open and now teach at and where my wife, Susan, and I now happily reside. Yet how can it be that fifteen years have passed and that over a quarter million copies have been sold of what is now simply referred to in chat groups as the *BBA*? I've even heard of a number of *BBA* Challenge groups, in which bakers attempt to make every bread in the book, one per week, and then blog about their progress. When the first edition was published, the word *blog* had barely entered the language. The learning just never seems to ends, and despite all that I and other baker authors have written, there is still more to do, more to learn, and more to teach.

Now, as I read again what I wrote then, I have moments of pride and also some of "oops." During these fast fifteen years, the world of bread has not only gone through a dramatic and ongoing evolution but has also endured threats to its very validity by the movement against the consumption of wheat and other grains. In the original introduction to the book, which follows this preface, I'm pleased to see that so many of what later became my core themes are already expressed. In fact, I think I may have never stated them as well in any of their later iterations. I often tell people that the plot of all of my books is bread but that the theme is *connectedness*, and I've managed to ride that message, in its many variations and subsequent books, like a sturdy steed. As I reread the words in the original introduction, I wondered at times if a revised edition was even necessary. But such thoughts were soon dashed. Although the universal ideas of bread and connectedness have not and never will change, a whole lot has happened in those blink-of-an-eye years with regard to how we go about our bread making. As the final line of chapter 1 says (and it may be one of my best lines ever), "Even after six thousand years, we are still on a quest with no end in sight, trying to figure out how to make bread even better." You can now make that six thousand *and* fifteen years, and still the quest continues.

The young woman on the original cover, Fumie Shibazaki, was a nineteen-year-old freshman in my bread-baking class when photographer Ron Manville took that now-iconic shot. It was not planned; she happened to pick up the loaf to move it for us when I heard Ron say, "Wait, Fumie, don't move." Snap! It was a Polaroid, and sixty seconds later we all looked at it—Nancy Austin, our art director; Linnea, our prop stylist; a few other student helpers; my wife, Susan—and someone said (I can't remember who; after all, it was fifteen years ago!), "That's our cover."

The current editors and I had to make some decisions about how to approach this "anniversary, revised edition." Should we reshoot the photos, add new formulas, change the existing formulas, or leave well enough alone? And here's an important question faced by all publishers and authors when creating a new edition: should we shoot a new cover in order to give the book a fresh look? These are all valid questions, yet in the end we decided that the original photography was so strong and timeless that a reshoot wasn't needed. And we knew we could never top that cover. Fumie is now, like me, also fifteen years older and a pastry chef in Japan. I wanted to fly her back to shoot a new cover. My idea was that she would still be in her JWU uniform, but this time she would be holding a little child in a chef's jacket who is holding a look-alike large *miche*. It would have been epic but, then again, why mess with a classic? (However, if you look at the very end of the book, you will see an updated photo of Fumie with her nephew.)

Rather than rewrite the chapter introductions and the headnotes for each of the breads, we decided that I would add new comments, where appropriate, to support the existing text. If I have tweaked a recipe, a note of explanation will usually appear. I have, however, added some new text regarding methodology improvements, such as more use of the stretch-and-fold method, which can be applied in place of, or in addition to, the original mixing method (see page 58). The sourdough method, beginning on page 238, has also been updated, which is a result of my own learning curve, helped along by other professionals as well as a slew of non-professional SBEs ("Serious Bread Enthusiasts," otherwise known as home bakers). Finally, as a bonus, I have added three new recipes/formulas to help further narrow the gap of that fifteen-year learning curve.

One of my proudest achievements in the original *BBA* was the introduction of the delayed fermentation method, which was inspired by Philippe Gosselin in Paris and is illustrated in the recipe for *pain à l'ancienne* on page 199. I predicted it could and would have huge implications for bakers, and I enjoyed watching that prediction come true through the works of Jim Lahey (the *New York Times*'s famous No Knead Bread), Zoë François and Jeff Hertzberg (the *Artisan Bread in Five Minutes a Day* series), Nancy Baggett (*Kneadlessly Simple*), and other authors and bakers, especially those now using these methods in their bakeries. Looking back, it all seems so obviously intuitive, applying the advanced techniques of fermentation, pre-fermentation, and enzyme activity in their infinite variations of manipulating time, temperature, and ingredients. Yet when we compare the recent books with the many that preceded them, it's immediately apparent how far we've all come.

I started my bakery in 1986, making all my breads by measuring the ingredients in scoops and cups. It took me another seven years to discover ratios and percentages, the invaluable baker's math that turns a recipe into a formula. That one piece of fundamental information changed my life and opened a universe of possibilities. When I became a bread instructor and first-time author, it was the question that my students asked—what would happen if I did this instead of that?—or the question that interviewers frequently asked—what is it about bread that makes it so special?—that forced me to grow in search of answers. These were the questions that drove me deeper into the craft and made me realize that although some of the knowledge was already out there, perhaps some of it was still waiting to be discovered. It was surprising at first to find out that, despite thousands of years of baking knowledge behind us, there were more bread frontiers to be explored. This book, this *BBA*, blew those doors open for me and initiated a quest that keeps leading to new and newer frontiers. The one thing I now know with certainty is that the quest for knowledge, especially for self-knowledge, never ends. Being an eternal apprentice, I have learned, is a state of mind.

INTRODUCTION

Acorns were good enough until bread was invented.
—DECIMUS JUNIUS JUVENALIS, AD 125

I used to be a professional baker, happily making bread in beautiful Sonoma County, California. Somehow, through a series of events complexly intertwined with many other facets of my life, I found myself serving as a teacher of bread baking at the world's largest culinary school, Johnson & Wales University, in Providence, Rhode Island. Rhode Island itself isn't much bigger than Providence, the entire state seeming like a large metropolitan area consisting of the city and its suburbs, the whole of which is smaller than Sonoma County. Rhode Island is quite beautiful in its own way, but it is not the charm and beauty that brought me to either Sonoma County or Providence. I chronicled this journey in a previous book, so I won't rehash its intricacies, but I will sum up one of the themes: Having learned so much from many teachers during my own life's apprenticeships, I find a great deal of meaning and purpose in transmitting knowledge, whether it be about bread or any other aspect of life. Producing successful students gives me even more pleasure than producing successful bread.

Since my first book, *Brother Juniper's Bread Book: Slow Rise as Method and Metaphor*, was published more than twenty-five years ago, dozens of superb bread books have appeared. These include recipe collections with hundreds of variations on every type of bread imaginable, from every culture, with infinite shapes and blends of grains. *The Baker's Catalogue*, produced by the good people at King Arthur Flour (see Resources, page 314), has grown from a sort of underground journal to a popularly discussed source of supplies and folklore among the thousands of "bread-heads" sprouting like malted barley across the country. Bread machines have become common household gadgets, and many of them are actually

◂ Baguettes proofing on a *couche*.

1

being used and are not just sitting on the counter like last year's toy. The recipe books for bread machines are among the best sources for esoteric single-loaf recipes, some of them of the family-heirloom variety. Whenever I want quick information on the "backstory" of a particular type of bread, usually in response to a question from one of my students, one of the first places I check is my collection of bread-machine recipe books. "World encyclopedia" books on bread, "ultimate" books on bread, books on artisan breads and the bakers who make them, and numerous websites and e-groups dedicated solely to the growing national passion for bread baking have also become part of the bread landscape.

I wanted to call one of my recent books *The Bread Revolution,* but that sounded too militant ("After all, what are they revolting against?" one editor asked me). We tried *Bread Renaissance,* but I thought that sounded too elitist, and the most famous person who made a snobbish remark about bread, Marie Antoinette, lost her head over it ("Let them eat brioche," she was reported to have shouted when asked for her final words). After serious brainstorming, we came up with *Crust & Crumb: Master Formulas for Serious Bread Bakers,* and I'm glad we did. I loved the sound of that title and so did many readers who commented on its aptness. It allowed me to pursue what I think of as my personal teaching mission: synthesizing information and reformulating it into usable knowledge for current times. The "master formula" concept helped home bakers, and even some professional ones, take a step away from recipe dependence toward thinking like a baker. This means thinking formulaically and structurally and then baking by an elusive quality called feel, not just blindly following a recipe without knowing the reasons behind certain steps. (Interestingly, many years later, in 2014, I did publish a book called *Bread Revolution* with the same publisher, which reminded me never to give up on a good title.)

Knowledge is power, and I think a teacher's job is all about the empowerment of his or her students, regardless of the subject. A bread baker, like any true artisan, must have the power to control outcomes. This concept of empowerment is a universal principle and one of the reasons I love teaching. It's what made ancient craft guilds so important and powerful. Whether the aspiring artisan was a baker, carpenter, mason, butcher, candlestick maker, or chef, a guild apprenticeship put initiates on common ground with others, establishing a shared understanding of what made life meaningful. Coupled with religious influences, and the basic three R's, guild training was a foundation peg in keeping the spirit of quality, beauty, and goodness alive in the world. With this book, I want to forge into the next frontier with you, beyond simply making bread, and on to explore its possibilities from the inside out to

BAGUETTE
$2.25

SEVEN
STARS
BAKERY

empower you to control the outcomes of your bread-baking pursuits. My goal is to teach you to fly without controls, by feel, the way a good pilot must from time to time.

When I began writing this book, my working title was *Deconstructing Bread*. It is a cute phrase, but as any philosophy student knows, true deconstructionism is a rather austere course. It means stripping away romance and myth and looking at the thing itself, without preconceived biases and notions. As anyone who has read my previous work knows, I am not a deconstructionist. I love myth and romance, and I think bread is the perfect mythic symbol to explain the meaning of life. If making bread were simply clinical, bread would not have such a powerful influence in our lives, both historically and spiritually. So my goal in breaking

it down to its essence runs into treacherous ground. I want to pop out on the other side, like our baking guild forebears, into a place where the mythic and romantic have even more power and bring us even more joy, because we have achieved a new level of understanding.

In *The Bread Baker's Apprentice,* we examine bread through the framework of the classic twelve stages of baking. This is the structure that forms the broad strokes of our inquiry and gives us a context. Within that context we will go deeper and deeper, establishing infrastructure along the way. My goal is not to make you into a dogmatically doctrinal baker, what I call a letter-of-the-law baker. Instead, I want to help you become a spirit-of-the-law baker, that is, one who has a sense of what the options are and is thus free to choose the options that will bring about the desired outcomes. I want to turn you into a baker who might even transcend structure and break through into new frontiers, applying knowledge to make bread that pushes the envelope. This kind of freedom can only come, as the universal principles converge with baking principles, when you have mastered the outer form and structures or at least understand them. Mastery comes with practice. Understanding comes from hanging in there with me, keeping an open mind, and also revisiting your other baking books with a fresh eye (don't ever abandon those classics!).

There aren't hundreds of formulas in this book, but there are many (more than fifty) enough to empower you to make extraordinary versions of these classics, sometimes using innovative techniques that can then be applied to any other recipe or formula you encounter elsewhere. After years of baking, I have discovered that while everyone has certain favorite breads, some sentimental preferences related to taste memories or some for cultural reasons, it is not the exotic flavor or the innovative ingredient that brings one back again and again to a particular loaf. It is the perfect execution in that bread of the manipulation of time and temperature, evoking the fullest potential of flavor from the grain. That is what creates excitement and buzz. I have long contended that pizza will be memorable, regardless of how fancy the toppings are, only if the crust is truly great (and how few there are that meet this standard). It is the same with all bread.

Since I have promised you an adventure, the first chapter opens with a story and then it gets into the nuts and bolts of the process. After that, I explain my baking assumptions and choices so that you will understand how to follow the master formulas that follow. And finally, we begin the process itself, applying the unfolding concepts to a number of master formulas.

ONE

What Is It About Bread?

On August 7, 1999, on a drizzly, chilly day typical of the region, thousands of pilgrims flooded a four-block area of southwest Portland, Oregon, in a park near Portland State University. They didn't come for religious reasons but rather to venerate with religious zeal their newly emerged passion for the world's most symbolically evocative food-stuff: bread. And it was not just bread, but good-as-it-gets bread, made by artisans of the Pacific Northwest using techniques discovered either accidentally or from the dissemination of arcane knowledge brought to this country only recently by European bakers through the Bread Bakers Guild of America, itself a throwback to days of yore. The Summer Loaf Festival, as it was called, was among the first of what soon became a nationwide parade of trib-utes to the hottest food trend since, well, sliced bread. (Note: The actual first bread festival, which had been held two years earlier in Sonoma County, California, was cleverly called the Grainaissance Fair.)

The French call it simply *pain ordinaire*, "ordinary bread." What the new, young American bakers had discovered, and what they proudly displayed in dozens of booths at Summer Loaf, is that many layers of flavor are hidden within the four ingredients of flour, water, salt, and yeast that make up the sole components of true French bread. They have taken up the timeless baker's challenge of evoking from the wheat its fullest potential, finding ways of unraveling the tasteless starch molecules that comprise the bulk of a loaf by attempting to spring free the simple sugars that are woven within the complex but unassailable starch carbohydrates. When they successfully accomplish this, using bakers' tricks that are both ancient and mod-ern, layers of flavor emerge as if from one of those magic-eye, three-dimensional, there-it-is-wait-where-did-it-go paintings. Flavors slowly come into focus as the palate, with its five flavor zones, aided by the chewing process and the release of salivic enzymes, encounters it first in the sweet zone, eliciting an "ahhh, this is nice," reaction. Then the salty zone kicks in, an "oohhh," followed by another level of either sweetness or sourness (depending on the bread), along the sides of the tongue, calling forth a "hmnnn, whoaa. . . ." Finally, just at the swallowing point, the mouth floods in the umami, or rich zone in the back central region, with a nutlike flavor that perfumes its way into the sinuses, where it lingers for as long as fifteen to thirty minutes, re-creating with every inhalation the inimitable finish of a proper, world-class bread—the inevitable "yessss!" (accompanied by appropriate victorious arm pumping, in some instances). This flavor joy is in addition to the various auditory pleasures of the sound of crust, crackling and crumbling under the pressure of the chew, and the visual satisfaction caused by both the rich, dusty, reddish-gold caramelization of crust and the blooming of the loaf along the slash marks. The blooming produces what the French call the *grigne,* an ear of crisp crust that neatly separates from the loaf like a proudly curled lip. Bread this good must also be beautiful; after all, in our culinary schools it is taught that we eat first with our eyes.

I teach bread baking in a large culinary school. My students are mostly young wannabe and soon-to-be pastry chefs and bakers, and I have less than nine days to teach them everything—or nearly everything—I know about bread. What I'd like to do is first send them to Summer Loaf and Grainaissance festivals, or to Paris with its hundreds of bread shops, so they can be swept into the romance of the bread revolution as I have been. Instead, what I am required to do is teach them formulas and how to safely work the ovens and use stationary and spiral mixers, powerful tools that will rip off their hands if they get too anxious and prematurely feel their dough. Since feeling the dough is really where the magic begins, I rapidly make my way through the boring but necessary safety requirements to get to the stuff of which baker's dreams are made. Usually somewhere around the third or fourth day, it—the magic—happens for most of my students.

In *Zen and the Art of Motorcycle Maintenance,* a book that came out, coincidentally, around the same time as the Tassajara Bakery began selling bread made by American Zen Buddhist students in San Francisco, Robert Pirsig wrote of two kinds of motorcycle riders. Some like to tinker with their bikes, making sure they are tooled just right, and the others just like to ride and feel the wind against their cheeks. Bread bakers are like that, too. The more technical and mechanical bakers often go to Manhattan, Kansas, where there is a superb school called the American Institute of Baking. There they learn all about the properties of wheat and the effect of multitudinous sugars upon various strains of yeast. They learn dough formulas, and they learn about equipment options and methodologies. Graduates of this program become valuable technical bakers, usually for large companies, and earn good salaries, troubleshooting problems and guaranteeing consistency in operations that may produce forty thousand or more loaves a day.

The other type of baker, the wind-on-cheek baker, often opens a small bakeshop and makes what has become known as artisan bread, the term *artisan* having been driven, sadly, to near meaninglessness by its recent ubiquity. These are the bakers who tend to rhapsodize about their loaves. ("They are *loaves;* please don't call them products.") Many of them travel to Europe, making pilgrimages to the house of Poilâne or Ganachaud or Kayser, and gather at bread bakers' guildhall meetings, held whimsically throughout the year, to discuss the merits of various baguette-shaping techniques or the hydration potential of their latest experimental ciabatta. They philosophize, read and write books, and argue about the ever-shifting line between the true artisan and the mass producer or the merits of supporting small-scale wheat farmers who grow heirloom strains. These bakers get very excited every time they learn a new technique or hear that the French professor Raymond Calvel might be coming to town. (Note: When I first wrote these words, the esteemed bread teacher of bread teachers was in his late eighties and had already committed his knowledge to a superb series of videos he made with the Bread Bakers Guild of America in 1994. He passed away in 2005.) When they go to France, Germany, or anywhere where good bread might be found, these artisans come back with new ideas and add ever more dialogue to the still-building buzz.

My students, being younger than these entrepreneurial bakers who have now changed the American bread paradigm, may become either technical or romantic bakers, or a hybrid of the two, or they may never get grabbed by the bread-*geist*. Many of them initially view my class as a necessary prerequisite to get them to the plated-dessert or wedding-cake class, but then find themselves inexplicably falling under the spell of *pain au levain, ciabatta al funghi,* or *pain à l'ancienne*. Some fight against the discipline of repetitive drills, shaping baguette after baguette—not a simple matter—and trying in vain to match their slashes, or scoring cuts, in a consistent pattern. I never know on the first day who of my twenty or so students will emerge on the ninth day as bread revolutionaries, but I know some of them will. It usually happens before they taste the *pain à l'ancienne,* but if it hasn't happened by then, that is the bread that seduces them. If it still doesn't happen, I pray, having taken my best shot, that they will discover their culinary awakening in the chocolate or cake class.

Many of my former students have long since graduated and are working in the field, sending e-mails or dropping in from time to time to share their "war" stories. A number of them tell me it was the *pain à l'ancienne* that first grabbed hold of their imagination, and now that they are out and exposed to even more varieties, they can't seem to get bread out of their systems, even if they have become pastry chefs rather than bakers.

I learned about *pain à l'ancienne* in Paris in 1996, when I went over to collect on my prize for winning the James Beard National Bread Competition in 1995. I won with a simple sourdough, a country *boule* (ball), made with an unusually high proportion of sourdough starter. I baked my winning loaves at Amy's Breads on the west side of Manhattan, rushing them straight from Amy's many-thousand-dollar Bongard steam-injected oven into the trunk of my friend Joel's car. He's a locksmith and thus knows the fastest ways through town, and he safely delivered me and the bread to the James Beard House in Greenwich Village.

The Beard House is one of the meccas of the American food scene. When James Beard, the rotund food writer and America's most famous gourmand, died in 1982, a group of his friends and colleagues started a foundation in his memory to perpetuate interest in the burgeoning American culinary explosion. They eventually paid off the mortgage on his house and turned it into a sort of museum and dining showcase for up-and-coming and seminal chefs, regularly hosting theme meals prepared by various culinary artists brought to town for the occasion. They also bestow prestigious cookbook awards and honor the top American chefs every year at their gala, an Oscar-like ceremony aptly called the James Beard Awards.

The bread competition was organized for the Beard Foundation by author and teacher Nick Malgieri, the head baking instructor at the Peter Kump's New York Cooking School (renamed the Institute of Culinary Education, or ICE, in 2001) and a onetime acquaintance of the late James Beard. Prior to the finals, Nick traveled around the United States staging regional competitions, inviting the eight regional winners to New York for the final bake-off in January 1995.

I had won the California regional in October by unexpectedly defeating Craig Ponsford, who a few months later would win the world championship of breads at the Coupe du Monde de la Boulangerie competition in Paris, the so-called Bread Olympics. I believe the California regional Beard competition was the only time Craig ever lost a head-to-head competition. When I, in false modesty, whispered to him after my name was announced, "I can't believe it," he understandably responded, "Me neither." His loaves were a multigrain sourdough, perfectly formed, loaded with complex flavors, made at Artisan Bakers, his bakery in Sonoma. My two large sourdough *boules*, made from a starter I'd been cultivating for about three months, were baked at home on a pizza stone and spritzed with water from a plant mister. It was an experimental dough, using a ratio of about 80 percent starter to fresh flour, very unusual as most sourdoughs use only about 25 to 35 percent starter to flour. The loaves came out of the oven somewhat misshapen, having spread sideways and upward. The cuts were okay but not particularly attractive, blooming to form only a slight *grigne* but without creating any ears. The crust had a wonderful golden glow and was blistered from the long overnight proofing in my refrigerator. By true French standards this would not have been a winning bread, but on that particular day, with those particular judges, the rustic quality and the bold sour flavors gave it a small edge over Craig's perfect, but less rustic, loaves. I happily collected my regional prize, which was a free trip to New York City to compete in the finals, knowing I would have to do better to stand any chance of winning the real prize: a week in Paris to study with the *boulanger* of my choice.

There is a huge difference between baking bread in a real bread oven and a home oven, but even the best oven cannot produce great bread if the dough itself is not fermented properly. Fermentation is the key to world-class bread, assuming that the flour and other ingredients are good. I was able to win the regional event because I had great dough going into the less-than-great electric oven in my home. Compensating for a lack of real steam with plant misters and other oven tricks to simulate the blast of steam a good Bongard, Tibiletti, or Werner & Pfleiderer hearth oven produces was an audacious, but successful, attempt to prove a point. In my opinion, the quality of the dough is responsible for at least 80 percent of the finished product, while the oven is worth only about 20 percent. When I got to Amy's Breads, I was able to create an even better dough than my regional batch, having had three months of practice to refine my formula and mixing times.

Amy Scherber and Toy Dupree, the owners of Amy's Breads, were kind enough to let me work around their production schedule during the competition. Amy is one of the leading personalities in the American bread revolution, a founding board member of the Bread Bakers Guild of America, and a smart businesswoman. One of the signature items at Amy's Breads is a semolina twist that simply flies off the shelf. Tasting her bread confirmed my own growing interest in semolina bread, or *pane siciliano*, as I call it on page 207, which is a good example of how the bread revolution spreads.

Making bread in someone else's bakery is a challenge, and I had to estimate fermentation times based on ambient temperature because Amy's did not, at that time, have a temperature-controlled proof box. One of the keys to my formula is leaving the shaped loaves in the refrigerator overnight for their final slow-rise fermentation (known as retarding the dough). This allows the bacterial fermentation to catch up to the wild-yeast fermentation (two types of fermentation plus a whole lot of enzyme action are at the heart of sourdough bread) and allows the starches to unwind into sugars as the dough slowly rises to its appropriate pre-bake size. When I arrived the following morning to bake off the loaves, I discovered I had miscalculated the temperature of the walk-in refrigerator, and my loaves were far from ready to go into the oven. I had to find a way to warm them, to wake them up, so that they could complete their rise. Without a proof box on a cold, snowy New York morning, I was at the mercy of ingenuity. Amy told me the warmest place in the bakery was at the top of the stairs leading to the basement. "That's where I put my doughs when they're too small," she advised. "But watch out for the stairs—don't let the racks roll down" was her final warning. I rolled my two racks of shaped bread dough, each loaf nestled in a canvas-lined bentwood willow basket (or *banneton*, as it is called in France) to the top of the stairs where a warm breeze drifted from the basement. It was 8:00 a.m., and I needed to have finished bread ready to transport by noon, when Joel would arrive to wend us through the icy streets to the Village. There was nothing I could do but wait and hope the dough would wake up and respond to

Finished country *boules* emerge from Seven Stars Bakery's Spanish-made oven in Providence, Rhode Island.

the warmth with some movement. I parked the rolling racks at the top of the stairs, warning everyone on the production team not to jostle them lest they tumble into the abyss. I then went across Ninth Avenue to get a bagel and read the Sunday *Times*, a pleasure I had been denied during the twenty-five years I lived in California.

Two hours later I returned to the bakery, relieved to find the racks still at the top of the stairs, but the dough was still undersized. I decided that 11:00 a.m. was my drop-dead time. I killed the hour by hanging out with the bakers, shaping loaves with them, talking bread philosophy—the usual baker stuff—and then took my loaves, still looking too small, to the oven, hoping they'd give me a good oven spring when the steam engulfed them. I had made two sizes: a nineteen-ounce *bâtard*, or torpedo-shaped loaf, and some three-pound *miches*, or large *boules*. I lined them up on the conveyor loader, scored them with either crosshatch pound signs, angled slashes, or asterisk stars, and pushed the conveyor into the eight-foot-deep oven deck. This action engaged the flanges of the loader into special brake slots, and then I pulled the conveyor out of the oven as it neatly dropped the loaves, one by one, onto the stone deck. After the deck was loaded, I pushed the steam button, causing a large blast of steam to billow out into the oven for twenty seconds. The steam moistened the skins of the dough to prevent them from gelatinizing too quickly, allowing the loaves to spring to their full size as the yeast completed its final feeding frenzy, at least until the center of the loaves reached 140°F (60°C), killing the last of that most useful of fungi. The oven kick, as it's called, usually produces a size increase of 10 to 15 percent. But on this particular day, in that particular oven, with my particular dough, the loaves kicked a whopping 20 percent, bloomed open perfectly, producing *grignes* distinct enough to allow me to carry each loaf by its ear. The caramelization of the crust, the distinct Maillard reaction unique to bread and just a few other products, was a rich golden brown with tones of red, so soothing to the eye, so appealing and appetizing that it could, and did, induce tears.

As if on cue, Joel pulled up to the shop, moved his locksmithing tools around in the trunk to make room, and helped me load the bread, about thirty loaves, into empty flour sacks. Then it was hugs to the bakers, good luck, good luck, good luck, thank you, thank you, thank you, and we were off to the Beard House. Once there, we chose the two most perfect specimens for the judges, placed the others under the table, went around the corner to a café for cappuccino and hot chocolate, and, knowing there was nothing more we could do but wait for the judging, caught up on old times. Joel had just sold a book of locksmith stories to a publisher, and I had just sold a bread-book concept to a different publisher, so we talked writer talk instead of bread talk. It's very similar.

An hour later, we went back for the announcements. The competitor whose bread impressed me the most was Biagio Settepani of the Bruno Bakery in Brooklyn. His loaves were not as visually stunning as mine, but the flavor was spectacular, with a sweet, creamy crumb that was as satisfying as a bowl of Cream of Wheat on a cold winter morning. He and his young son worked at the opposite side of the table from me as we, and the other finalists, cut small slices of our loaves for the hundreds of guests and spectators to taste. The other competitors had flown in from Texas, Oregon, Washington, St. Louis, and Boston. All the breads were wonderful. One was a four-pound rye bread with a cocoa-stenciled floral design baked onto the crust. Another looked just like my loaves, but the inside, the crumb, was tighter and a little dry. Mine were probably the best I'd ever baked: The inside and outside, the crumb and the crust, were perfectly matched; the flavor and texture of the crumb, its mouthfeel, was cool and creamy even while still warm from the oven (with bread, the antithesis of cool is not warm but dry). The sour was properly complex, changing flavors in the mouth with each chew. What I call the "loyalty factor" kicks in just after swallowing, as the lactic and acetic acids produced by the bacterial fermentation work their way into the sinuses for the "thirty-minute finish." When the judges announced that I had won, I was relieved but not shocked. If not then, then never. I called my wife, Susan, in Santa Rosa, and when she answered the phone, I sang the first few words of "La Marseillaise." She squealed with delight. We were going to France.

．　．　．　．　．

It took a year and a half to arrange the logistics for the trip. The prize money made available from Godiva Chocolate through the James Beard Foundation was supposed to be used to underwrite a one-week *stage*, or training session, with a baker of my choice in Paris. Stephanie Curtis, an American living in Paris, was the liaison, and I was told to contact her to work out the details. I asked her if it would be possible to meet with five bakers for one day each, rather than one baker for five days. I didn't really want to spend my time in Paris making bread while Susan went out alone to sightsee and shop. What I really wanted was a crash tour of the best bread bakers and enough time to interview them and pick their brains. I figured two hours per baker. My interest was as a writer and teacher more than as a commercial baker, and I was looking for a thread, something to bring back to my students that I didn't know and that they might not hear about any other way.

Stephanie was kind enough to rent us her second apartment, in Montmartre, and we took possession on a clear day in early June, excited to be in an exciting part of town, totally intimidated by the Parisian reputation and our own lack of worldliness. On our first foray to a café, Susan ordered us two bottles of "*avion.*" When the bartender started making engine sounds and flapping his arms, she realized her gaffe, correctly ordered "Evian," and, actually, it broke the ice for us. After that, Stephanie served as our translator and escorted us on the various bakery tours so we encountered no more "aeroplanes."

We got off to a rather weird beginning by getting thrown out of the Centre de Formation Technologique Ferrandi, the national academy of baking. Apparently, the instructor who approved our visit forgot to inform his superior, who was extremely upset when he saw us observing a class in session. No amount of explanation by either Stephanie or the instructor could convince him it was a simple communication error. He insisted we leave, which we did, but not before I had a chance to witness the young students. They were between sixteen and eighteen years old, doing some of their daily drills, each student responsible for shaping about fifty perfect baguettes and an equal number of croissants or Danish pastries, an exercise they would do for the two years of their training. I realized in that brief moment, before getting tossed out, the yin and yang of the French national training. On the one hand, every graduate would have outstanding fundamental skills; on the other, he (and there were only men) would be too invested in certain methods to be open to unconventional or alternative approaches. Since only a rare apprentice would ever have the desire to break from the pack, this concern would seem, especially at such an early stage, to be of little consequence. The upside of such rigorous training highlighted the vast difference between the French and American systems. (Well, there actually isn't an existing American system, which is my point.)

Ferrandi's Monsieur B., as I shall call him, confirmed our initial fears that the French would be arrogant and nasty. Fortunately, he turned out to be the exception. No other visit on our tour was anything but warm and pleasant. Stephanie took us to the Ritz Hotel where we had a tour of the bakeshop with master *boulanger* and executive pastry chef Bernard Burban, who showed us, among other things, how the Ritz bakers made their signature *clafouti* tartlets with brioche crusts.

The next day I visited L'Autre Boulangerie, the bakery of Michel Cousin. What makes his operation unique is the unconventional variety of his bread offerings. Throughout the week, he makes as many as thirty different types of bread, not all on the same day of course, but according to a menu of daily specials. He makes multigrains, sun-dried tomato loaves, various herb-and-cheese *bâtards,* and gigantic loaves of rye that appear to weigh about six pounds each. He was the only baker I met who was interested in what American bakers were doing, where they were getting their ingredients, and how they came up with their ideas. In this sense, Cousin's bakery was American in spirit in that it reached for distinction instead of conformity, pushing the envelope of local customs and taking conceptual risks.

One of the things about American bread bakers that has allowed us to catch up so quickly to our better-trained and tradition-steeped European brethren is our unshackled nature. The yang of Ferrandi, its anchorage in very specific methodologies, is the yin of the American approach. In a society that values its bread a certain way, as the French do, it is not easy to break from the pack. In the States we haven't quite established if there is a pack and what it ought to look like. Having shared his vision of unbounded bread possibilities, I was pleased to be able to give back to M. Cousin the name of a friend of mine who produces sun-dried tomatoes in Healdsburg, California. "It is amazing how expensive it is to bring them in from Italy even though it's so close," Cousin remarked.

The next day we made one of our most anticipated visits, to the Latin Quarter and the Cherche-Midi location of Lionel Poilâne's mother-house bakery. The window was filled with two-kilo *miches,* the famous flour-crusted *pains Poilâne* that have become the icon of the bread revolution. This is what the new breed of bread freak calls "real bread," made with mostly whole grain flour and wild-yeast pre-ferments. The loaves are big, heavy, crusty, and reputed to taste better on the third day than the first (Poilâne's own assessment of the flavors). He greeted us warmly with steaming coffee, tea, and croissants in his small office, the walls covered with dozens of canvases of bread art and the ceiling hung with a working bread-dough chandelier he'd made for Salvador Dali thirty-some years ago.

After the initial greetings, Poilâne escorted us down an old, flour-dusted, stone-and-mortar spiral staircase to the cavelike oven room in the basement of the building. Here we met one of his young apprentices, or disciples, since one of the Poilâne rules of hiring is that his apprentices not have worked at another bakery or been trained in one of the formal academies. "I have a vision, the Poilâne vision, of how bread should be made. It is too difficult to train one who has picked up the habits of the schools," he told us without pretension. In pressing for more details, I was able to discern some of the critical points that drive this personal vision. Much has to do with commitments to the ingredients and to the baking process. As much of the work as possible should be done by hand, by one person taking responsibility for his loaves from start to finish—no assembly line. Each loaf is the expression of an artisan accurately following the methodology determined by Lionel Poilâne as he (and his brother Max, who also has quite a following at his own *boulangeries*) learned it from his father. The wood-fired oven, designed by Lionel, has no temperature gauge on it, forcing the baker to determine by feel when it is time to put in the loaves. Much of the training that a Poilâne apprentice gets involved developing a feel for the dough, the baker's touch.

The cave was barely big enough for the four of us and the apprentice. We watched the young baker work his station, peeling two dozen two-kilo loaves into the small aperture and onto the hot stone hearth. The stone deck was heated by bringing up the flames from the firebox below the baking deck. The flames made their way through a connecting hole filled by a curved metal tube that swiveled around to direct them into all the corners of the oven chamber. After the oven reached the proper temperature, the swivel was removed and the hole was covered by a metal bowl filled with water. As the water heated up, it provided a touch of moisture and preserved the even distribution of the heat.

The Poilâne loaves, these two-kilo country *miches*, have become so distinctively associated with Poilâne that it is easy to forget that hundreds of other bakers throughout France make similar loaves called the same thing. They are round, not too high, about four inches thick and twelve inches in diameter, dusty with the excess surface flour from the *bannetons* in which the unbaked dough has its final rise. The cut marks are done in a broad pound (#) sign (now often referred to as a hashtag sign), scored close to the edge of the loaf so as almost to square the circle. The dough includes some whole wheat flour, unlike the more common baguette that is Paris's other great bread treasure. It is naturally leavened by a wild-yeast starter, passed from batch to batch, creating a distinctively sour, but not too sour, chewy, crusty bread designed to last a family for close to a week, the flavors changing each day as the bread tempers. The French do not prize sourness as, say, San Franciscans do. Poilâne insists that the peak flavor comes forth on the third day. I found it tasted best about three hours after it emerged from the oven, but I am, after all, an unsophisticated American with an American's palate and thus less susceptible to the third-day subtleties of the well-tempered loaf.

M. Poilâne invited us to take a tour of his *manufacture* in Bièvres, about fifteen miles outside of Paris. It is here that Poilâne's arguably greatest contribution to the craft of modern artisan baking is found. In a round building in this suburban town, Poilâne has made a statement and a fortune producing thousands of his *miches* for distribution throughout France and into foreign lands, including a few dozen shipped regularly to select American clientele in New York and Chicago. Here is how he does it: Twenty-four ovens are strategically placed around the circumference of the building, each one an exact replica of the older oven we saw in action back at Cherche-Midi. Each oven exists in a space—not as dungeonlike and charming as in Paris, but equally functional—that includes a dough mixer, a fermentation bin, an old-time baker's balance scale, a stack of *bannetons,* and some long metal pans for the signature sandwich rye breads also made here. In the large arenalike center of the building, accessible by truck through big doors that open as needed, is the most impressive pile of firewood I have ever seen. Cord after cord after cord of hard French oak circumnavigate the hall, and above the woodpile, hovering like a master of ceremonies, is a claw on a track. Upon command, the claw scoops up some of the wood and transports it to a chute (there are twelve around the walls). Like an arcade gift game, the prized wood slides to an awaiting baker on the other side of the wall. The chutes deposit the wood in the space between every two bakeshops, from which the bakers collect it and stack it and eventually build their own fires timed to peak and heat just when the dough is ready to be baked.

This ingenious design allows Poilâne to stay true to his vision of handcrafted loaves, with each loaf made by one and only one baker. Each baker is responsible for three hundred loaves per day, which adds up to quite a number when all ovens are fired. At the time of our visit, only sixteen ovens were actually being used because, as Poilâne's production manager explained to us, the *manufacture* (which literally means "made by hand") was designed with a ten-year growth plan in mind. It opened two years prior to our visit with only fourteen of the ovens in use, and each year one of the unused ovens is to be fired up and added to the operation. Each year a new baker must also be trained and added to the flock of what I call *le culte de Poilâne.* Eight years of growth potential remained for this location, at which time all the ovens will be in use and it will max out. If demand for the bread continues to exceed production, this will be accommodated not by forcing more production from each baker but by building a new facility. When I did the math, figuring that at wholesale prices of about ten dollars a loaf, plus the few other products like the rye bread and Poilâne's famous apple tarts, Boulangerie Poilâne must be doing close to twenty million dollars a year. (Note: Lionel and his wife, Iréna, died tragically in a helicopter crash off the coast of Brittany in 2002; the bakery is now run by their daughter Apollonia.)

With the Poilâne bakery sales numbers dancing in my head, I took my two gift loaves home, the street folk of Montmartre staring with envy as they recognized not one but two loaves of Poilâne gold under my arm. One of the loaves lasted us the rest of the week. The other I took with me to dinner the following night along with a baguette from the Boulangerie Gosselin, where, with my head still swimming with *la vision de Poilâne*, I learned how to make *pain à l'ancienne*. Learning that technique was perhaps the single most important thing—at least bread thing—that happened to me on this trip.

Gosselin is a young man, perhaps in his early thirties, who presides over a small, not-too-fancy bakeshop on rue Saint-Honoré, not too far from the Louvre. Like many bakers, his revenue is derived in equal proportion from three main categories: bread, pastries, and lunch items, primarily sandwiches. The pastries and sandwiches appeared rather typical, and I wondered why Stephanie chose this place as one of the five definitive stops in my itinerary. The baguettes looked like those in most other shops, but next to them was a second rack of breads, looking like baguettes, only dustier with surface flour and not as deeply browned nor as distinctively scored (slashed). She pointed to those and said, "That's why I brought you here. This baguette, the *pain à l'ancienne,* won the award for best in the city this year. You must try it."

Gosselin himself brought us into the back of his shop, proud to show off the improvements he'd made since taking over the operation and buying the place from the master baker with whom he'd apprenticed for five years. He led us down a staircase to an underground bakeshop, where we followed a strange-looking tube device that hugged the walls through the catacomb until it and we popped out into a perfect little pastry kitchen, with new ceramic tile walls and floors, climate controlled to maintain the ideal temperature of 60°F (16°C) so necessary for chocolate and for butter-laminated pastries such as croissants and Danish pastries. It was clear that Gosselin was proud of this underground oasis, but I was still wondering about the wormy tube that we followed through the corridors.

"That," he explained through Stephanie, "is where the flour comes in." Eventually we were able to grasp the cleverness of the system. No one wants to carry fifty-pound sacks of flour down a staircase to a storeroom, so instead, a few times a week, a flour truck pulls up and blows the flour through the tube to a holding silo in the basement. From there the flour can be released through a gravity-fed device and scaled for mixing. Very easy, no heavy lifting, and voilà, everyone is happy.

In a room separate from the pastry shop, clearly not renovated, was the bread shop. Unlike some of the other *boulangeries* we visited, like Boulangerie Ganachaud, birthplace of the *poolish* (sponge-method) baguette, where wood-fired baking was an important part of the artisan image, Gosselin relied on a standard four-deck, gas-heated hearth oven with a conveyor loader. The oven is not where the Gosselin *pain à l'ancienne* magic takes place, but in the fermentation technique. It is the most unique, and most improperly named, technique I had seen, relying on a method that cannot possibly be *à l'ancienne* because it depends completely on the power of the refrigerator, a modern invention. The bread should probably be called *pain moderne,* but then who would value it? The important difference between this dough and most others is that it is made by a delayed-fermentation technique caused by using ice-cold water to mix it, without yeast or salt, and then immediately refrigerating it. The dough is held overnight and then remixed with the yeast and salt and slowly awakened to begin its first, or bulk, fermentation. This technique evokes a whole different range of flavors and textures than is usually found in the standard 60-2-2 baguette, so-called because it is, and has been for generations, made with 60 percent water, 2 percent salt, and 2 percent yeast to 100 percent flour. It is only in recent years, or at least in the post-Ganachaud years commencing in the 1960s, that bakers have played around with this sacred formula, pushing the envelope to create better bread. Gosselin's *pain à l'ancienne* was the best baguette I'd ever had, even better than the version made by Professor Raymond Calvel that I tasted at his French bread seminar in Berkeley in 1994.

Calvel is generally regarded as the teacher of teachers, the chemist who quantified the internal processes of dough fermentation, and then applied that knowledge as a baker to set the bar for French bread excellence in the 1950s. His was the best I'd ever tasted until Gosselin's, and the good professor, then deep into his eighties, never mentioned the *à l'ancienne* technique during our seminar. As Gosselin generously explained the method, confident that the other local bakers wouldn't steal it because every baker in Paris hubristically thinks that his own bread is the best, I wondered if I had stumbled upon the next great thing, cold-dough delayed fermentation, the new frontier of bread making. I couldn't wait to get back home and try out Gosselin's method.

That evening I went to dinner at the home of an American who lives in Paris, where he translates, subtitles, and sometimes dubs French films into English and English-language films into French. I told him on the phone that I'd bring the bread. He said, "That's okay, we have a great *boulangerie* around the corner. I love their baguettes. I'll pick one up."

"But I have some *pain Poilâne* and also a very special baguette I want you to try," 21I countered.

"Ohhh, *pain Poilâne.* Yes, do bring that, but don't worry about the baguette, really."

"You don't understand," I pressed, "this really is very special."

"Well, okay, if you must."

When I arrived I noticed a fresh baguette sitting on the counter next to the pot of *boeuf bourguignon* he had made. I laid my *pain à l'ancienne* next to it and saw him smile. He took the Poilâne loaf and rushed it into the living room to show his wife, a sweet Parisian woman who nodded happily when she saw it. "Oh, Poilâne. Max or Lionel?"

"Lionel, from Bièvres, not Cherche-Midi," I said. She raised her eyebrows, indicating that she didn't know about Bièvres. "It's the same, just a new facility," I assured.

Another friend arrived, also an American, a writer and performer who had found much success in France where it had eluded him in the States. We sat down to eat and Michael, our host, brought out the bread with the stew. Howie, the writer-performer said, "Ah, *pain Poilâne,* I see. But what's with the two baguettes?"

I explained about the Gosselin, and Michael said, "Well, let's see. Try this; we're quite proud of it here in the neighborhood."

I tore off a piece and chewed it well. It was pleasant, not unlike the bread I purchased in Montmartre across from our apartment. In fact, not unlike most of the good baguettes in Paris, better than almost any found in the States, but. . . .

"Okay, try the Gosselin," I said, pushing it over to Michael and Howie. They tore off chunks, and the first thing we all noticed was how much bigger the holes were than in typical baguettes. It was also creamier, not as white. Michael chewed off a bite, the crackle of crust slightly cracklier than the local bread's. I watched his face as he chewed, the realization that there was another level, never experienced even here in the baguette center of the universe, that was now entering his orbit. He displayed a series of emotions on his face, swinging from smiling sublimity to furrowed anger, then back the other way. He was on a pendulum ride as the room grew silent and all attention focused gravitationally on him, getting weightier by the second. In my memory I see lights getting dimmer, with a spotlight on Michael's face, but I know this is just a trick of my own mind. But what did happen was this: He slowly picked up his local baguette and looked at it, then looked at the *à l'ancienne* baguette on the table, then back to the one in his clenched hand. As if in slow motion, he threw the local loaf against the wall where it smashed and fell to the floor. His wife said sharply, "Michael!"

Michael turned to me and said, "You've ruined me. Are you happy?"

"Yes, actually, I am happy," I said.

Then we all smiled and enjoyed dinner.

· · · · ·

I often participated in an event called the Book and the Cook, in Philadelphia, where cookbook authors collaborated with local chefs to stage a meal built around the author's latest books. For five years I collaborated with chef Philippe Chin at his two popular restaurants, Chanterelles and Philippe on Locust, where I was able to test out my new bread concepts on sophisticated foodies. At the year 2000 event, we featured wild mushroom ciabatta (*ciabatta al funghi)*, made according to my version of the Gosselin *pain à l'ancienne* method. We also introduced *pane siciliano,* a bread that one of my former students at the California Culinary Academy, Peter DiCroce, brought to my attention. He wanted to re-create his Sicilian American childhood memories of semolina bread, so we worked together applying pre-ferment techniques I was teaching to come up with the best version possible. After months of tinkering with it, we finally nailed down the formula and now make what I think is one of the finest versions of this bread. The key is using lots of pre-fermented dough plus the addition of an overnight rise. The semolina flour gives the bread a sweet and nutty flavor that is unique and delightful.

In preparation for these forays to Philadelphia to try out my latest ideas, I corresponded about the Gosselin technique with many of my own mentors and influences. These include Jeffrey Steingarten, food columnist at *Vogue* and author of *The Man Who Ate Everything,* and Ed Behr, the publisher and author of *The Art of Simple Eating,* one of the more popular food journals. They had both visited Gosselin, were familiar with his bread, and were impressed with its quality and distinctiveness. Although they both write about all aspects of food, they seem to share a particular passion for good bread. A whole network of bread fanatics exists out there, on the Internet, in the newsletters, and in the pages of *Vogue* and other mainstream journals. Behr and Steingarten are two of the more articulate spokespersons for the bread revolution, yet when it came to the Gosselin method, we all came away with different impressions of it. (Was he just messing with us, giving us partial versions, or did we each change it in our minds?) I know my interpretation and version is now quite different from even Gosselin's; like any baker worth his Normandy salt, I've tinkered and tweaked. I discovered that the true Gosselin method, which requires two mixings, can be consolidated into one mixing without adverse results. I began playing with variations and applications and now think of the *pain à l'ancienne* technique in its generic, deconstructed sense as a delayed-fermentation cold-mixing method.

This technique has the potential to change the entire bread landscape. I've begun teaching it to my students, both at Johnson & Wales University and across the country in my classes for home bakers. Within the next few years I fully expect to see variations of this method

Bentwood *bannetons*, or proofing baskets.

appearing in both artisan bakeshops and at the industry level. It is the next frontier in breads. (Note: When I wrote these words in 2001, it was well before the so-called no-knead and refrigerator methods swept the bread world in popular books by others. I've since found myself often using the term *next frontier* in my subsequent books, as today's frontier becomes tomorrow's mainstream. Next frontiers just seem to keep on appearing.) When we deconstruct the process, it takes us beyond fermentation, actually beneath fermentation, down to the level of enzymes. It is the enzyme that serves as the catalytic converter, freeing up sugars that are bound up in the complex starches of flour. The delayed-fermentation technique, revealed to me by Gosselin, and intuited by many others without knowing why, is all about how enzymes affect fermentation and release flavor. At culinary schools, we teach a fundamental principle: flavor rules. But to release flavors, remember enzymes.

· · · · ·

At the Summer Loaf Festival of 2000, I again taught a class and spoke at the Speaker's Corner, and talked about cold fermentation and enzymes. Thousands of bread revolutionaries attended, hungry for baking tips and tricks, or just hungry, as food writer John Thorne says, for bread that is good beyond belief. We know that bread is a metaphor, we sense it in our bones, we eat it as the body of God in our worships, and we believe that it truly is the staff of life.

It has been six thousand years since some Egyptian applied heat to beer and initiated the concept of leavened bread. The process clearly has its traditional and neotraditional aspects. To make great bread, we have learned from the patriarchs of the bread world the time-honored methods of the Old World. But they did not have refrigerators back then; they did not have access to ice chips and water coolers. We are writing new chapters, diving and deconstructing, and nibbling at the finer points, the microbial points, of the process.

What is it about bread that makes it such a hot topic these days? Whether master baker or young upstart, we are all apprentices, still learning and excited about sharing our findings with one another as we break into new frontiers. Even after six thousand years, we are all on a quest with no end in sight, trying to figure out how to make bread even better.

{ TWO }

Deconstructing Bread: A Tutorial

ASSUMPTIONS AND RATIONALES

Several assumptions and choices are fundamental to the way I bake bread. The assumptions represent ideas that will recur throughout the book and, rather than repeat them over and over in each formula, I am grouping them here for easy reference.

I begin with an overview of basic bread classifications and a discussion of ingredients, then move on to equipment, and conclude with the baker's math system (much easier than it sounds, I promise!).

Explanation of Weight and Measure Conversions

I've noticed that various cookbooks list contradictory information regarding the weight of various ingredients. Every formula in this book lists both the volume measure (teaspoons, tablespoons, and cups) and weight. Obviously, a cup of flour does not weigh the same as a cup of water or of salt or of yeast. In fact, 1 cup of flour scooped by one person may not weigh the same as 1 cup scooped by another. That is why professional bakers prefer to use weight measures, since 1 pound of flour, regardless of how many scoops or cups it took to get there, will weigh the same 1 pound (454g) from person to person. Many home bakers are now baking by weight rather than measure, but as home bakers, we face another problem not faced

WEIGHTS AND MEASURES
of COMMON INGREDIENTS

INGREDIENT	WEIGHT	VOLUME
Unbleached bread or all-purpose flour	16 ounces/454g	3½ cups
	4.5 ounces/128g	1 cup
Whole wheat flour	16 ounces/454g	3½ cups
	4.5 ounces/128g	1 cup
Coarse whole wheat flour	16 ounces/454g	3¾ cups
	4.25 ounces/120.5g	1 cup
Cornmeal (coarse)	16 ounces/454g	2⅔ cups
	6 ounces/170g	1 cup
Rolled oats	16 ounces/454g	4 cups
	4 ounces/113g	1 cup
Salt (table grind)	1 ounce/28g	4 teaspoons
	0.25 ounce/7g	1 teaspoon
Salt (kosher)	1 ounce/28g	7 teaspoons
	0.25 ounce/7g	1¾ teaspoons
Salt (sea)	1 ounce/28g	6 teaspoons
	0.25 ounce/7g	1½ teaspoons
Instant yeast	1 ounce/28g	3 tablespoons
	0.25 ounce/7g	2¼ teaspoons
	0.11 ounce/3g	1 teaspoon
Active dry yeast	0.25 ounce/7g	2½ teaspoons
	0.11 ounce/3g	1 teaspoon
Granulated sugar, baking powder, baking soda	1 ounce/28g	2 tablespoons
	0.25 ounce/7g	1½ teaspoons
Oil, butter, shortening, milk, water, most liquids	8 ounces/227g	1 cup
	1 ounce/28g	2 tablespoons
Powdered milk (DMS, or dry milk solids)	8 ounces/227g	1½ cups
	1 ounce/28g	3 tablespoons
Eggs	1.65 ounces/47g	1 large egg (without shell)
Egg yolk	0.75 ounce/21g	1 yolk from large egg
Raisins	16 ounces/454g	2⅔ cups
	6 ounces/170g	1 cup
Barm (sourdough sponge), *poolish* (yeasted sponge)	16 ounces/454	2⅓ cups
	7 ounces/198g	1 cup
Firm starter, *biga*, *pâte fermentée*	16 ounces/454g	3 cups
	5.4 ounces/153g	1 cup
Honey, molasses, corn syrup	1 ounce/28g	1½ tablespoons

by professional bakeries: the size of our batches is much smaller, and some ingredients are so light that our kitchen scales cannot weigh them accurately, such as 0.11 ounce (3g), a common weight for yeast in these recipes. So, to make sure we're all on the same page, at left is a chart of the weights and measures that I've used in these formulas. If you are following formulas from another baking book, some of which might list 1 pound of flour as 4 or 4½ cups instead of the 3½ cups I use, remember that the weight, not the volume, is always the preferred amount. You might want to weigh out 1 pound of flour yourself and see exactly how many cups of flour it takes when you do the scooping. Otherwise, these formulas do work with the weights given and, especially in the small-quantity items like salt, sugar, and yeast, with the volume measures as well.

Salt is always a tricky ingredient because various brands and types weigh out differently. Some salt is coarser than other salt or, as in kosher salt, the crystals are hollow and very light. For the purposes of this book, I have used table salt as the benchmark because everyone has it on hand. However, if you prefer to bake with sea salt or kosher salt, remember that the weight will remain the same, but the spoon equivalent will differ. My table salt, and I believe yours, requires 4 teaspoons to the ounce, or 0.25 ounce (7g) per teaspoon. This is what I use in the formulas. If you happen to use kosher salt, it will take nearly, but not quite, double that in volume, or 1¾ teaspoons, to make 0.25 ounce. Sea salt is somewhere in the middle, about 1½ teaspoons per 0.25 ounce. Rather than list every variable in each formula, I refer you back to this chart if you need to make a substitution.

Most of us know that a liquid ounce of water also equals a volume ounce. That is, 8 ounces (227g) of water by weight equals 1 cup. Liquid oil and milk, while not exactly the same weight as water, are close enough to follow the same weight-volume conversion as water.

You will also notice that coarse flour takes more volume to equal a pound than finely milled flour. This is because the coarser particles make the flour less dense and, as we all know, air is lighter than most ingredients. Again, some brands of flour may weigh out slightly differently than other brands per cup, so when in doubt, weigh it out. The baker's percentage system is always based on weight, not volume, so this is where the accuracy is to be found.

Types of Flour

Flour is the core of bread, the body containing its heart and spirit. Wheat is the grain of choice from which bread flour is milled. This is because wheat contains more gluten, a type of protein, than other grains. There are many international breads made from grains other than wheat, and there are many grains that can be added to wheat breads to make them interesting and nutritious. But the breads in this book are, for the most part, totally dependent on flour milled from wheat, regardless of the brand or the milling method.

Milling crushes wheat berries, which are the seeds or grains of mature wheat grass, into various degrees of powder. The three main components of a wheat berry are the outer skin, called bran; the oily, vitamin E–rich embryo, or germ; and the starch- and protein-laden nutritional cushion, called the endosperm. An analogy to this is an egg with its shell, yolk, and white.

Flour, whether whole wheat or sifted into clear (once sifted or bolted) or patent (twice sifted or bolted) bleached or unbleached white flours (see page 28), is called the "100 percent ingredient," against which all other ingredients stand in ratio. In the United States, one of the ways wheat flour is designated is by the amount of gluten protein (derived from the endosperm) it contains. Thus, cake flour has 6 to 7 percent gluten, pastry flour has 7.5 to 9.5 percent gluten, all-purpose flour has 9.5 to 11.5 percent gluten, bread flour has 11.5 to 13.5 percent gluten, and high-gluten flour has 13.5 to (rare but possible) 16 percent gluten. The gluten amount is determined by the type of wheat used in the flour. There is hard wheat and soft wheat, red wheat and white wheat, winter wheat and spring wheat. These various strains all contain different qualities, or specifications (bakers refer to these qualities as specs), and the job of the mill is to blend various strains of wheat into flours suitable for the bakers' requirements.

European flours use other keys to define the type of flour, often assigning numbers that refer to ash content (related to fiber) or extensibility. For example, the French type 55 flour is the standard baguette flour. It has moderate ash and is very extensible (as opposed to elastic and springy; see page 73, Extensibility, Elasticity, and Tolerance). Some French breads now use type 65 flour, which is higher in ash and thus has a more earthy, wheatlike coloration, similar to what American bakers call clear flour.

Professional bakers use the designations clear flour and patent flour for types of white flour (as opposed to whole wheat flour, a category unto itself in which the entire wheat berry is preserved in the flour). They indicate what part of the wheat berry has been sifted through and packaged. Clear flour, which means the flour that clears the first sifting (millers prefer the term bolting, to separate the bran and germ), still retains some of the finer bran fiber from the outer endosperm of the wheat berry and is thus coarser and contains higher levels of ash. This flour is often used in rye breads and is usually made from very strong, high-protein wheat. Regular markets rarely stock clear flour, but it is a good value for professional bakers who can use it in whole grain and high-fiber breads.

Patent flour, sometimes called second clear, is flour that has passed through a second sifting, thus retaining only the pure inner endosperm, or white interior, of the wheat berry. It is the purest grade and shows up in stores as bleached or unbleached all-purpose, pastry, bread, or high-gluten flour.

Picking the right flour is one of the joys and challenges that bakers face, and sometimes it is what distinguishes one bakery's products from another's. Artisan bakers are as passionate about their choice of flour as they are about their formulas, and many professional bakeries are now contracting with small specialty farmers to grow specific types of wheat, hoping to match the specifications and functionality of European flour. This is one of the most exciting aspects of the bread movement, but one that has yet to trickle down to home bakers other than through a favorite local mill, a specialty packager like King Arthur, or a miller like Bob's Red Mill in Oregon (see Resources, page 314). Flour availability will no doubt increase as demand grows; in the meantime, if you have a local bakery that makes a bread you really love, ask the baker the name of the flour and see if you can buy some from the bakery.

Although home bakers have a more limited menu of flours from which to choose, as long as you use the type of flour called for in a formula, your breads will not suffer. The formulas in this book will work with any brand of commercially available bread flour and even, in

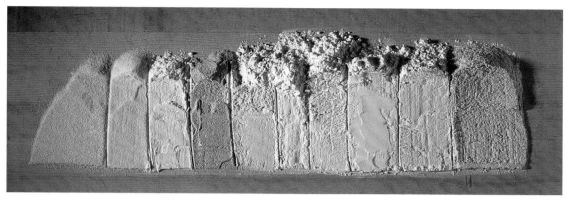

It is easy to see the subtle difference in color and texture of various flours when they are placed side by side. These are, from left to right, cornmeal, semolina flour (coarse durum), fancy durum, dark rye, white rye, bleached cake flour, unbleached pastry flour, unbleached bread flour, clear flour, and whole-wheat flour.

most instances, with all-purpose flour. The performance of the formula may vary from brand to brand, and the dough will certainly absorb water differently depending on the flour. As a general rule, a higher percentage of protein (gluten) in flour translates to more water absorption and slightly longer mixing times. But since each brand of flour has slightly different specifications, including ash content, protein percentage, and the particular blend of wheat strains, we are left again with that important feel quality. I find that King Arthur's unbleached all-purpose flour is comparable, for instance, to Gold Medal's bread flours (marketed as Better for Bread and also as Harvest King).

WHY USE UNBLEACHED FLOUR

Although it is possible to make good bread with bleached flour, it is preferable to use unbleached. This is because the yellowish tint in unbleached flour is caused by the building blocks of beta-carotene, the same substance we associate with vitamin A. While the nutritional value is compromised during the baking process, the real reason we prefer the presence of beta-carotene pigments is that it contributes better aroma and better flavor to the bread (it also lends a visually appealing, creamy tint to the crumb, which is far more appetizing than pure white). This subtle difference can be discerned clearly if we taste and smell bread made from bleached versus unbleached flour side by side. In our efforts to evoke the fullest potential of flavor from the wheat, it is important to utilize every tool at our disposal. Flour, being the 100 percent ingredient in our baker's math system, is a major player in our ability to control outcomes.

The use of unbleached flour is especially important in simple lean breads, the *pains ordinaire*, such as baguettes, and other French-, Italian-, and Vienna-style breads where the entire flavor is determined by the quality of the wheat coupled with the baker's ability to draw out flavor through fermentation and baking technique. In highly enriched breads, such as pullman, challah, general sandwich, and soft dinner roll, the advantage of unbleached flour is nullified somewhat by such enrichments as fat, egg, and milk. However, if you have only bleached flour on hand and want to make baguettes or other lean breads, by all means go ahead. When in doubt, follow what I consider the golden rule of all home-baked bread: it will always be a hit no matter how it turns out.

The formulas specify unbleached flour for the reasons specified above and, for the most part, almost all bread flour is now unbleached (some brands are still bleached, so read the label to be sure). All-purpose flour is widely sold bleached and unbleached. High-gluten flour, with its protein level of about 14 percent, is hard to find in supermarkets, but it can often be purchased at natural foods markets and through specialty sources. Using this stronger flour makes a difference in some breads, but feel free to use bread flour in its place if you cannot find a source. (Do not underestimate the power of begging at your favorite bakery for a dip into their bin.)

WHOLE WHEAT FLOUR

Whole wheat flour, which still contains the oily wheat-germ nucleus, is always best if less than a few months old, but it does last for many months if kept at average room temperature. During warm spells, you might want to consider keeping it tightly sealed in your refrigerator or freezer. The type of grind—regular, medium, or coarse—is specified in some formulas. If not, use regular grind or a blend of regular and either medium or coarse if you want more texture.

Why Instant Yeast

The reasons I prefer instant yeast are simple: it's more concentrated than fresh or active dry yeast, it has a longer shelf life, and it can be added to the flour instead of hydrating it first. I believe in the old baker's axiom to use only as much yeast as it takes to get the job done and no more. Instant yeast is concentrated because of the method by which it is produced and packaged. There are 25 percent more living yeast cells per teaspoon than in an equal amount of active dry yeast, and there are three times (300 percent) more living cells than in an equal amount of fresh compressed yeast. Instant yeast, even though it may be called rapid-rise, bread machine, or fast- or quick-rising yeast on some packaging, is actually a potent but slow-to-awaken yeast, which I find to be an advantage in many instances (slower is better, as you will see). When the yeast does awaken, the cells do their work as any other type of yeast would, digesting sugar and creating carbon dioxide and ethanol as by-products. It is the number of viable cells, along with the temperature and dough environment (yeast needs three things to grow: food, warmth, and moisture), that determines the rate of fermentation. Instant yeast is the easiest to use, is now readily available, and requires the least amount of volume per formula (usually about 0.66 percent of the flour weight as opposed to 2 percent for fresh compressed yeast).

Instant yeast, as well as active dry yeast, can be kept for months in the refrigerator in an airtight container without losing potency. Fresh yeast, on the other hand, because of its high moisture content, will degrade after about 2 weeks and will be completely over the hill within 4 weeks. The formulas specify instant yeast, but, as you will see on page 63, any type of yeast can be substituted. Regardless of the type of yeast you use, always keep it in an airtight container or wrapped completely in plastic wrap.

Water

There is little advantage to using expensive bottled water if your regular tap water is drinkable. Any chlorine taste will bake out of the finished bread. Only if your water is particularly hard or soft should you consider using bottled water. As a general rule, I suggest everyone consider putting a filter on the tap, since drinking water as a whole has declined in quality and is vulnerable to contamination or an excessive chlorine taste. Even then, however, the baking process itself will kill any microorganism and bake out the chlorine taste.

For the record, I do not believe, as many New Yorkers do, that their bagels are better because of the water. New York City water does happen to be very good, but that is not what makes their bagels better. In fact, I believe that if you make the bagels in this book (page 121), you will come to agree with me on this point.

Hand Kneading, Electric Mixers, Bread Machines, and Food Processors

The mixing instructions for most of the formulas in this book call for either hand mixing (kneading), using an electric mixer, or both. As you will see in the section on mixing (page 58), the method you use is less important than the final result, so I will leave this choice to you.

I almost always mix by hand because I love working the dough. Since one of the goals of this book is to help you develop that elusive quality called feel, I recommend mixing by hand whenever possible. Many people are intimidated by kneading dough, which means they miss out on one of bread making's most valuable pleasures. The mixing time is nearly the same whether mixing by hand or machine, depending on how steady your pace (well, maybe it takes a minute or two longer by hand).

Many people now own a KitchenAid or other brand of stand mixer with dough hook and paddle attachments. Most, but not all, of the formulas will fit in a standard-size KitchenAid or comparable mixer. In the case of those who don't, instructions are given for hand mixing or for using a larger machine, such as a Magic Mill.

I am definitely not against bread machines. In fact, I love them. But when you use a bread machine, you are limited to single-loaf recipes, so feel free to reduce larger formulas to fit your machine. Typically, a 1-pound machine will take dough made with about 2 cups of flour, while a 1½-pound machine usually incorporates about 3 cups of flour. Some people now use their bread machine to mix and ferment the dough, and then they perform the dividing and shaping by hand and the baking in a conventional oven. This is a great use for bread machines as it allows you to form the loaf in the shape of your choice.

Many home bakers have discovered that most bread dough can be made in a food processor with good results. On page 57, you will find general guidelines for using a processor for mixing. If a dough works particularly well in a processor, I indicate that in the notes accompanying the formula.

Thermometer

I highly recommend that you use an instant-read food thermometer (sometimes called a probe thermometer), any brand, when baking. You will need it for checking the temperatures of your ingredients, of the dough, and of the baked loaves. Every formula in the book refers to temperatures, and even though you will eventually be able to estimate temperatures by feel, it is important to develop that skill by discovering how particular temperatures, as registered on the thermometer, actually feel to the touch. Make sure the thermometer is calibrated accurately or follow the directions on the package to calibrate it before using.

Shaping and Proofing Equipment

Many years ago, when I was still teaching in Northern California, I took a class on a field trip to Craig Ponsford's marvelous Artisan Bakers in Sonoma, shortly after Craig had won the world championship of bread in Paris at the 1995 Coupe du Monde de la Boulangerie. One of my students noticed that the bakery had only a few dozen French *bannetons*, the bentwood willow baskets so popular for shaping breads during the proofing stage. The bakery did have, however, hundreds of little wicker baskets, the type often used in restaurants for serving rolls or crackers. The student asked Craig why he proofed his dough in those baskets instead of the real *bannetons*. He answered by holding up one in each hand. "These," he said, nodding toward the French *banneton,* "cost about fourteen dollars each, wholesale, and probably thirty dollars retail. These, on the other hand," as he looked toward the wicker, "cost me one dollar apiece at Cost Plus. They both do the job; you do the math."

Admittedly, the bentwood baskets are much sturdier than wicker and, frankly, feel good just to handle. But they are costly, and, as with almost any other aspect of bread making, the professional tool can be improvised at home for far less money.

If you don't have professional *bannetons*, you can use stainless-steel or glass mixing bowls, as shown on page 35. The size of the bowl will depend on the size of the loaf, but since most of the formulas specify 1- or 1½-pound loaves, the bowls need not be big. A bowl does need to be twice as large as the piece of dough going into it to accommodate the rise, however.

The same improvisation can be used for *couches*, the linen proofing cloths used in many bakeries for freestanding loaves.

Wicker, muslin-lined *bannetons.*

If you do not want to buy the actual heavy-duty beds (*couche* means "bed") from *The Baker's Catalogue* (see Resources, page 314) or a bakery supply house, you can use a white tablecloth, preferably one that you no longer use for company, or an old pillowcase. To ensure against sticking, lightly mist the surface with spray oil and dust the cloth with flour before lining up your loaves. Once the loaves are on the cloth, bunch the cloth between the pieces to make a wall and cover with cloth or plastic wrap.

The cloth is helpful with soft dough because it provides walls and structure to prevent the dough from spreading sideways or flattening. But much of the dough usually raised on cloth will do perfectly fine on a sheet pan that has been lined with baking parchment, misted with spray oil, dusted with cornmeal or semolina, and loosely covered with plastic wrap or slipped into a food-grade plastic bag. Food-grade plastic bags are usually clear or translucent and are designed to store food without leaching any petrochemicals into it. The shiny, vinyl-like trash bags are not food grade, though many people use them for this purpose.

▲ These *boules* from Seven Stars Bakery are proofed in *bannetons* that leave a distinctive pattern on the top of the loaf.

With just a few basic tools, spray oil being one of them, you can pretty much replicate at little expense many of the processes used in bakeries. Or you can go whole hog and outfit your kitchen with the authentic tools, most which are now available for home chefs. As Craig Ponsford puts it, "You do the math."

Baking Parchment and Silicone Baking Mats

Another baking tool that I use extensively and highly recommend is baking parchment. I do not like the parchment that comes on a roll, however, because it tends to curl up easily and is a hassle to cut. Instead, I prefer precut sheets, which are now becoming more readily available and certainly can be found at baking supply stores (or ask to buy a few dozen sheets from your favorite bakery). One sheet can be cut in half for home sheet pans (which are technically half-sheet pans as far as professional kitchens are concerned).

Not everyone knows that baking parchment is silicone treated and that it does not perform like greased or waxed paper. The silicone does not cause a release until it heats up to about 160°F (71°C), so if you plan to move products around on the parchment, it is best first to mist the paper with spray oil. In many instances, you will also dust the parchment with

* IMPROVISED PROOFING BOWLS

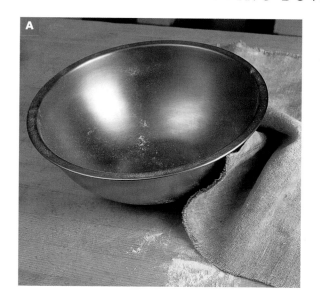

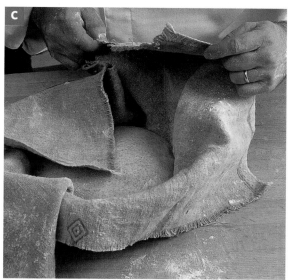
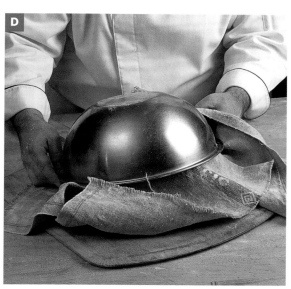

(A) Mist a stainless-steel or glass mixing bowl with spray oil and then line with a cloth napkin, scrap fabric, or smooth towel (not terry cloth). Mist the fabric with spray oil and lightly dust with flour. (B) Place the loaf in the bowl, seam side up, and mist the top of the dough with spray oil. (C) Cover with the flaps of the fabric or a separate cloth. (D) When you are ready to bake the loaf, gently invert the bowl onto a peel or the back of a sheet pan that has been dusted with semolina flour or cornmeal. Carefully peel off the fabric and proceed with scoring and baking.

Fumie prepares a *couche* to proof a batch of rustic dough.

cornmeal or gritty semolina for both texture and release value. This is not always necessary and applies to particular breads only, but it does provide a nice bottom to hearth breads.

One of the best features of baking parchment is that you can slide it right into the oven, directly onto a baking stone. This makes it possible to transfer bread to the oven without having to lift it off the proofing pan, thus diminishing the possibility of damaging the dough while it is at its most vulnerable.

Many home bakers are now using silicone-treated baking mats, with Silpat the most popular brand. These are useful for some breads, especially if you plan to bake directly on the sheet pan. I never use them for baking directly on a hot stone, however, for fear of melting the silicone or wearing out the mat prematurely. The best thing about these baking mats is that they are reusable.

Why Spray Oil Works Best

Spraying a mist of oil over the dough prevents the dough from sticking to plastic wrap or other coverings before baking and, of course, releases the product from the baking pan once it is done. I use spray oil more than almost anyone I know, but it really makes life easier. It doesn't matter what brand you choose, though some are pure vegetable oil and others have food-grade pan-release additives. Always keep a can on the counter because every formula in this book requires it at some point. You can make your own by using vegetable or olive oil in a pressurized pump-style kitchen mister. The main advantage of spray oil is that you are able to use a minimum amount of oil to create the necessary release effect. If you do not have spray oil, lightly brush on liquid oil with either a paper towel or a pastry brush.

Baking Stones

I highly recommend using a baking stone for many of the breads in this book. Stones retain heat much more effectively than sheet pans do and thus promote a more even bake and a crispier crust. In tandem with the double-steaming technique described on page 98, a stone is the home baker's best means of replicating the hearth ovens used by artisan bakers.

I prefer the thick, rectangular stones available now in most housewares departments or cooking stores. These stones retain their heat longer than thin, round pizza stones. The unglazed quarry tiles that many of us used before stones became so available are also good, though they tend to slide around and are more prone to cracking when they get wet. If you have already outfitted your oven with tiles and are happy with them, feel free to continue using them. The key is to get the stone (or tiles) as hot as possible before you transfer the dough to the oven, so be sure it is in place when you preheat the oven, and allow 45 minutes to get the stone as hot as the oven. I always heat to at least 50°F (10°C)—and sometimes 100°F (38°C)—higher than is actually necessary to compensate for all the heat that will be lost during the steaming action and door opening. After I finish steaming, I reset the oven to the desired temperature.

Since every oven bakes differently, you will have to be the judge as to the best location for the stone. Some people prefer to put it on the floor of the oven, while others use one of the racks. I usually place it on an oven rack in the lower third of my electric oven, which leaves headroom for tall loaves and delivers a pretty even baking performance.

If you want to make hearth breads but do not have a stone, you can invert a regular sheet pan and use it as a baking deck. Simply slide the pan into the oven on the regular oven rack and proceed with steaming. (Note: A new option, the Baking Steel, has become available. It is a solid steel plate that works even better than a baking stone, but it is also, of course, quite a bit more expensive. Unlike a stone, it is indestructible. See Resources, page 314, for details.)

Ovens

No two ovens bake the same, so all baking times are approximate and based on conventional radiant-heat ovens. You will almost always need to rotate your breads 180 degrees about halfway through the estimated baking time for even baking. If you are using a wood-fired oven, all bets are off and you will know better than I how long to bake your breads. If you are using a convection oven, I recommend lowering the suggested temperature by 25°F to 50°F (4°C to 10°C), depending on the intensity of the convection, and decreasing the baking time by about 10 to 20 percent.

Fermentation and Proofing Temperatures

As you begin making some of the breads in this book, you will notice that almost all of them are fermented and proofed at room temperature, not in a warm place. To artisan bakers, room temperature is a warm place. Yeast will double its rate of fermentation for every increase of 17°F (8°C), up to the killing point (about 140°F/60°C). In most cases, slower is better. Bread that might rise in 1 hour in a commercial proof box at 90°F (32°C) will take 2 hours if the room temperature is 73°F (23°C). But during that extra hour, more flavor is being elicited from the flour by the organic activity that is going on invisibly inside the dough.

However, you do have the power to control the fermentation and may find, for various reasons, that you want to speed up the final rise (or slow it down), and you are free to do so if it meets your needs. See page 92 for advice on improvising a proof box in the home kitchen.

The Baker's Math-Formula System

Professional bakers view recipes as formulas, meaning that they conceive of them as ratios and percentages rather than as cups and spoonfuls. Measuring by weight is far more accurate than measuring by volume (or scoop), but even more important, the ratios of ingredients to one another reveal patterns that allow bakers to be creative and to control the outcomes of their efforts. Home bakers tend to avoid thinking mathematically (and my full-time students also try, unsuccessfully, to dodge this bullet), but I can assure you that possession of this knowledge will strengthen your ability to control the outcome of your baking. The baker's percentage formulas that accompany each recipe in this book are designed with just such a goal in mind. Each can be easily rescaled for larger batch sizes and adjusted within a given batch size to refine a recipe.

To understand the baker's math system, it is important to know that all ingredients are viewed in ratio to the total flour weight (TFW). The TFW always equals 100 percent, and all other ingredients are figured as a percentage against that figure. For example, if the flour weight is 1 pound (16 ounces) and the salt weight is ¼ ounce (.25 ounce), the percentage of salt to flour is determined by dividing the salt weight by the flour weight and multiplying by 100 (.25 ÷ 16 = .0156 × 100 = 1.56 percent). An experienced baker knows that salt is usually 1.5 to 2.5 percent of flour weight, so this ratio, 1.56 percent, indicates an appropriate amount of salt.

Water or other liquids also fall within norms in particular types of breads, such as 55 to 68 percent for French breads, sandwich bread, or rolls, and 68 to 80 percent for ciabatta and focaccia. For example, if a recipe for baguettes made with French flour calls for 2 pounds of flour (TFW), the water should be about 60 percent. We can calculate this by multiplying 2 pounds by 60 percent (2 × 0.60 = 1.2). To convert this pound weight to ounces, simply multiply by 16 (since there are 16 ounces to a pound). So, 16 × 1.2 = 19.2 ounces, or just slightly more than 19 ounces of water is needed. To check the accuracy, divide the 19.2 ounces of water by the 32 ounces (2 pounds) of flour. It will come to 0.60, or 60 percent. The same math works for metric weights such as grams. In fact, for those who are comfortable working in metric grams, baker's math is actually easier, more intuitive, and even more accurate because a gram is a smaller unit than an ounce (28.35g) or even a 0.25 ounce (about 7g).

Following are other principles to keep in mind:

- Total Flour Weight (TFW) consists of all the flour in the recipe, so if there is a combination of white and whole grain flour, the total is 100 percent. Example: The recipe calls for 1 pound bread flour and 4 ounces rye flour. The total flour weight is 1 pound, 4 ounces (1.25 pounds), and this is the ratio to which all other ingredients relate. If there is a sponge (pre-ferment), it may weigh more than the total flour weight. For instance, some of the recipes call for 1 pound flour and 1.66 pounds of *poolish* (sponge). If you divide 1.66 pounds by 1 pound, you get 1.66, or 166 percent.

- The formula's Total Percentage (TP) does not add up to 100 percent—only the flour weight does. Every formula will have a different TP depending on the number of ingredients. It will begin with 100 percent and go up from there.

- If a formula is given to you with only the percentages and not the weights, it is possible to figure out the weight of each ingredient, as long as you know how much total dough you need.

For example, you need 10 pounds of bread (total weight, or TW) for a party, and the recipe is a classic French bread dough: 100 percent flour, 60 percent water, 2 percent salt, 2 percent fresh yeast. Therefore, the TP is 164 percent. Here is how you then figure each ingredient weight:

First, divide the TW by the TP (divide 10 pounds by 164 percent, or 1.64) to determine the TFW. This will give you a TFW of 6.097 pounds, or 6 pounds plus .097 × 16 = 1.55 ounces). To make things easy, and to give you some buffer, round the number up to an easy-to-work-with figure, such as 6.25 pounds (6 pounds, 4 ounces) and use that as the TFW. (It is always better to round up and have too much dough than too little.)

Then, find the water weight by multiplying 6.25 pounds (TFW) × 60 percent = 3.75 pounds (3 pounds, 12 ounces).

Do the same with the yeast and salt (6.25 × 2 percent = 0.125 pound or 0.125 × 16 = 2 ounces).

This recipe now reads:

6 pounds, 4 ounces flour
3 pounds, 12 ounces water
2 ounces salt
2 ounces yeast

The column totals 10 pounds, 4 ounces. This is 4 ounces more than we need (the buffer), so that's good.

This system will come in handy as you become familiar with more breads based on the categories discussed on page 46, especially if you want to control flavor or texture or trouble-shoot a performance problem. For instance, if your dinner rolls are too hard and the percentage of fat is only 6 percent, you might want to increase that to 10 percent by multiplying the TFW by 10 percent. Or, if the dough is rising too slowly and you discover the yeast is only at 2 percent, you may decide, if appropriate for the dough, to increase the yeast to 3 percent by doing the math. If the dough tastes salty and you discover, by doing the math, that the salt is 3 percent, you can confidently reduce the salt to 2 percent by doing the math. (Yeast percentage in professional bakeries, by the way, is usually based on fresh compressed yeast. If you are using instant yeast, as is the case throughout this book, plan to reduce the amount to one-third the amount of fresh yeast; if you are using active dry yeast, reduce the amount to half the amount of the fresh yeast. Also, if the formula calls for instant yeast and all you have is active dry yeast, increase the amount of active dry yeast by 25 percent more than the instant yeast.)

Initially, this formula system may seem confusing. It takes practice to get the hang of using the baker's percentage, but even a rudimentary understanding will strengthen your bread-baking skills.

Just remember these primary baker's math formulas:

TFW = TW ÷ TP
Total Flour Weight equals Total Weight divided by Total Percentage

IW = IP × TFW
Ingredient Weight equals Ingredient Percentage times Total Flour Weight

IP = IW ÷ TFW × 100
Ingredient Percentage equals Ingredient Weight divided by Total Flour Weight times 100

To illustrate these concepts, let's look at a master formula as it might be presented in one of my classes (a variation on the format used in this book). This is for the standard white sandwich bread called *pain de mie* in France and sometimes referred to in American bakeries as pullman bread. This recipe is for 10 pounds of dough. (On page 285, we'll see this formula recalculated for use at home in a smaller mixer.) We use pounds and ounces in this example, but it works just as well in grams (comparable metric weights are provided in all the formulas).

A final reminder before we walk through this exercise: knowledge is power, the power to affect outcomes, in life and in baking, so I encourage you to dive into this process as one of empowerment as well as culinary enjoyment.

PULLMAN (WHITE) BREAD

	WEIGHT	VOLUME MEASURE	%
Bread flour	5 pounds, 4 ounces	18⅓ cups	100
Salt	1.5 ounces	2 tablespoons	2
Granulated sugar	8 ounces	1 cup	8
Powdered milk (DMS)	5 ounces	⅔ cup	6
Yeast (fresh)	2.5 ounces (.88 ounce if using instant yeast)	must be weighed (3½ tablespoons)	3 (1 if instant yeast)
Large eggs	4 ounces	2 to 3 large eggs	4
Shortening	8 ounces	1 cup	8
Water	3 pounds	6 cups	58
TOTAL	10 pounds		189

In a 20-quart mixer, mix all ingredients on low speed for 2 minutes. Then mix on second speed for 6 to 8 minutes, until the dough sets up and is approximately 80°F (27°C). Follow the twelve stages to complete.

Here are a few things that immediately become evident: The dough contains a ratio of 8 percent shortening (fat) to flour (notice that the weight of the flour represents 100 percent). This immediately tells us the dough falls in the enriched category (as explained on page 46), especially since it also contains milk (in powdered form), sugar, and eggs. The formula contains a ratio of 2 percent salt to flour and of 3 percent fresh yeast to flour. These ratios are right in line with this kind of bread, but the 3 percent yeast indicates a fast-moving dough (French bread, for instance, usually only contains 2 percent yeast to flour). Such dough offers no opportunity for extended punch downs or long fermentation cycles. This is meant to be a rather fast, easy-to-make bread, the flavor of which is determined more by the enrichments than by the fermentation. Being enriched, it is designed to be a soft bread, tender to chew. The eggs, milk, and sugar add various degrees of sweetness, fat, and protein to the bread. This means the dough will caramelize easily and thus should be baked at a lower temperature than, say, lean French bread, which contains no added sugar or enrichments and will therefore brown, or caramelize, more slowly, and thus requires a hotter oven temperature.

The dough has a hydration ratio of 58 percent water to flour (plus a few extra percentage points for the liquid in the eggs—figure about 3 percent since eggs are about 75 percent water). This information clearly places pullman bread in the standard range rather than rustic or stiff. The dough should be pliable and tacky, but not sticky. It should be easy to handle, needing only a minimum amount of dusting flour.

During its primary fermentation it will probably double in size in 1 to 1½ hours, depending on the temperature at which it is held. Once it ferments, it will quickly be brought through the dividing, rounding, benching, and shaping stages so that it can undergo its final fermentation, or proofing, which should again take 1 to 1½ hours. It is then baked at approximately 350°F (177°C) until it is done, meaning that the crust has caramelized, the proteins have coagulated and formed a distinctive gluten webbing, and the starch has gelatinized. The internal temperature of the bread should be 185°F to 190°F (85°C to 88°C) when it comes from the oven, thus ensuring a full, but light, gelatinization and little deep protein roasting. This kind of bread is designed to be consumed with other condiments or foods, such as butter, jam, and/or sandwich fillings, offering little resistance to the tooth and providing sweetness more from the sugar than from the flour. (This is different from French bread in which all the sweetness is evoked from the natural wheat sugars.)

Please refer back to the pullman formula and look at the percentage column. Try to grasp the relationship of each ingredient to the flour weight. Notice that the way we determined the flour weight was by dividing the total weight of all the ingredients (10 pounds) by the total percentage of the formula (189 percent, or 1.89), and then rounding the answer to 5 pounds, 4 ounces.

NOTE ON BAKER'S PERCENTAGE FORMULAS

There are two ways a formula can be broken up into percentage ratios. The first, used in most of the recipes in this book, is to count only the flour in the final dough to represent the TFW as the 100 percent ingredient. With this approach, we do not count the flour in a pre-ferment as part of the TFW. The second approach is to use the flour in both the pre-ferment and the final dough as the TFW. Both are valid methods with advantages and disadvantages.

The primary advantage of the first method, which we can call the final dough formula, is that the pre-ferment is seen as a distinct ingredient in ratio to the flour in the final dough. This is helpful for breads made with a *poolish, biga, pâte fermentée,* or wild-yeast (sourdough) pre-ferment, all of which can be made in any size and then measured off as needed. The disadvantage is that this approach does not represent each of the other ingredients as a ratio against the true amount of flour used, or the total dough formula. The flour in a *poolish*, for example, is, in reality, part of the actual total flour weight but not part of the official 100 percent ingredient, the TFW, as listed in the final dough. In the ciabatta formula, for instance, the *biga* (or *poolish*, depending on which formula you follow) is a distinct ingredient, listed separately and in ratio to the TFW.

The main advantage of the second approach, or the total dough formula, is that it allows us to see every ingredient in ratio to the full amount of flour. This approach makes more sense when using a fast-acting pre-ferment that has been calculated specifically for that formula, as with the recipes for bagels, brioche, *casatiello*, and stollen. This fast-acting pre-ferment is generally called a *sponge*, and the final dough is made by building upon all of the sponge. Very often in dough made with a fast sponge, all of the yeast and much of the hydrating liquid is introduced during the sponge stage with only part of the total flour. The disadvantage of this approach to calculation is that some ingredients, such as flour and perhaps water or yeast, get split and listed more than once in the percentage formula, which can be confusing.

In the formulas that follow, I will list the baker's percentage of each ingredient as part of a "final dough formula" with the recipe. When a *poolish, biga,* or sourdough pre-ferment is used, I will also list a "total dough formula" in a separate box, factoring in the flour and water from the pre-ferment (based on the pre-ferment formulas on pages 110 to 113) as part of a total ingredient ratio.

Classifications of Breads

There are many ways to frame the classifications of bread, as you will see on the chart on page 46. For instance, one classification system defines breads according to three categories based on hydration, or water content. These are the *stiff doughs* (bagels, pretzels—50 to 57 percent hydration of liquid to flour), *standard doughs* (sandwich bread, rolls, French and other European-style breads—57 to 68 percent hydration), and *rustic doughs* (ciabatta, pizza, focaccia—above 68 percent hydration). All breads will fall into one of these categories.

Another classification system defines breads by hardness or richness. *Lean dough* (from which French, Italian, sourdough hearth, and bagels are made) has little or no fat or added enrichments. *Enriched dough* has some fat, dairy, eggs, or sugar—enough to tenderize and add a little sweetness or flavor. This category includes most sandwich breads, soft rolls, and braided breads such as challah. Rich dough includes breads with more than 20 percent fat-to-flour ratio, such as brioche, some holiday breads, and sweet rolls and breads. Within this category is a subcategory called laminated bread. This term refers to croissants, Danish pastry, puff pastry, and even some types of biscuit and pie dough. They all have a high percentage of fat that is laminated between layers of dough through a series of folds. The dough puffs when it is baked, resulting in a flaky texture.

A large classification called *flat breads* includes both yeasted and unyeasted doughs whose primary attribute is low height. This family embraces, but is not limited to, pizza and focaccia, crackers, matzo, lavash, and tortillas. These breads may be crisp, airy, soft, flaky, or tender, depending on the style. The dough can be lean, enriched, or rich.

Another classification is composed of breads made with no pre-ferment and in one mixing cycle. These are called *direct* or *straight doughs*. Breads made with a pre-ferment, which are known as *indirect* or *sponge breads*, are the counterpoint.

Finally, there are the classifications of *commercially yeasted breads, naturally leavened breads* (wild yeast or sourdough), and *unyeasted doughs* that may or may not be chemically leavened by baking soda or baking powder. The latter includes quick breads, a subcategory of its own with tortillas, biscuits, muffins, and pie doughs.

As we encounter specific breads in this book, it will be necessary at times to refer to them within their categories to make certain points about the process. Armed with this information, including knowledge of the baker's math system, it will be possible for you, whether a home baker or professional, to confidently create numerous original recipes with infinite variations.

BREADS BY CATEGORY

The following chart lists all the breads in this book by the categories in which they fall. Because every bread falls within more than one category, depending on the method of classification, it's helpful to see all the profiles together. Similarities and differences among breads emerge, and the patterns will help you to better understand and control the baking process.

Here is the key to the categories:

STIFF: Has 50 to 57 percent hydration; very firm, dry, and satiny, not tacky

STANDARD: Has 57 to 67 percent hydration; tacky but not sticky, supple

RUSTIC: Has 68 to 80 percent hydration; wet, sticky

LEAN: Little or no fat or sugar added; hard dough

ENRICHED: Less than 20 percent fat; may also include sugar, milk, or eggs; medium-soft dough

RICH: More than 20 percent fat; may also include sugar, milk, or eggs; soft dough

FLAT: May be leavened or unleavened, crisp or soft, but always baked thin

DIRECT: Mixed without pre-ferment in one mixing session (also called the straight dough method)

INDIRECT: Uses a pre-ferment (sponge) made with commercial yeast, wild yeast, or a soaker (also called the sponge method)

YEASTED: Made with commercial yeast of any type (instant, active dry, or fresh compressed)

LEAVENED: Made exclusively with a wild-yeast starter (also called natural leaven or sourdough)

MIXED METHOD: Made with both a wild-yeast starter and commercial yeast (also called spiking the dough)

CHEMICAL: Made with a chemical leavening agent (baking soda or baking powder)

NAME	STIFF	STANDARD	RUSTIC	LEAN
Anadama Bread		X		
Artos		X		
Bagels	X			X
Brioche		X		
Casatiello		X		
Challah		X		
Ciabatta			X	X
Cinnamon Buns		X		
Cinnamon Raisin Walnut Bread		X		
Corn Bread				
Cranberry-Walnut Celebration Bread		X		
English Muffins		X		
Focaccia			X	
French Bread		X		X
Italian Bread		X		
Kaiser Rolls		X		
Lavash Crackers	X			
Light Wheat Bread		X		
Marbled Rye Bread		X		
Multigrain Bread Extraordinaire		X		
Pain à l'Ancienne			X	X
Pain de Campagne		X		X
Pane Siciliano		X		
Panettone		X		
Pizza Napoletana			X	X or
Poolish Baguettes		X		X
Portuguese Sweet Bread		X		
Potato Rosemary Bread		X		
Pugliese			X	X
Basic Sourdough		X		X
New York Deli Rye		X		
100% Sourdough Rye Bread		X		X
Poilâne-Style *Miche*		X		X
Pumpernickel Bread		X		
Sunflower Seed Rye		X		X
Stollen		X		
Swedish Rye (*Limpa*)		X		
Tuscan Bread		X		
Vienna Bread		X		
White Breads		X		
Whole Wheat Bread		X		
Potato, Cheddar, and Chive Torpedoes		X		
Roasted Onion and Asiago *Miche*			X	
Sprouted Wheat and Brown Rice Bread		X	X	
Sprouted Whole Wheat Onion and Poppy Seed Bialys			X	X
Beyond Ultimate Cinnamon and Sticky Buns		X		

ENRICHED	RICH	FLAT	DIRECT	INDIRECT	YEASTED	LEAVENED	MIXED METHOD	CHEMICAL	NAME
X				X	X				Anadama Bread
X				X	X or		X		*Artos*
				X	X				Bagels
	X			X	X				Brioche
	X			X	X				*Casatiello*
X			X		X				Challah
				X	X				Ciabatta
X			X		X				Cinnamon Buns
X			X		X				Cinnamon Raisin Walnut Bread
X								X	Corn Bread
X			X		X				Cranberry-Walnut Celebration Bread
X			X		X				English Muffins
X		X	X or	X	X				Focaccia
				X	X				French Bread
X				X	X				Italian Bread
X				X	X				Kaiser Rolls
X		X	X		X				Lavash Crackers
X			X		X				Light Wheat Bread
X			X		X				Marbled Rye Bread
X				X	X				Multigrain Bread Extraordinaire
			X		X				*Pain à l'Ancienne*
				X	X				*Pain de Campagne*
X				X	X				*Pane Siciliano*
	X			X			X		Panettone
X		X	X		X				*Pizza Napoletana*
				X	X				*Poolish* Baguettes
X				X	X				Portuguese Sweet Bread
X				X	X				Potato Rosemary Bread
				X	X				Pugliese
				X		X			Basic Sourdough
X				X			X		New York Deli Rye
				X		X			100% Sourdough Rye Bread
				X		X			Poilâne-Style *Miche*
X				X			X		Pumpernickel Bread
				X			X		Sunflower Seed Rye
	X			X	X				Stollen
X				X	X				Swedish Rye (*Limpa*)
X				X	X				Tuscan Bread
X				X	X				Vienna Bread
X			X or	X	X				White Breads
X				X	X				Whole Wheat Bread
X				X			X		Potato, Cheddar, and Chive Torpedoes
X				X			X		Roasted Onion and Asiago *Miche*
			X		X				Sprouted Wheat and Brown Rice Bread
			X		X				Sprouted Whole Wheat Onion and Poppy Seed Bialys
	X		X			X			Beyond Ultimate Cinnamon and Sticky Buns

THE TWELVE STAGES OF BREAD: EVOKING THE FULLNESS OF FLAVOR FROM THE GRAIN

In my first lecture, on the first day of the nine-day bread lab that I teach at Johnson & Wales University, I tell my students, "Your mission as a bread baker is to evoke the full potential of flavor from the wheat." Everything else we do flows from this statement. Some of the students grasp this concept at the beginning, and some grasp it by the end of the course (and a few, regrettably, never quite get it, though in those instances I consider it a seed planted for future harvest). Most important, though, is that this goal provides the focal point through which everything I teach makes sense. Deconstructing bread making can be a tedious process if you don't have a compelling reason to do so. Fortunately, what I've discovered in my travels across the country teaching home bakers, and also with my full-time students, is that an amazingly strong interest exists in this mission.

This section summarizes all twelve stages of bread production and gives a brief overview of how to build a loaf in order to accomplish the baker's mission. Ultimately, this is done by unwinding the complex carbohydrates to release their foundational sugars through mastery of fermentation, and by roasting the proteins to draw forth their nutlike flavors, while fully gelatinizing the starches so that they do not mask any of the flavor. To understand how to do this, we will review the basic principles underlying world-class bread, including the use of sponges, pre-ferments, starters, oven technique, and wild versus commercial yeast. Much of this has been previously presented in *Crust & Crumb: Master Formulas for Serious Bread Bakers*, as well as in books by other authors. However, I want to take these techniques further than in previous books, so we will metaphorically follow the bread baker's axiom that the best loaves are made by building dough in stages. To this end, we will layer new knowledge upon foundational principles and then extend this knowledge into frontier territory.

In the table opposite, you will see the twelve stages of bread. All bread goes through these stages, which form the framework of the bread-baking process. Understanding this structure does not ensure great bread; neither does failure to understand this structure mean you will not make great bread. Most commercial bread bakers, many who have had no formal training, do not have the slightest clue about these twelve stages, but they do know that if they explicitly follow directions, they can produce adequate bread. However, in our quest to control outcomes and have the power to push beyond adequacy to world-class quality, understanding this structure as the foundation of bread baking is the first layer of knowledge. In the pages to come, we will build on this foundation into more advanced concepts.

1.	2.	3.	4.
MISE EN PLACE in which the organizing principle is "everything in its place"	**MIXING** in which three important requirements must be met	**PRIMARY FERMENTATION** also called bulk fermentation, in which most of the flavor is determined	**PUNCHING DOWN** also called degassing, in which the dough begins to enter its secondary fermentation and individuation
5.	6.	7.	8.
DIVIDING in which pieces are weighed, or scaled, while continuing to ferment	**ROUNDING** in which the pieces are given an interim shaping prior to their final shape	**BENCHING** also called resting or intermediate proofing, during which time the gluten relaxes	**SHAPING AND PANNING** in which the dough is given its final shape prior to baking
9.	10.	11.	12.
PROOFING also called secondary or final fermentation, in which the dough is leavened to its appropriate baking size	**BAKING** which may also include scoring the dough and steaming, but in which three vital oven actions must occur	**COOLING** which is really an extension of baking but must occur before cutting into the bread	**STORING AND EATING** in which the primary emphasis for production baking is storage, but for home baking is usually, ahem, eating

All bread goes through twelve stages in its journey from raw ingredients to consumable loaf (I now call it "the journey from wheat to eat"). In some instances, such as sandwich breads, certain of these stages happen almost simultaneously, while in other instances, bagels for example, there are slight variations in how the dough journeys through the stages. What is universal, though, is that some form of transformation occurs, changing a lifeless lump of flour-based clay into a living, growing organism. What was once a tasteless pile of flour, like sawdust on the tongue, is miraculously transformed into a multilayered series of flavors and textures that bring joy to both the palate and the soul. How does this happen? Is it chemistry or alchemy?

Eighty percent of the quality of the finished bread will be determined during the primary fermentation stage (Stage 3), and the other 20 percent will be primarily determined during the baking, or oven, stage (Stage 10). Some of the in-between stages affect the outcome in subtle and important ways, but they cannot undo choices made during the fermentation and baking stages. Even these vital stages are totally dependent on the first stage, however, the *mise en place*, and the success of your personal bread-baking experience, not just the finished product, begins with organization. If you get off to a good start, the rest will take care of itself.

Stage 1: Mise en Place

We begin our exploration of this transformational process with *mise en place*, both as a stage of bread baking and as a principle of life and knowledge. *Mise en place* is the primary organizational principle in all cooking. It means first things first or, literally, "everything in its place." It is the first stage in the transformational journey of how flour becomes bread.

The baker's "altar of transformation" requires only a few essentials: properly measured or weighed ingredients, a sturdy work bench, bowls or a machine for mixing, a decent oven, and room to perform the various activities through which the dough will traverse its twelve stages. There are, of course, refinements to this list that include additional tools, such as a thermometer, baking stone, water mister, and the like.

KEYS TO MISE EN PLACE

Here are keys to Stage 1 of bread making, *mise en place*:

- Refer to the *mise en place* checklist at right, making sure in advance that you have everything you need.

- Read the instructions from start to finish and visualize how you plan to make the formula at each stage. Many times this mental preparation will reveal a missing tool or a time conflict (such as the roast that will be in the oven when you need to bake the bread!).

- Decide whether you are going to weigh or scoop your ingredients. There are many inexpensive digital scales available that are accurate to within two decimal places (0.25 ounce or 0.01 gram). If you are scooping, refer to the chart on page 26, but remember that everyone has a different touch when it comes to scoops. Many of my friends claim that it takes 4 cups of flour to make a pound, while I always end up with 3½ cups to the pound. The difference means that, for me, 1 cup of flour weighs just over 4.5 ounces, while my friend's cup of flour weighs only 4 ounces. The flour amount will take care of itself during the mixing stage as you make adjustments based on the feel of the dough. But salt and yeast are more difficult to adjust. There is a great difference between a rounded and a level teaspoon (or tablespoon). Remember that a bread recipe, that is, the measurements for a specific batch as opposed to a formula (which consists of percentages rather than weights and measures), is strictly a guideline, not an absolute. The brand or age of your flour may make it necessary to adjust the flour or liquid even when you have scaled the ingredients precisely. But by starting with accurate measurements, your adjustments will be minimal and your margin for error will be reduced.

• *Mise en place* is as much a mental organization as it is about scaling ingredients. Arrange to have as few distractions as possible, or factor them in as required. Minimize conversation or you will surely make mistakes or forget an ingredient. Success in bread making, as in any facet of life, comes down to one word: focus.

• Scale (weigh or scoop) all your ingredients before starting to assemble the dough.

MISE EN PLACE CHECKLIST

I have divided this checklist into "must have" and "ought to have," and by that I mean that many tools can be improvised, but there are some, at least for the formulas in this book, that really need to be part of your setup. Spray oil and baking parchment are good examples. Here's one organizational tip: never start making bread without first setting up a bowl of extra flour for dusting and adjustments. Also, have a plastic bowl scraper and a metal dough scraper (sometimes called a bencher or pastry blade) in place, and keep a bowl of water available both for adjustments and for dipping hands or tools to keep dough from sticking. If you don't have any of these in place before you start mixing the dough, you will soon know, when you go to reach for something or, later, when you are cleaning bread dough off everything, why you need them in place ahead of time.

MUST HAVE

☐ Measuring tools
☐ Spray oil, any brand or homemade
☐ Baking parchment
☐ Plastic bowl scraper
☐ Metal dough scraper (aka bencher, pastry blade)
☐ Rubber spatula
☐ Various-size mixing bowls
☐ Wooden and metal mixing spoons
☐ Sturdy work counter
☐ Extra flour
☐ Extra water
☐ Instant-read (probe) thermometer
☐ All the ingredients for the formula weighed or measured in advance
☐ Sheet pans that fit your oven
☐ Bread pans in two sizes: 8½ by 4½ inches (for 1-pound loaves) and 9 by 5 inches (for 1½- and 2-pound loaves)

OUGHT TO HAVE

☐ Stand mixer with paddle and dough hook attachments or food processor
☐ Sharp serrated knife, French *lame* (scoring blade), or single-edge razor
☐ Pizza cutter (rolling blade)
☐ Cornmeal or semolina for dusting
☐ Proofing *couche* or cloth substitute
☐ Proofing baskets (*bannetons*) or bowl substitutes
☐ Kitchen scale, includes both pound and gram weighing modes and accurate to at least two decimal places
☐ Steaming devices
☐ Cooling racks
☐ Plastic wrap or food-grade plastic bags
☐ Baking stone or quarry tiles
☐ Wooden or metal peel

Stage 2: Mixing

Mixing is sometimes referred to as kneading, especially if it is performed by hand rather than in a machine. Regardless of the name given to it, mixing has three purposes: distributing the ingredients, developing the gluten, and initiating fermentation. Of course, how the three goals of mixing are achieved depends greatly on the raw materials that go into the thing that is being mixed—that is, the dough. So, let's first look at the two distinct categories of doughs: direct and indirect.

DIRECT DOUGH VERSUS INDIRECT DOUGH

Direct dough is mixed with ingredients that have not undergone any previous mixing or fermentation. Breads made with direct dough usually rely more on the flavor of the ingredients than on the flavor developed through fermentation, and the recipes often have enough yeast to bring about the necessary leavening in a minimal amount of time. Examples of typical direct-dough breads include standard enriched white bread, flavored dough like cheese bread or spiced bread, and most (but not all) sandwich bread and soft rolls.

Indirect dough is built in two or more stages, utilizing one of many types of pre-fermented dough. There are some breads that greatly benefit from this building approach, while others may show no discernible improvement beyond the direct-dough method. The indirect method is particularly effective when extended fermentation is necessary for flavor or texture development, such as in lean *pain ordinaire*. Breads such as French bread, whole grain (especially 100 percent whole wheat) bread, and rye bread usually turn out better if made with a pre-ferment because the extended fermentation makes the bread more digestible and coaxes more flavor from the grain.

Pre-ferments

A pre-ferment is a powerful tool in the creation of superior bread. Pre-ferments extend fermentation time, allowing for more flavor to be coaxed out of the complex wheat molecule. Four types of pre-fermented dough are commonly used, with variations of each creating the possibility of endless types of pre-ferments. There are two types of firm, or stiff, pre-ferments and two types of wet, or sponge, pre-ferments. The firm pre-ferments are known under their European names, *pâte fermentée* and *biga*. The wet pre-ferments are called *poolish* and regular sponge, or *levain levure* (leaven of the yeast) in French.

Pâte fermentée is the French name for pre-fermented, or old, dough. It can be made, for example, by saving a piece of dough from one batch, after the dough has had its primary fermentation, to use later in a different batch or by simply making a piece of dough specifically to be used later, perhaps the next day. Adding the *pâte fermentée* has the effect of immediately aging a newly made dough. This method is often used in bakeries to improve simple lean breads.

A *biga*, an Italian style of firm pre-ferment, differs from a *pâte fermentée* in that it doesn't have any salt in it. Also, rather than cutting off a piece of finished bread dough to hold back as an improver, a *biga* is made specifically to be used as a pre-ferment. By leaving out the salt, a *biga* can be made with less yeast than a finished bread to accomplish its necessary fermentation. Salt serves as a yeast inhibitor, making fermentation more difficult to achieve (which

DESIRED DOUGH TEMPERATURE

A question that often comes up is how to determine the temperature of the water or other liquid when mixing the dough. Many of the doughs in this book call for water at about room temperature, anywhere from 68°F to 72°F (20°C to 22°C). But in colder or warmer climates, the other ingredients may require a warmer or cooler liquid in order to achieve the desired dough temperature (in most cases) of 77°F to 81°F (25°C to 27°C). Here's the method, known as the 240 factor, that many bakers use to determine water temperature.

To illustrate how it works, we will use 80°F (27°C) as a target for the desired dough temperature. The four factors that most directly influence this temperature are the temperature of the flour, the general ambient temperature, the water or liquid temperature, and the friction caused by mixing. The one ingredient we can most easily control is the liquid temperature. So the formula for calculating the liquid temperature is to add up the flour temperature, the ambient temperature, and the friction factor (which for

most mixers is 30, if very little mixing is involved, and thus no heat-generating friction, the number can be as low as 20, as is more likely when using short mixing coupled with stretch and folds). Once you have determined these three numbers and totaled them, subtract that total from 240. The number 240 is based on the number of known factors (flour temperature, ambient temperature, and friction)—3—multiplied by the desired dough temperature, 80, thus 240. Subtract the total of these factors from 240, and the remaining number is the desired water temperature. Here's an example:

Flour temperature:	65°F
Ambient temperature:	69°F
Friction factor:	30°F
Total	164

Therefore, 240 − 164 = 76°F (24°C)

Thus, with a lightly mixed dough followed by a series of stretch and folds and very little friction, the water temperature should be about 76°F (24°C). If you

are using a stand mixer with a long mix (more than 6 minutes total), you would increase the friction factor to 40, which would bring the total to 174, and then subtract 174 from 240; the liquid temperature would need to be 66°F (19°C).

Although most of the instructions in this book provide the temperature for the liquid, feel free to calculate it yourself using this formula and adjust the liquid temperature as needed based on your temperature conditions and the mixing method you are using.

NOTE: The 240 factor doesn't translate into Celsius calculations at each step of the way, so it is best to calculate all the numbers in Fahrenheit first and then convert the final water temperature number if you are working in Celsius. If you don't have access to an electronic conversion program, you can subtract 32 from the Fahrenheit number and then multiply by 0.5556 (or ⁵⁄₉) to determine the Celsius equivalent.

is why it is such a good preservative in certain foods). In the absence of salt, the yeast has no restrictions in its quest to digest all available sugar, so very little yeast is needed.

Why is using less yeast good? Remember that our mission is to evoke from the wheat the fullness of its flavor. The flavor of bread comes from the grain, not from the yeast. Leaven should not draw attention to itself but to the grain. Therefore, a baker's maxim is to use only as much yeast as is necessary to get the job done. This minimizes the flavor of the yeast and maximizes the flavor of the grain. Thus a *biga* may have as little as 0.5 percent fresh yeast to flour (and even less if using instant or active dry yeast) to ferment the dough successfully.

A *poolish* (right) is very wet and sticky, while a *biga* (left) looks and feels like French bread dough.

Poolish is a term that was coined by the French to honor the Polish bakers who, centuries ago, taught them this technique for improving bread. A *poolish* is a wet sponge, usually made with a ratio of equal weights of water and flour, no salt, and only 0.25 percent or less of fresh yeast to flour, even less than for a *biga*. The wet sponge offers far less resistance to fermentation than does firm dough, so the yeast has an easy time converting the available sugars into carbon dioxide and ethanol. For this reason, a little yeast goes a long way, and a long fermentation ensues. When a *poolish* is used as a pre-ferment, it is usually, but not always, necessary to use additional yeast during the mixing of the final dough to complete the leavening.

Sourdough starters made with wild yeast, which we will cover in more depth later, are also pre-ferments and can take the form of a wet, *poolish*-like sponge or as a firm, *biga*-like dough. They, too, are typically made without salt. A regular sponge, on the other hand, is usually faster than a *poolish* because it front-loads all or most of the yeast in the sponge itself. This kind of sponge, often used in whole grain and rich breads, improves flavor and digestibility of the grain, and in less time than a *poolish*. The flavor improvement is not as drastic as in the slower pre-ferments, but the trade-off is that the breads can be made in a relatively short time frame. The final mixing, for instance, can be done approximately 1 hour after the sponge is made.

Soaker is the name for another type of pre-dough that appears in some of the formulas. This is a nonyeasted ingredient, usually made with coarsely milled whole grain such as cornmeal, rye meal, or cracked wheat, that has been soaked overnight in water or milk. Its purpose is to activate the enzymes in the grains in order to break out some of the trapped sugars from the starches. It also softens the coarse grain. Although little or no actual fermentation takes place in a soaker, its effect in the final dough is dramatic. Instructions for soakers are provided in the formulas in which they are used.

The real question behind these pre-ferment techniques, and one that you are hopefully asking at this point, is why does extended fermentation improve flavor? This is where deconstructing bread gets really interesting because you enter into the realm of enzymes and the concept of sugar breakout, the real key to evoking flavor from the grain. We'll get deeper into the world of enzyme activity at Stage 3, primary fermentation.

Note: Confusion often exists among bakers regarding the terminology surrounding pre-ferments. Some bakers refer to all pre-ferments as sponges, whether they are made with commercial yeast or wild yeast, whether they are firm and dry or wet and sticky. Other bakers use the term *sponge* only for wet, fast-acting pre-ferments. Some breads are made with a fast-rising sponge (*levain levure*) and other breads with a slow-acting sponge (the *poolish,* for example). All pre-fermented dough can be called a sponge, however, or by any other of the international names that are associated with sponges. Regardless of how they are made or what they are called, they are all part of the family called pre-ferments, that is, dough that has been fermented or conditioned in advance and added to another dough as part of a building process. For our purposes, when we refer to sponges, we mean wet pre-ferments, whether made with commercial yeast (like a *poolish*) or wild yeast (like a barm or sourdough starter). Firm, dry pre-ferments will be referred to by name, such as *biga,* or simply as firm starters (usually in sourdough bread). Whether called sourdough starter, *levain,* barm, *desum,* mother, or *chef,* these are all variations of pre-ferments leavened by wild yeast rather than commercial yeast. This category of pre-ferments will be explained, beginning on page 110.

MACHINE MIXING VERSUS HAND KNEADING

Whether a dough is made using the direct or indirect method, the three purposes of mixing—distribution of ingredients, development of gluten, and initiation of fermentation—must be fulfilled. The "how" question reveals the philosophical divide that exists in the baking world between those who are die-hard by-hand kneaders and the opposing camp of mixing-machine loyalists. There is a certain romantic, spiritual cachet to the idea of hand kneading, and

I wouldn't deny the meditative, spiritual component of the process. Looked at from a strictly utilitarian or functional perspective, however, each method can get the job done.

In batches larger than 10 pounds (4.5kg), it is more practical to use large mixing machines, of which there are several designs, than to mix by hand (although I do know a few bakers who mix even large batches by hand). Small batches can be mixed in the following machines:

- KitchenAid or other planetary mixer (2.2 pounds/1kg flour is usually the maximum).

- Food processor (1 pound/454kg flour is the maximum, unless you have a very large processor).

- Magic Mill mixer (5 pounds/22kg flour is the maximum).

- Other electric mixers, such as Kenwood and Hamilton Beach (2 to 4 pounds/908g to 1.8kg flour, depending on the model); like the KitchenAid, these are called planetary mixers because the hook or paddle rotates around the bowl like the planets around the sun.

- Any brand of electric bread machine designed to knead 1- to 2-pound loaves (454g to 908g). Some may even take up to 2.5 pounds (1.13kg)

If you are using an electric mixer, here are a few things to keep in mind:

- Mixers tend to walk on the counter, especially under the stress of mixing bread dough, so do not leave the machine unattended.

- You can use the paddle attachment in the beginning to gather the ingredients, and then switch to the dough hook. This is not necessary in bakery operations, but small batches sometimes are hard to get started with a dough hook because the ingredients tend to hug the walls of the bowl.

- If the mixer seems to be laboring or straining, dribble in a few drops of water or liquid to lubricate the bowl and soften the dough. Some mixer brands now include instructions suggesting that you mix for no longer than 4 minutes to reduce stress on the motor. If you want to protect your machine, you can allow the dough to rest after 4 minutes of mixing and then resume 5 or even 20 minutes later, or knead by hand. Remember the baker's maxim: mix only as long as it takes to get the job done. If the dough meets the mixing criteria after 4 minutes, there is no need to continue, but there are many ways to extend mixing time, if needed, without damaging your machine.

- Most stand mixers seem to work best with doughs that call for less than 8 cups flour (approximately 36 ounces/1kg). If the dough rides up close to the top of the dough hook, take it out and finish it by hand.

- Mixers and food processors can overheat and overwork the dough if left unattended, so stay close by.

If you decide to mix by hand, to knead in other words, a number of methods will accomplish the job. First, I prefer to stir everything together in a mixing bowl until the ingredients form a coarse ball of dough, transfer it to a lightly floured counter, and then use the mellow two-handed press-roll-turn method. Some of my friends prefer to slap the dough around like a rag doll, whacking it on the counter until it stretches out, folding it up, and then slapping it around again, giving the gluten a good workout. Between those two extremes are numerous other styles, such as the one-handed press and the roll-press-roll method. There is also the two-handed, squeeze-it-long, and then-work-it-in-sections technique. Some people prefer doing it all in the mixing bowl as shown on page 58, with either one hand plunged into the dough (like a dough hook) while the other turns the bowl, or using a large metal or wooden spoon or plastic dough scraper in place of your hand. Rustic doughs are well suited to this method since their higher hydration makes them harder to work with on a counter.

HOW TO MIX IN A FOOD PROCESSOR

Many bread bakers are now using food processors to mix dough and, if properly used, they work well. The key is to use the pulse mechanism and not to mix for long cycles. Also, because the processor mixes ingredients faster than they can actually hydrate, you need to let the dough rest for at least 5 minutes after the initial hydration, or gathering of ingredients into a ball. During this time, the gluten will begin to set up and all the ingredients will absorb the moisture to their fullest capacity. When you begin pulsing again, it will not take very long to finish mixing. You can turn the machine to "on" rather than "pulse," but do not mix for more than 45 seconds. The mixing should be finished by then. I usually wait to perform this longer mixing until I've made all the flour and water adjustments and the dough has the correct feel. Some dough, especially wet, rustic dough, gets caught under the blade. If that happens, stop mixing, remove the dough with a plastic bowl scraper or rubber spatula (dipping it into water repeatedly to prevent sticking), and then remove the blade. Clean the mixing bowl before returning the blade and dough to it and then mix again to finish.

NOTE: There has been ongoing discussion as to the relative merits of the metal versus the plastic dough blade. The plastic blade was developed specifically because it was believed to be gentler on the dough, but very few people who have used it find it effective. I agree with the recent consensus that the metal blade is superior to the plastic blade, assuming that you follow the mixing suggestions above.

*MIXING RUSTIC DOUGH BY HAND

(A) Using a large spoon, distribute the ingredients and initiate mixing. You can then continue to stir with a spoon, or you can dip one hand in water and (B) use it like a dough hook, rotating the bowl as shown above.

Once the three purposes of mixing have been accomplished, there is usually no reason to continue mixing and an important reason, in some instances, to stop immediately and proceed to the third stage of bread production (primary fermentation).

MIXING METHODS

In professional bread-baking operations, three mixing methods can be used: the intensive method, the improved method, and the simplified or short method. Each has its advantages, depending on the type of dough being made. For instance, rich sweet dough usually requires long, intensive mixing on high speed to accomplish fat incorporation and gluten development fully. Lean French-style dough does better with either the improved mixing method (a combination of slow and fast speeds) or a long, gentle simplified mixing on slow speed followed by a series of stretch and folds. Home bakers most often find themselves using a modified improved method (if using electric mixers) or the simplified method. This is especially true when kneading by hand, since it is impossible to replicate sustained high-speed mixing when it's just your hands and the dough.

Whichever method you use, the goals of mixing must be met without damaging or degrading the dough. The most common form of degrading comes from overmixing and overheating (which leads to overfermenting).

Each type of dough has its own parameters and requirements. Some require cold water and some warm water. Some set up quickly, and others take longer for the gluten to bond properly. The type of mixing equipment or mixing method directly relates to the mixing time, so choices must be made by the baker to optimize the success of the mixing, and the quality of these choices will be reflected in the final product.

It is particularly important to remember that how a dough absorbs water will vary depending on climatic conditions and the brand and age of the flour. Therefore, the water (hydration) percentage in a formula can never be more than an approximation. For this reason, I strongly advise you always to withhold a small amount of the liquid in the first stages of mixing until you are certain the dough needs it. Likewise, if you have added all the required liquid and the dough still seems too stiff, adjust by adding more than the required amount. The dough, not the written formula, must dictate its needs. If it seems as though you have added too much liquid and your dough is too slack or sticky, then add more flour to make it right.

Before moving onto primary fermentation, here are some tips for accomplishing the three goals of mixing.

Ingredient Distribution

Each of the mixing methods described will adequately distribute the ingredients. When adding ingredients to the mixing bowl, it is a good idea to avoid placing the yeast and the salt in direct contact with each other, as salt will kill the yeast in such concentrated contact. Instead, you can stir the salt into the flour, and then do the same with the yeast, or simply place the yeast and salt on opposite sides of the bowl prior to hydration and mixing. If you are adding pre-fermented dough or a firm sourdough starter, break it up into smaller pieces, which can be more easily incorporated and distributed evenly.

STRETCH AND FOLD

A few years after the original publication of this book, I became more interested in the effectiveness of what I call the stretch-and-fold technique. The method was included in that first edition but was not emphasized to the degree that I later used it. In many of the instructions that follow, I have suggested the stretch-and-fold technique in place of longer mixing times. It not only saves on mixing but also reduces oxidation of the beta-carotene pigments and promotes better oven spring and dough development. The method is simple, not unlike the photo shown on page 24 and also shown in the Ciabatta recipe on page 146. But to make it even simpler, I have also added a step called the oil slick, which allows you to make the fold without extra flour and without the dough sticking to your hands or the work surface.

First, place a small amount of vegetable or olive oil (about ¼ teaspoon) on the work surface and spread it into a circle or square about 10 inches (25cm) across. Using oiled hands or an oiled plastic bowl scraper, transfer the dough to this slick. Next, pat the dough to flatten it, pull a section from one side to stretch it out slightly, and then flop that stretched section on top of the dough so that it lands in the center of it and reaches about halfway across. Repeat this same action from the other side of the dough, folding it to land on top of the first fold, covering it completely. Repeat this same action from both the top and the bottom of the dough. The dough will now have been stretched and folded from all four sides. Now, flip the dough over so the folded sides are down and the smooth underside is facing up. At this point, you can either return the dough to a lightly oiled bowl or cover the dough with the bowl. This completes one stretch and fold (s&f).

The intervals between these s&f's vary from dough to dough, so follow the prompts in the instructions. They can be as short as 1 to 5 minutes and up to 20 or even 45 minutes. Typically, a lean hearth dough will benefit the most from three or four s&f's, and the dough will become stronger and smoother with each one.

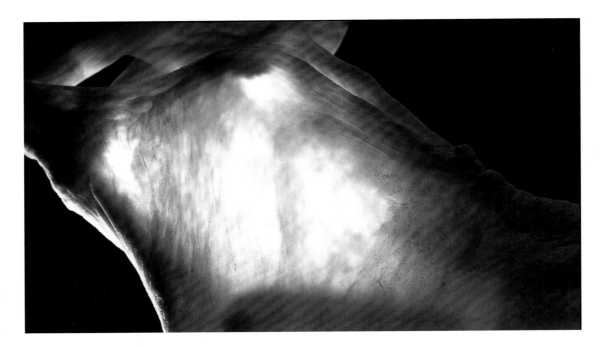

The windowpane test reveals valuable information about gluten development.

Gluten Development

Gluten is the primary protein in wheat, providing both structure and flavor. It is composed of two partial proteins, gliadin and glutenin, which are able to link to each other when hydrated. When they bond, they create the more complex protein called gluten. Flour is defined by the amount of potential gluten it contains (remember, there is no gluten, per se, in flour until it is hydrated and the gliadin and glutenin link up). As discussed on page 27, each flour variety has a different gluten percentage. Regardless of the type of flour or its protein, every brand has its own capacity to develop gluten within a predictable window of time. Most commercial flour will develop gluten within 6 to 8 minutes of hydration. Typically, the higher the protein, the longer it takes for the gluten to bond fully, so high-gluten flour may require 8 to 12 minutes of mixing to develop.

One of the techniques that bakers often use to minimize mixing (and thus to reduce oxidation that causes natural bleaching of the flour) is to mix the flour and water for only a few minutes, enough time to hydrate the flour fully, and then let the dough rest for 20 minutes. During this resting, or what the French call the *autolyse*, the protein molecules complete their hydration and begin bonding on their own. Then, when the mixing resumes and the other ingredients are added, it takes only 2 to 4 additional minutes to complete the mixing process, during which the newly formed gluten molecules continue to bond to one another in more complex ways.

The most reliable method to determine when gluten development is sufficient is called the windowpane test, sometimes referred to as the membrane test. This is performed by cutting off a small piece of dough from the larger batch and gently stretching, pulling, and turning it to see if it will hold a paper-thin, translucent membrane (see photograph, opposite). If the dough falls apart before the windowpane forms, continue mixing for another minute or two and test again. It is very difficult to overmix bread dough, that is, to overwork the gluten to the point of breaking the molecular bond. It can happen in professional mixing equipment if the dough overheats, or in a food processor, which can overheat dough very quickly, but most home-kitchen mixers will overheat themselves before overmixing bread dough. If you are hand kneading, you will probably cramp up well before your dough breaks down. I've never seen anyone overknead dough by hand, but I have seen dough oxidize and lose some flavor from overmixing.

Initiating Fermentation

Yeast activation and the initiation of fermentation is, like gluten development, also triggered by hydration (hydration can come from either water or some other liquid, such as milk or juice). Regardless of the type of yeast used, it must be hydrated and distributed throughout the dough in order perform its leavening magic.

With the exception of active dry yeast, which must be hydrated in water first, both fresh and instant yeast will absorb enough moisture during the mixing and kneading process to activate. You can soften it in water if you like, but it is not necessary to do so. I prefer mixing it into the flour before adding the liquid.

Stage 3: Primary Fermentation

> *What many bakers don't realize is that good wheat can make*
> *bad bread. The magic of bread baking is in the manipulation*
> *and the fermentation. What has been lost . . . is this method.*
> —LIONEL POILÂNE

Baking great bread really comes down to one skill: how to manipulate time and temperature to control outcomes. Control is a very important concept here, since every decision that the baker makes is reflected in the finished loaf. If the bread is underbaked or overbaked, it shows up. If it is improperly fermented, either for too long or not long enough, this also reveals itself.

The baker's ability to respond and adjust to external conditions reveals the skill of the baker and is also one of the most fun and challenging components of the craft.

Fermentation is the single most important stage in the creation of great bread. As we will see later, the baking stage (Stage 10) also employs manipulation of time and temperature, but no matter how good your oven is or how perfect your shaping technique, if the bread is not properly fermented, it can never be better than average. It is in this, the primary fermentation stage, that dough is transformed from a lifeless lump of clay into a living organism.

Every dough has its own fermentation requirements based on a delicate balance among the amount of yeast, yeast nutrients, and enzymes at work; the temperature of both the dough and the room in which it is fermented; and the length of fermentation. Some doughs are raised (fermented) in covered bowls or tubs at room temperature or warmer, typically for 1 or 2 hours, while others are chilled immediately after mixing, thus slowing (or retarding) the fermentation activity in order to draw forth more flavor from the dough through extended enzyme activity. (The latter is the principle at work in the *pain à l'ancienne* technique I learned from Philippe Gosselin and featured on page 199.) Professional bakeshops usually have controlled environments and closely monitor dough and room temperatures, but home bakers often have to improvise. Finding a warm place on a cold day can be a challenge as can timing fermentation and proofing cycles to coincide with your schedule. When I make bread at home, I often set a timer to keep me mindful of the dough.

Whatever fermentation specifications a dough may require, it always comes down to a dance between time, temperature, and ingredients, especially sugar. Sugar is the one necessary ingredient for fermentation to occur, as it is ultimately converted into alcohol and carbon dioxide by the yeast. The sugar can be added as an ingredient or it can be derived (as it is, for example, in French bread) exclusively from the complex flour starch molecules as they break apart into simpler sugar molecules. Typically, the fewer enrichments in a dough, the longer the fermentation will take because most of the flavor will come exclusively from the wheat, the starches of which need time to release their natural sugars. In a dough that is enriched with added sugar, dairy, or fat, much of the bread flavor is derived from the enrichments rather than from the flour, so shorter fermentation time is preferable.

The following discussion is designed to empower you as a baker by giving you information that will inform the choices you make during the bread-baking process.

METHODS OF FERMENTATION AND TYPES OF YEAST

Here I am referring specifically to yeast fermentation. Bacterial fermentation also affects bread, especially sourdough or wild-yeast breads, but it will be discussed later in this chapter (see page 67). Yeast fermentation in bread is a result of yeast cells, primarily from the Saccharomycetaceae family of fungi, more specifically, the species known as *Saccharomyces cerevisiae*, feeding on the simple sugars of glucose and, to a lesser extent, fructose and maltose (but not sucrose, or table sugar). Several strains of wild yeast given the general name *S. exiguus* can also ferment bread, but this species generally comes into play in sourdough breads. Commercially produced *S. cerevisiae* yeast is used in most home and professional baking for fermenting almost every standard bread.

Professional bakers are used to working with fresh yeast but are also comfortable with active dry yeast and instant yeast, substituting according to the following standard formula:

100 percent fresh yeast = 40 to 50 percent active dry yeast = 33 percent instant yeast

Fresh yeast is available to home bakers in some specialty and natural foods stores, but its shelf life is only 2 to 3 weeks. Active dry yeast and instant yeast have the advantage of almost unlimited shelf life. As a general rule, if a recipe calls for one type of yeast, it is usually acceptable to substitute another type following the substitution ratio described above.

SAF Products packages a type of instant yeast called osmotolerant. It was developed for use in either very sweet or very acidic dough, as it is able to tolerate the high acid or sugar that normally slows down regular yeast strains. It is packaged in a gold wrapper, and most bakers call it SAF Gold. There are only a few dough formulas in which this yeast strain is appropriate. Although it will take longer to activate, regular instant yeast will also work in those formulas, so feel free to make those breads even if you don't have the osmotolerant yeast.

More facts about yeast:

- Commercial yeast is grown and packaged under very strict hygienic regulations. The yeast cells are grown in a nutrient base that usually contains molasses and other carbohydrates. Yeast multiplies by budding (mitosis), and the manufacturing companies have perfected the ability to grow the cells rapidly and keep them alive in both dry and moist forms.

- Large bakeries sometimes use cream yeast, a type not available to home bakers. The yeast and nutrient base are in liquid form, which makes them easier to blend in high-speed mixing systems. Cream yeast is seen rarely except in bakeries producing tens of thousands of pounds of dough a day.

- All the commercial yeast brands are fairly comparable in strength. Instant yeast contains about 25 percent more living yeast cells per spoonful than active dry yeast, regardless of the brand, due to the processing method. This is why you need less of it than active dry yeast. Also, active dry yeast forms larger grains that have to be dissolved first in warm water (this is called proofing the yeast). Instant yeast comes in such small grains that it instantly hydrates when the dough hydrates, so it can be added directly to the flour. This is the best reason to use it and why it is the preferred yeast in these formulas. However, you can certainly substitute active dry yeast or even fresh yeast if that's what you have on hand.

- Once a yeast package is opened, the yeast will begin to absorb moisture from the air and slowly come to life. For this reason, it will lose strength as it sits unless you keep it in an airtight container in the refrigerator or the freezer. Some people think that freezing yeast will kill it, but I've kept a viable container in my freezer for over a year without it losing any discernible potency.

WHAT HAPPENS DURING FERMENTATION AND HOW IT CHANGES THE DOUGH

Here is the most basic piece of information to know about yeast fermentation: the yeast feeds on sugars, converting the sugar to carbon dioxide and alcohol (ethanol) as a digestive by-product. The ethanol evaporates during baking while the carbon dioxide leavens, or raises, the dough, and then it too bakes out of the bread.

Among the axioms of bread making is this: use only as much yeast as it takes to get the job done. Too much yeast will speed the leavening of the dough, but it will also exhaust the available sugars and create an alcohol aftertaste. As the yeast starves for sugar, it begins turning inward upon itself, causing the yeast to create a less desirable by-product, glutathione, which creates an ammonia-like taste that adversely affects the dough and weakens the gluten bonds. Most standard recipes are formulated for a 1- to 1½-hour primary fermentation with a similar time frame for the secondary fermentation, or final proofing and rise. If the dough ferments faster than this, due to warm conditions or too much yeast, it is easy to lose control of the dough and end up with inferior bread.

THE IMPORTANCE OF ENZYMES

Enzymes are proteins that, according to food scientist Harold McGee, "are organic catalysts. That is, they selectively increase the rate of chemical reactions that otherwise would occur only very slowly." This is incredibly important information for a bread baker and serves differently for bakers than for cooks. In the case of most cooking, enzymes are responsible for hastening the degradation of food, in other words, spoilage. This is because in most foods, unlike bread (or beer and wine), fermentation is bad, not good. But in bread baking, we are trying to ferment grain in order to leaven it. We are also trying to release sugars trapped in the complex starch molecules. Some of this released sugar becomes yeast food, but much of it becomes available to the palate as flavor and to the crust as color (caramelization).

Imagine a starch molecule, what we call a complex carbohydrate, as a ball of yarn composed of many threads of sugar molecules interwoven to create an almost impenetrable fortress. When we taste raw flour, or even raw bread dough, very little flavor is perceived by the palate because all the threads are wrapped around one another, making them difficult to discern. Flour tastes like sawdust because its sugar components are too complex to differentiate on the tongue. Now introduce a catalyst, an enzyme, that acts like a wedge breaking apart that ball of yarn, freeing the various threads so that they become accessible, even vulnerable, to our palates or to other organisms such as yeast and bacteria. This is the degradation process of food, proteins, starches, and even sugars that ultimately reduces all foods to simple sugars and thus makes them fermentable.

Bread bakers, knowingly or unknowingly, avail themselves of this natural process, interrupting it midstream during baking (Stage 10) to capture the optimum flavors inherent in the complex carbohydrates and proteins. The outcome is that the freed sugars are manifest as a golden crust and a sweetness that was not present in the raw flour or the raw dough. When I repeat over and over the importance of manipulating time and temperature, it is this process to which I am referring.

Enzyme science is a large and complex matter in its own right and thus could use an enzymatic catalyst to deconstruct it for laypeople like us, so this will be a very brief explication. The particular enzyme type that affects flour carbohydrates is called amylase, of which there is both an alpha- and a beta-amylase category. Whenever you see a term ending in "ase," it usually denotes an enzyme that acts upon the corresponding sugar ending in "ose," such as amylose, or lactase acting upon lactose (milk sugar). (There are also protein-acting enzymes, or proteases, that cause the same chain reaction in proteins such as gluten, initiating a process that affects structure more than flavor.) Amylose is a large category of sugar that includes subcategories, such as maltose, sucrose, glucose, fructose, and dextrose. For instance, there is a type of alpha-amylase enzyme called diastase that breaks down some complex sugars into maltose, or malt. If one of the ingredients on a label is malted barley flour, or if you see the term *diastatic malt*, it refers to the presence of active diastase enzymes within the flour. There is also such a thing as nondiastatic malt in which the enzymes have been heated to the point of deactivating or denaturing, usually to around 170°F (77°C). This type of malt is used as a flavor enhancer but not as an enzyme catalyst (it is often used in bagels).

During yeast fermentation, the yeast can feed properly only on the most simple sugars like glucose and, to a lesser extent, fructose. There is a small amount of these simple sugars naturally present in flour, mostly due to starch damage caused during the milling process in which some of the glucose strands are bruised. This is what allows French bread to rise even though no sugar is added to the dough (and even if it were, the yeast can't feed on sucrose, or table sugar, because it is a two-chain sugar and thus too complex for the yeast). While the dough is fermenting, the amylase and diastase enzymes go to work on the starches, breaking down the complex starch molecules into simpler components by breaking out the sugars. Given enough time, all the starch would degrade into sugar and eventually be consumed by yeast and bacteria, but the baking stage interrupts this process well in advance, and at the optimum time for flavor and texture—if a good baker is at work. (A natural built-in ceiling also exists regarding the extent to which enzymes alone can degrade starches, so there is a point beyond which even enzymes cannot go on releasing all the inherent sugar. But now we are talking rocket science. . . .)

What happens in a properly fermented dough is that the maximum amount of sugar for flavor and color is released while retaining enough starch and protein to attain optimum texture. The full-spectrum bread-baking process is an acting out of this drama, this race against and within time to achieve maximum results in the areas of flavor, appearance, and texture.

Most bread flour now comes already enhanced with malted barley flour. Barley is sprouted, which activates the enzymes and begins the conversion process of barley starch to barley sugar (what we commonly call malt). This is then dried and milled into powder or melted into syrup. A small amount of the powder, loaded with diastatic alpha-amylase enzymes, is added to bread flour to promote the catalytic action referred to earlier. It takes a number of hours for the enzyme activity to accomplish its mission fully, which is another reason why long, slow fermentation produces better bread. As already noted, there is a built-in automatic brake mechanism in the enzyme-catalyzing process, limiting the degree of degradation that enzymes can accomplish on their own. For this reason, it is not necessary to use a lot of malt; usually 0.5 to 1 percent is enough to do the job. Any more than that can cause the dough to become gummy.

One appropriate use of diastatic enzyme–rich malted barley flour is to promote better color in the crust. A small addition of diastatic malt (0.5 percent) will dramatically improve caramelization by breaking out more maltose from the flour starch. Most of the time this is not necessary because of the malted barley flour added to the bread flour by the mill, but some formulas are improved further by the addition of a little more during the mixing stage.

Another result of this enzyme action is that more natural sugar previously trapped in the wheat is now made available to the palate. This is really the most important piece of information regarding enzymes, upon which we will soon create some interesting breads. To evoke the maximum flavor potential from the grain takes time. There are enough enzymes naturally occurring in flour that it is not always necessary to add them in the form of malted barley, as long as you are able to stretch time long enough to allow them to do their job. This is, in a nutshell, why pre-ferments create superior bread: they are a way to manipulate time, to stretch it, so that the wondrous chemical activity going on at the cellular level can fulfill its mission.

It is up to the baker to utilize the various fermentation options to their best effect. Almost any bread can be made in a variety of ways, and the formulas that have been passed down to us are not always the best ones. For example, access to refrigeration and other ways to control temperature is a modern phenomenon. Also, it is only in the past 50 years or so that chemists have figured out some of the internal drama that has been so blithely summarized in the past few pages. French breads, which were once made strictly by the 60-2-2 method (60 percent water, 2 percent salt, 2 percent yeast), can now be made by any number of formulas, using various types of pre-ferments, or with no pre-ferment at all, such as Philippe Gosselin's *pain à l'ancienne* (page 199). The required method for making baguettes for the Coupe du Monde bread competition (the so-called Bread Olympics) calls for using a *poolish*, but a *biga*, a *pâte fermentée*, and even combinations of these and other techniques also can make a superior baguette.

SOURDOUGH (WILD YEAST) AND BACTERIAL FERMENTATION

To complete this section on fermentation, we must discuss wild-yeast bread, better known as sourdough bread. The previous pages have focused on yeast fermentation enhanced by enzyme activity. But simultaneous to the yeast activity is a secondary fermentation, bacterial, that has a different effect on the flavor of bread. On page 238, you will learn a method for making wild-yeast starters, followed by a number of bread formulas that use this method, but here are some questions and answers that explain the broad strokes of this important process.

All About Wild Yeast and Bacterial Fermentation

What makes sourdough different from regular bread? Most people think the difference is caused by a special wild yeast, but that is only part of the answer. Yes, a variety of wild-yeast strains aggregated under the name *Saccharomyces exiguus* is used to make sourdough bread, as opposed to the *S. cerevisiae* strains used in regular breads. But the complex sour flavor is not created by the wild yeast. Other microorganisms, bacteria, specifically lactobacillus and aceto-bacillus, create lactic and acetic acids as they feed off the enzyme-released sugars in the dough, and these are responsible for the sour flavor. San Francisco sourdough bread, for example, has a particular type of local bacteria called *Lactobacillus sanfranciscensis* (what a coincidence!) that gives this bread a different quality, more sour with a thicker crust, than any other wild-yeast bread made in other parts of the world. (Note: *L. sanfranciscensis* exists throughout the world and shows up in other regions' sourdough breads, but just not in such abundance.)

What does the wild yeast do? Regular commercial yeast (*S. cerevisiae*), which is the same yeast used in beer making (which might explain why beer has been called "liquid bread"), does not like an acidic, or sour, environment. If bacterial activity creates too much acid, this type of yeast will die and make the bread taste funny, with an ammonia-like aftertaste and a weakened gluten structure caused by the glutathione released by the yeast. Most regular *S. cerevisiae*–leavened breads have a pH level of 5.0 to 5.5.

On the other hand, wild yeast (*S. exiguus*) likes acidic environments (pH of 3.5 to 4.0) and therefore thrives when bacteria do their work creating lactic and acetic acids. Since it takes about twice as long for the bacteria to create flavor as it takes for the yeast to leaven the dough, it requires a hearty strain of yeast to endure. This is why wild yeast is required to make good sourdough bread.

How do you make or grow wild yeast? We do not have to make it since it already lives all around us in the air and on plants, grains, and fruits (it's in the white powdery "bloom" found on the skin of grapes, plums, and wheat berries). We do need, however, to capture and cultivate it to make bread. We do this by making a sourdough starter or what some bakers call a barm or a *levain*. A good bread baker knows how to keep the starter alive and healthy from batch to batch and how to add just the right amount to make a tasty bread. This is part of the craft of baking.

The main trick in cultivating a starter is to feed it regularly with fresh flour and water, thus providing it with the nutrients and grain sugars it needs to stay alive. You can also keep a starter alive, but dormant, by refrigerating or freezing it, which also slows down fermentation by putting the yeast to sleep (yeast fermentation practically stops below 40°F/4°C). A healthy starter can be kept alive forever with proper cultivation. Some of the bread companies in

CHEMICAL LEAVENING

With the exception of one formula (Corn Bread, page 157), this book is not about chemically leavened quick breads, but I think it is important to clarify a few points about chemical leavening because so many bakers use it. We teach culinary students that there are three types of leavening: biological or natural (in other words, yeast or wild yeast); physical (that is, steam or aeration); and chemical (baking powder, baking soda, and ammonium carbonate or ammonium bicarbonate, which is rarely used by home bakers). Physical leavening is at work in just about every baked product, since as soon as trapped air warms up, it begins to cause dough to rise. But the items we associate it with the most are laminated doughs like puff pastry, Danish, and croissants, as well as popover dough and cream puff dough (*pâte à choux,* also called choux paste).

The most often-used chemical leavening is baking powder, with baking soda also used in many recipes. One form of ammonium carbonate is derived from the horn of a deer and thus is called hartshorn. When it is used by bakeries, it is usually for crisp, dry items like crackers, as all moisture must evaporate in order to expel the ammonia taste.

Chemical leavening creates carbon dioxide, just as biological, organic leavening does, but it accomplishes this not through fermentation, but through a chemical process called neutralization. Simply stated, acid, which has a low pH factor (below 7 on a scale of 1 to 14), reacts to alkaline, which has a high pH factor (above 7). As the acid and alkaline react, or neutralize each other, the by-product of this action is carbon dioxide. Baking soda is very alkaline, and tartaric acid (cream of tartar) is very acidic. Mix the two in a glass of water, throw in an aspirin, and you have instant Alka-Seltzer (leave out the aspirin, and you have carbonated water).

In any formula that contains baking soda, you are likely to see a corresponding acidic ingredient, such as citrus juice, honey, vinegar, buttermilk, or sour cream. Typically, the amount of baking soda in a formula will range between 0.5 and 1.5 percent of the flour weight. Baking powder, which contains its own blend of acid and alkaline ingredients in a stable base, activates either when it gets wet or when it gets hot. Double-acting baking powder, which is what we mostly use in home baking, contains at least two types of acids. One type delivers what

we call bowl action, meaning that it begins neutralizing the alkaline (usually sodium bicarbonate, which is baking soda) as soon as the two hydrate. This is commonly tartaric acid or monocalcium phosphate monohydrate. The remaining acid, such as sodium aluminum sulfate, is heat sensitive but not water sensitive, so it doesn't activate with the baking soda until it reaches about 150°F to 160°F (66°C to 71°C). We call this oven action. Typically, a formula will contain 1 percent to 5 percent baking powder to flour, but some formulas contain as much as 7 percent baking powder. Since much of this book is devoted to understanding ratios, these percentages, along with this rudimentary understanding of chemical leavening, should be an important part of your knowledge bank.

For more information on how these chemical leavenings work, I recommend Shirley Corriher's *CookWise* (Morrow, 1997) and *BakeWise* (Scribner, 2008) or Harold McGee's *On Food and Cooking* (MacMillan, 1984, or Scribner, 2004).

San Francisco have been using the same starter, fed daily, for more than 150 years! We will go more deeply into the process of making a wild-yeast starter in specific formulas.

Stage 4: Punching Down (Degassing)

Punching down dough, while sounding very dramatic, is more accurately called degassing. There are four reasons for degassing dough. The first is that it expels some of the carbon dioxide trapped in the gluten network, and too much carbon dioxide will eventually choke off the yeast. Second, it allows the gluten to relax a bit. Third, the temperature on the outside of the dough is usually cooler than the interior, so the punch down helps equalize the interior and exterior temperature. Finally, when the dough is degassed, it allows for redistribution of the nutrients and triggers a new feeding cycle.

While many types of bread dough require a full degassing in preparation for the second rise, there are also many that benefit from a gentle handling, retaining as much gas as possible in order to produce large, irregular holes in the final product. French baguettes and other shapes of French bread are often judged by the quality of the holes, or webbing (also called the crumb).

When making lean, crusty breads, it's important to employ gentle handling to retain as much of the carbon dioxide as possible after the primary fermentation. These small pockets of holes become the foundation for the large, irregular holes formed during proofing and during baking that are the hallmark of high-quality hearth breads.

Some fermentation cycles require a punch down and then a second bulk rise, such as in long-fermentation lean dough like French bread. Technically speaking, as long as the dough stays in bulk, it is still in primary fermentation regardless of how many times it is punched down. Secondary fermentation (aka proofing) only begins once the dough is divided into smaller units (Stage 5). For this reason, when the degassing stage is mentioned, it is specifically the degassing just prior to dividing and scaling. The degree or severity to which this is done is entirely dependent on the type of bread being made. There will be times when the punch down is simply the transfer of the dough from the bowl to the counter. Often this is enough action to release carbon dioxide and accomplish the four primary objectives outlined above. In other instances, where bread with medium-size even holes is desired, such as in sandwich bread or dinner rolls, the punch down will involve total degassing.

I love transferring soft, rustic dough like ciabatta or focaccia from the bowl to the counter and watching it sink beneath its own weight, gently expelling gas but retaining enough to keep a nice, airy gluten network. The key to working with dough like this is to be gentle,

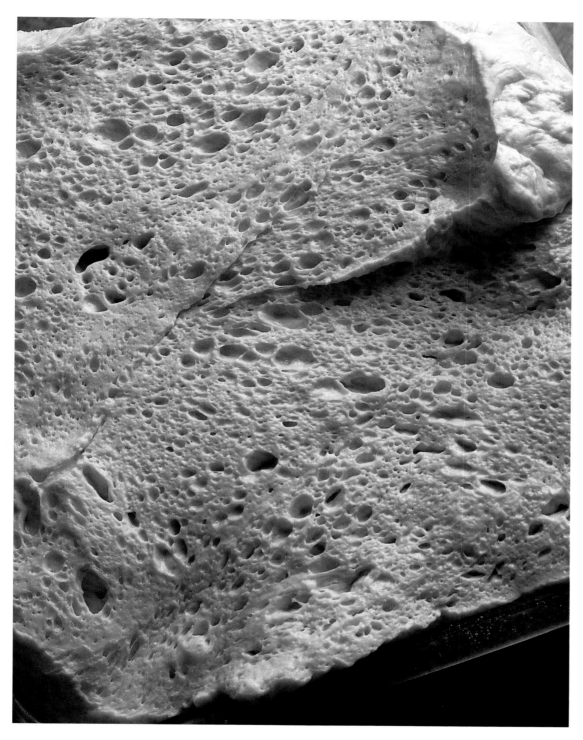

A cross section of raw French bread dough with large pockets of gas that will eventually become the irregular hole structure of the finished bread.

handling it as little as possible to retain as much gas as possible. This can be done by keeping the dough well floured or by keeping your hands wet (wet dough will not stick to wet hands). This kind of wet dough does not get rolled so much as gently folded. Again, the objective is to retain as much gas as possible so that in the secondary fermentation, the proofing stage, the newly generated gas will stretch the dough out farther, resulting in large, irregular holes in the final bread and thus a tastier loaf. The challenge facing those wishing to emulate the world-class breads now being produced at artisan bakeries is to handle the dough with, as the teacher of bread teachers Professor Raymond Calvel says, "an iron hand but a velvet glove."

Stages 5, 6, and 7: Dividing, Rounding, and Benching (the Middle Cycle)

Most commercially yeasted and naturally leavened (wild-yeast) breads require two fermentation cycles. As a rule, dough is fermented in bulk (primary fermentation) and then again after it has been divided and shaped (secondary fermentation, or proofing). Between these two fermentation cycles, the dough goes through three important stages.

Dividing the dough into individual pieces is the first stage of the secondary fermentation, quickly followed by rounding (preliminary shaping), and benching (a rest period, sometimes referred to as intermediate proofing). These three stages follow so closely together that we'll examine them in one section.

DIVIDING

First, the dough must be divided and scaled (weighed). This can be the final size or an intermediate size in preparation for subsequent dividing (for example, first weighing 16-ounce/454g pieces to be divided later into eight 2-ounce/57g rolls). When dividing, try to cut the dough cleanly (cut, don't rip) and with as few cuts as possible. Each time dough is cut, weak spots are created. These affect the final loaf if you have to combine two or more pieces to achieve the desired weight. Use either a metal pastry scraper or a serrated bread knife to make the clean cuts.

ROUNDING

The dough is then given a preliminary shaping, usually into a *boule* (ball) or *bâtard* (torpedo). This is called rounding, and it stretches the gluten yet again and helps to form surface tension on the skin of the dough, which aids the dough in retaining its shape during the final rise. If the finished bread is to have large, irregular holes, the shaping should be gentle, with minimum degassing. If it is for a sandwich loaf or rolls, it is okay to degas fully during the rounding.

The rounding stage is best viewed as preliminary shaping toward the final shape (though sometimes rounding is the final shape if you are making round loaves). When the final shape is to be a long loaf, like a baguette, I recommend forming the pieces into *bâtards* rather than into *boules*, as they make the final shaping easier. For illustrated instructions on making preliminary shapes, see pages 76 to 91.

BENCHING

Depending on the type of bread being made, the dough can again be handled quickly, almost immediately going into final shaping, or it may need to rest for up to 30 minutes or more to allow the gluten to relax. This is called benching, or resting, the dough. Although many of the breads in this book go directly from dividing to final shaping, you can apply the benching principle to any dough that resists shaping. The sole purpose of this stage is to relax the gluten after its workout during rounding, so that it will be easier to handle during final shaping. Whether a dough requires benching depends on three characteristics that affect final shaping, extensibility, elasticity, and tolerance, all of which are determined by the condition of the dough's gluten.

Extensibility, Elasticity, and Tolerance

If the gluten is tight, it will make the dough very elastic or springy. The opposite of elasticity is extensibility, meaning pliable and stretchy. Bread shaping is always dependent on the relationship of these two attributes, plus one other, tolerance. Extensibility is the dough's ability to stretch and hold a shape, elasticity is its tendency to spring back like a rubber band, and tolerance is its ability to be handled without breaking down. The elasticity and extensibility factors are primarily determined by the type of wheat or flour, but they are also influenced by the amount of handling the dough has undergone. Like a muscle, when the gluten protein is worked, it tightens up to the degree of its natural, inherent elasticity. Tolerance is determined by the strain or blend of wheat.

Two other factors that influence these three attributes include the amount of hydration (wetter dough is more tolerant and extensible, drier dough is more elastic and less tolerant) and the temperature of the dough (warmer dough is more extensible but loses some of its tolerance).

For example, when dividing a bulk pullman bread dough into smaller units for individual loaves, the units are first rounded into either *boules* or *bâtards*, then allowed to bench for 5 to 20 minutes before undergoing their final shaping. This benching gives the gluten time to relax so the final loaf shapes will not spring back into *bâtards*. When shaping baguettes or other long loaves, it sometimes is necessary to give the cut pieces two or even three benching cycles, extending the dough in stages to the desired length. Each time the elasticity kicks in, let the dough relax so it will become more extensible. The longer the benching, the more relaxed and extensible the dough will be.

What is important to understand throughout these stages is that the objective here is to both shape and prepare the dough for its final rise, or leavening cycle. Most of the flavor has already been developed during the primary fermentation. This is because the initial transformation that takes place when the dough ferments creates the most dramatic change in the flavor. The secondary fermentation continues some of the flavor development, but its effect is less noticeable than in the primary fermentation.

Stage 8: Shaping and Panning (Variations on Many Themes)

There are dozens of traditional shapes for bread and multiple techniques for achieving them. Some are classics and appear under various names throughout the world, like *boules*, *bâtards*, baguettes, and 12-inch (30cm) *pains parisiens* (also called stick bread in the United States and the most common shape for sourdough and French bread). Others are less common or very regional or seasonal. With the recent interest in traditional breads, home bakers have expressed a growing desire to learn the fancier, more difficult shaping techniques. There is even a surge in interest in artistic show breads.

One of the most difficult breads to shape properly is, surprisingly, the baguette. As ubiquitous as it is, and as inexpensive and simple in concept, this is the first shape by which apprentice bakers are judged. Again, many ways are used to achieve the iconic shape, so it is important to view the following instructions as a starting point. You may have already mastered another approach or seen it demonstrated another way. Please understand that this is just one of many methods. As you make more and more bread, you will eventually add your own twists and turns to your technique. You will, knowingly or unknowingly, develop a shaping style that is distinctively your own. However, the methods that follow will get you well on your way.

The shapes that are demonstrated in the following pages include *boule* (ball), *bâtard* (torpedo), baguette, *couronne* (crown), *épi* (sheaf of wheat) and other scissor cuts, *fendu* (split), *fougasse* (ladder), *tabatière* (pouch), *auvergnat* (cap), and pretzel, as well as sandwich loaves, *pistolets* (torpedo rolls), dinner rolls, pull-apart rolls, knotted rolls, and braids. Not every dough lends itself to all of these shapes, but most dough can be shaped in a variety of styles.

(Some recipe-specific shapes, such as bagel and brioche, are shown alongside the formula for the bread.) Accompanying the bread formulas are recommendations for which shapes are preferable.

Some shapes benefit from the use of special shaping devices such as proofing bowls or forms, canvas or muslin cloths, and shaped pans. However, even though these devices make life easier, it is possible to improvise and convert some common kitchen tools into useful shaping tools (see pages 32 to 35 for examples).

Most bread shapes begin with a *boule* or a *bâtard* shape, so I'll demonstrate these first.

* BOULE (BALL)

The *boule* is the fundamental shape from which many other shapes can be made. For this reason, we start here with one important principle: surface tension. The whole exercise of giving loaves this shape is based on creating a tight surface tension to allow the loaf to rise *up* and not just *out*; the tight skin causes the dough to retain its cylindrical shape rather than spreading and flattening. That is why the key step in shaping a *boule* is to press firmly on the bottom crease to tighten the surface (like getting the wrinkles out of a sheet). This can be done in a number of ways, the most common of which is to use either the edge of your hand or your thumbs to pinch the crease closed and exert pressure on the surface. Once you've grasped this step, you can follow the photographs and, with minimal practice, become proficient.

(A) Gather the dough to form a rough ball. (B) To create surface tension, stretch the outside of the dough into an oblong, being careful not to squeeze out the gas trapped in the dough any more than necessary. (C) Repeat this stretching motion, bringing the opposite ends together to make a ball. Tighten the surface tension by pinching to seal the bottom of the dough where the creases converge. (D) Set the *boules* aside for proofing or to rest for further shaping.

∗ BÂTARD (TORPEDO)

A *bâtard* (literally, "bastard") is a torpedo-shaped loaf 6 to 12 inches (15 to 30cm) in length. Aside from being a viable and popular shape in its own right, delivering a nice balance of both crust and crumb, it is also a good intermediate shape for making other forms. For example, rather than make a *boule* as a preliminary step to forming a baguette or sandwich loaf, I prefer to make a *bâtard*, so that I am already part of the way there and will need less effort to finish the extension after the dough rests briefly.

Gently pat the dough into a rough rectangle. **(A)** Without degassing the dough, fold the bottom third of dough, letter style, up to the center and press to seal, creating surface tension on the outer edge. **(B)** Fold the remaining dough over the top so that a new seam is formed on the edge, and **(C)** use the edge of your hand, or your thumbs, to seal the seam closed and to increase the surface tension all over. **(D)** Set the *bâtards* aside either for proofing or to rest before further shaping.

✳ BAGUETTE

This is the shape made famous in Paris and is thus the ultimate city bread. The length varies from region to region, but for home bakers, the real determining factor is the size of the oven. So while you may be able to make a perfect baguette shape as long as 3 feet (1m), your oven may only be able to handle 12- or 18-inch (30 to 46cm) lengths. For this reason, the instructions that follow are for 8-ounce (227g), 15-inch (38cm) baguettes designed for home ovens and baking stones. If you have access to a full-size commercial oven, you can increase the weight to 14 ounces (397g) and the length to 24 inches (61cm). And if you have access to a bakery oven, you can make 28- to 36-inch (71 to 91cm) baguettes scaled at 16 to 19 ounces (454g to 539g), which will result in spectacular loaves.

Before referring you to the instructional photos, it is again important to stress the necessity of surface tension, as explained in the *boule* and *bâtard* instructions. This not only enables the dough to rise in a tubular shape, but also makes it easier to score the loaf prior to baking.

After resting the *bâtard* to relax the gluten, lift the dough and gently pull it out from the ends. **(A)** Crease the dough down the middle and fold it as in the *bâtard*, like a letter. **(B)** Seal the crease against the counter to create surface tension. **(C)** Working from the center of the loaf and moving to the outside edges, gently but firmly rock and roll out the dough to extend it to the desired length. If the dough is too elastic and springs back to less than the desired length, allow it to rest for another 5 minutes and then repeat the rocking and rolling motion. **(D)** Set the baguettes aside for proofing.

* COURONNE (CROWN)

Make a *boule* and poke a hole in the center. **(A)** Gently stretch it into a large, circular, doughnutlike shape. Lay it down on a counter that has been dusted with flour and **(B)** crease the four quadrants with a dowel or thin rolling pin; dust the cracks with flour to prevent them from sealing closed. **(C)** Set the *couronne* aside for proofing.

* ÉPI (SHEAF OF WHEAT) AND OTHER SCISSOR CUTS

Shape and proof the dough as for a baguette. **(A)** Just before baking, cut the dough with scissors at a sharp angle, nearly parallel to the loaf, cutting almost, but not quite, through to the bottom of the dough (the loaf must stay connected). **(B)** Swing the cut sections out and away from the loaf, spreading them as wide apart as possible from one another. Bake directly on the parchment-lined sheet pan. You can make a wreath shape using the *épi* cut by making a ring with a baguette and then cutting it as described above. **(C, D)** Scissors can also be used to create interesting designs for any hearth bread shape, such as the dinner roll pictured.

★ FENDU (SPLIT BREAD)

Sprinkle flour over the top of a *bâtard* or short baguette and **(A)** crease it with a dowel or thin rolling pin, pushing to the bottom of the dough without severing it. Remove the pin and **(B)** sprinkle flour into the crack. Crease the dough a second time with the dowel or pin, slightly widening and reinforcing the split. Again sprinkle flour in the crack. **(C)** Gently lift the dough, turn it over, and proof it, crack side down. When proofed, roll it back over and bake it split side up.

*FOUGASSE (SOMETIMES CALLED LADDER BREAD)

Method 1: **(A, B)** Use a pastry scraper to slit open and spread a proofed baguette just prior to baking it.

Method 2: **(A, B)** Flatten a proofed *bâtard*, then slit it with a knife in a pattern of your choice, spreading the cuts open just prior to baking.

✳ TABATIÈRE (POUCH)

Make a *boule* and let it rest for 10 minutes to relax the gluten. Dust the top with flour. **(A)** Using a rolling pin, flatten half of the ball into a thin flap. **(B)** Brush vegetable oil on the top of the ball and **(C)** fold the flap back over the top. Set aside for proofing.

✳ AUVERGNAT (CAP)

Make a *boule* with a piece of dough. Cut another piece of dough one-quarter the size of the *boule* and flatten it into a disk. **(A)** Roll the disk into a circle the size of the top of the *boule*. Brush a small amount of vegetable oil on the top of the *boule* and lay the circle over the top. **(B)** Press the circle into the *boule* with your finger, making a depression in the center to seal the two together. (You can also put a small bead of dough into the depression and sprinkle poppy or sesame seeds on top.) Set aside for proofing.

✳ PRETZEL

Roll out 3 to 5 ounces (85g to 142g) of dough into a strand 12 to 15 (30 to 38cm) inches long. **(A)** Cross the ends to make a loop and give the loop an additional twist to anchor it. **(B)** Lift the two ends together, bringing them up to the widest parts of the loop, resting the tips just over the edge of the dough.

✳ PISTOLET (TORPEDO ROLL OR HOAGIE)

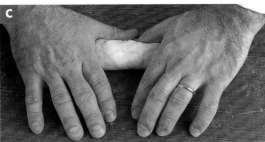

(A, B) Gently flatten the measured piece of dough and fold in the sides to square it off. Roll it up and seal the crease like a *bâtard*, creating surface tension. **(C, D)** Rock and roll the dough into a torpedo shape, exerting extra pressure on the ends to taper them. (For a more unusual look, you can split the roll in the style of a *fendu*.)

* SANDWICH LOAF

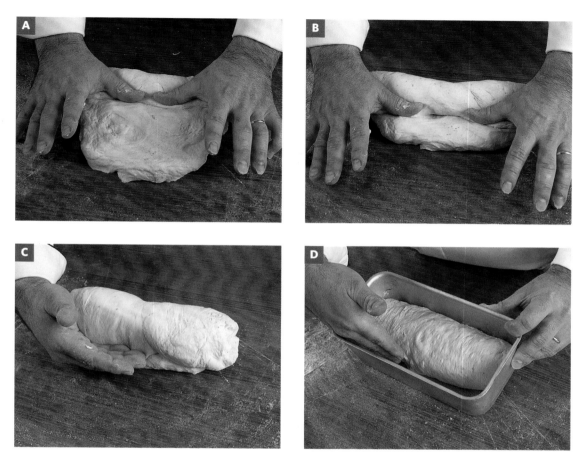

Flatten the measured piece of dough with your hand, folding in the edges to make an even-sided rectangle about 5 inches (13cm) wide and 6 to 8 inches (15 to 20cm) long. (A, B) Working from the short side of the dough, roll up the length of the dough one section at a time, pinching the crease with each rotation to strengthen the surface tension. The loaf will spread out as you roll it up, eventually extending to a full 8 to 9 inches (20 to 23 cm). (C) Pinch the final seam closed with the back edge of your hand or with your thumbs. Rock the loaf to even it out; do not taper the ends. Keep the surface of the loaf even across the top. (D) Place the loaf in a lightly oiled loaf pan. The ends of the loaf should touch the ends of the pan to ensure an even rise.

Clear the counter of all flour and swipe with a damp cloth to increase friction. Form your hand into a cup and place the dough inside. **(A)** Firmly press the dough into the counter as if trying to push it through the counter, simultaneously rotating your hand in a circular motion, driving the dough with the outer edge of your hand. **(B)** The dough should pop up into your palm and form a tight round ball. (With practice this shaping technique can be done with both hands at the same time.) **(C)** Assemble any number of rounded pull-apart dinner rolls on a parchment-lined sheet pan, just touching, so they will rise into one another. After they bake, the rolls will easily pull apart.

⋆ KNOTTED ROLL

(A) Roll out a measured piece of dough into a 6- to 8-inch (15 to 20cm) strand (2 ounces/57g for a dinner roll, 3 or 4 ounces/85g to 113g for a sandwich or kaiser-style roll). (B, C) Tie a simple knot. (D, E) Loop the two ends through the center a second time, by imagining the face of a clock. One end should come through at what would be 7 o'clock, the other end should come through at 5 o'clock (one end will go down through the loop and the other will come up through the loop, leaving a small nub in the center).

✴ BRAIDED LOAF

The most important principle in braiding loaves is to be sure each strand is the same weight and length. Also keep in mind that position numbers refer to the actual position of the strands on the counter (starting from your left) rather than to the strands themselves (thus, the number of a given strand changes as you move through the braiding process). To form the strands, use the same rocking-and-rolling hand motion used in shaping baguettes.

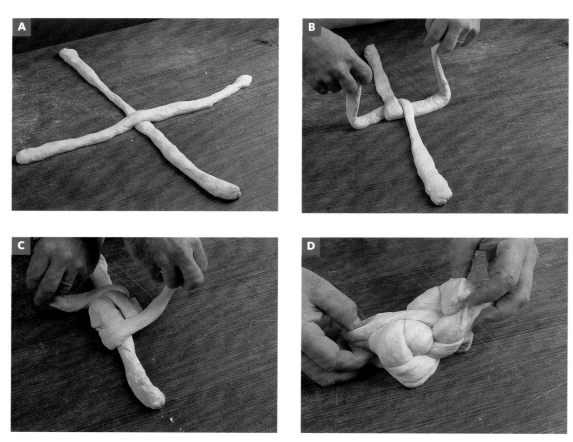

✴ TWO-BRAID

(A) Cross two strands of equal weight and length, and then take the two ends of the underneath strand and cross them again. (B) Cross the ends of the other strand in the same manner. (C) Continue crossing in this alternating manner until there is no more dough. (D) Pinch all the tips into one another to seal off the ends. Lay the braid on its side.

✷ THREE-BRAID AND DOUBLE BRAID

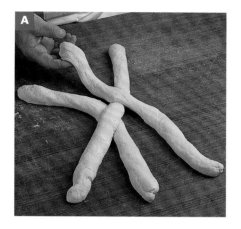

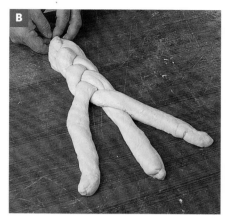

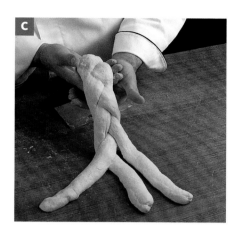

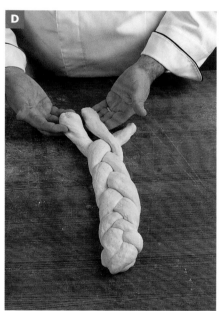

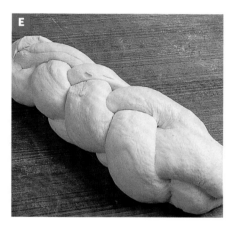

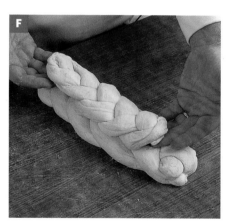

This is the only braid that begins in the middle. Place three strands of equal weight and length perpendicular to you and parallel to one another. From the left, number the strands 1, 2, 3. Beginning in the middle of the loaf and working toward you, follow this pattern: right outside strand over the middle strand (3 over 2); **(A)** left outside strand over the middle strand (1 over 2). Repeat until you reach the bottom end of the dough. **(B)** Pinch the end closed to seal and **(C)** rotate the loaf 180 degrees so the unbraided end is facing you. **(D)** Continue braiding but now weave the outside strand under the middle strand until you reach the end of the loaf. **(E)** Pinch together the tips at both ends to seal the finished loaf. For a double braid (festival or celebration loaf), make two three-braids, with the strands of the first braid weighing twice as much as those of the second braid (example: three 6-ounce strands and three 3-ounce strands). **(F)** Lay the smaller braid down the center of the top of the larger braid.

* FOUR-BRAID

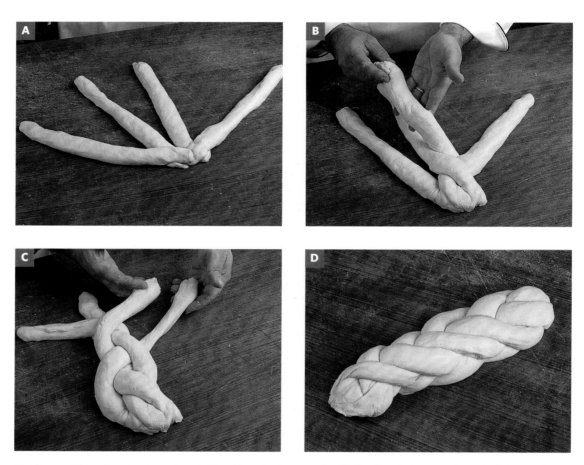

(A) Connect four strands of equal weight and length at one end, with the tips facing you. From the left, number the strands 1, 2, 3, 4. (B, C) Follow this pattern: 4 over 2, 1 over 3, and 2 over 3. Repeat until you run out of dough. (D) Pinch the tips together when you get to the end.

✳ FIVE-BRAID

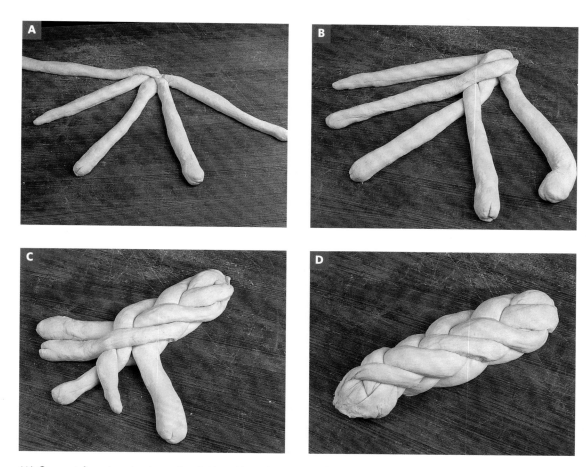

(A) Connect five strands of equal weight and length at one end, with the tips facing you. From the left, number the strands 1, 2, 3, 4, 5. (B) Follow this pattern: 1 over 3, 2 over 3, and 5 over 2. (C) Repeat until you run out of dough. (D) Pinch the tips together when you get to the end.

✳ SIX-BRAID   *not pictured*

(A) Connect the 6 strands of equal weight and length at one end, with the tips facing you. From the left, number the strands 1, 2, 3, 4, 5, 6. (B) Bring strand 6 over strand 1 to build up the connected end (6 has now become 1 and 5 has now become the new 6). (C) Follow this pattern: 2 over 6, 1 over 3, 5 over 1, and 6 over 4. (D) Repeat until you run out of dough, pinching the tips together when you get to the end.

Stage 9: Proofing (Secondary Fermentation)

Proofing is the baker's shorthand term for the ending phase of secondary fermentation. Both primary and secondary fermentation are a form of proofing (that is, proving that the yeast has enlivened the dough), and both stages are rightly called fermentation. But in professional settings, fermentation usually refers to the primary fermentation while proofing refers to the secondary fermentation.

From the moment the bulk dough is divided (Stage 5), the secondary fermentation cycle begins. Proofing is the climax of this secondary fermentation, where the dough is given its final rise in preparation for baking. For the dough to rise, the fermentation must create carbon dioxide as well as alcohol. As a result, more flavors are developed in the dough, but not as dramatically as in the first fermentation where the initial transformation occurred. The most important function of the proofing stage is to bring the dough to the appropriate size for baking. In many cases, this is 80 to 90 percent of the desired finished size, with the expectation of additional rising in the oven, known as the oven spring or oven kick. In some cases, however, the dough rises to its full size with the expectation of little or no oven spring. In general, doughs proofed in freestanding form, such as for rolls or baguettes, are taken to the baking stage before they double in size, anticipating a nice spring in the oven. (If the dough is proofed until fully doubled, it may collapse when it is scored.)

Proofing can involve loaf pans, proofing bowls or forms, or flat sheet pans covered with parchment (see Shaping and Proofing Equipment, page 32). It is important to use a size appropriately matched to the weight of the dough. The recipe instructions will offer guidance in choosing the correct-size form and preparing it for proofing.

PROOF BOX IMPROVISATION

Professional bakeshops often use atmosphere-controlled proof boxes. These boxes control both temperature and humidity and allow the baker to predict the proofing time accurately. They are usually set to around 90°F (32°C) and approximately 80 percent humidity. Control is especially important in production situations because the oven needs to be ready to receive the bread at the moment the bread is ready to go into it. If the dough isn't ready, then the bakery loses time and money; if the dough is ready too soon, it may overferment while waiting for the oven to clear and may miss quality expectations because of either deflating or failing to spring as hoped. In bread baking, as in life, timing is everything.

The home baker usually does not have to contend with these issues but does have to be vigilant in overseeing this stage. Without the controls of an expensive proof box, the options are either to proof at room temperature or in an improvised controlled environment. Temperature is extremely important in controlling proofing time. Every 17°F (about 8°C) effectively doubles or halves the proofing time. For example, if dough will double in size in 1½ hours at 70°F (21°C), or average room temperature, then it will only take 45 minutes if the temperature is 87°F (31°C). Conversely, it will take 3 hours if the temperature is lowered to 53°F (12°C). Any temperature variation within these extremes will affect rising time proportionately.

Proof boxes also control humidity. This is important because if the surface of the dough develops a skin, it will restrict the ability of the dough to rise, acting as a restraint. It also will affect the finished product, creating a tough, chewy crust. The presence of moist air keeps the surface soft and supple. There are a number of ways to replicate this effect in a home situation.

Food-grade plastic bags provide a somewhat controlled atmosphere. The bag protects the dough from any moving air that could dry the skin and traps humidity to keep the dough surface soft. Another advantage of a bag as opposed to plastic wrap, which also protects the surface of the dough, is that it fits loosely and therefore does not restrict the growth of the dough.

You can also use an inverted bowl large enough to cover the rising dough, such as a stainless steel mixing bowl or a large salad bowl. If the bowl is large enough, you can even increase the temperature and moisture by placing a cup of just-boiled water next to the dough before covering it with the bowl.

This same trick can be done in an oven or in the cabinet of a microwave oven. (If your oven has a pilot light, the temperature is probably too warm for proofing, so proceed cautiously, perhaps using it for only about 15 minutes on a cool day and then removing the dough to finish proofing at room temperature.) In a microwave, you can bring a cup of water nearly to a boil, and then place the dough inside and close the door.

An even more dramatic trick, especially good on cold days and taught to me by bread author Lora Brody, is to use an electric dishwasher. First run a cycle (without soap) to turn it into a steam cabinet. Then place the shaped dough inside and close the door. The temperature will be warmer than any other improvised technique, so the rate of leavening will be faster, usually about twice as fast as at room temperature. This is especially good for enriched sandwich breads in which the fermentation flavor is not as critical as in leaner breads. The cabinet is a little too warm for long bulk fermentation and will ferment most dough too quickly for the best flavor, but it is excellent for final proofing, raising the loaf in 30 to 45 minutes.

When time is not a factor, it is still best to proof slowly and gradually at room temperature, as most of the formulas suggest. This provides maximum control and the best flavor, but usually requires at least 1 to 2 hours, or longer in some instances. Finding warm locations, such as the top of a refrigerator or near a sunbeam, can accelerate the proofing time if desired.

WASHES AND GARNISHES

In some instances, it is appropriate to wash the surface of the dough with a whole egg or egg white wash, as in challah or brioche, or to garnish with seeds or other toppings such as Dutch crunch (see page 283). It is usually best to do this before the dough has reached its full size, as it becomes too fragile to tolerate the pressure of the brush and may degas and fall. Catching the dough at just the right point is probably the most valuable skill required at this stage. For example, waiting until French bread is at full size and then scoring it for the bake will result in flat bread. But if you catch it on the rise, the bread will spring mightily in the oven and bloom open at the cut points, as we will discuss in Stage 10, baking.

There are some washes and garnishes that are appropriate to specific breads. For example, it is common to wash the outside of rye bread with beaten egg white to give it a clear gloss. Dinner rolls and brioche often call for a wash made from beaten whole egg, the yolk adding browning qualities to the sheen of the white. Water is the most common wash because it doesn't affect the browning, allows for the application of seeds and flakes such as rolled oats or bran, and also promotes oven spring and shine. I've seen instructions that call for white vinegar washes but do not use them myself, having seen little value in them. Likewise, I do not use water-cornstarch washes. However, I do like the Dutch crunch garnish on top of Vienna bread and sometimes on sandwich bread.

The most common garnishes for breads are poppy, sesame, and occasionally caraway or other seeds. Also popular are rolled oats and other grain flakes and sometimes wheat bran or a dusting of flour. These garnishes are held on by spraying or brushing the top of the dough with water (or egg wash) and sprinkling on the garnish, or by rolling the dough on a wet towel and then dipping it into a bed of the garnish. The first option can be done before or after the final proofing rise, while the second option must be done before the dough has proofed.

When garnishing a loaf of bread, remember the general culinary rules that govern the practice. A garnish must be functional (edible), it must be beautiful, and it must enhance the taste. Garnishing gets young cooks into more trouble than most people imagine, sometimes costing them points on practical exams and even costing them jobs when improperly done. For example, mint leaves might supply the proper tone of green to complement the appearance of a dessert but will the flavor complement the taste? The same goes for bread garnishes. We do eat first with our eyes, so any choice of a garnish must enhance the eye appeal. But please be sure that the flavor of the garnish enhances and does not compete with or over-power the flavor of the bread, or even worse, does not obscure the flavor of the bread, as can often happen with excess flour or dry grain flakes.

Stage 10: Baking

There are many activities that take place during this stage, including scoring the dough, pre-paring and loading the oven, baking, and testing for doneness. The crux of the baking stage takes place, of course, in the oven, where three vital reactions occur: the **gelatinization** of the starches, the **caramelization** of the sugars, and the **coagulation** and roasting of the proteins. These are the final critical control points in determining the quality of the finished bread.

First the practical advice and then the hard science.

SCORING THE LOAVES

The purpose of scoring bread before baking is to release some of the trapped gas. This pro-motes a proper oven spring and an attractive finished look, making the cuts both functional and aesthetic. Often, they protect against trapped gas making tunnels or caverns in the bread ("the room where the baker sleeps," as this flaw is teasingly described among bakers). When done artfully, the cuts greatly enhance the line of the bread. Strong lines, whether straight or curved, are a hallmark of all food presentation.

Most of the time, cuts are made just prior to baking, but occasionally they are made earlier. In this sense, scoring, cutting, slashing, or docking, as this process is interchangeably called, falls somewhere between Stages 9 and 10. We'll place the scoring as part of the baking stage because the cuts, for all their aesthetic value, also provide a distinct functional benefit during the baking period.

The most characteristic cuts are the ones associated with baguettes and other hearth-style European breads. They are best made with a razor-sharp blade, such as a safety razor or a double-edged blade on a stick (the French call this a *lame*; see photograph, page 96). The cut is made with just the tip of the blade to avoid dragging the back part of the blade through the dough (which would rip it rather than slit it). I often tell my students to say the word *slit* when they make the cut to emphasize this action—like slitting open an envelope—over any other notion of cutting. The cut should be on an angle, not straight down, so the slit is almost parallel to the surface of the bread. This will encourage a separation between the crust side of the cut and the rest of the loaf, resulting in what is called an ear. As the loaf bakes, it

Baguettes scored with *lames* (scoring blades).

will spring in the oven, releasing some of the trapped gas through the weakest points, the cut points, causing the loaf to open in what the French call *la grigne*, or "the grin," and we call the bloom. In competitions, the loaves are largely judged on the uniformity and consistency of the cuts and the quality of the bloom.

In some instances the cuts are distinctive to a particular village or baker. Similar types of bread may be scored in dissimilar styles. For instance, a *boule* can be scored with a pound sign (#) or in a spiral or with vertical side-wall cuts either intersecting or not intersecting, such as an asterisk or a sunburst. In other words, although there are conventions and protocols in the traditional European systems, there are really no rules other than what will serve the beauty and functionality of the bread best.

If you prefer to use a sharp serrated knife, or another type of blade, remember to let the knife do the work, that is, resist the urge to press down on the dough. Instead, let the knife bite into the dough and then gently slide it through, letting the weight and sharpness of the blade do the cutting without any downward pressure on your part. This will slit the bread more cleanly, allowing it to pucker open rather than collapse under the pressure of your hand.

*LOADING THE OVEN

(A) Jennifer uses the back of a sheet pan to slide the loaves directly onto a baking stone. **(B)** Alex uses a peel, generously dusted with semolina flour, to slide the baguettes directly onto the stone.

PREPARING THE OVEN FOR HEARTH BAKING AND LOADING THE DOUGH

Many of the breads in this book are hearth breads, that is, breads baked directly on the hearth or a hot deck of the oven, and instructions will often call for preparation of the oven for hearth baking. The purpose of hearth baking is to radiate heat directly into the bread as immediately as possible in order to promote oven spring and a crisp crust. Hearth baking may also employ steam to promote spring and contribute a shiny finish to the crust. Most professional ovens have steam generators that create a mighty blast of steam with the push of a button. Most home ovens do not offer this feature, although some home ovens are now being built with a steaming mechanism.

There are a number of ways to replicate a professional hearth oven in your home, though none quite matches the professional oven's ability to retain heat and deliver a tremendous blast of steam. The first is the use of a baking stone (or Baking Steel) or unglazed quarry tiles as discussed on page 37. You can slide your hearth breads directly onto the stone or tiles using either (A) an overturned sheet pan or (B) a peel that has been generously dusted with semolina, cornmeal, or flour. (In some cases it's fine to leave the dough on parchment during baking, which the recipe instructions will indicate.) Although nearly all breads can be baked directly on a baking stone, there are some that I prefer to leave on the sheet pan. These include enriched doughs (like the Potato Rosemary Bread on page 229) that tend to burn if they aren't

∗ DOUBLE-STEAMING METHOD

(A) Add hot water to the preheated pan for a burst of steam. **(B)** Spray the walls of the oven with a mister to create extra steam.

insulated from direct contact with the stone, and doughs that are difficult to slide due to their shape, like an *épi*-cut baguette. If you have confidence in your hearth-bread abilities, feel free to overrule my instructions for pan baking and go for the total hearth experience.

The second way to replicate a professional hearth oven is to use the double-steaming technique. Steam is not required for all breads, but it is definitely important for hearth breads. The steam delays the onset of gelatinization, allowing the bread additional time to spring in the oven. It also lends an attractive glaze, or shine, to the bread. Its value is only realized during the first half of the baking process. After that, the bread needs a dry environment in which to develop its crisp crust properly. For this reason, all of the steam is generated during the first few seconds of the bake, with its lingering effects fading out as the bread continues to cook. There is no advantage to steaming late in the process, or even after the first few minutes—that is, once the crust has set.

I used to advocate just spraying the oven walls with water to create steam, but then I discovered a better way. While the oven is preheating, place a steam pan, such as an empty heavy-duty sheet pan or, even better, a cast-iron frying pan, on either the top shelf or on the oven floor (a thin sheet pan will buckle at high temperatures). Before putting the bread in the oven, have hot water standing by, the hotter the better (simmering is fine). You can use ice cubes instead of water, but I think they rob too much heat from the oven to convert them to steam. What we want is instant steam, not just water. As shown on page 98, image (A), the hot water is added to the steam pan when the bread is placed in the oven. When you pour the hot water into the hot steam pan, work at an angle and use hot pads to prevent steam burns.

In addition to the steam pan, use a plant mister, as seen in image (B), or go for the big statement and use a garden pressure sprayer. These cost fifteen to twenty dollars, hold a lot of water, and require some serious pumping to create pressure. The amount of water they spray creates great blasts of steam in a short amount of time. Keep in mind that the idea is to make steam and vapor, not to wet the dough, which causes splotches. Fill the mister or sprayer with room-temperature water. Aim for the side and back walls of the oven so the water hits the walls and instantly vaporizes. Stay away from light fixtures or any glass. I learned the hard way to lay a towel over the oven window when I pour the water into the steam pan and when I spray. A little drop of water on hot glass, even on tempered oven glass, can begin that awful sound of crackling that sinks the heart and costs money. After spraying, quickly shut the door and wait 30 seconds, then spray again. I usually do three sprays at 30-second intervals to replicate as closely as possible the steam of a bakery oven, but each time the oven will lose heat. This is why its helpful to set the oven 50°F to 100°F (10° to 38°C) above the required temperature during the preheat stage. Only after the final spray do I lower the oven setting to the specified baking temperature, usually 450°F or 425°F (232°C to 218°C), depending on the bread. The oven will probably be below that temperature after all the steaming but won't take nearly as long to recover as it would have had I set the temperature at 450°F (232°C) to start.

In most, though not all, home ovens, it is necessary to rotate the loaves 180 degrees in order to get an even bake. This is usually done about halfway through the suggested baking time. But every oven bakes differently, so baking times are just suggested, not written in stone. The best way to determine doneness is by placing an instant-read thermometer into the center of the loaf and bake to the suggested internal temperature.

UNDERSTANDING OVEN REACTIONS

Gelatinizing the Starches
Flour consists of approximately 80 percent starch, some of which reverts to various sugar chains during the fermentation stage, but most of which remains as complex starch molecules and granules. As Shirley Corriher explains in her wonderful book, *Cook Wise*, starch is basically a configuration of "hundreds, even thousands, of molecules of glucose linked together."

In other words, according to Corriher, "They are simply sugars hooked together." In the case of wheat and most bread grains, these are called amylose starches (the other kind of starch is called amylopectin, or waxy starch, and it predominates in tapioca, arrowroot, and cornstarch). Gelatinization, or gelation, is the chemical reaction that begins when starch and liquid are heated, and continues as the internal temperature increases until the starch absorbs and traps as much liquid as it can hold and then bursts, flooding the liquid with starch molecules and thickening the mixture. The bursting point of most amylose starches is between 180°F and 212°F (82°C and 100°C). This explains why 180°F (82°C) is the minimum temperature that the center of a loaf must reach (and it will never exceed 210°F/99°C). As starches reach their maximum bursting point, they clarify, becoming translucent or semiopaque and set into a mass solid enough to cut.

From the perspective of the baker's mission to evoke the full flavor from the grain, gelatinization is important for two reasons. The first is the obvious necessity to thicken the mass, transforming it from dough to bread. The second is that the palate responds to gelled starch in a different way than when the starches are not gelled. The glucose, or sugar molecules, of complex carbohydrates are so bound up, like a ball of yarn, that they taste like sawdust when eaten as flour and like paste when eaten as raw dough. The fermentation process and amylase enzymes trigger a breakout of the sugar from the starch, as discussed in Stage 3. But it is heat that transforms the remaining starches into a clarified gel as it gelatinizes the dough. This replaces the tastelessness of raw dough with a clear, cool, and clean mouthfeel. The starches don't have a taste of their own, but when gelled, they get out of the way and reveal the other flavors, thus releasing the hidden flavors usually obscured by the complex starches.

Caramelizing the Sugars

When sugar approaches 325°F (163°C), it begins to harden and darken during the process of caramelization. We know from the explanation of gelatinization that the internal temperature of the dough will only reach between 180°F and 210°F (82°C and 99°C), which is not hot enough to caramelize the sugars, but the outside of the loaves are exposed to the full heat of the oven. The crust will nearly reach the temperature of the oven setting, causing the sugars on the surface to caramelize, which is why crust is usually brown. Furthermore, as the sugars heat up, their molecules recombine in various combinations with other ingredients, including proteins. In certain configurations these sugar-protein bonds brown at a lower temperature. This is known as the Maillard reaction, named after Dr. L. C. Maillard, who first discovered this type of caramelization, which actually occurs at a lower temperature than normal caramelization.

The multitude of sugar chains brown, or caramelize, in different shades. A young 4-hour *pain ordinaire* dough caramelizes as a yellow-gold shade. However, a *pain ordinaire* dough made with 50 to 100 percent pre-ferment, or retarded overnight in the refrigerator, caramelizes as a reddish gold shade because the enzymes have had a chance to break out more of the maltose and glucose sugars trapped in the amylose starches. The effect of these various caramelization reactions shows up both visually and on the palate and is affected by the fermentation time, enzyme activity, and the oven temperature.

Coagulating and Roasting the Proteins

The third oven reaction begins with denaturing, then coagulating the proteins, but extends further into the roasting of these proteins as the dough reaches higher and higher temperatures. Denaturing happens first as a protein molecule is cooked. The tightly coiled molecules unwind and straighten when they reach 140°F to 145°F (60°C to 63°C), but soon after that, they wrap themselves up with other, similarly denatured molecules and create tightly bound protein chains. This is called coagulation and is most easily demonstrated in a scrambled or fried egg as the liquid and translucent raw egg gradually becomes opaque and firm. The same process unfolds in bread as it bakes. Since bread flour is approximately 12 percent gluten protein, and it is this protein that forms the skeleton structure that traps the carbon dioxide gas for leavening, as the bread bakes hotter and hotter, the proteins get cooked more deeply than mere coagulation. Baking, which means the application of heat to a food product in an oven, drives off whatever moisture isn't trapped in the gelled starches. This acts almost like a reduction, concentrating flavors. As the protein bonds become exposed to higher heat, more of the subtle, nutlike flavors emerge from the strands of gluten holding the loaf together. Once again, and true to the baker's mission, we are coaxing flavor from the ingredients.

HOW TO TELL WHEN THE BREAD IS DONE

Each of the formulas gives instructions for judging doneness, but here are a few general rules:

- Hard, crusty bread is baked until the center of the loaf registers 200°F to 210°F (93°C to 99°C). In most instances, I shoot for 205°F (96°C). Of course, if the outside is changing from golden brown to black, that is, from caramel to carbon, you might have to pull the bread out before it reaches that internal temperature. Or, you can make a tent of aluminum foil or even of baking parchment and cover the bread with it to buy a few more minutes of baking time. The whole point of intense baking is to drive off excess moisture in order to concentrate the flavors. Also, the higher heat ensures full gelatinization of the starches, thus drawing out more flavor from the grain.

- Soft bread, such as enriched dinner rolls and sandwich bread, needs to exceed at least 180°F (82°C) in the center. Small items like rolls will usually set as soon as they pass 180°F (82°C), but I prefer to wait until the dough registers 185°F to 190°F (85°C to 88°C) for full-size loaves to be sure they are free of underbaked doughy sections. Also, thump the bottom of the loaves and listen for a hollow reverberation rather than a dull quietness. The sides should be firm rather than soft and crushable, golden with caramelization rather than white or uncolored.

- Always test the internal temperature by probing to the center of the center. By this I mean place the thermometer through the center of the bottom or the top of the loaf and go to the center of the dough. This will be the last place to receive the heat and will thus be the coolest section. If it registers the temperature you seek, the rest of the loaf will also be at least that hot.

Cooling is an important part of baking, but we will go into that in the next stage.

Stage 11: Cooling (Patience Is a Baking Virtue)

Most people think that the job is done when the loaves are baked. Some systems list only ten stages, ending with baking. But in reality, the cooling stage is important to understand because it is a continuation of the baking stage.

The loaves come out of the oven at a minimum of 180°F (82°C) at their center, usually higher. Depending on the size of the breads, it may take up to 2 hours for them to cool down to room temperature. During this time they continue to evaporate moisture, drying out and, thus, intensifying in flavor. While the loaves are still above 160°F (71°C), they are technically still gelatinizing. This is why if you cut into a loaf right out of the oven, even one that is 200°F (93°C) in the center, it will seem doughy or underbaked. The starches, though fully saturated and swelled with moisture, are still in the process of setting. The trapped steam either evaporates off through the crust, or it will re-form as moisture and be absorbed by the crumb of the bread. This process needs to complete itself for optimum results. If the process is interrupted by cutting or breaking the bread while it is still hot, the loaf will seem soggy.

Flavor intensity, though, is most critical. In culinary schools around the world, students are taught that flavor comes first (Flavor Always Rules! is the motto). The steps in the formulas presented in this book are designed to deliver breads of the finest flavor within their type. I encourage my student bakers to push their loaves, that is, to bake them as long as possible, but I also encourage them to push when cooling them. This means, in a word, patience.

The optimum time to eat most bread, and some people feel that sourdough may be the exception to this rule, is at the moment it cools to about 80°F (27°C) in the center. There will be no residual warmth to cover or blunt the flavor on the palate. Of course, many people like to eat bread warm so that it melts the butter and tastes comforting in the mouth. There is nothing wrong with this, but if you want to taste fully the bread itself, with all its subtle nuances, then cool it completely, preferably by allowing it to sit at room temperature on a cooling rack. The rack will prevent condensation from forming on the bottom of the loaf or on whatever side it is leaning.

If you want to accelerate the cooling process, it is acceptable to aim a fan at the bread while it cools. The moving air draws off the heat and blows away moisture. This will cut cooling time in half, but it does tend to dry out the surface slightly. There is no advantage, as some people think, to putting hot bread into the refrigerator or freezer. This cools only the surface without effectively drawing out the heat. Moving air is far more effective. Many bakeries set up banks of fans to blow on the racks of bread that seem to fill up instantly every hour or so. The higher-volume bakeries even pass the loaves through wind chambers on conveyor belts. This allows the bakeries to begin packaging the bread before the next batch comes out of the oven.

Stage 12: Storing and Eating

In the previous section, I noted that bread usually tastes best just after it cools down completely. It is at this point that the flavor-baffling warmth is gone, the moisture has evaporated, thus intensifying flavor, and the bread is still fresh so that it is soft and creamy on the palate. It is never difficult to advise people what to do with fresh bread: eat it and enjoy it. However, it becomes more problematic to advise what to do with the bread that is in excess of what can be enjoyed after that perfect bread moment passes.

This final stage of the bread-making process is, technically speaking, storing; eating is the grace note. But in production operations, storing is the realistic issue. The following few words will address storing methods, but after that I will offer some thoughts on how to recognize the attributes of a well-made loaf.

STORING TIPS

• Lean, crusty breads are stored differently than soft, enriched breads. If you want to preserve the crustiness in lean breads, store them in paper, though they will become stale within a day and are best eaten on the day they are baked. If you want to preserve them for more than a day, "cater wrap" the cooled loaves in plastic wrap (this means wrap them completely in both directions to prevent any air from getting to them). Then, either freeze them or place them in a cool, dark place. You can also use zipper-style plastic bags, squeezing out all the air before sealing. When planning to freeze the bread, it is acceptable to preslice the loaf so you can remove only what you need rather than defrosting the entire loaf. Snack-size zippered bags are useful for individual slices.

• Soft, enriched bread, such as sandwich bread, is always best stored in plastic and either frozen or kept in a cool, dark place (exposure to sunlight causes the loaf to sweat, creating condensation in the wrapper and, eventually, mold on the loaf). Presliced sandwich loaves are best for freezing, allowing the removal of only as many slices as you need, which will also thaw much more quickly than whole loaves.

• If you have a frozen unsliced loaf and want to thaw it, pull it from the freezer at least 2 hours before you need to use it. Do not try to accelerate the thawing by putting it into the oven or microwave. This will only dry it out. Of course, in an emergency, when you have to get bread on the table and have forgotten to thaw it in advance, you can quickly thaw it in the microwave or in a hot oven. The best way to prevent it from drying out is to place it under a wet towel. Heat the oven to 400°F (204°C), place the bread in a pan, and cover the pan with a towel that has been soaked in warm water and then wrung out. Check on the towel every 10 minutes to see if it needs rewetting. It should take 20 to 30 minutes to thaw out a standard-size loaf, 10 to 20 minutes for a baguette. If you want to restore a crackly crust to the bread, remove the towel for the final few minutes and turn the oven up to 450°F (232°C).

STORING DON'TS

• Don't store bread in the refrigerator. It dries out, even when packaged in sealed plastic bags.

• Don't store crusty breads in plastic bags or in plastic wrap unless you plan to recrisp the crust in the oven.

- Don't store soft, enriched breads in paper bags unless you intend to dry them out for bread crumbs or croutons.

- Don't store any bread that you intend to dry for crumbs in plastic bags or plastic wrap. If the moisture cannot escape, the bread will eventually mold.

- Don't store warm bread in plastic bags or plastic wrap. To prevent condensation from forming in the bag, which will accelerate mold development, wait until the bread has cooled down completely (no warmth at all).

EATING

Culinary-school training involves a lot of palate development. Just as wine expertise involves learning to discern subtle flavors in wine and match them with appropriate foods, so does any kind of cooking and baking also depend on understanding how the palate accesses flavor. The art of cooking is really about how flavors work together to create synergies, harmonies, or even disharmonies.

Bread baking is no different, especially in relationship to other foods and flavors. The challenge for a baker is converting a relatively tasteless raw starch into the sweet, nutty, multilayered flavor we call good bread. This is accomplished mainly during the primary and secondary fermentation cycles and brought to fruition in the baking stage.

When we eat properly baked bread, there are a few things we should notice. The first is that the bread will be cool and creamy on the palate. The phrase *cool and creamy* is in contrast to *dry and dusty*. The opposite of cool in bread is not warm but dry. If there is any starch left in the crumb, it will manifest to the palate as a dry taste, and instead of tasting creamy on the tongue, it will have a dusty, almost gritty texture. This occurs not only in underbaked bread but also in underfermented bread. One reason for this is that during fermentation much of the starch is undergoing a slow conversion to simpler forms of sugar. The palate also cannot access the flavors trapped in the complex carbohydrates that we call starch. In a well-made loaf of bread, much of the sugar has sprung free from the starches, and some of these have been converted into food for the yeast. Some of the sugar has caramelized in the crust, and many of the previously trapped sugar molecules are now accessible by the five flavor zones of the palate (sweet, salty, bitter, sour, and, the most recent addition, umami). Just as gravy becomes clear and shiny when it reaches the gelatinization point (recipes usually say to bring it almost to a boil), so too does the crumb of bread. When a thin slice is held up to a light, it will reflect and sparkle and sometimes, in breads that are baked to 205°F (96°C) or more at the center, it will even be translucent.

Add to this flavor development the roasting of the gluten proteins, a process that begins when the loaf reaches approximately 145°F (63°C) and continues to add more and more flavor as the dough heats up to the 180°F to 205°F (82°C to 96°C) range. It is like a coffee bean that releases new layers of flavor as it roasts, or like meat and other protein foods that also reveal hidden flavor as they roast. The protein in bread, which falls somewhere between 12 and 20 percent of the flour weight, depending on the type of flour and other protein-rich ingredients in the formula, also releases subtle layers of flavor due to the release of amino acids during fermentation and their reaction to the baking process. The deeper the bread is roasted, the more complex the flavor. This is why soft bread, usually baked to 180°F to 190°F (82°C to 88°C), does not tend to have the same intensity of flavor and is more dependent for its flavor on the enrichment ingredients than on the fermentation and baking technique. Crusty leaner bread, dependent almost entirely on fermentation and the skill of the baker for its flavor, benefits much more dramatically from intensified baking times and temperatures.

Much of how a bread's flavor develops through the three oven reactions is determined by the quality of the final rise. As noted, crusty lean breads are improved by retaining a large, irregular hole structure, or crumb. The larger the holes, the easier it is for moisture to evaporate out of the loaf while it is baking, thus intensifying flavor by deeper roasting of the proteins and the fullest possible gelatinization of the starches. The tighter the holes are, the more difficult it is for the interior moisture to evaporate and thus the more difficult it becomes to raise internal temperatures to the extremes of 205°F to 210°F (96°C to 99°C). During the baking stage, the crust is engaged in a race with the crumb to accomplish their necessary processes in the same time frame. While the sugars in the crust are caramelizing, the starches of the crumb are gelatinizing and the proteins are roasting. When all of these converge and reach their peak at the same time, which is within the control of the baker's mastery of the oven and the baking stage, world-class bread is the result. Soft, enriched breads, usually formed with even, medium-size holes, are not designed to reach the high temperatures required for world-class lean breads. Therefore, the flavor profile of a bread is within the context of that particular bread. Rich breads like brioche or panettone, sandwich loaves like white bread (*pain de mie*), or tighter-holed rye and 100 percent whole wheat breads are not all held to the same flavor and palate criteria.

What is important, though, is that bakers understand the outcome they seek in each particular bread and use the knowledge gained in the study of the twelve stages of bread making to empower them to achieve it. If the baker's challenge is to evoke the fullest potential of flavor from the grain, then understanding how to manipulate time and temperature in all of the stages is the key to achieving this outcome. The knowledge and ability to meet the baker's challenge are now within your grasp—to the victors go the crumbs!

THREE

Formulas

The formulas are arranged in alphabetical order to help you find them easily. The sourdough and sourdough rye breads are grouped by theme, since the introductory information provided will apply to all the breads within that cluster. At the head of each formula you will find a brief bread profile and time estimates for the various preparation stages. The profile recaps the information from the bread classifications chart on pages 46, and the time estimates give approximate times for each stage of dough preparation to help you plan your baking schedule. The baker's percentages listed in each recipe are based on the final dough, not the total dough (see page 39 for a detailed explanation of these terms). The total dough formula ratios are given in a separate box.

Before you dive into any of the formulas, please take the time to read the previous sections to ensure that we are all on the same page regarding terminology, concepts, and theory. You may already know this information, though maybe in a different way or from a different system. There are many ways to approach the teaching of bread, and mine is only one of them. I have no doubt that if you apply the knowledge gained in the previous instructional sections to the formulas that follow, you will make amazing bread and, perhaps, even be able to revisit some of your favorite bread recipes and take them to the next level. At the very least, you will be able to troubleshoot problems with your bread and better understand the processes at work inside it.

Remember, my goal is to make you a spirit-of-the-law, not a letter-of-the-law, baker. This comes about as you develop a feel for your dough, adjusting as you knead until it feels just right (and you will know when it feels right!). As you develop this feel, you will also develop the confidence to make other adjustments, tweaking the formulas to suit your individual tastes and desires. Ultimately, I want you to own these formulas, to use them as templates for your own creative variations. As you embark on the adventure of making these breads, I send you off with what I call the baker's blessing: may your crust be crisp and your bread always rise!

PRE-FERMENTS: PÂTE FERMENTÉE, POOLISH, AND BIGA

Many of the formulas in this book call for a version of pre-ferment, one of the baker's most effective tools for manipulating time. A pre-ferment's main purpose is to improve flavor and structure, as discussed beginning on page 52. The amount of pre-ferment required for each bread varies, so I am going to suggest approaches to preparing the pre-ferments that accommodate different batch-size requirements, especially with the main pre-ferments: *pâte fermentée, poolish,* and *biga.*

The very presence of *pâte fermentée* in a formula immediately improves most bread, quantum leaping it in maturity and flavor. One way to make it is to make a batch of dough (as shown opposite)—which is, in fact, simply French bread dough—and put it in the refrigerator overnight. In the French bread formula on page 174, you will use this whole piece in the final dough, but other formulas in the book might require more or less. So, in the following formula, as is true with every formula, the most important information is the percentage ratio of each ingredient. With this, you can customize your batch sizes, making exactly the amount you need.

The other option is to save back a portion of every batch of French bread that you make to use as pre-ferment in future batches. The dough will keep for 3 days in the refrigerator and at least 3 months in the freezer if you store it in an airtight freezer bag.

Poolish, a wet sponge, is easy to make and is best when made fresh each time you need it. It will, however, also be good for up to 3 days in the refrigerator, or it can be frozen if you choose to do so. It is inexpensive to make, so it is okay to make more than you need and discard any excess. The formula is the easiest of the pre-ferments to make, since the flour and water weigh the same and it can be mixed with a spoon or a whisk.

Biga, the Italian version of a firm pre-ferment, is as easy to make as French bread dough and should feel about the same (the main difference from *pâte fermentée* is the absence of salt and, therefore, the need for less yeast). Again, the percentages are most important; with them you can make this in any size, as needed.

A *poolish* and a *biga* are interchangeable in a recipe (you may have some leftover from one batch and be looking for a dough in which to use it). However, you will have to adjust the water content in the final dough to compensate for the difference in hydration between them.

Interchangeability also applies to wet starters (barms) and firm wild-yeast starters, again as long as you remember to adjust the water in the final dough. Such substitutions will result in a different flavor and structure in the final dough, so we're in the realm of baker's choice here. In most of my sourdough formulas, I use a wet starter to make a firm starter and then the final dough, but there are other times when I use the wet starter to make the final dough, as explained on page 246. The point here is that it is okay to interchange pre-ferments, and I encourage you to experiment to learn which options you prefer.

Pâte Fermentée

Makes approximately 16.5 ounces (468g), enough for 1 batch of French Bread, page 174; Pain de Campagne, page 203; or Pane Siciliano, page 207

MEASURE	OUNCES	GRAMS	INGREDIENTS	%
1⅛ cups	5	142	unbleached all-purpose flour	50
1⅛ cups	5	142	unbleached bread flour	50
¾ teaspoon	0.19	5.5	salt	1.9
½ teaspoon	0.055	1.5	instant yeast	0.55
¾ cup plus 1 tablespoon	6.5	184	water, at room temperature	65
TOTAL				167.5

1 Stir together the flours, salt, and yeast in a 4-quart mixing bowl (or in the bowl of an electric mixer). Add the water, stirring until everything comes together and makes a coarse ball (or mix on low speed for 1 minute with the paddle attachment). Adjust the flour or water, according to need; the dough should be neither too sticky nor too stiff. (It is better to err on the sticky side, as you can adjust more easily during kneading. It is harder to add water once the dough firms up.)

2 Sprinkle some flour on the counter and transfer the dough to the counter. Knead for 3 to 4 minutes (or mix on medium speed with the dough hook for 3 to 4 minutes), or until the dough is soft and pliable, supple, and tacky, but not sticky. The internal temperature should be 77°F to 81°F (25°C to 27°C).

COMMENTARY
You can use this pre-ferment on the same day that you make it if you ferment it at room temperature for 2 hours instead of refrigerating it. I prefer to give it the overnight treatment, however, as it brings out more flavor.

• • •

If you have only bread flour or only all-purpose flour, you can make this pre-ferment with that flour exclusively, but I have found that the blend brings about the best results. The amount of water is always, at best, an approximation, as it may need to be slightly adjusted, up or down, depending on the brand of flour you use. But 65 percent water to flour should be a good starting point.

(continued)

3   Lightly oil a bowl and transfer the dough to the bowl, rolling it around to coat it with oil. Cover the bowl with plastic wrap and ferment at room temperature for 1 hour or until it begins to swell.

4   Remove the dough from the bowl, knead it lightly to degas, return it to the bowl, and cover the bowl with plastic wrap. Place the bowl in the refrigerator overnight. You can keep this pre-ferment in the refrigerator for up to 3 days or in the freezer in an airtight plastic bag for up to 3 months.

Poolish

Makes about 23 ounces (652g), enough for Ciabatta, Poolish Version, page 143

Makes about 23 ounces (652g), enough for Ciabatta, Poolish Version, page 143

MEASURE	OUNCES	GRAMS	INGREDIENTS	%
2½ cups	11.25	319	unbleached bread flour	100
¼ teaspoon	0.03	1	instant yeast	0.27
1½ cups	12	340	water, at room temperature	107
TOTAL				207.3

COMMENTARY

You can make this pre-ferment in larger or smaller batches, depending on the formula in which you plan to use it, or you can make more than you need and use the leftover in another bread, such as Poolish Baguettes (page 223).

• • •

You can use this sponge as soon as it ferments, but, as with other pre-ferments, I prefer to give it an overnight retarding to draw out more flavor. If using it on the same day, give it 2 to 4 extra hours of fermentation at room temperature before adding it to the final dough.

• • •

It is acceptable to substitute *biga* for *poolish* and vice versa as long as you adjust the water in the final formula to compensate for the change.

Stir together the flour, yeast, and water in a mixing bowl until all of the flour is hydrated. The dough should be soft and sticky and look like very thick pancake batter. Cover the bowl with plastic wrap and ferment at room temperature for 3 to 4 hours or until the sponge starts to become bubbly. Immediately refrigerate it, where it will continue to ferment while it cools down. It will keep for up to 3 days in the refrigerator.

Biga

Makes about 18 ounces (510g), enough for Ciabatta,
Biga Version, page 147 or Italian Bread, page 178

MEASURE	OUNCES	GRAMS	INGREDIENTS	%
2½ cups	11.25	319	unbleached bread flour	100
½ teaspoon	0.055	1.5	instant yeast	0.49
¾ cup plus 3 tablespoons	7.5	213	water, at room temperature	66.7
TOTAL				167.2

1   Stir together the flour and yeast in a 4-quart mixing bowl (or in the bowl of an electric mixer). Add the water, stirring until everything comes together and makes a coarse ball (or mix on low speed for 1 minute with the paddle attachment). Adjust the flour or water, according to need; the dough should be neither too sticky nor too stiff. (It is better to err on the sticky side, as you can adjust more easily during kneading. It is harder to add water once the dough firms up.)

2   Sprinkle some flour on the counter and transfer the dough to the counter. Knead for 3 to 4 minutes (or mix on medium speed with the dough hook for 3 to 4 minutes), or until the dough is soft and pliable, tacky, but not sticky. The internal temperature should be 77°F to 81°F (25°C to 27°C).

3   Lightly oil a bowl and transfer the dough to the bowl, rolling it around to coat it with oil. Cover the bowl with plastic wrap and ferment at room temperature for approximately 2 hours, or until it swells noticeably, but to no more than 1½ times in size.

4   Remove the dough from the bowl, knead it lightly to degas, return it to the bowl, and cover the bowl with plastic wrap. Place the bowl in the refrigerator overnight. You can keep this pre-ferment in the refrigerator for up to 3 days or in the freezer in an airtight plastic bag for up to 3 months.

COMMENTARY

You can use this *biga* as soon as it ferments, but just as for the *poolish* and the *pâte fermentée,* I prefer to give it an overnight retarding to bring out more flavor. If you want to use it the same day, allow it to ferment for an extra 1 to 2 hours at room temperature before adding it to the final dough.

• • •

In Italy, nearly every pre-ferment, including wild yeast or sourdough, is called a *biga.* So if you are making a recipe from another source that calls for a *biga,* make sure you check to see exactly what kind of *biga* it requires. In this book, *biga* refers to the particular ratio of ingredients listed here.

• • •

You can substitute all-purpose flour for the bread flour, if you prefer, or you can blend all-purpose and bread flour as in the *pâte fermentée.*

Anadama Bread

BREAD PROFILE
Enriched, standard dough;
indirect method; commercial
yeast

• • •

DAYS TO MAKE: 2
DAY 1: 5 minutes soaker

DAY 2: 1¼ hours sponge;
15 minutes mixing; 2¾ to
3¼ hours fermentation,
shaping, and proofing;
40 to 50 minutes baking

• • •

COMMENTARY
The brand or type of molasses
will make a difference in the
final flavor. People who tested
this formula preferred Brer
Rabbit Mild Flavor Molasses
for its lightness. Molasses is
high in iron and other minerals, but some brands are
harsher and darker. I suggest
using the lightest, most
refined brand you can find,
unless you like the stronger
flavor tones of darker brands.
Sorghum syrup can also be
used for a lighter flavor.

• • •

The amount of flour you use
may vary depending on the
type of molasses you use, so
do not be concerned if you
have to add more flour to firm
up the dough. Let the dough
dictate how much flour it
needs. You want a dough that
is slightly tacky but not sticky,
and supple enough for easy
shaping.

When I moved to Providence in 1999, after 22 years in California, I felt duty bound to revisit one of the great New England breads, anadama, and to come up with a definitive version. There are conflicting stories concerning the origin of the name. Judith and Evan Jones, in their wonderful *The Book of Bread*, tell the story of a Rockport, Massachusetts, man who was upset with his wife not only for leaving him but also for leaving behind only a pot of cornmeal mush and some molasses. The angry husband tossed the mush and molasses together with some yeast and flour and muttered, "Anna, damn 'er!" This was later amended by the more genteel local Yankees, as they retold the story, to anadama. Sounds likely to me.

Traditional formulas for this bread are usually given as a direct-dough method, but this version utilizes a soaker and a sponge to evoke more flavor from the grain. Corn is chock-full of natural sugars, trapped in the complex carbohydrate starch base, so any trick we can employ to break the sugars free can only improve the already wonderful flavor.

Makes two 1½-pound (680g) loaves or three 1-pound (453g) loaves

SOAKER (DAY 1)

MEASURE	OUNCES	GRAMS	INGREDIENTS	%
1 cup	6	170	cornmeal, preferably coarse grind (also packaged as "polenta")	29.5
1 cup	8	227	water, at room temperature	39.5
TOTAL				n/a

DOUGH

MEASURE	OUNCES	GRAMS	INGREDIENTS	%
4½ cups	20.25	574	unbleached bread flour	100
2 teaspoons	0.22	6	instant yeast	1.1
1 cup	8	227	water, lukewarm (90°F to 100°F/32°C to 38°C)	39.5
Use all	14	397	soaker	69
1½ teaspoons	0.38	11	salt	1.9
6 tablespoons	4	113	molasses (see Commentary)	19.8
2 tablespoons	1	28	vegetable oil or unsalted butter	4.9
Cornmeal for dusting (optional)				
TOTAL				236

Multigrain loaf and slices on left (see page 195), anadama loaf in bread pan with anadama slices on right.

1   The day before making the bread, make the soaker by mixing together the cornmeal and water in a small bowl. Cover with plastic wrap and let sit overnight at room temperature.

2   The next day, to make the dough, stir together 2 cups (9 ounces/252g) of the flour, the yeast, water, and soaker in a mixing bowl (or in the bowl of an electric mixer). Cover the bowl with a towel or plastic wrap and ferment for 1 hour, or until the sponge begins to bubble.

3   Add the remaining 2½ cups (11.25 ounces/272g) of flour, the salt, molasses, and oil and stir (or mix on low speed with the paddle attachment) until the ingredients form a ball. Add water if necessary to make a soft, slightly sticky mass.

4   Sprinkle flour on the counter, transfer the dough to the counter, and begin kneading (or mix on medium speed with the dough hook), sprinkling in more flour as needed to make a tacky, but not sticky, dough. The dough should be firm but supple and pliable and definitely not sticky. It will take about 10 minutes of kneading to accomplish this (or 4 to 8 minutes in the electric mixer). The dough should pass the windowpane test (page 61) and register 77°F to 81°F (25°C to 27°C).

5   Lightly oil a bowl and transfer the dough to the bowl, rolling it around to coat it with oil. Cover the bowl with plastic wrap and ferment the dough at room temperature for about 1½ hours, or until it doubles in size.

6   Remove the dough from the bowl and divide it into 2 equal pieces of 24 ounces (680g) each, or 3 pieces of about 16 ounces (454g) each. Shape the dough into loaves, as shown on page 85, and place them into bread pans that have been lightly oiled or misted with spray oil (the larger loaves should go into 9 by 5-inch/23 by 13-cm pans and the smaller loaves into 8½ by 4½-inch/22 by 11-cm pans). Mist the tops of the loaves with spray oil and cover loosely with plastic wrap.

7   Proof at room temperature for 1 to 1½ hours, or until the loaves crest fully above the tops of the pans. (If you want to hold back any of the loaves, place them in the refrigerator without proofing, where they will hold, or retard, for up to 2 days. Remove them from the refrigerator about 4 hours before baking and proof them at room temperature, or until ready.)

8   Preheat the oven to 350°F (177°C) with the oven rack on the middle shelf. Place the pans on a sheet pan and remove the plastic wrap. Mist the tops with a spray of water and dust with cornmeal.

9   Place the sheet pan in the oven and bake for 20 minutes. Rotate the sheet pan 180 degrees for even baking and continue to bake for 20 to 30 minutes, or until the loaves are golden brown (including along the sides and bottom), and register at least 185°F to 190°F (85°C to 88°C) in the center. They should make a hollow sound when thumped on the bottom.

10 When the loaves are done, remove them immediately from the pans and let cool on a rack for at least 1 hour before slicing or serving.

Artos: Greek Celebration Breads

When it comes to holiday and festival breads, the varieties and secret family recipes are endless. But when broken down to their basic components, they are pretty much variations on a theme. This is especially evident in the various Greek breads. *Artos* is the general name for Greek celebration breads, but they are given particular names and twists and turns for specific festivals. It is the twists and turns that make the breads special, bringing visual drama, history, and family tradition into the process. For instance, the color of the fruit is different for Christmas breads than for Easter because Christmas is a festival of incarnation and Easter is a festival of resurrection and transformation. The breads are often taken to the local church by home bakers, where they are blessed by the priest, and then brought back home to the table or given to the needy. I love the designs of the nativity *christopsomos*, with its bread-dough cross laminated on top of a round loaf, and of the Easter egg–braided *lambropsomo*, also called *tsoureki* (a Turkish variation). The orange and brandied *vasilopita*, served on New Year's Day in honor of Saint Basil, often has a gold coin hidden in it, not unlike the three kings cake of New Orleans and Spanish cultures.

The following master formula can be used as the base for any of these breads, and some specific holiday variations follow. The formula uses a wild-yeast starter, along with a spiking of commercial yeast, to create a manageable dough that bakes up into an authentic-tasting bread. Nowadays, most versions use commercial yeast, but this is a recent innovation. If you do not have any barm (mother starter) on hand, you can replace it with an equal amount of *poolish*. The fermentation and proofing times will remain the same.

(continued)

BREAD PROFILE

Enriched, standard dough; indirect method; commercial yeast or mixed leavening method

. . .

DAYS TO MAKE: 1 OR 2

BARM VERSION: 1 hour to de-chill barm; 15 minutes mixing; 2¾ to 3¼ hours fermentation, shaping, and proofing; 40 to 45 minutes baking

POOLISH VERSION:

DAY 1: 3 to 4 hours *poolish*

DAY 2: 1 hour to de-chill *poolish*; 15 minutes mixing; 2¾ to 3¼ hours fermentation, shaping, and proofing; 40 to 45 minutes baking

. . .

COMMENTARY

If you can find authentic Middle Eastern ingredients, *mahlab* (also called *mahlepi* seed, extracted from the pits of Saint Lucie cherries) and ground mastic (a plant resin), you can substitute them in equal measure for the spices listed (*mahlab* for the cinnamon, nutmeg, and allspice; mastic for the clove).

Greek Celebration Bread

Makes 1 large loaf

MEASURE	OUNCES	GRAMS	INGREDIENTS	%
1 cup	7	198	barm (mother starter, page 241) or *poolish* (page 112)	43.8
3½ cups	16	454	unbleached bread flour	100
1¼ teaspoons	0.31	9	salt	2
1½ teaspoons	0.17	5	instant yeast	1.1
1 teaspoon	0.11	3	ground cinnamon	0.7
¼ teaspoon	0.03	0.85	ground nutmeg	0.2
¼ teaspoon	0.03	0.85	ground allspice	0.2
¼ teaspoon	0.03	0.85	ground cloves	0.2
1 teaspoon	0.16	4.5	minced orange or lemon zest or orange or lemon extract	1
1 teaspoon	0.16	4.5	almond extract	1
2 large	3.3	93.5	eggs, slightly beaten	20.6
¼ cup	2.67	76	honey	16.7
¼ cup	2	57	olive oil	12.5
¾ cup	6	170	whole or low-fat milk, lukewarm (90°F to 100°F/32°C to 38°C)	37.5
TOTAL				237.5

OPTIONAL GLAZE

2 tablespoons water				
2 tablespoons granulated sugar				
2 tablespoons honey				
1 teaspoon orange or lemon extract				
1 teaspoon sesame seeds				

1 Remove the measured amount of barm or *poolish* from the refrigerator 1 hour before making the dough. (If using *poolish*, make it the day before.)

2 Stir together the flour, salt, yeast, cinnamon, nutmeg, allspice, and cloves in a large mixing bowl (or in the bowl of an electric mixer). Add the barm or *poolish*, citrus zest or extract, almond extract, eggs, honey, oil, and milk. Stir together with a sturdy spoon (or mix on low speed with the paddle attachment) until the dough forms a ball.

3   Sprinkle flour on the counter, transfer the dough to the counter, and begin kneading (or mixing on medium speed with the dough hook), adding more milk or flour as needed to form the dough into a soft but not sticky ball. It should be tacky and very supple. It will take about 10 minutes of kneading (or about 6 minutes in an electric mixer). The dough should pass the windowpane test (page 61) and register 77°F to 81°F (25°C to 27°C).

4   Lightly oil a bowl and transfer the dough to the bowl, rolling it around to coat it with oil. Cover the bowl with plastic wrap and ferment the dough at room temperature for 1½ to 2 hours, or until it doubles in size.

5   Remove the dough from the bowl and shape it into a *boule*, as shown on page 76. Transfer it to a sheet pan that has been lined with baking parchment. Mist the dough with spray oil and loosely cover with plastic wrap.

6   Proof at room temperature for 1 to 1½ hours, or until the dough nearly doubles in size.

7   Preheat the oven to 350°F (177°C) with the oven rack on the middle shelf.

8   Bake the loaf for 20 minutes. Rotate the pan 180 degrees for even baking and continue to bake for 20 to 25 minutes, or until the loaf is golden brown and registers 190°F (88°C) in the center. It should make a hollow sound when thumped on the bottom.

9   You may glaze the loaf (optional) as soon as it comes out of the oven, while it's still on the pan. To make the glaze, combine the water and sugar in a saucepan and bring to a boil. Add the honey and citrus extract and turn off the heat. Reheat the glaze, if necessary, before applying it to the bread. Brush the loaf with the glaze and immediately sprinkle with the sesame seeds.

10   Transfer the bread to a rack and let cool for at least 1 hour before slicing or serving.

Christopsomos

Makes 1 large loaf

Greek Celebration Bread (opposite)

½ cup (3 ounces/85g) dark or golden raisins, or a combination

½ cup (3 ounces/85g) dried cranberries, dried cherries, or chopped dried figs, or a combination

½ cup (2 ounces/57g) chopped walnuts, lightly toasted

Prepare the dough for the celebration bread, mixing in the raisins, dried fruit, and walnuts during the final 2 minutes of the mixing in step 3. Proceed as for the celebration bread, but before shaping the dough into a *boule*, divide it into 2 pieces, 1 piece twice as big as the other. Shape the larger piece into a *boule*, as shown on page 76, and proof as described in steps 5 and 6. Place the smaller piece in a plastic bag and chill in the refrigerator. When the larger piece is ready to bake, remove the smaller piece from the refrigerator, divide it in half, and roll each half into a 10-inch-long (25-cm-long) strand. Shape the final dough as shown below.

*SHAPING CHRISTOPSOMOS

(A) Cross the 2 strands of dough over the top of the *boule*. (B) Using a pastry scraper, split the ends of each strand and coil them to form a decorative cross.

Lambropsomo

Makes 1 large loaf

Greek Celebration Bread (page 118)

¾ cup (4.5 ounces/128g) golden raisins

¼ cup (1.5 ounces/43g) chopped dried apricots

½ cup (2 ounces/57g) slivered blanched almonds, lightly toasted

3 hard-cooked eggs, dyed red

Prepare the dough for the celebration bread, mixing in the raisins, apricots, and almonds during the final 2 minutes of the mixing in step 3. Proceed as for the celebration bread, but instead of shaping into a *boule*, divide the dough into 3 equal pieces and braid using the three-braid method shown on page 89. Nestle the eggs in the spaces among the braided strands.

Bagels

There are two kinds of people in the world: those who like chewy water bagels and those who prefer softer steamed bagels. Having grown up on the East Coast in a predominantly Jewish neighborhood, I am naturally inclined toward what I think of as the true bagel, the thick-crusted, dense, boiled version, called the water bagel because it is poached in a kettle of boiling alkalized water. (I also like egg bagels, which call for enriching the dough with eggs, but they are still boiled.)

Most people who like the new style of softer bagels, and many such adherents exist, do not realize that what makes them so big and soft is that they are an airier dough, formed after a long proofing. This makes them impossible to boil because they are too soft to sustain their shape in the roiling cauldron. They are perfect for commercial steam-injected rotating rack ovens, however, because they do not have to be handled twice. (The oven lifts the entire rack of sheet pans and rotates it for even baking, after blasting it with a bath of steam to replace the boiling.)

According to folklore, bagels were invented in seventeenth-century Austria as a tribute to the wartime victories of King John III Sobieski of Poland (also known as King Jan) and were modeled after the stirrup of his saddle. They were a bread for the masses, popular also in Germany and Poland, but they were introduced into the United States by German and Polish Jewish immigrants, so we think of them as a Jewish bread. Now, because of the softer steamed versions, bagels have once again become a bread for the masses. The modern steaming method lends fuel to the debate of authenticity, however, and battles against our nostalgic desire for the real deal. Everyone who loves bagels seems to have a theory as to why even properly boiled bagels seem to fall short of those memories. Some think it depends on the quality of the water. "New York bagels can't be duplicated because of that great New York water," say New Yorkers, while others think it has something to do with the quality of the flour, or of whatever else they put into the kettle to flavor the crust. Others blame the automatic bagel-shaping machines invented by Tom Atwood in the 1950s. (Tom, who was in his eighties when I met him a number of years ago, told me that prior to his invention, all bagels were shaped by hand using the wrap-around method shown on page 126.) My theory is that nothing can top the taste of memory, but it is quite possible to find and make bagels every bit as good as those of yesteryear, albeit never as good as those of our memories.

As a professional baker, a bread instructor, and a water-bagel guy, I've been working on making the perfect bagel for a number of years. Just as the steam technique is a totally modern

BREAD PROFILE
Lean, stiff dough; indirect method; commercial yeast

. . .

DAYS TO MAKE: 2
DAY 1: 2 hours sponge; 10 to 15 minutes mixing; 1 to 1½ hours fermentation, shaping, and proofing

DAY 2: 10 minutes boiling and topping; 15 to 20 minutes baking

. . .

COMMENTARY
It is possible to make a sourdough version of these bagels by replacing the sponge with 5 cups (35 ounces/992g) wild-yeast barm (mother starter, page 241) and then increasing the instant yeast in the final dough to 1½ teaspoons (0.17 ounce/5g) or, for a bagel that's more sour, leave the yeast out entirely. Treat the dough the same as instructed for regular bagels from that point on. The flavor will have the distinctive tang of sourdough bread while retaining the chewy character of a classic bagel. Before you make a sourdough version, however, make the version that follows to master the technique.

NOTE: Nearly every one of my books includes a new formula for bagels, some with pre-ferments and some without, along with whole grain variations and even ancient- and sprouted-grain versions. They are all excellent and each of them proves that you can make fabulous bagels anywhere in the world—even without New York City water—if you have good flour and know just one trick: overnight fermentation, the key to a great bagel. Something almost magical happens to dough during long, cool fermentations, and bagels, which are a very simple product, rely on that magic to turn an ordinary dough into a deeply satisfying, beloved bread.

innovation that opened the bagel to the mainstream marketplace, there are many techniques that are now available to both professional and home bakers that did not exist in the days of King John. Even the bagel bakers of our parents' generation did not fully understand bread science as we now know it, though their feel for the product and their intuition was sharpened to a fine edge. What I have been working on is the application of some of the artisan techniques recently introduced by the new generation of bread bakers to the production of a definitive water bagel good enough to challenge our childhood memories and overcome our nostalgic biases. You will have to be the judge. This version is an improvement on the formula given in *Crust & Crumb*, which at the time I thought was as good as it gets. Here, I use an easier-to-make sponge, yet still employ the overnight fermentation that maximizes flavor. My students at Johnson & Wales University are too young to have had a "good old days" experience with bagels, so even though they love these bagels, their frame of reference is limited. But my wife, Susan, who, like me, grew up in the food and bagel mecca of Philadelphia, and some of my friends who grew up in New York City (the self-declared bagel center of the universe) feel that this is a bagel for the ages.

Most bagel shops use two ingredients that are hard for home bakers to find. One is high-gluten flour and the other is nondiastatic malt syrup. High-gluten flour, which contains up to 14 percent gluten protein as opposed to the 12.5 percent found in bread flour and the 10.5 percent in all-purpose flour, provides the elasticity and chewiness associated with classic water bagels. This flour can be purchased in at least three ways. One is through mail order, such as *The Baker's Catalogue* (see Resources, page 314). Another option is at specialty or natural foods stores (ask for unbleached hard spring-wheat flour). The third option, and not as unusual as you might think, is to throw yourself upon the mercy of your local bagel shop, explaining that you are a home baker on a quest to make a great bagel and would love to buy just a few pounds of flour from its stock. You'd be surprised how well this works. If all else fails, feel free to use regular bread flour, which still delivers a great, though not quite as chewy, bagel.

Malt syrup can be obtained in the same three ways (at natural foods stores, it is found under the label "barley syrup.") Most bagel shops use liquid nondiastatic malt, a thick, sticky molasseslike syrup. The word *diastatic* refers to diastase enzymes found in barley malt that help break down carbohydrates and release flavors trapped in the flour. Nondiastatic malt has been heated to the point of denaturing the enzymes, so the malt is used strictly for its flavor. However, I often use active diastatic malt, available in powder or crystal form from mail-order catalogs or at beer-making–supply stores. This "live" malt provides the added ability to

improve flavor enzymatically by hastening the release of natural sugars bound up in the flour starches. Regardless of the type of malt you use, it will give the bagels the familiar bagel shop flavor. If you cannot find malt and want to proceed anyway, you can substitute honey, agave, or brown sugar for wonderful, though less authentic, flavor.

In all of my bread travels, I have never found a bagel shop that uses the following sponge technique. But I am convinced that it not only gives the bagels a better flavor and texture but also ensures that they freeze and thaw better than commercially produced bagels because of the increase of natural acid produced by the method. The operating premise is that longer, slower fermentation improves both the flavor and shelf life of the product. The sponge, or pre-ferment, technique is one way to extend fermentation as is the overnight retarding technique used in any respectable bagel shop. It is impossible, in my opinion, to make a decent bagel without the overnight method, though I've seen many recipes in cookbooks that leave out this vital step. Believe me, you will never achieve a legendary bagel without the benefits of a long, slow cold fermentation, which allows the naturally occurring enzymes (and any additional enzymes provided by the malt) to release flavors. Making a bagel without this step is like drinking a fine wine just after it's been put in the bottle. The flavors are there in potential but are not fully realized. (This binding of flavors in immature wine or bread is due to the same circumstances: sugars that have not had time to unwind from their complex-carbohydrate base.)

Another important principle in understanding the uniqueness of a bagel is that it is probably the stiffest dough in the bread kingdom. Typically, most dough consists of a 55 to 65 percent liquid-to-flour ratio. Bagels, on the other hand, are usually 50 to 57 percent liquid to flour. This stiffness is what allows the dough to tolerate the brutality of boiling without deflating or losing shape. If you try to make a bagel with, say, French bread dough, it will flop around in the water and come out both flat and oblong. The hydration range never can be given as an exact ratio because each brand of flour absorbs liquid differently, and it may even vary within the same brand from batch to batch. So I always advise my students to feel their way into the dough and let it dictate exactly how much liquid or flour it will need in the final adjustment. It is always easier to add extra flour than extra water, especially in stiff dough, so the following instructions suggest gradually stiffening the dough by working in the last bit of flour little by little. The final dough should be stretchy but not tacky, unlike French or any lean bread dough, which is usually tacky to the touch.

Finally, the boiling, or poaching, is another one of those controversial techniques that runs up against family customs. Some people insist on putting baking soda, salt, sugar, honey, malt syrup, or milk, or some combination of them, into the water. Many bagel shops use food-grade lye, and many others use absolutely nothing but the water. I've boiled bagels all sorts of ways and have found that the final result is not as dependent on any add-in as it is on the time in the water. However, I prefer to use a small amount of baking soda to alkalize the water, as it is readily available and replicates closest the flavor of the lye baths used commercially. The alkalizing of the water causes a slightly different quality of gelatinization of the outer starches on the surface of the dough, inducing more shine and a richer caramelization of the crust when it bakes. It is but a subtle effect, and one that most of the people eating the bagels won't notice (and you may prefer to also add honey, malt syrup, or sugar to the water instead, all of which add flavor value). But it may be the final piece of the puzzle that will convert the diehards who continue to insist that no bagel is quite as good as the bagel they remember from the New York, Chicago, Philadelphia, Los Angeles, or you-fill-in-the-blank of their youth. I agree with my wife and friends: this is a bagel, a true water bagel, for the ages.

Makes 12 large or 24 mini bagels

MEASURE	OUNCES	GRAMS	INGREDIENTS	%
SPONGE				
1 teaspoon	0.11	3	instant yeast	0.31
4 cups	18	510	unbleached high-gluten or bread flour	51.4
2½ cups	20	567	water, at room temperature	57.1
DOUGH				
½ teaspoon	0.555	1.5	instant yeast	0.16
3¾ cups	17	482	unbleached high-gluten or bread flour	48.6
2¾ teaspoons	0.7	20	salt	2
2 teaspoons, or	0.33	9.5	malt powder	0.94
1 tablespoon	0.5	14	dark or light malt syrup, honey, or brown sugar	
TOTAL				160.5

TO FINISH

1 tablespoon baking soda, added to the boiling water (optional; or substitute 1 tablespoon honey or malt syrup)

Cornmeal or semolina for dusting

Sesame seeds, poppy seeds, kosher salt, rehydrated dried minced garlic or onion, or chopped fresh onion tossed in oil (optional)

＊SHAPING BAGELS

METHOD 1: (A) Poke a hole in a ball of bagel dough and **(B)** gently rotate your thumb around the inside of the hole to widen it to approximately 2½ inches (6cm) in diameter (1½ inches/4cm for mini-bagels). The dough should be as evenly stretched as possible (try to avoid thick and thin spots).

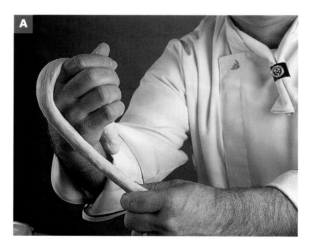 

METHOD 2: Roll the dough into an 8-inch-long (20-cm-long) rope. If the pieces are too elastic and snap back, roll part of the way, let the pieces rest for 3 minutes, and then extend them again to bring to full length. **(A)** Wrap the dough around the palm and back of your hand, between the thumb and forefinger, overlapping the ends by several inches (5cm). **(B)** Press the overlapping ends on the counter with the palm of your hand, rocking back and forth to seal.

1. To make the sponge, stir the yeast into the flour in a 4-quart mixing bowl. Add the water, whisking or stirring only until a smooth, sticky batter (like pancake batter) forms. Cover the bowl with plastic wrap and leave at room temperature for approximately 2 hours, or until the mixture becomes very foamy and bubbly. It should swell to nearly double in size and collapse when the bowl is tapped on the countertop.

2. To make the dough, in the same mixing bowl (or in the bowl of an electric mixer), add the additional yeast to the sponge and stir. Then add 3 cups (13.5 ounces/383g) of the flour and all of the salt and malt. Stir (or mix on low speed with the dough hook for about 3 minutes) until the ingredients form a ball, slowly working in the remaining ¾ cup (3.5 ounces/99g) flour to stiffen the dough.

3. Transfer the dough to the counter and knead for at least 8 to 10 minutes (or for about 6 minutes on low speed with the dough hook). The dough should be firm, stiffer than French bread dough, but still pliable and smooth. There should be no raw flour, that is, all the ingredients should be hydrated. The dough should pass the windowpane test (page 61) and register 77°F to 81°F (25°C to 27°C). If the dough seems too dry and rips, add a few drops of water and continue kneading. If the dough seems tacky or sticky, add more flour to achieve the stiffness required. The kneaded dough should feel satiny and pliable, but it should not be tacky.

4. Immediately divide the dough into 4½-ounce (128g) pieces for standard bagels, or 2.5-ounce (71g) pieces for mini bagels. Form the pieces into balls, as shown on page 86.

5. Cover the balls with a damp towel and allow them to rest for approximately 20 minutes.

6. Line 2 sheet pans with baking parchment and mist lightly with spray oil. Proceed with one of the following shaping methods.

7. Place the shaped pieces 2 inches (5cm) apart on the prepared pans. Mist the bagels very lightly with the spray oil and slip each pan into a food-grade plastic bag, or cover loosely with plastic wrap. Immediately place the pans in the refrigerator to chill overnight. They can remain in the refrigerator for up to 3 days, but they are best if used the following day.

GRACE NOTE

CINNAMON RAISIN BAGELS

For cinnamon raisin bagels, increase the yeast in the final dough to 1 teaspoon (0.11 ounce/3g) and add 1 tablespoon (0.5 ounce/14g) ground cinnamon and 5 tablespoons (2.5 ounces/71g) granulated sugar to the final dough. Rinse 2 cups (12 ounces/340g) loosely packed raisins with warm water to wash off surface sugar, acid, and natural wild yeast. Add the raisins during the final 2 minutes of mixing. Proceed as directed but do not top the bagels with a garnish. When the bagels come out of the oven and are still hot, brush the tops with melted butter and dip them in cinnamon sugar to create a cinnamon-sugar crust, if desired.

CINNAMON RAISIN BAGELS

SPONGE	
Instant yeast	.31
High-gluten flour	51.4
Water	57.1
DOUGH	
Instant yeast	.31
High-gluten flour	48.6
Salt	2
Malt powder	1
Raisins	34.3
Cinnamon sugar	8.6
TOTAL	203.6

8 When you are ready to bake the bagels, preheat the oven to 500°F (260°C) with 2 racks set on the middle shelves. Bring a large pot of water to a boil (the wider the pot the better) and add the baking soda. Have a slotted spoon or skimmer nearby.

9 Remove the pans from the refrigerator and check to see if the bagels are ready by using the "float test." Fill a small bowl with cool or room-temperature water. The bagels are ready to be boiled when they float within 10 seconds of being dropped into the water. Take 1 bagel and test it. If it floats, immediately return the tester bagel to the pan, pat it dry, cover the pan, and return the pan to the refrigerator until the water is boiling. If the bagel does not float, return it to the pan, pat it dry, and continue to proof the dough at room temperature, checking back every 10 to 20 minutes or so until a tester floats. The time needed to accomplish the float will vary depending on the ambient temperature and the stiffness of the dough. If the water comes to a boil before the bagels pass the float test, turn down the heat and cover the pot with a lid to keep the water hot.

10 Remove the bagels from the refrigerator and gently drop them into the water, boiling only as many as fit comfortably (they should float within 10 seconds). After 30 seconds, flip them over and boil for another 30 seconds. If you like very chewy bagels, you can extend the boiling time to 1 minute per side. While the bagels are boiling, sprinkle the same parchment-lined sheet pans with cornmeal or semolina. (If you decide to replace the paper, be sure to spray the new paper lightly with spray oil to prevent the bagels from sticking to the surface.) If you want to top the bagels, do so as soon as they come out of the water, while they are still wet. You can use any of the suggestions in the ingredients list or a combination. I usually make a seed-and-salt blend.

11   When all the bagels have been boiled, place the pans on the 2 middle racks in the oven. Bake for approximately 7 minutes, then switch the pans between the racks and rotate the pans 180 degrees. (If you are baking only 1 pan, leave it on the center rack and rotate it 180 degrees.) After the rotation, lower the oven temperature to 450°F (232°C) and continue to bake for about 7 to 8 additional minutes, or until the bagels turn light golden brown. You can bake them darker if you prefer.

12   Remove the pans from the oven and let the bagels cool on a rack for 15 minutes or longer before serving.

Brioche and Brioche Relatives

BREAD PROFILE
Rich, standard dough;
indirect method; commercial
yeast

• • •

DAYS TO MAKE: 1 OR 2
DAY 1: 20 to 45 minutes
sponge; 20 minutes mixing
(for Poor Man's Brioche:
3 hours for fermentation,
shaping, and proofing; 15 to
50 minutes baking)

DAY 2: 2½ hours for
shaping and proofing;
15 to 50 minutes baking

• • •

COMMENTARY
When a formula calls for
lots of fat, whether butter,
shortening, or oil, it is usually
beneficial to wait until the
gluten has had an opportunity to develop before adding
the fat. If the fat is added at
the beginning, it coats the
protein fragments (gliadin
and glutenin) and makes it
difficult for them to bond into
the longer, stronger gluten
molecule. Wait for 5 minutes
before incorporating the fat
to allow complete hydration
to occur. Of course, there
are cakelike variations of
brioche in which the butter is
intentionally added with the
flour to create a very tender,
tight-crumbed bread, almost
like pound cake. If you desire
this texture or application,
simply add the butter early
on and ignore the chill-down
step, transferring the batter
with a spoon or spatula to a
greased pan right after the
primary fermentation.

Brioche is the standard by which all rich breads are judged. In fact, whenever rich breads are described, they are often compared to brioche or called a relative. Brioche is actually simple in character: it is enriched with a small amount of sugar, substantial amounts of egg, and lots of butter—at least in excess of 20 percent (butter-to-flour ratio) but usually 50 percent or higher.

I have rarely seen brioche made commercially with more than 75 percent butter, but I have seen formulas that call for up to 100 percent. There are countless formula variations. Some are made with sponges or other pre-ferments, some by the direct-dough method. Some versions are immediately fermented and then shaped and baked, and some require overnight chilling.

The anecdotal history of this bread includes allusions to Queen Marie Antoinette, whose last words are reputed to be properly translated as "Let them eat brioche," and not "Let them eat cake." There are a lot of reasons to assume that either translation is more myth than fact, but it does beg the question, why would anyone even think to make such a statement? This may be because brioche had two distinct expressions in pre-Revolution France. One version, for the wealthy and thus called rich man's brioche, was loaded with butter (70 percent or more). The other, made for the huddled masses and therefore called poor man's brioche, was butter challenged (20 to 25 percent). As so often happens with bread, it makes a perfect symbol for many things, not the least of which is the class struggle between the haves and the have-nots. So, it would make sense that if the queen was about to lose her head because the revolutionaries were, for the most part, have-nots, why not offer them rich man's brioche. "Yeah, we can do that, sure." But, alas, it was too late, too futile, and probably too arrogant a gesture.

When we examine the formula for rich man's brioche, one thing becomes evident: it has almost the same flour-to-fat-to-sugar ratio as pie dough. The main difference is the yeast and eggs. Most pie dough, whether *pâte brisée* (plain) or *pâte sucrée* (sweet), and whether flaky or mealy, is made by some variation of what is known as the 1-2-3 method. This means 3 parts flour, 2 parts fat, and 1 part water (and also, in sweet dough, or *pâte sucrée*, sugar). The ratio translates as 66.6 percent fat to 100 percent flour. Brioche, rich man's brioche at least, has between 50 and 80 percent butter, right in the pie-dough range. This means that brioche can, in principle, be used to make a very nice tender pie or tart dough, which is often done in French *pâtisseries*. It is a wonderful alternative to the flaky or mealy pie dough under quiche or other custard tarts, as I have witnessed in the *clafouti* sold in the pastry shop of

Paris's Ritz Hotel. Apparently, hundreds of these tartlets are made everyday for the hotel's guests, and the kitchen can barely keep up with the demand.

Other applications of brioche include loaf breads for the definitive French toast, tea and café rolls, wraps for meat- or vegetable-filled molds, and, most famously, small fluted rolls with "heads" (*petites brioches à tête*). Beyond that, there are the infinite regional and holiday expressions of the bread, from the Italian *pandoro* and panettone, to the *Kugelhopf* of Alsace, stollen of Germany and Switzerland, and the amazing meat-and-cheese-filled Italian version called *casatiello*.

The following versions of brioche give you three options, depending on the amount of butter you feel ready to tackle. In the spirit of Queen Marie, we will call them rich man's, middle-class, and poor man's brioche, all of which have valid applications in the bread canon.

· · ·

To make *brioche à tête*, you will need a special fluted brioche mold, available at gourmet kitchen shops. These molds come in many sizes, but I find the small 2-ounce (56g) molds to be the most functional. The larger molds are nice for special holiday or festive breads like panettone. Remember to increase the baking time to account for the dough size. (All three brioche variations can be made as standard rolls; see page 86 for shaping.)

· · ·

The Rich Man's Brioche that follows is even richer than the version presented in *Crust & Crumb*. That one was about 70 percent butter to flour; this version is about 88 percent butter to flour. The yeast percentage is thus higher to provide the necessary push, and the sponge is very fast, needing only 20 minutes to develop. It is best if mixed in an electric mixer with the paddle attachment, but it can also be mixed by hand with a sturdy spoon and a strong arm.

Rich Man's Brioche

Makes 16 to 24 petites brioches à tête, 2 to 4 large brioches
à tête, or three 1-pound (453g) loaves

MEASURE	OUNCES	GRAMS	INGREDIENTS	%
SPONGE				
½ cup	2.25	64	unbleached bread flour	12.3
1 tablespoon	0.33	9.5	instant yeast	1.8
½ cup	4	113	whole milk, lukewarm (90°F to 100°F/32°C to 38°C)	22
DOUGH				
5 large	8.25	234	eggs, slightly beaten	45.2
3½ cups	16	454	unbleached bread flour	87.7
2½ tablespoons	1.25	35	granulated sugar	6.8
1½ teaspoons	0.38	11	salt	2
2 cups	16	454	unsalted butter, at room temperature	87.7
1 egg, whisked until frothy, for egg wash				
TOTAL				265.5

1   To make the sponge, stir together the flour and yeast in a 4-quart mixing bowl (or in the bowl of an electric mixer). Stir in the milk until all the flour is hydrated. Cover with plastic wrap and ferment for 20 minutes, or until the sponge rises and then falls when you tap the bowl.

2   To make the dough, add the eggs to the sponge and whisk (or beat on medium speed with the paddle attachment) until smooth. In a separate bowl, stir together the flour, sugar, and salt. Add this mixture to the sponge and eggs and stir (or continue to mix with the paddle on low speed for about 2 minutes) until all the ingredients are hydrated and evenly distributed. Let this mixture rest for 5 minutes so that the gluten can begin to develop. Then, while mixing with a large spoon (or on medium speed with the paddle attachment), gradually work in the butter, about one-quarter at a time, waiting until each addition of butter is incorporated before adding more. This will take a few minutes. Continue mixing for 6 minutes longer, or until the dough is very well mixed. You will have to scrape down the bowl from time to time as the dough will cling to it. The dough will be very smooth and soft.

3   Line a sheet pan with baking parchment and mist lightly with spray oil. Transfer the dough to the sheet pan and spread it into a large, thick rectangle measuring about 6 by 8 inches (15 by 20cm). Mist the top of the dough with spray oil and cover the pan with plastic wrap or place it in a large food-grade plastic bag.

4   Immediately put the pan into the refrigerator and chill overnight, or for at least 4 hours.

5   Remove the dough from the refrigerator and shape it while it is very cold. If it warms up or softens, return it to the refrigerator. If you are making *brioches à tête*, lightly oil or use spray

oil to grease the fluted molds. Divide the dough into 12 to 16 portions for *petites brioches à tête* and 2 to 4 portions for larger shapes. (The size of each portion should correspond to the size of the molds; *petites brioches à tête* are typically 1½ to 2 ounces (42.5g to 57g) each, while larger versions can range from 1 to 2 pounds (454g to 907g). Whatever size you are making, the molds should be no more than half full with the larger section of dough to allow for expansion during proofing.) Shape the *petites brioches à tête* into small balls (below) and the larger ones into *boules* (see page 76). Proceed with the shaping instructions shown below. Place the molds on a sheet pan after the final shaping. If you are making loaves, lightly oil or use spray mist to grease three 8½ by 4½-inch (22 by 11cm) loaf pans. Divide the dough into 3 pieces (or two pieces for 2 larger loaf pans) and shape the dough into loaves, as shown on page 85.

✳ SHAPING BRIOCHES À TÊTE

METHOD 1: Dust your hands with flour and, using the edge of your hand, **(A)** divide a ball of dough into a large and small ball by rolling down, but not quite all the way through, the dough. **(B)** Place the large ball into the oiled brioche mold and use the tips of your fingers to indent the top and to round and center the smaller ball.

METHOD 2: Roll the dough into a strand that tapers at one end. **(A)** Poke a hole in the thick end of the strand and **(B)** loop the tapered end through it so that it pops out and forms a cap. Round the cap into a ball and center it on the larger portion. Place it in the oiled brioche mold.

6   Mist the top of the dough with spray oil and loosely cover with plastic wrap, or slip the pan(s) into a food-grade plastic bag. Proof the dough until it nearly fills the molds or loaf pans, 1½ to 2 hours for *petites brioches à tête* and longer for larger shapes. Gently brush the tops with egg wash. Cover the dough with plastic wrap that has been lightly misted with spray oil. Continue proofing for another 15 to 30 minutes, or until the dough fills the molds or pans.

7   Place the oven rack on the middle shelf of the oven and preheat the oven to 400°F (204°C) for *petites brioches à tête* or 350°F (177°C) for larger shapes.

8   Bake for 15 to 20 minutes for *petites brioches à tête* or 35 to 50 minutes for larger shapes. The internal temperature should register above 180°F (82°C) for the small ones and about 190°F (88°C) for the larger shapes. The bread should sound hollow when thumped on the bottom and be golden brown.

9   Remove the brioches or loaves from the pans as soon as they come out of the oven and let cool on a rack for at least 20 minutes for small brioches and 1 hour for larger shapes before serving.

Middle-Class Brioche

Makes 12 to 16 petites brioches à tête, 2 to 4 large brioches à tête, or two 1-pound (453g) loaves

COMMENTARY
Middle-Class Brioche, made with a 50 percent butter-to-flour ratio, is a versatile dough, perfect for cinnamon or sticky buns, soft loaves, and *brioche à tête*. It is the most common form of brioche because it costs less than Rich Man's Brioche and requires less gym time to work off the butter (though 50 percent fat to flour is still workout worthy!). It is also easier to handle than the richer version.

MEASURE	OUNCES	GRAMS	INGREDIENTS	%
SPONGE				
½ cup	2.25	64	unbleached bread flour	14
2 teaspoons	0.22	6	instant yeast	1.4
½ cup	4	113	whole milk, lukewarm (90°F to 100°F/32°C to 38°C)	25
DOUGH				
5 large	8.25	234	eggs, slightly beaten	51.6
3 cups	13.75	390	unbleached bread flour	86
2 tablespoons	1	28	granulated sugar	6.25
1¼ teaspoon	0.31	9	salt	1.9
1 cup	8	227	unsalted butter, at room temperature	50
1 egg, whisked until frothy, for egg wash				
TOTAL				236.2

Proceed as directed for Rich Man's Brioche, extending the fermentation for the sponge to 30 to 45 minutes.

Poor Man's Brioche

Makes 12 to 16 petites brioches à tête, 2 to 4 large brioches à tête, or two 1-pound (453g) loaves

MEASURE	OUNCES	GRAMS	INGREDIENTS	%
SPONGE				
½ cup	2.25	64	unbleached bread flour	13.2
2 teaspoons	0.22	6	instant yeast	1.3
½ cup	4	113	whole milk, lukewarm (90°F to 100°F/32°C to 38°C)	23.5
DOUGH				
4 large	6.6	187	eggs, slightly beaten	38.8
3¼ cups	14.75	418	unbleached bread flour	86.8
2 tablespoons	1	28	granulated sugar	5.9
1¼ teaspoons	0.31	9	salt	1.8
½ cup	4	113	unsalted butter, at room temperature	23.5
1 egg, whisked until frothy, for egg wash				
TOTAL				194.8

COMMENTARY
Poor Man's Brioche is especially useful for wraps or en croûte applications, since it is by far the easiest version to handle. It also makes a very nice pain de mie, or sandwich bread. It is still a rich bread, in excess of 20 percent butter to flour, but it lacks the melt-in-your-mouth buttery flake of the richer versions.

1 To make the sponge, stir together the flour and yeast in a large mixing bowl (or in the bowl of an electric mixer). Stir in the milk until all the flour is hydrated. Cover with plastic wrap and ferment for 30 to 45 minutes, or until the sponge rises and then falls when you tap the bowl.

2 To make the dough, add the eggs to the sponge and whisk (or beat on medium speed with the paddle attachment) until smooth. In a separate bowl, stir together the flour, sugar, and salt. Add this mixture to the sponge and eggs and stir (or continue to mix with the paddle on low speed for about 2 minutes) until all the ingredients are hydrated and evenly distributed. Let this mixture rest for 5 minutes so the gluten can begin to develop. Then, while mixing with a large spoon (or on medium speed with the dough hook), gradually work in the butter, about one-quarter at a time, waiting until each addition of butter assimilates before adding more.

3 Transfer the dough to the counter and knead for about 10 minutes, adding small amounts of flour as needed, or until the dough is very smooth and soft but not too sticky to handle—kind of like French bread dough. (Or continue mixing with the dough hook on low speed for 6 to 8 minutes, or until the dough is very well mixed and clears the sides and bottom of the bowl.)

4 Lightly oil a bowl and transfer the dough to the bowl. Mist the top of the dough with spray oil and cover the bowl with plastic wrap. Ferment for about 1½ hours, or until the dough doubles in size.

5 Proceed with the shaping instructions described in Rich Man's Brioche, reducing the proofing time to about 1 hour. Bake and cool as directed.

Casatiello (foreground) and *petites brioches à tête* (back left).

Casatiello

This is a rich, dreamy Italian elaboration of brioche, loaded with flavor bursts in the form of cheese and bits of meat, preferably salami. Since first reading about it in Carol Field's wonderful *The Italian Baker,* I've also made it with bacon bits, different types of fresh or cured sausage, and even with nonmeat substitutes. The bread is traditionally baked in paper bags or panettone molds, but it can also be baked in loaf pans. Perhaps the best way to think of it is as a savory version of panettone, with cheese and meat replacing the candied fruit and nuts. Serve it warm and the cheese will still be soft; serve it cool and each slice will taste like a sandwich unto itself.

This is one of my most popular formulas. Even 15 years after first publishing this recipe in the original edition of *The Bread Baker's Apprentice,* I still get e-mails from folks who rave about it.

Makes 1 large loaf or 2 small loaves

MEASURE	OUNCES	GRAMS	INGREDIENTS	%
SPONGE				
½ cup	2.25	64	unbleached bread flour	12.3
1 tablespoon	0.33	9.5	instant yeast	1.8
1 cup	8	227	whole milk or buttermilk, lukewarm (90°F to 100°F/32°C to 38°C)	43.8
DOUGH				
3½ cups	16	454	unbleached bread flour	87.7
1 teaspoon	0.25	7	salt	1.4
1 tablespoon	0.5	14	granulated sugar	2.7
2 large	3.3	93.5	eggs, slightly beaten	18
¾ cup	6	170	unsalted butter, at room temperature	32.9
1 cup	4	113	dry-cured Italian salami or other meat (see Commentary)	22
¾ cup	6	170	coarsely shredded or grated provolone or other cheese (see Commentary)	32.9
TOTAL				255.5

BREAD PROFILE
Rich, standard dough; indirect method; commercial yeast

• • •

DAYS TO MAKE: 1
1 hour sponge; 12 minutes mixing; 3 hours fermentation, shaping, and proofing; 40 to 60 minutes baking

• • •

COMMENTARY
Other types of cheese can be substituted for the provolone, but the cheese should be a good "melter" with distinctive flavor of its own, such as Swiss, Gouda, or Cheddar or their infinite cousins. I rarely use mozzarella or Jack because they are somewhat bland, or Parmesan or other hard cheeses because they are too salty and do not melt into a creamy pocket. However, if that is what I have on hand, blending mozzarella or Jack with a grated hard cheese brings the melting and flavor perks of each together into an excellent substitute.

• • •

This is a fast sponge and the entire bread can be made in about 5 hours from start to finish. The dough can also be made a day ahead, and then shaped and baked the following day, like brioche, but you must chill it as soon as it comes off the mixer to avoid overfermenting.

The formula calls for whole milk, but I often substitute buttermilk because I like the slightly acidic flavor.

• • •

The meat can be any flavorful substitute that you have on hand or prefer. Italian salami and pepperoni are ideal because their flavor intensifies as they cook, and little bits go a long way, especially if they are lightly sautéed before they are added to the dough. Cooked and crumbled bacon and pancetta are also superb in this bread, and the rendered fat can be added to the dough as a substitute for an equal part of the butter for even more flavor intensity. Other substitutes include crisped chorizo, Italian sausage, or other crisped fresh sausage; fresh all-beef salami (diced and then cooked until slightly crisp); imitation bacon bits (soy); or firm smoked tofu cut into bits.

• • •

You can cut the butter in half if you prefer, but you may have to increase the milk slightly to achieve the proper consistency.

1. To make the sponge, stir together the flour and yeast in a bowl. Whisk in the milk to make a thin batter. Cover with plastic wrap and ferment at room temperature for 1 hour. The sponge will foam and bubble and should collapse when you tap the bowl.

2. While the sponge is fermenting, cut the salami for the dough into small cubes and sauté it lightly in a skillet to crisp it slightly. (Alternatively, cook and crumble the bacon or sauté fresh sausage or salami substitutes until crisp, saving the rendered fat.)

3. To make the dough, in a mixing bowl (or in the bowl of an electric mixer), stir together the flour, salt, and sugar with a spoon. Add the eggs and sponge and mix together (or mix with the paddle attachment on low speed) until all the ingredients form a coarse ball. If there is any loose flour, dribble in a small amount of water or milk to gather it into the dough. Stir (or mix) for about 1 minute, then let the dough rest for 10 minutes to allow the gluten to develop. Divide the butter into 4 pieces. Begin working the butter into the dough, one piece at a time, stirring vigorously with the spoon (or mixing on medium speed). The dough will be soft but not a batter. Continue mixing with the spoon, or switch to your hands but keep them floured as you knead, working the dough into a smooth, tacky mass. It will take about 12 minutes. (In the electric mixer, scrape down the bowl with a plastic bowl scraper or rubber spatula and then switch to the dough hook after 4 minutes. The dough will change from sticky to tacky and eventually come off the sides of the bowl. If not, sprinkle in more flour until the dough forms a ball and clears the sides of the bowl.)

4. When the dough is smooth, add the meat pieces and knead (or mix) until they are evenly distributed. Then gently knead (or mix) in the cheese until it too is evenly distributed. The dough will be soft and stretchy, very tacky but not sticky. If it is sticky, sprinkle in more flour until it firms up. Lightly oil a large bowl and transfer the dough to the bowl, rolling it around to coat it with oil. Cover the bowl with plastic wrap.

5. Ferment at room temperature for about 1½ hours, or until the dough increases in size by at least 1½ times.

6. Remove the dough from the bowl and leave as 1 piece for 1 large loaf or divide into 2 pieces for smaller loaves. The loaves can be baked in white or brown sandwich-size paper bags set in metal cans just large enough to hold them, such as a no. 10 can or a coffee can. Or they can be baked in 1 large or 2 small loaf pans. (You can also use paper or metal pannetone molds, available at specialty cookware stores, or an 8-inch cake pan, as shown by the loaf in the photo on page 136.) If you are baking in bags, generously spray the inside of 1 or 2 small brown or white sandwich- or lunch-size paper bags with spray oil. Lightly dust your hands and the dough with flour and shape the dough (or dough pieces) into a *boule*, as shown on page 76. Place a ball of dough in the prepared bag, and roll the top of the bag back to make a collar about 2 inches above the top of the dough. Place the bag in a metal can just large enough to hold it. If you are baking in loaf pans, mist one 9 by 5-inch (23 by 13cm) or two 8½ by 4½-inch (22 by 11.5cm) pans with spray oil. Lightly dust your hands and the dough with flour and shape the dough into 1 or 2 loaves, as shown on page 85, and place in the pans. Mist the top of the dough with spray oil and loosely cover the bags or pans with plastic wrap or a towel.

7   Proof for 1 to 1½ hours, or until the dough just reaches the top of the bags or just crests to the top of the pans.

8   Preheat the oven to 350°F (177°C) with the oven rack in the lower third of the oven.

9   Place the can(s) or pan(s) with the dough in the oven and bake for 20 minutes and then rotate them 180 degrees. If you are baking in cans, reduce the oven temperature to 325°F (163°C). Do not reduce the oven setting if you are baking in loaf pans. Bake for an additional 20 to 30 minutes for loaf pans or about 40 minutes for cans, or until the center of the loaves registers 185°F to 190°F (85°C to 88°C). The dough will be golden brown on top and on the sides, and the cheese will ooze out into crisp, little brown pockets. The bread will rise to just above the tops of the bags.

10   When the bread is done, remove it from the oven and transfer to a cooling rack. If you are baking in bread pans, remove the bread from the pans; if you are baking in bags, remove the bags from the cans and either remove the bread from the bags or cut slits in the bags to allow the steam to escape. Let the bread cool for at least 1 hour before slicing or serving.

Challah

BREAD PROFILE
Enriched, standard dough; direct method; commercial yeast

· · ·

DAYS TO MAKE: 1
10 to 15 minutes mixing; 3½ hours fermentation, shaping, and proofing; 20 to 45 minutes baking, depending on size

Challah, the braided Sabbath bread of Judaism, is a European celebratory loaf symbolic of God's goodness and bounty. The braids traditionally separate the loaf into twelve distinct sections representing the twelve tribes of Israel. The use of eggs in the bread was probably a way to use up excess eggs before the strict Judaic Sabbath day of rest made it impossible to gather new eggs, one of many activities considered work in Orthodox Jewish communities.

I've made challah many different ways, but this is a great formula that produces a soft golden loaf, radiant when brought to the table. The key to a beautiful challah, one that stops conversation and holds everyone's attention, is to braid it so that it is tapered at the ends and plump in the middle.

This version is different from the one in the original edition, as I recently discovered how more egg yolks and a few other tweaks make it even better. Save the egg whites for the egg wash or other uses. Also, the water is approximate and should be adjusted as needed, since eggs can vary in weight. The final dough should be supple but firmer than French bread dough and barely tacky, so that it will hold the distinct shape of the braided strands.

Makes 1 large braided loaf, 2 smaller loaves, or 1 large double-braided celebration loaf

MEASURE	OUNCES	GRAMS	INGREDIENTS	%
4 cups	18	510	unbleached bread flour	100
2½ tablespoons	1.25	35	granulated sugar	6.9
1¼ teaspoons	0.3	8	salt	1.6
1½ teaspoons	0.18	5	instant yeast	1
2½ tablespoons	1.25	35	vegetable oil	6.9
1 large	1.65	47	egg, slightly beaten	9.2
4 large	3	85	egg yolks	16.7
¾ cup plus 2 tablespoons	7	198	water, at room temperature (see note below)	39
1 egg white, whisked with 1 tablespoon water, for egg-white wash				
Sesame or poppy seeds for garnish				
TOTAL				181.3

Note: If the whole egg and egg yolks are cold, use lukewarm (90°F to 100°F/32°C to 38°C) water to compensate.

1   Stir together the flour, sugar, salt, and yeast in a large mixing bowl (or in the bowl of an electric mixer). In a separate bowl, whisk together the oil, eggs and yolks, and the water. Pour the egg mixture into the flour mixture. Mix with a spoon (or on low speed with the paddle attachment) until all the ingredients gather and form a ball. Add more water, if needed, to make a coarse, slightly tacky dough.

2   Sprinkle flour on the counter, transfer the dough to the counter, and knead for 6 to 10 minutes (or mix on medium-low speed with the dough hook for 4 to 6 minutes), sprinkling in more flour or water, if needed, to make a dough that is soft and supple, slightly tacky but not sticky. The dough should pass the windowpane test (page 61) and register approximately 77°F to 81°F (25°C to 27°C).

3   Lightly oil a large bowl. Form the dough into a *boule*, as shown on page 76, and transfer it to the bowl, rolling it around to coat it with oil. Cover the bowl with plastic wrap. Ferment for 1 hour at room temperature.

4   Remove the dough from the bowl and knead for 2 minutes to degas. Re-form it into a ball, return the ball to the bowl, cover the bowl with plastic wrap, and ferment for an additional hour. It should be at least 1½ times its original size.

5   Remove the dough from the bowl and divide it into 3 equal pieces for 1 large loaf or 6 equal pieces for 2 loaves. (Or, for a celebration challah, divide the dough into 3 equal pieces, combine 2 of the pieces, and form them into 1 large dough. Take this larger piece and divide it into 3 equal pieces. Take the smaller dough and divide it into 3 pieces as well; in the end, you will have 3 large pieces and 3 small pieces.) Regardless of the size of the loaves you decide to make, form each of the pieces into a *boule*, as shown on page 76, cover them with a towel, and let them rest on the counter for 10 minutes. (Note: You can divide the dough into other equal sizes for 4, 5, or 6-braid loaves and shape them as shown on pages 90 and 91.)

6   Roll out the pieces into strands, each the same length, thicker in the middle and slightly tapered toward the ends. Braid them using the three-braid method shown on page 89. (If making the celebration challah, lay the smaller braid on top of the larger braid, gently pressing the smaller braid onto the larger to adhere.) Line a sheet pan with baking parchment and transfer the loaf or loaves to the pan. Brush the loaves with the egg wash. Mist the loaves with spray oil and cover loosely with plastic wrap or place the pan in a food-grade plastic bag.

7   Proof at room temperature for 1 to 1¼ hours, or until the dough has grown to 1½ times its original size.

8   Preheat the oven to 350°F/177°C (or 325°F/163°C for the celebration challah) with the oven rack on the middle shelf. Brush again with egg wash and sprinkle sesame seeds on top.

9   Bake for 20 minutes. Rotate the pan 180 degrees and continue baking for 20 to 45 minutes, depending on the size of the loaf. The bread should be a rich golden brown and register 190°F (88°C) in the center.

10 When done, transfer the bread to a rack and let cool for at least 1 hour before slicing or serving.

COMMENTARY

A double-braided celebration challah is often made for weddings and bar and bat mitzvahs. This double-decker version, with a smaller braid laminated to the top of the larger loaf, makes a dramatic centerpiece.

. . .

One of the people who tested this recipe, Ellen Fenster, reminded me that the braided dough also can be curled into a round loaf, especially for Rosh Hashanah, the Jewish New Year. The round shape symbolizes that the world has no beginning and no end; the three strands symbolize truth, peace, and beauty; and the spiral coil indicates the ascent to God. It is also customary to sweeten the loaf with additional sugar (you can double it) as a sign of beginning the New Year in a sweet way. Ellen told me that garnishing the loaves with seeds, such as poppy or sesame, symbolizes the falling of manna from heaven, and the covering of the challah with a cloth as it is served at the Sabbath meal represents the heavenly dew that protects the manna. Thank you, Ellen!

Ciabatta

BREAD PROFILE
Lean, rustic dough; indirect
method; commercial yeast

• • •

DAYS TO MAKE: 2
DAY 1: 2 to 4 hours *poolish*
or *biga*

DAY 2: 1 hour to de-chill *poolish* or *biga*; 10 to 15 minutes
mixing; 3 to 4 hours fermentation, shaping, and proofing;
20 to 30 minutes baking

This bread, with its big, shiny holes and amorphous shape, has taken America by storm, just as it did Italy during the past 50 years. Although it hails from an age-old tradition of rustic, slack-dough breads, according to one of its many origin stories, the name *ciabatta* was not applied to this loaf until the mid-twentieth century. An enterprising baker in the Lake Como region of northern Italy observed that the bread resembled a slipper worn by dancers of the region and thus dubbed his loaf *ciabatta di Como* (slipper bread of Como). A new tradition was born. During the second half of the century, this *ciabatta* became the unofficial national bread of Italy, so closely identified is it with the chewy, rustic peasant breads of the Italian countryside. As with pugliese bread, the dough is not unlike that of many other Italian and French rustic breads, including pizza and focaccia, and can thus be made into many shapes other than the Lake Como slipper.

You can make this dough with a large amount of either *poolish* or *biga,* and formulas for both versions follow. It can also be made with the addition of milk and olive oil to tenderize the dough. In other words, there are many variations, all valid, and as long as you make a slipper shape, you can call it ciabatta.

Since writing *Crust & Crumb,* I have continued to fine-tune these rustic breads, pushing the limits of time and temperature manipulation, trying to evoke every bit of flavor trapped in the flour. In the *pain à l'ancienne* formula on page 199, we will make a similar dough but with no pre-ferment and a long cold fermentation. Each variation in technique brings forth slightly different flavor tones from the wheat, and everyone seems to have their own preferences. In this version, the use of 165 to 180 percent pre-ferment seems to be the magic amount to maximize a same-day bread in a 4- to 5-hour window. It yields a slightly acidic and yeasty edge, a flavor that many people love. They say, "This tastes like real bread!" I have found little difference between the *biga* and *poolish* versions; both are amazing.

This rustic bread dough can be formed into a number of shapes beyond the classic slipper, such as the long *stirato*, stubby *pain rustique*, or round pugliese style.

Ciabatta, Poolish Version

Makes two 1-pound (453g) loaves or 3 smaller loaves

MEASURE	OUNCES	GRAMS	INGREDIENTS	%
3¼ cups	22.75	645	*poolish* (page 112)	168.5
3 cups	13.5	382	unbleached bread flour	100
1¾ teaspoons	0.44	12.5	salt	3.25
1½ teaspoons	0.17	5	instant yeast	0.75
¾ cup plus 3 tablespoons	7.5	213	water (or substitute whole milk or buttermilk for all or part of the water, see Commentary), lukewarm (90°F to 100°F/32°C to 38°C)	44.5
Semolina or cornmeal for dusting				
TOTAL				317

TOTAL DOUGH FORMULA AND %

	OUNCES	GRAMS	INGREDIENTS	%
	25	709	bread flour	100
	0.44	12.5	salt	1.8
	0.17	5	instant yeast	0.7
	18.75	532	water	75
TOTAL				177.5

1   Remove the *poolish* from the refrigerator 1 hour before making the dough to take off the chill.

2   To make the dough, stir together the flour, salt, and yeast in a 4-quart mixing bowl (or in the bowl of an electric mixer). Add the *poolish* and the water and, using a large metal spoon (or on low speed with the paddle attachment), mix until the ingredients form a sticky ball. If there is still some loose flour, add additional water as needed and continue to mix. If you are mixing by hand, repeatedly dip one of your hands or the metal spoon into cold water and use it, much like a dough hook, to work the dough vigorously into a smooth mass while rotating the bowl in a circular motion with the other hand (see page 58). Reverse the circular motion a few times to develop the gluten further. Do this for 5 to 7 minutes, or until the dough is smooth and the ingredients are evenly distributed. If you are using an electric mixer, mix on medium speed with the paddle attachment for 5 to 7 minutes, or as long as it takes to create a smooth, sticky dough. Switch to the dough hook for the final 2 minutes of mixing. The dough should clear the sides of the bowl but stick to the bottom of the bowl. You may need to add additional flour to firm up the dough enough to clear the sides of the bowl, but the dough should still be quite soft and sticky.

COMMENTARY

You can add ¼ cup (2 ounces/57g) olive oil to the formula and/or substitute whole milk or buttermilk for some or all of the water (even the *poolish* can be made with milk). The oil- or milk-enriched product will be softer and more tender than the lean, water-only version. If you are adding the oil, you may need to add a small amount of flour—as always, let the dough dictate if it needs any flour or liquid adjustments.

. . .

As you become comfortable with wet dough, you may want to try increasing the hydration and stickiness of the dough. The wetter the better, as long as it holds together enough to make the stretch-and-fold maneuvers. It is during the stretching and folding that the gluten has a chance to strengthen, resulting in the large holes so distinctive and prized in this bread.

. . .

This dough is very simple to make in a food processor. See page 57 for instructions.

. . .

There are a number of excellent variations that you can try, including adding mushrooms, cheese, or sautéed onions, as described on the following pages.

3   Sprinkle enough flour on the counter to make a bed about 8 inches (20cm) square (or use the oil slick method, as described on page 59). Using a bowl scraper or spatula dipped in water, transfer the sticky dough to the bed of flour and proceed with the stretch-and-fold method as described on pages 59 and 146. Mist the top of the dough with spray oil, again dust with flour, and loosely cover with plastic wrap or a food-grade plastic bag. Let rest for 30 minutes and then stretch and fold the dough again; mist with spray oil, dust with flour, and cover.

4   Allow the covered dough to ferment on the counter for 1½ to 2 hours. It should swell but not necessarily double in size.

5   Set up a *couche* as described on page 33 (or use a sheet pan dusted with bread flour or semolina). Carefully remove the plastic from the dough and proceed as shown on page 146 for shaping the dough. Mist the top of the dough with spray oil and dust the dough with more flour, then cover the cloth with a towel. Proof for 45 minutes to 1½ hours, or until the dough has noticeably swelled. Prepare the oven for hearth baking as described on page 97 making sure to have an empty steam pan in place. Preheat the oven to 500°F (260°C).

6   Generously dust a peel or the back of a sheet pan with semolina or cornmeal and very gently transfer the dough pieces to the peel or pan, using the pastry scraper if you need support. Lift the dough from each end and tug the dough out to a length of 9 to 12 inches (23 to 30cm). If the dough bulges too high in the middle, gently dimple it down with your fingertips to even out the height of the loaf. Slide the 2 doughs (or bake one at a time if you prefer) onto the baking stone (or bake directly on the sheet pan). Pour 1 cup hot water into the steam pan and close the door. After 30 seconds, open the door, spray the side walls of the oven with water, and close the door. Repeat twice more at 30-second intervals. After the final spray, turn the oven setting down to 450°F (232°C) and bake for 10 minutes. Rotate the loaves 180 degrees, if necessary, for even baking and continue baking for 5 to 10 minutes longer, or until done. The bread should register 205°F (96°C) in the center and should be golden in color (but the flour streaks will also give it a dusty look). The loaves will feel quite hard and crusty at first but will soften as they cool.

7   Transfer the bread from the oven to a cooling rack and let cool for at least 45 minutes before slicing or serving.

*STRETCH-AND-FOLD METHOD

(A) Dust the top of the dough liberally with flour, patting the dough into a rectangle. Wait for 2 minutes for the dough to relax. Coat your hands with flour and (B) lift the dough from each end, stretching it to twice its size. (C) Fold the dough over itself, letter style, to return it to a rectangular shape.

*SHAPING CIABATTA

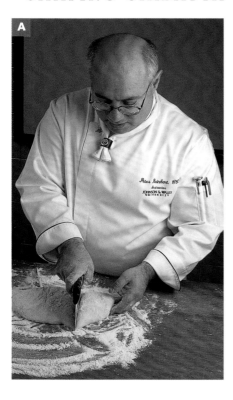

(A) Using a pastry scraper that has been dipped in water, divide the dough into 2 or 3 rectangles, taking care not to degas the dough. Sprinkle the dough generously with more flour and, using the scraper to get under the dough, gently lift each piece from the counter and then roll it on both sides in the loose flour to coat.

(B) Lay the loaves on the cloth and gently fold each piece of dough, from left to right, letter style, into an oblong about 6 inches (15cm) long.

(C) Bunch the cloth between the pieces to provide a wall. (For an alternative method, dust a sheet pan generously with flour or a blend of flours, such as rye, semolina, bread, or the like. Roll the formed ciabatta loaves on the pan to coat them with flour and then space them, seam side down, on the pan. Mist the loaves with spray oil and then cover loosely with plastic wrap or a towel. After 30 minutes, gently flip the loaves over, seam side up, and continue proofing before transferring the loaves to the oven to bake.)

Ciabatta, Biga Version

Makes two 1-pound (453g) loaves or 3 smaller loaves

MEASURE	OUNCES	GRAMS	INGREDIENTS	%
3 cups	16	454	*biga* (page 113)	178
2 cups	9	255	unbleached bread flour	100
1½ teaspoons	0.37	10.5	salt	4.1
1½ teaspoons	0.18	5	instant yeast	2
1 cup	8	227	water (or substitute whole milk or buttermilk for all or part of the water, see Commentary), lukewarm (90°F to 100°F/32°C to 38°C)	88
2 tablespoons	1	28	olive oil (optional)	11
TOTAL				383.1

TOTAL DOUGH FORMULA AND %

	OUNCES	GRAMS	INGREDIENTS	%
	18.5	524	bread flour	100
	0.37	10.5	salt	1.8
	0.18	5	instant yeast	0.7
	14.5	411	water	78.4
	1	28	olive oil (optional)	
TOTAL				180.9/186.4

1 Remove the *biga* from the refrigerator 1 hour before making the dough. Cut it into about 10 small pieces with a pastry scraper or serrated knife. Cover with a towel or plastic wrap and let sit for 1 hour.

2 To make the dough, stir together the flour, salt, and yeast in a 4-quart mixing bowl (or in the bowl of an electric mixer). Add the *biga* pieces, water, and oil (if using). With a large metal spoon (or on low speed with the paddle attachment), mix until the ingredients form a sticky ball. If there is still some loose flour, add additional water as needed and continue to mix. Proceed as directed in the *poolish* version.

Wild Mushroom Ciabatta (Ciabatta al Funghi)

Makes two 1-pound (453g) loaves or 3 smaller loaves

COMMENTARY
Probably the most popular
bread among my students
is wild mushroom ciabatta. I
included an excellent formula
for this in *Crust & Crumb*
but have developed a new
technique for making this and
other flavor variations using
the new formulas in this book.
Here are three examples,
but there are no limits to the
options.

5 dried shiitake or porcini mushrooms, broken into pieces and stems discarded

6 tablespoons water, warm (100°F/38°C)

1 pound (454g) fresh button or shiitake mushrooms, cut into ¼-inch-thick (6-mm-thick) slices
(stems discarded from shiitake)

4 cloves garlic, pressed or minced

¼ cup olive oil

Salt and freshly ground black pepper

Ciabatta, Poolish Version (page 143) or Ciabatta, Biga Version (page 147)

1   Soak the dried mushrooms in the water for 30 minutes (you can do this just prior to making
the final dough or the day before). Meanwhile, in a large skillet, sauté the fresh mushrooms
and garlic in the olive oil over medium heat just until the mushrooms are soft. Drain off the
pan juices and add them to the soaking dried mushrooms. Season the sautéed mushrooms
with salt and pepper and set them aside to cool.

2   Make the dough as directed in the master formula, adding the dried mushrooms and
soaking liquid as you mix the dough and using as much liquid as necessary to make a soft,
sticky dough.

3   Proceed as directed in the chosen version. When you perform the two stretch-and-fold turns,
sprinkle one-quarter of the sautéed fresh mushrooms (or less, if you are making 3 smaller
loaves) over each piece of dough each time and fold them in. If any fall out, simply add them
in the next time or slip them between the folds.

Ciabatta with Cheese (Ciabatta al Formaggio)

Makes two 1-pound (453g) loaves or 3 smaller loaves

Ciabatta, Poolish Version (page 143) or Ciabatta, Biga Version (page 147)

2 cups shredded or grated Parmesan, romano, mozzarella, Jack, Cheddar, provolone, Swiss, and blue cheese, in any combination

Make the dough as directed in the master formula. When performing the two stretch-and-fold turns, sprinkle one-quarter of the cheese blend (or less, if you are making 3 smaller loaves) over each piece of dough each time and fold them in. Proceed as described in the chosen version.

Caramelized Onion and Herb Ciabatta

Makes two 1-pound (454g) loaves or 3 smaller loaves

4 cups sliced yellow or white onions

¼ cup olive oil

2 tablespoons granulated sugar

1 tablespoon balsamic vinegar

1 cup chopped fresh herb blend (parsley, basil, oregano, tarragon, cilantro, or other favorite herb, in any combination)

Salt and freshly ground black pepper

Ciabatta, Poolish Version (page 143) or Ciabatta, Biga Version (page 147)

1   Prepare the onion-and-herb mixture at least 1 hour before making the dough or the day before. In a large skillet, sauté the onions in the olive oil over medium heat until they start to caramelize or turn brown (it will take 10 to 15 minutes). Add the sugar and continue to cook until the sugar melts and the onions turn golden brown. Add the balsamic vinegar and stir until the onions are evenly coated. Turn off the heat and add the herbs, tossing just until they are evenly distributed and wilted. Season with salt and pepper. Set aside to cool.

2   Make the dough as directed in the master formula. When performing the two stretch-and-fold turns, spread one-quarter of the onions (or less, if you are making 3 smaller loaves) over each piece of dough each time and fold them in. Proceed as directed in the chosen version.

Cinnamon Buns and Sticky Buns

BREAD PROFILE
Enriched, standard dough;
direct method; commercial
yeast

• • •

DAYS TO MAKE: 1
15 minutes mixing; 3½ hours
fermentation, shaping, and
proofing; 20 to 40 minutes
baking

• • •

COMMENTARY
This dough can be used
for other applications. For
instance, you can make
thumbprint sweet rolls, filled
with jam or jelly. You can also
make pastry logs. Roll out
the dough as you would for
cinnamon buns, but instead
of cutting pinwheel slices and
baking them face up, load the
logs with nuts, raisins, and
cinnamon sugar and bake
them whole, like *bâtards*. Slice
them after they've cooled
so that all the goodies inside
come tumbling out onto
the plate.

My students often ask me to teach them how to make a cinnamon bun as good as the ones they get at the mall from Cinnabon and other franchise shops. For my money, this version makes a cinnamon bun that outperforms anything you can buy at the mall. But those of us who grew up in eastern Pennsylvania have a soft spot in our hearts for sticky buns, such as the ones that originate in the Pennsylvania Dutch countryside. Frankly, everyone in the United States seems to have a favorite regional version, whether it is a cinnamon bun glazed with a sweet white-sugar fondant or a sticky bun with a caramel glaze. Regardless of side issues, such as white versus caramel glazes, the type of nut (usually walnuts versus pecans), or with or without raisins, the real key to this kind of comfort food is a soft, light, tender, slightly sweet dough baked just right.

This formula falls in the enriched, not the rich, dough category because the fat content is slightly under 20 percent. I've made versions of sweet dough that contain up to 50 percent fat, but then why eat the buns? You might as well strap them right onto your hips, since that's where they will end up (or, as one of my customers used to say, "They call them sticky buns because they stick to your buns!"). There are plenty of enrichments—shortening, eggs, sugar, milk—to tenderize this dough without additional fat. However, if you do want to make an even more decadent version of cinnamon or sticky buns, try using the formula for Middle-Class Brioche on page 134, or see the bonus formula on page 297, where I push the envelope even further.

Makes 8 to 12 large or 12 to 16 smaller cinnamon or sticky buns or other sweet rolls

MEASURE	OUNCES	GRAMS	INGREDIENTS	%
6½ tablespoons	3.25	92	granulated sugar	20
1 teaspoon	0.25	7	salt	1.6
5½ tablespoons	2.75	78	unsalted butter, shortening, or vegetable oil, at room temperature	17
1 large	1.65	47	egg, slightly beaten	10.3
1 teaspoon, or 1 teaspoon	0.18 0.1	5g 3	lemon extract grated zest of 1 lemon	1.1
3½ cups	16	454	unbleached bread or all-purpose flour	100
2 teaspoons	0.22	6	instant yeast	1.4
1 cup plus 2 tablespoons, or 3 tablespoons and 1 cup	9 1 8	255 28 227	whole milk or buttermilk, lukewarm (about 90°F/32°C) or powdered milk (DMS) and lukewarm water (about 90°F/32°C)	56.25
½ cup	4	113	cinnamon sugar (6½ tablespoons granulated sugar mixed with 1½ tablespoons ground cinnamon)	
TOTAL				207.65

White Fondant Glaze for Cinnamon Buns (page 153)

Caramel Glaze for Sticky Buns (page 153)

Walnuts, pecans, or other nuts (for sticky buns)

Raisins or other dried fruit, such as dried cranberries or dried cherries (for sticky buns)

1 Cream together the sugar, salt, and butter on medium-high speed in an electric mixer with the paddle attachment (or use a large metal spoon and mixing bowl and do it by hand); if you are using powdered milk, cream it with the sugar but add the water with the flour and yeast. Whip in the egg and lemon extract or zest until smooth. Then add the flour, yeast, and milk. Mix on low speed (or stir by hand) until the dough forms a ball. Switch to the dough hook and increase the speed to medium, mixing for approximately 6 minutes (or knead by hand for 6 to 8 minutes), or until the dough is silky and supple and tacky but not sticky. You may have to add a little flour or water while mixing to achieve this texture. The dough should pass the windowpane test (page 61) and register 77°F to 81°F (25°C to 27°C). Lightly oil a large bowl and transfer the dough to the bowl, rolling it around to coat it with oil. Cover the bowl with plastic wrap.

2 Ferment at room temperature for 1½ hours to 2 hours, or until the dough doubles in size.

3 Mist the counter with spray oil or rub it lightly with vegetable oil and transfer the dough to the counter. Proceed as shown on page 152 for shaping the buns.

*SHAPING CINNAMON BUNS AND STICKY BUNS

(A) Roll out the dough with a rolling pin, lightly dusting the top of the dough with flour to keep it from sticking to the pin. Roll it into a rectangle about ⅔-inch (17mm) thick and 14 inches (35cm) wide by 12 inches (30cm) long for larger buns, or 18 inches (46cm) wide by 9 inches (23cm) long for smaller buns. Don't roll out the dough too thin, or the finished buns will be tough and chewy rather than soft and plump. **(B)** Sprinkle the cinnamon sugar over the surface of the dough and **(C)** roll the dough up into a cigar-shaped log, creating a cinnamon-sugar spiral as you roll. With the seam side down (see page 150), cut the dough into 8 to 12 even pieces each about 1¾-inches (4.5cm) thick for larger buns; or 12 to 16 pieces each 1¼-inch (3cm) thick for smaller buns.

4   For cinnamon buns, line 1 or more sheet pans with baking parchment. Place the buns, with a spiral side face-up, approximately ½ inch (13mm) apart. They should be close together but not touching. For sticky buns, coat the bottom of 1 or more baking dishes (or baking pans) with at least 1½-inch (4cm) sides with a ¼-inch-thick (6mm) layer of the caramel glaze. Sprinkle on the nuts and raisins. You do not need a lot of nuts and raisins, only a sprinkling. Lay the dough pieces, with a spiral side face- up, on top of the caramel glaze, spacing them about ½ inch (13mm) apart. Mist the dough with spray oil and cover the dish(es) loosely with plastic wrap or place in a food-grade plastic bag.

5   Proof at room temperature for 1¼ to 1½ hours, or until the pieces have grown into one another and have nearly doubled in size. You can also retard the shaped buns in the refriger-ator for up to 2 days, pulling the pans out of the refrigerator 3 to 4 hours before baking to allow the dough to proof.

6   Preheat the oven to 350°F (177°C) with the oven rack on the middle shelf for cinnamon buns or on the lowest shelf for sticky buns.

7   Bake the cinnamon buns for 20 to 30 minutes or the sticky buns for 30 to 40 minutes, or until golden brown. If you are baking sticky buns, remember that they are really upside down (regular cinnamon buns are baked right side up), so the heat has to penetrate through the pan

and into the glaze to caramelize it. The tops will become the bottoms, so the buns may appear dark and done, but the real key is whether the underside is fully baked. It takes practice to know just when to pull the buns out of the oven.

8   For cinnamon buns, cool the buns in the pan for about 10 minutes and then streak white fondant glaze across the tops while the buns are warm but not too hot. Remove the buns from the pans and place them on a cooling rack. Wait for at least 20 minutes before serving. For sticky buns, let the buns cool in the pan for 5 to 10 minutes, then invert a platter over the top of a baking dish, flip the dish and platter together, place on the counter, and lift off the dish. Be careful, as the glaze will still be very hot. Using a rubber spatula, carefully scoop any run-off glaze or any glaze remaining in the baking dish over the buns. If more than 1 baking dish was used, repeat with the second dish. Wait for at least 20 minutes before serving.

GRACE NOTES

WHITE FONDANT GLAZE FOR CINNAMON BUNS

Cinnamon buns are usually topped with a thick white glaze called quick fondant or flat icing. There are many ways to make fondant glaze, but here is a delicious and simple version, enlivened by the addition of citrus flavor, either lemon or orange. You can substitute vanilla extract or rum extract for the citrus or you can make the glaze without any flavoring.

Sift 4 cups powdered sugar into a bowl. Add 1 teaspoon lemon or orange extract and 6 tablespoons to ½ cup warm milk, briskly whisking until all the sugar is dissolved. Add the milk slowly and use only as much as is needed to make a thick, smooth paste that falls in a ribbon from the whisk.

When the buns have cooled but are still warm, streak the glaze over them by dipping the tines of a fork or a whisk into the glaze and waving the fork or whisk over the tops. Or, form the streaks by dipping your fingers in the glaze and then letting the glaze drip off as you wave your fingers over the tops of the buns. (Remember to wear latex gloves.)

CARAMEL GLAZE FOR STICKY BUNS

Caramel glaze is essentially some combination of sugar and fat, cooked until it caramelizes. The trick is catching it just when the sugar melts and lightly caramelizes to a golden amber. Then it will cool to a soft, creamy caramel. If you wait too long and the glaze turns dark brown, it will cool to a hard, crack-your-teeth consistency. Most sticky bun glazes contain other ingredients to influence flavor and texture, such as corn syrup to keep the sugar from crystallizing and flavor extracts or oils, such as vanilla or lemon. This version makes the best sticky bun glaze of any I've tried. It was developed by my wife, Susan, for Brother Juniper's Café in Forestville, California.

In the bowl of an electric mixer fitted with the paddle attachment, or a food processor, combine ½ cup each granulated sugar and firmly packed brown sugar, ½ teaspoon salt, and 1 cup unsalted butter, at room temperature. Cream together for 2 minutes on high speed in the mixer or pulse for about 1 minute if using a food processor.

Add ½ cup corn syrup and 1 teaspoon lemon, orange, or vanilla extract and continue to cream for about 5 minutes in the mixer or about 1 minute in the food processor, or until light and fluffy.

Use as much of the glaze as you need to cover the bottom of the pan with a ¼-inch-thick (6-mm-thick) layer. Refrigerate the excess in an airtight container for future use; it will keep for months.

Cinnamon Raisin Walnut Bread

BREAD PROFILE
Enriched, standard dough;
direct method; commercial
yeast

• • •

DAYS TO MAKE: 1
15 minutes mixing; 3½ hours
fermentation, shaping, and
proofing; 40 to 50 minutes
baking

• • •

COMMENTARY
An alternative to the method
described here is to add a
cinnamon swirl. To make
cinnamon sugar, stir together
a ½ cup (3½ ounces/100g) of
granulated sugar and 2 tablespoons ground cinnamon.
When shaping the dough, roll
out each piece with a rolling
pin to a rectangle 5 inches
(13cm) wide by 8 inches
(20cm) long and approxi-
mately ⅓ inch (8.5mm) thick.
Sprinkle cinnamon sugar
evenly over the surface of
the rectangles and then roll
up the dough into a tight
sandwich-style loaf (page
85), pinching the seam closed
with your fingers. When you
slice the baked bread, there
will be a cinnamon swirl that
not only looks pretty but will
also add additional cinnamon-
sugar flavor.

• • •

Another way to add flavor is
to brush the tops of the baked
loaves with melted butter as
soon as they come out of the
bread pans and then roll them
in the cinnamon sugar. When
the bread cools, the top will
have an additional sweet and
crunchy flavor burst.

In *Brother Juniper's Bread Book,* I included a recipe for a variation of this bread, but I believe this version is even better, encompassing all the qualities one wants from a raisin bread. It is light, flavorful, loaded with raisins, and it has a wonderful finish, filling your mouth with the satisfying aftertaste of roasted walnuts. If you prefer not to use nuts, you can eliminate them from the formula without any further changes. You can also substitute other nuts, such as pecans or hazelnuts, for the walnuts.

Makes two 1½-pound (680g) loaves

MEASURE	OUNCES	GRAMS	INGREDIENTS	%
3½ cups	16	454	unbleached bread flour	100
4 teaspoons	0.66	19	granulated sugar	4
1¼ teaspoons	0.31	9	salt	1.9
2 teaspoons	0.22	6	instant yeast	1.4
1¼ teaspoons	0.16	4.5	ground cinnamon	1
1 large	1.65	47	egg, slightly beaten	10
2 tablespoons	1	28	unsalted butter, melted or at room temperature, or vegetable oil	6.25
½ cup	4	113	buttermilk or whole milk, at room temperature	25
¾ cup	6	170	water, at room temperature	37.5
1½ cups	9	255	raisins, rinsed and drained	56
1 cup	4	113	chopped walnuts	25
TOTAL				268

1   Stir together the flour, sugar, salt, yeast, and cinnamon in a mixing bowl (or in the bowl of an electric mixer). Add the egg, melted butter or oil, buttermilk, and water. Stir together with a large spoon (or mix on low speed with a paddle attachment) until the ingredients come together and form a ball. Adjust with flour or water if the dough seems too sticky or too dry and stiff.

2   Sprinkle flour on a counter, transfer the dough to the counter, and begin kneading (or mixing on medium speed with the dough hook). The dough should be soft and pliable, tacky but not sticky. Add flour as you knead (or mix), if necessary, to achieve this texture. Knead by hand or machine for approximately 6 minutes. Sprinkle in the raisins and walnuts during the final 2 minutes of kneading (or mixing) to distribute them evenly and to avoid crushing them too

Cinnamon Raisin Walnut Bread with a cinnamon swirl and cinnamon sugar crust (see Commentary).

much. (If you are mixing by machine, you may have to finish kneading by hand to distribute the raisins and walnuts evenly.) The dough should pass the windowpane test (page 61) and register 77°F to 81°F (25°C to 27°C). Lightly oil a large bowl and transfer the dough to the bowl, rolling it to coat it with oil. Cover the bowl with plastic wrap.

3   Ferment at room temperature for approximately 2 hours, or until the dough doubles in size.

4   Divide the dough into 2 equal pieces and form them into loaves, as shown on page 85. Place each loaf in a lightly oiled 8½ by 4½-inch (22 by 11.5cm) pan, mist the tops with spray oil, and cover loosely with plastic wrap.

5   Proof at room temperature for 1 to 1½ hours, or until the dough crests above the lips of the pans and is nearly doubled in size.

6   Preheat the oven to 350°F (177°C) with the oven rack on the middle shelf. Place the loaf pans on a sheet pan, making sure they are not touching each other.

7   Bake the loaves for 20 minutes. Rotate the pan 180 degrees for even baking and continue baking for another 20 to 30 minutes. The finished breads should register 190°F (88°C) in the center and be golden brown on top and lightly golden on the sides and bottom. They should make a hollow sound when thumped on the bottom.

Corn Bread

The single most vivid taste memory I associate with Thanksgiving is the flavor of crisp turkey skin. I almost always get first dibs on the wing tips and sneak into the kitchen to peel off the crispiest pieces of golden, salt-and-peppery cracklings, before the carvers go to work. The intensity of flavor means it doesn't take a lot of skins to satisfy my craving, but by the end of the meal, I usually find myself yearning for just one more piece.

This corn bread is designed to take the pressure off that yearning, substituting the smoky, salty flavor of crisp bacon for the turkey skin. However, I often make a variation of this, buying a half-pound of chicken or turkey skins from the butcher, laying them out on a sheet pan, seasoning them with salt and pepper, and baking at 350°F (177°C) until they render their fat and become very crisp and crumbly, just like bacon.

The use of sugar, honey, buttermilk, lots of corn kernels, and polenta-grind cornmeal (rather than the usual finely ground cornmeal) gives this bread moisture, texture, and sweet yet tart flavor bursts. The bacon (or cracklings) on the top is the final payoff, complementing any Thanksgiving dinner or re-creating Thanksgiving flavor memories throughout the year.

I have an ongoing love affair with good corn bread. By good I mean moist and sweet, with crunch and texture. This recipe is my favorite, and it is the best corn bread I have ever made or eaten. Corn bread falls into the category of quick breads, since it is leavened by baking powder (see page 69 for information on chemical leavening). Even though this book is not about chemically leavened quick breads, I couldn't resist adding it to the collection because, frankly, I just don't think it gets any better than this. (Note: For this revised edition, I have added a new suggestion, recently learned, that allows the baker to push the flavor profile even further into true corn greatness by substituting sprouted cornmeal for the regular cornmeal. See Resources, page 314, for where to order it.)

BREAD PROFILE
Enriched, batter dough; chemical leavening (baking powder and baking soda)

• • •

DAYS TO MAKE: 2
DAY 1: 5 minutes cornmeal soaker

DAY 2: 45 minutes to prepare bacon; 15 minutes mixing and heating the pan; 30 minutes baking

• • •

COMMENTARY
As with all quick breads, this batter can be used to make muffins. Fill the greased muffin cups to the top and bake at 350°F (177°C) for about 30 minutes, or until the center of a muffin is springy and a toothpick inserted into the center comes out clean.

(continued)

Makes one 10-inch (25cm) round bread

MEASURE	OUNCES	GRAMS	INGREDIENTS	%
1 cup	6	170	coarse-grind cornmeal (also packaged as "polenta") or sprouted cornmeal	42.9
2 cups	16	454	buttermilk	114
10 slices	8	227	bacon	51.1
1¾ cups	8	227	unbleached all-purpose flour	57.1
1½ tablespoons	0.75	21	baking powder	5.4
¼ teaspoon	0.05	1.5	baking soda	0.36
1 teaspoon	0.25	7	salt	1.8
¼ cup	2	57	granulated sugar	14.3
¼ cup	2	57	firmly packed brown sugar	14.3
3 large	5	142	eggs	35.7
2 tablespoons	1.5	42.5	honey	10.7
2 tablespoons	1	28	unsalted butter, melted	7.1
2½ cups	16	454	fresh or thawed frozen corn kernels	114
2 tablespoons	1	28	rendered bacon fat, unsalted butter, or vegetable oil	7.1
TOTAL				475.86

1   The night before baking the corn bread, soak the cornmeal in the buttermilk. Cover and leave at room temperature overnight.

2   The next day, to prepare the bacon, preheat the oven to 375°F (190°C). Lay the bacon slices in a single layer on 2 sheet pans. Bake the bacon for 15 to 20 minutes, or until it is crisp. Using tongs or a fork, transfer the slices to a pan lined with paper towels to cool. Drain off the fat into a can or stainless-steel bowl and save for greasing the corn bread pan. When the bacon has cooled, crumble it into coarse pieces.

3   Lower the oven setting to 350°F (177°C). Sift together the flour, baking powder, baking soda, and salt into a large mixing bowl. Stir in the granulated sugar and brown sugar. In another bowl, lightly beat the eggs. Dissolve the honey in the melted butter and then stir the warm honey-butter mixture into the eggs. Add this to the soaked cornmeal mixture. Add the wet mixture to the flour mixture and stir with a large spoon or whisk until all the ingredients are evenly distributed and the batter is blended and smooth. It should be the consistency of thick pancake batter. Stir in the corn kernels until they are evenly distributed.

4   Place 2 tablespoons of the rendered bacon fat (or melted butter) into a 10-inch (25cm) round cake pan (you can also use a 9 by 13-inch (23 by 33-cm) baking pan or a 12-inch (30cm) square pan). Place the pan in the oven for 2 to 3 minutes, or until the fat gets very hot. With good pot holders or oven mitts, remove the pan, tilt it to grease all the corners and sides, and pour in the batter, spreading it from the center of the pan to the edges. Sprinkle the crumbled bacon pieces evenly over the top, gently pressing them into the batter.

5   Bake for about 30 minutes, or until the corn bread is firm and springy (the baking time will depend on the size of the pan) and a toothpick inserted into the center comes out clean. The top will be a medium golden brown. The center of the bread should register at least 185°F (85°C).

6   Allow the bread to cool in the pan for at least 15 minutes before slicing it into squares or wedges. Serve warm.

Cranberry-Walnut Celebration Bread

BREAD PROFILE
Enriched, standard dough;
direct method; commercial
yeast

• • •

DAYS TO MAKE: 1
15 minutes mixing; 3¾ hours
fermentation, shaping, and
proofing; 50 to 55 minutes
baking

• • •

COMMENTARY
There are a lot of dried cranberries and walnuts in this
bread, which makes it seem
difficult to incorporate them
evenly, but they will all fit
with patient kneading. Don't
worry if some fall out during
the shaping stage (just put
them back in the dough) or
during baking (discard the
burned ones).

• • •

You can freely substitute
raisins or other dried fruits for
the cranberries, and pecans
or other nuts for the walnuts,
but I think the combination
of cranberries and walnuts is
a classic! You can also lightly
toast the walnuts before
chopping them to inten-
sify their flavor, but this is
optional.

I've long believed that the connecting link in any Thanksgiving dinner is the cranberry relish. It ties all the other flavors together, its juices running in every direction on the plate, blending with the gravy, potatoes, and dressing, and then finally enlivening the turkey itself with its sweet-and-sour flavor tones. Of course, it has to be good cranberry relish, made with coarsely chopped berries and walnuts and fresh orange juice, not just the canned jelly slices. This bread captures those flavors and can be used to supplement the relish (which always seems to run out before I've had my fill). It also makes a beautiful table presentation, with its double-decker braiding, evocative of a traditional celebration challah (page 140).

Makes 1 large braided loaf

MEASURE	OUNCES	GRAMS	INGREDIENTS	%
3 cups	13.5	382	unbleached bread flour	100
3 tablespoons	1.5	42.5	granulated sugar	11.1
¾ teaspoon	0.19	5	salt	1.4
3½ teaspoons	0.39	11	instant yeast	2.9
1½ tablespoons	0.75	21	orange or lemon extract	5.6
2 large	3.3	93.5	eggs, slightly beaten	24.4
½ cup	4	113	buttermilk or any kind of milk, at room temperature	29.6
2 tablespoons	1	28	unsalted butter	7.4
¼ to ½ cup	2 to 4	57 to 113	water, at room temperature	22.2
1½ cups	9	255	dried sweetened cranberries	66.7
¾ cup	3	85	coarsely chopped walnuts	22.2
1 egg, whisked until frothy, for egg wash				
TOTAL				293.5

(continued)

Cranberry-Walnut Celebration Bread   161

This dough can also be baked in regular loaf pans or as freestanding *boules* or *bâtards*. Follow the shaping instructions on pages 76 and 77. Sweetened, enriched breads such as this one should always be baked in the lower temperature range of 325°F to 350°F (163°C to 177°C), regardless of the shape, in order to avoid burning the outside of the loaf before the inside sufficiently gelatinizes.

1 Stir together the flour, sugar, salt, and yeast in a large mixing bowl (or in the bowl of an electric mixer). Add the citrus extract, eggs, buttermilk (or milk), and butter. Stir (or mix on low speed with the paddle attachment), slowly adding just enough water to make a soft, pliable ball of dough.

2 Sprinkle flour on the counter and transfer the dough to the counter. Knead (or mix on medium speed with the dough hook) for about 5 minutes, or until the dough is smooth and only slightly tacky, but not sticky. It should have a soft, pliable quality, not stiff and resistant. If it is too stiff, knead (or mix) in small amounts of water until it softens; if the dough seems too sticky, sprinkle in small amounts of flour as needed. Add the dried cranberries and knead (or mix) for another 2 minutes, or until they are evenly distributed. Then gently knead (or mix) in the walnut pieces until they are evenly distributed. Lightly oil a large bowl and transfer the dough to the bowl, rolling it to coat it with oil. Cover the bowl with plastic wrap.

3 Ferment at room temperature for about 2 hours, or until the dough doubles in size.

4 Transfer the dough to the counter and divide it into 6 pieces: 3 pieces of 10 ounces (284g) each and 3 pieces of 4 ounces (113g) each. Roll out the larger pieces into strands about 9 inches (23cm) long that are thicker in the middle and slightly tapered toward the ends. Roll the smaller pieces into strands about 7 inches (18cm) long and similarly tapered. Braid the large strands using the three-braid technique shown on page 89, and then braid the small strands in the same pattern. Line a sheet pan with baking parchment. Place the large braid on the pan. Center the smaller braid on top of the large braid in double-decker fashion. Brush the entire assembly with half of the egg wash and refrigerate the remaining egg wash to be used later.

5 Proof uncovered at room temperature for about 1½ hours, or until the dough nearly doubles in size. Brush the loaf a second time with the remaining egg wash.

6 Preheat the oven to 325°F (163°C) with the oven rack on the middle shelf.

7 Bake for approximately 25 minutes. Rotate the pan 180 degrees for even baking and then continue baking for another 25 to 30 minutes, or until the loaf is a deep golden brown, feels very firm, and sounds hollow when thumped on the bottom. The internal temperature at the center of the loaf should register between 185°F (85°C) and 190°F (88°C).

8 Remove the bread from the pan and let cool on a rack for at least 1 hour before slicing or serving.

English Muffins

These are fun to make, especially with kids. Instead of baking the bread in the oven, the muffins are first baked in a skillet or on a griddle. If you want to get the big holes that the professionals get, the dough must be soft but not too sticky, and you will need to bake or grill the muffins at just the right time, catching them on the rise. The fairly straightforward enriched dough can also be used to make English muffin loaf bread, a holey white loaf that kids—well, not just kids—love.

Makes 6 English muffins or one 1-pound (453g) loaf

MEASURE	OUNCES	GRAMS	INGREDIENTS	%
2½ cups	10	284	unbleached bread flour	100
1½ teaspoons	0.25	7	granulated sugar	2.5
¾ teaspoon	0.19	5	salt	1.9
1¼ teaspoons	0.14	4	instant yeast	1.4
1 tablespoon	0.5	14	unsalted butter, at room temperature, or vegetable oil	5
¾ to 1 cup	6 to 8	170 to 227	milk or buttermilk, at room temperature	70
Cornmeal for dusting				
TOTAL				180.8

1   Stir together the flour, sugar, salt, and yeast in a mixing bowl (or in the bowl of an electric mixer). Stir in (or mix in on low speed with the paddle attachment) the butter (or oil) and ¾ cup (6 ounces/170g) milk until the ingredients form a ball. If there is still loose flour in the bowl, dribble in some of the remaining ¼ cup milk. The dough should be soft, tacky, and pliable, not stiff.

2   Sprinkle flour on the counter, transfer the dough to the counter, and begin kneading (or mixing on medium speed with the dough hook). Knead the dough for 8 to 10 minutes (or mix for about 8 minutes), sprinkling in more flour if needed to make a tacky, but not sticky, dough. It should pass the windowpane test (page 61) and register 77°F to 81°F (25°C to 27°C). Lightly oil a large bowl and transfer the dough to the bowl, rolling it to coat it with oil. Cover the bowl with plastic wrap.

BREAD PROFILE
Enriched, standard dough; direct method; commercial yeast

• • •

DAYS TO MAKE: 1
10 to 15 minutes mixing; 3 hours fermentation, shaping, and proofing; 15 to 25 minutes cooking and baking

• • •

COMMENTARY
Instead of cutting open the finished muffins with a knife, use a fork. The commercial brands like to trumpet this as "fork-split" English muffins. The advantage is that by running the tines of the fork into and around the edge of the bread, the famous nooks and crevices that are so much a part of the English muffin mystique are created.

• • •

For a larger baking spring and bigger holes, place a metal mixing bowl over the muffins while they are cooking on the stove top to trap steam and heat. Use the metal spatula to get under and lift the bowl off the pan.

3   Ferment at room temperature for 1 to 1½ hours, or until the dough doubles in size.

4   Wipe the counter with a damp cloth and transfer the dough to the counter. Divide the dough into 6 equal pieces of 3 ounces (85g) each (or shape into a loaf, as shown on page 85, and proceed as for white bread, page 286, beginning with step 5). Shape the pieces into small *boules*, as shown on page 76. Line a sheet pan with baking parchment, mist the parchment lightly with spray oil, and dust with cornmeal. Transfer the dough balls to the sheet pan, spacing them about 3 inches (8cm) apart. Mist them lightly with spray oil, sprinkle them loosely with cornmeal, and cover the pan loosely with plastic wrap or a towel.

5   Proof at room temperature for 1 to 1½ hours, or until the pieces nearly double in size and swell both up and out.

6   Heat a skillet or flat griddle to medium (350°F/177°C if you have a thermometer setting). Also, preheat the oven to 350°F (177°C) with the oven rack on the middle shelf.

7   Brush the pan or griddle with vegetable oil or mist with spray oil. Uncover the muffin rounds, then slide a metal spatula under a round and gently transfer it to the pan. Add more rounds the same way, spacing the rounds at least 1 inch (2.5cm) apart. Cover the rounds still on the sheet pan with the plastic wrap or a towel to prevent them from developing a skin. The dough rounds will flatten in the hot pan and spread slightly and then they will puff somewhat. Cook the round for 5 to 8 minutes, or until the bottoms cannot cook any longer without burning. The bottoms should be a rich golden brown; they will brown quickly but will not burn for a while, so resist the temptation to turn them prematurely or they will fall when you flip them over. Using the metal spatula, carefully flip each one over and cook on the other side for 5 to 8 minutes in the same manner. Both sides will now be flat. When the dough seems as if it cannot endure any further cooking without burning, transfer the pieces to a sheet pan and place the pan in the oven (don't wait for the still uncooked pieces, or the ones just out of the pan will cool down and will not respond to the oven stage). Bake for 5 to 8 minutes to ensure that the center is baked. Meanwhile, return to the uncooked pieces and cook them, then bake them, as you did the first batch.

8   Transfer the baked English muffins to a cooling rack and let cool for at least 30 minutes before slicing or serving.

Focaccia

With a few recent exceptions, the quality of most American focaccia is so poor that I'm surprised it has caught on as it has. Its survival and emergence is probably due to the few bakeries that really do it well, showcasing the honeycombed crumb that results from a properly executed rustic dough. Toppings, no matter how creative and flavorful, can never cover for an inadequate crust. This is true for pizza as well as its Ligurian cousin, focaccia. The main difference between them is that classic pizza (Neapolitan) has a thin crust, while authentic focaccia has a thicker crust, but not obnoxiously thick as seen in some American renditions. I prefer a thickness of 1 to 1¼ inches (2.5 to 3cm), with big, open, translucent holes, like a ciabatta or pugliese. There is really only one way to achieve such perfection, and that is through long fermentation of a wet, rustic dough by either generous use of a pre-ferment or by retarding the fermentation process through refrigeration. Either method will get you there, so I offer you two formulas. The results are comparable and demonstrate the possibilities presented by time and temperature manipulation. Following the formulas are some suggestions for variations and toppings. Please note, the formulas that appear here differ from those that appeared in the original *Bread Baker's Apprentice*, as they incorporate new tweaks that I continue to make in my never-ending search for the perfect focaccia.

BREAD PROFILE
Lean, rustic dough (enriched slightly with olive oil); flat; direct or indirect method; commercial yeast

• • •

DAYS TO MAKE: 2
DAY 1: 10 minutes mixing; 100 minutes stretch and fold, fermentation, and panning (Poolish Focaccia: 3 to 4 hours *poolish*)

DAY 2: 3 hours fermentation; 20 to 30 minutes baking (Poolish Focaccia: 1 hour to de-chill *poolish*; 15 minutes mixing; 3 hours fermentation, panning, and proofing; 20 to 30 minutes baking)

• • •

COMMENTARY
This dough makes great pizza as well as focaccia, but it is a little too slack for *stromboli*, or rolled and stuffed pizza. A popular hybrid is what can best be called pizza-style focaccia, small round pies that begin as pizzas but are allowed to proof and puff up and are then topped with intensely flavored toppings, rather than the customary cheese and sauce toppings of pizza. See page 172 for examples. The beauty of these, aside from their sheer eye appeal, is that they can be made ahead and served cold or lightly reheated. This dough can also be used for Sicilian-style pizzas in which the dough (rectangular or round) is parbaked, without a final rise, until firm, then cooled, topped, and rebaked for thick, crispy pan pizza.

Makes one 17 by 12-inch (43 by 30-cm) focaccia

MEASURE	OUNCES	GRAMS	INGREDIENTS	%
5 cups	22.5	638	unbleached high-gluten or bread flour	100
1⅞ teaspoons	0.46	13	salt	2
1¾ teaspoons	0.18	5	instant yeast	0.8
2 tablespoons	1	28	olive oil	4.5
2 cups plus 2 tablespoons	17	482	water, at room temperature	75.5
¼ to ½ cup Herb Oil (page 169), optional				
TOTAL				182.8

1   Stir together the flour, salt, and yeast in a 4-quart mixing bowl (or in the bowl of an electric mixer). Add the oil and water and mix with a large metal spoon until all the ingredients form a wet, sticky ball (or mix on low speed with the paddle attachment). If you are mixing by hand, repeatedly dip one of your hands or the metal spoon into cold water and use it, much like a dough hook, to work the dough vigorously into a smooth mass while rotating the bowl

in a circular motion with the other hand (see page 58). Reverse the circular motion a few times to develop the gluten further. Do this for 3 to 5 minutes, or until the dough is smooth and the ingredients are evenly distributed. If you are using a mixer, switch to the dough hook and mix on medium speed for 3 to 5 minutes, or as long as it takes to create a smooth, sticky dough. The dough should clear the sides of the bowl but stick to the bottom of the bowl. You may need to add additional flour to firm up the dough enough to clear the sides of the bowl, but the dough should still be quite soft and sticky.

2   Use the oil slick method, as described on page 59, using olive oil. Using a scraper or spatula dipped in water, transfer the sticky dough to the oil slick, rub olive oil on your hands, and pat the dough into a rectangle about 6 by 12 inches (15 by 30cm). Wait for 5 minutes for the dough to relax.

3   Coat your hands with oil and stretch the dough from each end until the rectangle is twice its length. Fold it, letter style, over itself to return it to a rectangular shape, as shown on page 146. Mist the top of the dough with spray oil, and loosely cover with plastic wrap.

4   Let the dough rest for 30 minutes. Stretch and fold the dough again; mist with spray oil and cover. After 30 minutes, repeat this one more time.

5   Allow the covered dough to ferment on the counter for 30 minutes. It should swell only slightly.

6   Line a 17 by 12-inch (43 by 30-cm) sheet pan with baking parchment and proceed with the shaping and panning instructions on page 168. Spray the top of the dough with spray oil or drizzle the top with olive or herb oil.

7   Loosely cover the pan with plastic wrap (or place the pan inside a food-grade plastic bag). Refrigerate the dough overnight (or for up to 3 days).

8   Remove the pan from the refrigerator 3 hours before baking. Drizzle additional olive or herb oil to taste over the surface and dimple it in. (You can use all of it if you want; the dough will absorb it even though it looks like a lot.) This should allow you to fill the pan completely with the dough to a thickness of about a ½ inch (13mm). Add any other pre-proof toppings desired (see page 172). Again, cover the pan with plastic and proof the dough at room temperature for 2½ to 3 hours, or until the dough doubles in size, rising to a thickness of nearly 1 inch (2.5cm) and to the top of the pan.

9   Preheat the oven to 500°F (260°C) with the oven rack on the middle shelf. Gently place any prebake toppings on the dough (see page 172).

. . .

Like most rustic dough with hydration in excess of 70 percent, mixing in a food processor is a valid and excellent alternative to the hand and mixer methods described here. See page 57 for instructions on using a food processor.

. . .

It will seem as though you are using way too much herb oil, but the dough will absorb it all as it bakes. If the amount seems excessive for your diet, however, feel free to cut back on how much you apply during the final dimpling stage.

. . .

One of my favorite variations is raisin focaccia (there is a long tradition of sweet, or breakfast-style, focaccia in Liguria). To make it, omit the herb oil. Add about 2 cups (12 ounces/340g) or more raisins during the final 2 minutes of mixing. (The more raisins the better—the dough should be dense with them. Fifty percent of the flour weight is a good guideline.) Use regular olive oil on top in place of the herb oil, dust lightly with kosher salt or coarse AA (sanding) sugar before baking, and prepare yourself for the best raisin bread you have ever eaten!

. . .

Some people prefer a crustier, chewier finished product. To accomplish this, reduce the oven temperature to 400°F (204°C) and bake for about 10 minutes longer.

(A) Drizzle 2 tablespoons olive oil over the paper and spread it with your hands or a brush to cover the paper and the inside walls of the pan. Lightly oil your hands and, using an oiled plastic or metal pastry scraper, lift the dough off the counter and transfer it to the sheet pan, maintaining the rectangular shape as much as possible. (B) Spoon about 2 tablespoons of the herb oil over the dough.

(C) Use your fingertips simultaneously to dimple the dough and spread it to fill the pan. Do not use the flat of your hands—only the fingertips—to avoid tearing or ripping the dough. Try to keep the thickness as uniform as possible across the surface. Dimpling allows you to degas only part of the dough while preserving gas in the nondimpled sections. If the dough becomes too springy, let it rest for about 15 minutes and then continue dimpling. Don't worry if you are unable to fill the pan 100 percent, especially the corners. As the dough relaxes and proofs, it will spread out naturally. Use more herb oil as needed to ensure that the entire surface is coated with oil.

10 Place the pan in the oven. Lower the oven setting to 450°F (232°C) and bake for 15 minutes. Rotate the pan 180 degrees and continue baking the focaccia for 5 to 10 minutes, or until it begins to turn a light golden brown. If you are using any during-bake toppings (see page 172), sprinkle them on at this point and continue baking an additional 5 minutes or so. The internal temperature of the dough, measured in the center, should register above 200°F (93°C), and cheese, if used, should melt but not burn.

11 Remove the pan from the oven and immediately transfer the focaccia from the pan to a cooling rack. If the parchment is stuck on the bottom, carefully remove it by lifting the corner of the focaccia and peeling if off the bottom with a gentle tug.

12 Allow the focaccia to cool for at least 10 minutes before slicing or serving.

GRACE NOTE

HERB OIL

The generous application of herb oil to focaccia will enhance the flavor of the dough more than any toppings. There are many ways to make this oil, and you can make it in any quantity. I try always to keep some on hand for cooking and dipping. You can use dried or fresh herbs or a combination. Do not heat the oil; instead, just let the herbs steep in the oil, infusing it with their wonderful flavors.

Here's one way to make it, but feel free to substitute your favorite herbs and spices. The olive oil you use does not have to be extra virgin because it will be cooked later, and the subtle flavor of extra virgin, for which you pay so much, will be lost.

Use 2 cups olive oil at room temperature. Add 1 cup chopped fresh herbs. The herbs may include basil, parsley, oregano, tarragon, rosemary, thyme, cilantro, savory, and sage, in any combination.

I recommend lots of fresh basil. (Substitute ⅓ cup dried herbs or a blend such as *herbes de Provence*, or use a combination of fresh and dried herbs.) Add 1 tablespoon coarse or flaky sea salt, or kosher salt, 1 teaspoon coarsely ground black pepper, and 1 tablespoon granulated garlic or 5 or 6 cloves fresh garlic, chopped or pressed. You can also add up to 1 teaspoon paprika, ½ teaspoon cayenne pepper, 1 tablespoon fennel seeds, 1 teaspoon onion powder, or 1 tablespoon dried minced onion. Store any leftover herb oil in the refrigerator for up to 2 weeks.

Poolish Focaccia

Makes one 17 by 12-inch (43 by 30-cm) focaccia

MEASURE	OUNCES	GRAMS	INGREDIENTS	%
3 cups	20	567	*poolish* (page 112)	167
2⅔ cups	12	340	unbleached bread flour	100
1⅞ teaspoons	0.46	13	salt	3.8
1½ teaspoons	0.17	5	instant yeast	1.4
2 tablespoons	1	28	olive oil	8.3
¾ cup plus 2 tablespoons	7	198	water, lukewarm (90°F to 100°F/32°C to 38°C)	58
TOTAL				338.5

TOTAL DOUGH FORMULA AND %

	OUNCES	GRAMS	INGREDIENTS	%
	21.8	618	bread flour	100
	0.46	13	salt	2.1
	0.2	6	instant yeast	1
	17.2	488	water	79
	1	28	olive oil	4.5
TOTAL				186.6

1   Remove the *poolish* from the refrigerator 1 hour before making the dough to take off the chill.

2   Stir together the flour, salt, and yeast in a 4-quart mixing bowl (or in the bowl of an electric mixer). Add the oil, *poolish,* and water and mix with a large metal spoon until the ingredients form a wet, sticky ball (or mix on low speed with the paddle attachment). If you are mixing by hand, repeatedly dip one of your hands or the metal spoon in cold water and use it, much like a dough hook, to work the dough vigorously into a smooth mass while rotating the bowl in a circular motion with the other hand (see page 58). Reverse the circular motion a few times to develop the gluten further. Do this for 3 to 5 minutes, or until the dough is smooth and the ingredients are evenly distributed. (If you are using an electric mixer, switch to the dough hook and mix on medium speed for 4 to 5 minutes, or as long as it takes to create a smooth, sticky dough.) The dough should clear the sides of the bowl but stick to the bottom of the bowl. You may need to add additional flour to firm up the dough enough to clear the sides of the bowl, but the dough should still be quite soft and sticky.

3   Sprinkle enough flour on the counter to make a bed about 6 inches (15cm) square (or use the oil slick method, as described on page 59). Using a scraper or spatula dipped in water, transfer the sticky dough to the bed of flour (or oil slick), dust liberally with flour, and pat the dough into a rectangle, about 6 by 12 inches (15 by 30cm). Wait for 5 minutes for the dough to relax.

4   Coat your hands with flour or oil and stretch the dough from each end to twice its size. Fold it, letter style, over itself to return it to a rectangular shape, as shown on page 146. Mist the top of the dough with spray oil and loosely cover with plastic wrap.

5   Let rest for 30 minutes. Stretch and fold the dough again; mist with spray oil, and cover. After 30 minutes, repeat this one more time.

6   Allow the covered dough to ferment on the counter for 1 hour. It should swell but not necessarily double in size.

7   Line a 17 by 12-inch (43 by 30cm) sheet pan with baking parchment and proceed with the foccacia shaping and panning instructions on page 168, adding any pre-proof toppings at this time (see page 172).

8   Loosely cover the pan with plastic wrap. Proof at room temperature for about 2 hours, or until the dough fills the pan.

9   About 15 minutes before baking, drizzle on more herb oil, if desired (you can use all of it; the dough will absorb it even though it seems like a lot), and dimple it in along with any pre-bake toppings (page 172). This should allow you to fill the pan completely with the dough to a thickness of about ½ inch (13mm). Let the dough relax for 15 to 30 minutes before baking to allow the gas to build back up. It will rise to almost 1 inch (2.5cm) in thickness.

10   Preheat the oven to 500°F (260°C) with the oven rack on the middle shelf. Place the pan in the oven and lower the oven setting to 450°F (232°C). Bake for 10 minutes. Rotate the pan 180 degrees and continue baking for 5 to 10 minutes, or until the dough begins to turn a light golden brown. If using any during-bake toppings (see page 172), sprinkle them on at this point and continue baking for an additional 5 minutes or so. The internal temperature of the dough, measured in the center, should register above 200°F (93°C), and the cheese, if used, should melt but not burn.

11   Remove the pan from the oven and immediately transfer the focaccia out of the pan onto a cooling rack. If the parchment is still stuck on the bottom, carefully remove it by lifting the corner of the focaccia and peeling the parchment off the bottom with a gentle tug.

12   Allow the focaccia to cool for at least 10 minutes before slicing or serving.

Pizza-Style Focaccia

Makes 4 to 6 small breads

1   To make these beautiful pizza breads, follow the instructions for making Focaccia (page 165) or Poolish Focaccia (page 170), through the stretch-and-fold and bulk fermentation stages. Transfer the dough to a bed of flour and sprinkle flour over the top. Divide the dough into 4 pieces of 10 ounces (284g) each or 6 smaller equal pieces. Toss the pieces in a bed of flour to coat them (or rub them with olive oil) and gently round them into loose balls, degassing as little as possible. Mist the inside of 4 (or 6) plastic bags with spray oil and also mist the dough balls with spray oil. Place 1 piece in each bag, seal closed with a twist tie, and refrigerate overnight or for up to 3 days (you may also freeze the dough for up to 3 months).

2   Remove the desired number of dough balls from the refrigerator 3 hours before baking. Sprinkle about 2 tablespoons (1 ounce/28g) flour on the counter for each ball (or use the oil slick method, as described on page 59) and transfer each piece of dough to the counter.

GRACE NOTE

TOPPINGS FOR FOCACCIA

I have designated three types of toppings. Those that go on before proofing the dough (pre-proof), those that go on just before baking (pre-bake), and those that go on while the focaccia is baking (during-bake), usually in the last few minutes. Some toppings, such as sun-dried tomatoes, olives, and nuts, need to be surrounded by dough to protect them from burning and from falling off. Other ingredients are not so vulnerable and will stay on the dough without having the dough proof around them, including moist cheeses, like blue, or strips of meat, which should not sit out during proofing. The during-bake ingredients are usually various cheeses that would otherwise burn, such as grating cheeses.

Here is a sample list of topping ideas for your focaccia. If you have other ideas for toppings, match them to the category and place them on at the appropriate time.

PRE-PROOF TOPPINGS
Marinated sun-dried tomatoes; olives; roasted garlic; fresh herbs; walnuts, pine nuts, or other nuts; and sautéed mushrooms, red or green peppers, or onions.

PRE-BAKE TOPPINGS
High-moisture cheeses, such as blue, fresh mozzarella, and feta, and cooked ground meat or meat strips. Also coarse salt or sugar.

DURING-BAKE TOPPINGS
Dry or semihard cheeses, such as Parmesan, romano, regular mozzarella, jack, Cheddar, and Swiss.

Sprinkle a little more flour over the dough and gently press the dough with your fingertips (not your palms) into a disk 9 to 10 inches (23 to 25cm) in diameter. If the dough is too springy to extend to this diameter, mist it with spray oil, cover it with plastic wrap, let it rest for 15 minutes, and then press it to the full size.

3   Line a sheet pan with baking parchment and mist the parchment with spray oil. Sprinkle a small amount of cornmeal or semolina over the parchment and transfer the dough to the pan (you should be able to fit 2 rounds per pan). Rub some of the herb oil (or plain olive oil) over the top and press into the center of the dough any pre-proof toppings you plan to use (page 172). Cover the dough loosely with plastic wrap.

4   Proof at room temperature for 2 to 3 hours, or until the dough rises to about 1½ times its original size.

5   Preheat the oven to 550°F (290°C) or as high as it allows, up to 600°F (315°C). Place any prebake toppings (page 172) on the dough at this point.

6   Transfer each pizza-style focaccia, parchment and all, to a peel or to the back of a sheet pan. (If you are using a baking stone and it will only accommodate 1 pizza at a time, you can cut the parchment with scissors and transfer 1 pizza at a time, saving the others for a later bake or refrigerating for another time.) Slide the focaccia onto the baking stone (or bake directly on the sheet pan) and bake for 10 to 12 minutes, or until the edges of the dough are golden brown and the bottom is also caramelized to a light golden brown. You may remove the parchment after about 5 minutes by sliding it out from under the dough. Baking time will vary according to oven types, and you may need to rotate the focaccia 180 degrees to ensure even baking.

7   Transfer the focaccia to a cooling rack. Let cool for at least 10 minutes before slicing or serving. Remember to brush any flour or cornmeal off the baking stone before attempting a second bake.

French Bread

BREAD PROFILE
Lean, standard dough; indirect method; commercial yeast

. . .

DAYS TO MAKE: 2
DAY 1: 1¼ hours *pâte fermentée*

DAY 2: 1 hour to de-chill *pâte fermentée;* 10 to 15 minutes mixing; 4 to 4½ hours stretch and fold, fermentation, shaping, and proofing; 20 to 40 minutes baking

. . .

COMMENTARY
You can use only bread flour or only all-purpose flour if you choose, but I find a 50-50 blend results in a bread that has plenty of structure but is still tender, with a nice crackle to the crust.

Every book I've written includes a version of French bread, each attempting to close the gap between professional, artisan, and home-baked loaves. It's a never-ending learning process, and this updated version, based on all the things I've discovered since the original edition of this book, is, I believe, the best version yet and closest to the breads you will find at your favorite bakery. The key, as in many of these formulas, is the use of a large amount of pre-fermented dough, *pâte fermentée.* You will also find a *poolish* baguette variation in the new formulas section beginning on page 109, which is equally good.

My best previous version required holding the shaped loaves overnight in the refrigerator, a technique that still may be applied to improve many lean, slow-rising breads. But purists object because the technique causes blisters, sometimes called bird's-eyes, on the crust (due to carbon dioxide trapped just beneath the skin during the cold retarding stage). While I like that look, as do many consumers, it is not the way baguettes look in French *boulangeries* or in most bakeshops anywhere. (Note: Since writing these words for the original edition, I have witnessed the appearance of many bird's-eye loaves in bakeries, as the use of cold, overnight fermentation has grown in popularity.)

This method allows you to make a full-flavored French bread, from start to finish, in 4 to 5 hours (assuming you have the *pâte fermentée* made in advance). The pre-fermented dough gives the final dough the qualities of one that has been fermented for 7 to 9 hours, the standard of many professional operations. The crust will have a rich, reddish-gold caramelization rather than the more typical yellow-gold of younger dough. This richer color is a result of sugars released from the starches during fermentation. The bread also exhibits a sweetness that seems as if it must be from added sugar, but all the sugar in this bread is released from within the flour itself, broken free of the complex starch molecules by amylase and diastase enzymes during fermentation. As with most hearth breads, another key to the success of this bread is handling it gently, retaining as much gas as possible during shaping in order to promote large, irregular holes in the crumb that, again, release maximum flavor. This large, open crumb is one of the signs of a properly handled artisan loaf.

(continued)

Look carefully and you will notice that the amount of pre-fermented dough is equal to the amount of new dough. In other words, you can make the recipe once without the *pâte fermentée*, hold it in the refrigerator overnight to develop flavor and sugar breakout (retarding it immediately after the mixing stage), and then make it again the next day, using the first dough as the pre-ferment. This means that the pre-ferment represents 170 percent of the formula in the baker's math system, a very large amount since most bakeries rarely use more than 40 to 50 percent pre-ferment. But this is the key to making a bakery-quality baguette at home, as you will see.

• • •

If your flour is organic or does not contain malted barley flour, you should add ½ teaspoon diastatic barley malt powder to the flour blend. This malt powder will accelerate enzyme activity in the dough, resulting in a more colorful crust. You can purchase it through King Arthur Flour, Central Milling, and other suppliers (see Resources, page 314).

Makes 3 or 4 small baguettes (or experiment with other shapes and sizes)

MEASURE	OUNCES	GRAMS	INGREDIENTS	%
3 cups	17	482	*pâte fermentée* (page 111)	170
1¼ cups	5	142	unbleached bread flour	50
1¼ cups	5	142	unbleached all-purpose flour	50
¾ teaspoon	0.19	5.5	salt	1.9
½ teaspoon	0.05	1.5	instant yeast	0.55
¾ cup plus 2 tablespoons	7	198	water, lukewarm (90°F to 100°F/32°C to 38°C)	70
All-purpose or bread flour, semolina, or cornmeal for dusting				
TOTAL				342.45

TOTAL DOUGH FORMULA AND %

	OUNCES	GRAMS	INGREDIENTS	%
	10	284	bread flour	50
	10	284	all purpose flour	50
	0.38	11	salt	1.9
	0.11	3	instant yeast	0.5
	13.5	283	water	67.5
TOTAL				169.9

1   Remove the *pâte fermentée* from the refrigerator 1 hour before making the dough. Cut it into about 10 small pieces with a pastry scraper or serrated knife. Cover with a towel or plastic wrap and let sit for 1 hour to take off the chill.

2   Stir together the flours, salt, yeast, and *pâte fermentée* pieces in a 4-quart mixing bowl (or in the bowl of an electric mixer). Add the water, stirring until everything comes together and makes a coarse ball (or mix on low speed with the dough hook for 2 minutes). Adjust the flour or water, according to need; the dough should be neither too sticky nor too stiff. (It is better to err on the sticky side, as you can adjust more easily by adding more flour during kneading. It is harder to add water once the dough firms up.)

3   Sprinkle flour on the counter (or use the oil slick method, as described on page 59), transfer the dough to the counter, and begin to knead (or mix on medium speed with the dough hook). Knead for about 4 minutes (3 to 4 minutes by machine), or until the dough is smooth and supple, tacky but not sticky, and all the pre-ferment is evenly distributed. The dough should pass the windowpane test (page 61) and register 77°F to 81°F (25°C to 27°C). If the dough seems properly developed but is still cooler than 77°F (25°C), you can knead for a few minutes longer to raise the temperature or simply allow a lengthier first rise. Lightly oil a large bowl and

transfer the dough to the bowl, rolling it around to coat it with oil. Cover the bowl with plastic wrap. After 30 minutes, stretch and fold the dough (see page 59) and return it to the covered bowl. Repeat three times at 30-minute intervals, each time returning the dough to the covered bowl.

4   Ferment the dough for 1 hour, or until it doubles in size. If the dough doubles in size before an hour has elapsed, knead it lightly to degas and let it rise again, covered, until it doubles from the original size.

5   Gently transfer the dough from the bowl to a lightly floured (or oiled) counter. For baguettes, cut the dough into 3 or 4 equal pieces with a pastry scraper or serrated knife. Again, take care to degas the dough as little as possible. Form the pieces into baguettes, as shown on page 78 (or whatever shape you prefer). Prepare them for proofing as described on page 33, using either the *couche* technique or parchment dusted with flour, semolina, or cornmeal.

6   Proof at room temperature for 45 minutes to 1¼ hours, or until the loaves have grown to about 1½ times their original size. They should be slightly springy when poked with a finger.

7   Prepare the oven for hearth baking as described on page 97, making sure to have an empty steam pan in place. Preheat the oven to 500°F (260°C). Score the baguettes as shown on page 96.

8   Generously dust a peel or the back of a sheet pan with flour, semolina, or cornmeal and very gently transfer the baguettes to the peel or pan. Transfer the baguettes to the baking stone (or bake directly on the sheet pan). Pour 1 cup hot water into the steam pan and close the oven door. After 30 seconds, spray the oven walls with water and close the door. Repeat twice more at 30-second intervals. After the final spray, lower the oven setting to 450°F (232°C) and bake for 10 minutes. Rotate the loaves 180 degrees, if necessary, for even baking, and continue baking until the loaves are a rich golden brown and register at least 205°F (96°C) in the center. This can take anywhere from 10 to 20 additional minutes, depending on your oven and how thin your baguettes are. If they seem to be getting too dark but are not hot enough internally, lower the oven setting to 350°F (177°C)—or turn it off—and continue baking for an additional 5 to 10 minutes.

9   Remove the loaves from the oven and let cool on a rack for at least 30 minutes before slicing or serving.

Italian Bread

BREAD PROFILE
Enriched, standard dough;
indirect method; commercial
yeast

• • •

DAYS TO MAKE: 2
DAY 1: 3 to 4 hours *biga*

DAY 2: 1 hour to de-chill
biga; 12 to 15 minutes mixing;
3½ to 4 hours fermentation,
shaping, and proofing; 20 to
30 minutes baking

• • •

COMMENTARY
If you prefer a crustier loaf,
lower the oven temperature
to 400°F (204°C) after the
steaming and increase the
baking time. This will thicken
the crust and give it more
crunch.

• • •

The use of diastatic barley
malt powder produces better
color because it will accelerate the enzyme activity and
thus promote sugar breakout
from the starch. You can also
use nondiastatic barley malt
syrup, which will contribute
flavor more than color. This
bread can also be made
without the addition of any
malt, as malt is already added
to most brands of bread flour
(the *biga* pre-ferment will
contribute some enzymes of
its own). Both the powder and
the syrup can be purchased
through King Arthur Flour,
Central Milling, and other
suppliers (see Resources,
page 314).

In America, the term *Italian bread* has come to mean a loaf very similar to French bread, only usually a little softer. This has very little to do with reality, however, since many different types of authentic Italian bread exist.

What made the old-time Italian bakeries that were once a part of many American towns and cities special was that the bread was baked fresh daily and bought right at the shop. Today, even with the current bread revolution, much of the bread produced does not stand up to those long-ago Italian loaves, despite the love, care, and wonderful wood- or coal-fired ovens that we associate with many contemporary bakeries. This is because many bakeries, smitten with innovative modern ingredients that accelerate fermentation in order to save time and increase profits, have reverted to fast-rising methods that leave much of the potential flavor and color trapped in the starches. The Italian *biga* pre-ferment method is a step in the direc-tion of improving these breads, much as the *pâte fermentée* and *poolish* do for French bread.

The following formula pushes the *biga* method to its limits, and the result is an Italian bread as good as or better than any I've had in recent years. The use of a large amount of *biga* ensures maximum sugar breakout from starches, yielding a sweetness that goes far beyond the small amount of sugar in the formula. The finished bread will be slightly softer than French bread and less crusty. If you want it even softer, you can double the amount of olive oil.

Makes two 1-pound (453g) loaves or 9 torpedo (hoagie) rolls

MEASURE	OUNCES	GRAMS	INGREDIENTS	%
3½ cups	18	510	*biga* (page 113)	160
2½ cups	11.25	319	unbleached bread flour	100
1⅔ teaspoons	0.41	11.5	salt	3.7
1 tablespoon	0.5	14	granulated sugar	4.4
1 teaspoon	0.11	3	instant yeast	1
½ teaspoon	0.11	4	diastatic barley malt powder (optional)	1
1 tablespoon	0.5	14	olive or vegetable oil	4.4
¾ cup plus 2 tablespoons	7	198	water (or milk if making soft torpedo or hoagie rolls), lukewarm (90°F to 100°F/32°C to 38°C)	62
All-purpose or bread flour, semolina, or cornmeal for dusting				
TOTAL				336.5

	OUNCES	GRAMS	INGREDIENTS	%
	22	624	bread flour	100
	0.41	11.5	salt	1.8
	0.5	14	sugar	2.2
	0.16	4.5	instant yeast	0.72
	0.11	3	malt	0.5
	0.5	14	olive or vegetable oil	2.2
	14.25	404	water	64.7
TOTAL				172.12

1   Remove the *biga* from the refrigerator 1 hour before making the dough. Cut it into about 10 small pieces with a pastry scraper or serrated knife. Cover with a towel or plastic wrap and let sit for 1 hour to take off the chill.

2   Stir together the flour, salt, sugar, yeast, and malt powder (if using) in a 4-quart mixing bowl (or in the bowl of an electric mixer). Add the *biga* pieces, oil, and water or milk and stir together (or mix on low speed with the dough hook) for about 2 minutes, or until a ball forms, adjusting the water or flour according to need. The dough should be slightly sticky and soft but not batterlike or very sticky. If the dough feels tough and stiff, add more water to soften (it is better to have the dough too soft than too stiff at this point).

3   Sprinkle flour on the counter (or use the oil slick method, as described on page 59), transfer the dough to the counter, and begin kneading (or mixing on medium speed with the dough hook). Knead (or mix) for 4 to 6 minutes, adding flour or water as needed, or until the dough is smooth and supple, tacky but not sticky. The dough should pass the windowpane test (page 61) and register 77°F to 81°F (25°C to 27°C). Lightly oil a large bowl and transfer the dough to the bowl, rolling it to coat it with oil. Cover the bowl with plastic wrap. After 30 minutes, stretch and fold the dough (see page 59), form it back into a ball, return it to the bowl, and cover the bowl.

4   Ferment at room temperature for approximately 2 hours, or until the dough doubles in size.

5   Gently divide the dough into 2 equal pieces of about 18 ounces (510g) each for loaves, or into 9 pieces of about 4 ounces (113g) each for torpedo rolls. Carefully form the large pieces into *bâtards*, as shown on page 77, or the smaller pieces into rolls, as shown on page 86, degassing the dough as little as possible. Lightly dust with a sprinkle of flour, cover with a towel or plastic wrap, and let rest for 5 minutes. Then complete the shaping, extending the loaves to about 12 inches (30cm) in length or shaping the torpedo rolls as shown on page 84. Line a sheet pan with baking parchment and dust with flour, semolina, or cornmeal. Place the loaves or rolls on the pan and lightly mist with spray oil. Cover loosely with plastic wrap.

6   Proof at room temperature for about 1 hour, or until the loaves or rolls have grown to about 1½ times their original size.

7 Prepare the oven for hearth baking as described on page 97, making sure to have an empty steam pan in place. Preheat the oven to 500°F (260°C). Score the breads with 2 parallel, diagonal slashes or 1 long slash (see page 96).

8 Rolls can be baked directly on the sheet pan. For loaves, generously dust a peel or the back of a sheet pan with flour, semolina, or cornmeal and very gently transfer the loaves to the peel or pan. Transfer the dough to the baking stone (or bake on the sheet pan). Pour 1 cup hot water into the steam pan and close the door. After 30 seconds, spray the walls of the oven with water and close the door. Repeat once more after another 30 seconds. After the final spray, lower the oven setting to 450°F (232°C) and bake until done, rotating the loaves or pan 180 degrees, if necessary, for even baking. It should take about 20 minutes for loaves and 15 minutes for rolls. The loaves and rolls should be golden brown and register at least 200°F (93°C) in the center (for a crustier loaf, see Commentary, page 178).

9 Transfer the rolls or loaves to a cooling rack and let cool for at least 45 minutes before slicing or serving.

GRACE NOTE

BREADSTICKS: GRISSINI AND OTHERS

Breadsticks never go out of favor. I have seen sophisticated equipment designed for nothing else but making hundreds of thousands of breadsticks each day: long, thin ones or short, stubby ones; soft ones or crisp ones. *Grissini*, which originated in Turin in the Piedmont region of Italy, have become synonymous with crisp, thin Italian breadsticks, much as ciabatta has become generic for rustic bread (there is also a thicker, softer type of breadstick called *francesina*). But breadsticks are international in scope and, frankly, can be made from pretty much any bread dough. The question is, do you want them soft or crisp, long or short?

For soft breadsticks, you can use any of the white bread formulas (page 284), the kaiser formula (page 182), or English muffin dough (page 163). Also, French (page 174), Vienna (page 280), or Italian (page 178) bread dough baked hot and fast makes fine breadsticks. For crisp sticks, use bagel dough (page 125), lavash dough (page 186), or Italian bread dough. To drive off the moisture for crisp breadsticks, bake them for a long time at low temperatures (325°F to 350°F/163°C to 175°C) until dry and crisp. For soft breadsticks, bake at higher temperatures (400° to 425°F/200°C to 218°C) until golden brown and then immediately remove them from the oven. They will soften as they cool.

There are two ways to shape breadsticks. One is to roll out each stick individually, rolling them like strands to the desired length, laying them out on a pan, proofing, and then baking. This is great when you want each stick to be unique and distinctive, but it is time-consuming to make a lot of them. When making a large quantity of bread sticks, I've had great success with the following method.

*SHAPING BREADSTICKS

Roll out the dough to the desired thickness, and then **(A)** cut off individual sticks with a pizza cutter (rolling blade). To seed the breadsticks, you can either roll each unbaked breadstick on a wet towel and then in a bed of seeds, which is great for total seed immersion, or you can brush or mist the pan of breadsticks with water or an egg white wash and then sprinkle the seeds over the top just before the sticks go in the oven. **(B)** Sesame or poppy seeds are the most commonly used, but I like to those two seeds together along with a sprinkling of sea salt, paprika, and granulated garlic (or garlic salt) and a touch of coarsely ground black pepper. You can also add fennel, caraway, cumin, or aniseeds, but they are intense and a few seeds go a long way. These "everything" toppings are becoming more and more popular on bagels, cracker breads, and now on those ubiquitous, addictive breadsticks turning up in bread baskets all over the world. You can then either lay the sticks out on a baking parchment-lined sheet pan or individually stretch them further before laying them out, rolling them into swizzle twists, fashioning them into ovals, or curling them into distinctive shapes.

Kaiser Rolls

These are sometimes called by different names, such as New York hard rolls, bulkies, or even Vienna rolls. But the distinguishing characteristic of a kaiser roll is the star pattern on the top and a thin, slightly crisp crust that yields to the first bite and crumbles deliciously in the mouth around whatever sandwich filling it holds. Most bakeshops make them using a direct-dough method and knock them out by the thousands. This version, again pushing the limits of our newfound understanding of fermentation and enzyme activity, utilizes old dough, *pâte fermentée*, to improve flavor, texture, and color, making the resulting rolls significantly better than their commercial counterparts. While strangers will be complaining that they can't find a good old-fashioned New York hard roll, you will be spoiling your friends and family with these bulkies.

BREAD PROFILE
Enriched, standard dough; indirect method; commercial yeast

• • •

DAYS TO MAKE: 2
DAY 1: 1¼ hours *pâte fermentée*

DAY 2: 1 hour to de-chill *pâte fermentée;* 10 to 15 minutes mixing; 3½ to 4 hours fermentation, shaping, and proofing; 15 to 30 minutes baking

• • •

COMMENTARY
The traditional method for shaping a kaiser roll requires a series of overlapping folds, like making a paper flower. It is time-consuming and difficult to teach. Most people now use a commercial kaiser roll cutter, either metal or plastic, available at most cookware stores or through mail order (see Resources, page 314). Equally effective and fun and easy to make is a knotted roll design. The finished roll looks similar to the more difficult overlapping-fold technique.

Makes 6 large rolls or 9 smaller rolls

MEASURE	OUNCES	GRAMS	INGREDIENTS	%
1½ cups	8	227	*pâte fermentée* (page 111)	80
2¼ cups	10	284	unbleached bread flour	100
¾ teaspoon, plus a pinch	0.2	5.5	salt	2
1 teaspoon or 1½ teaspoons	0.17 0.33	5 9.5	diastatic barley malt powder or barley malt syrup	1.7 (3.3)
1 teaspoon	0.11	3	instant yeast	1.1
1 large	1.65	47	egg, slightly beaten	16.5
1½ tablespoons	0.75	21	vegetable oil	7.5
¾ cup	6	170	water, lukewarm (90°F to 100°F/32°C to 38°C)	60
1 egg white, whisked with 1 tablespoon water, for egg white wash				
Poppy or sesame seeds for garnish				
Semolina or cornmeal for dusting				
TOTAL				268.8 (270.4)

TOTAL DOUGH FORMULA AND %

OUNCES	GRAMS	INGREDIENTS	%
14.75	419	bread flour	100
0.3	8.5	salt	2
0.14	4	instant yeast	1
0.17	5	barley malt powder (or syrup)	1.2 (2.2)
1.65	47	egg	11.2
0.75	21	vegetable oil	5
9.25	262	water	62.5
TOTAL			182.9 (or 184)

1   Take the *pâte fermentée* out of the refrigerator 1 hour before making the dough. Cut it up into about 10 small pieces with a pastry scraper or serrated knife. Cover it with a towel or plastic wrap and let sit for 1 hour to take off the chill.

2   Stir together the flour, salt, malt powder, and yeast in a 4-quart mixing bowl (or in the bowl of an electric mixer). Add the *pâte fermentée,* egg, oil, and ½ cup plus 2 tablespoons (5 ounces/142g) water. Stir (or mix on low speed with the dough hook) for 2 minutes, or until the ingredients form a ball. If there is still some loose flour or the dough is stiff, add the remaining 2 tablespoons water.

3   Lightly dust the counter with flour (or use the oil slick method, as described on page 59), transfer the dough to the counter, and begin kneading (or mix on medium speed with the dough hook). Knead (or mix) for 4 to 6 minutes, adding flour, if needed, to make a dough that is smooth and supple, tacky but not sticky. The dough should pass the windowpane test (page 61) and the internal temperature should register 77°F to 81°F (25°C to 27°C). Lightly oil a large bowl and transfer the dough to the bowl, rolling it to coat it with oil. Cover the bowl with plastic wrap.

4   Ferment at room temperature for 2 hours, or until the dough doubles in size. If the dough doubles in size before 2 hours have elapsed, remove it, knead it lightly to degas it and let it rise again, covered, until it doubles from the original size or until 2 hours have elapsed.

5   Remove the dough from the bowl and divide it into 6 to 9 equal pieces (4-ounce/113g pieces for large rolls; 2⅔-ounce/76g pieces for smaller rolls). Form the pieces into rolls, as shown on page 87. Mist the rounds lightly with spray oil, cover with a towel or plastic wrap, and let the dough relax for 10 minutes. Meanwhile, line a sheet pan with baking parchment, lightly mist it with spray oil, and then dust with semolina or cornmeal.

6   Prepare the individual rolls by cutting them with a kaiser roll cutter (see page 185) or knotting them as shown on page 87. Place the rolls, cut side down, on the parchment, mist lightly with spray oil, and loosely cover the pan with plastic wrap or a food-grade plastic bag.

7 Proof the rolls for 45 minutes at room temperature and then flip them over so the cut or folded side is facing up. Mist again with spray oil, cover the pan, and continue proofing for another 30 to 45 minutes, or until the rolls are nearly double their original size.

8 Preheat the oven to 425°F (218°C) with the oven rack on the middle shelf. Uncover the rolls and prepare them for baking. If you want seeds on your rolls, brush them with egg white wash (or mist them with water) and sprinkle sesame or poppy seeds over the top. If not, just mist them with water or brush with egg wash.

9 Place the pan in the oven, spray the oven walls with water, and close the door. After 10 minutes, rotate the pan 180 degrees for even baking and lower the oven setting to 400°F (204°C). Continue baking until the rolls are a medium golden brown and register approximately 200°F (93°C) in the center. This will take 15 to 30 minutes for large rolls and less for smaller rolls.

10 Remove the rolls from the pan and transfer to a cooling rack. Wait for at least 30 minutes before serving.

You can use either a kaiser roll cutter (center) or the knotted-roll technique (left and right) to give your kaiser rolls their distinctive design.

Lavash Crackers

BREAD PROFILE
Enriched, stiff dough; flat;
direct method; commercial
yeast

• • •

DAYS TO MAKE: 1
10 to 15 minutes mixing;
2 hours fermentation,
shaping, and panning;
15 to 20 minutes baking

• • •

COMMENTARY
This dough, which is almost
as stiff as bagel dough, is
easier to knead by hand than
in a machine.

• • •

You can make a softer variation, used for making roll-up
pinwheel sandwiches, by rolling the dough a little thicker
than described and slightly
underbaking the uncut sheet,
so that the cracker is stiff but
not crackly crisp. When ready
to make the pinwheel sandwiches, mist the cracker with
water and it will magically
soften within 3 to 5 minutes
and be as workable as a flour
tortilla.

Here's a simple formula for making snappy Armenian-style crackers, perfect for breadbaskets, company, and kids. Lavash, though usually called Armenian flat bread, also has Iranian roots and is now eaten throughout the Middle East and around the world. It is similar to the many other Middle Eastern and North African flat breads known by different names, such as *mankoush* or *mannaeesh* (Lebanese), *barbari* (Iranian), *khoubiz* or *khobz* (Arabian), *aiysh* (Egyptian), *kesret* and *mella* (Tunisian), *pide* or pita (Turkish), and *pideh* (Armenian). The main difference among these breads is either how thick or thin the dough is rolled out or the type of oven in which they are baked (or on which they are baked, as many of these breads are cooked on stones or red-hot pans with a convex surface). Some of the breads, like pita, form a pocket; others, like the *injera* of Ethiopia and Eritrea, are thicker and serve as sponges to soak up spicy sauces.

The key to crisp lavash, which is one of the most popular of these flat bread variations, is to roll out the dough paper-thin. The sheet can be cut into crackers in advance or snapped into shards after baking. The shards make a nice presentation when arranged in baskets.

Makes 1 sheet pan of crackers

MEASURE	OUNCES	GRAMS	INGREDIENTS	%
1½ cups	6.75	191	unbleached bread or all-purpose flour	100
½ teaspoon	0.13	3.5	salt	1.9
½ teaspoon	0.55	1.5	instant yeast	0.8
1 tablespoon, or	0.75	21	honey or	11.1
1½ tablespoons	0.75	21	granulated sugar	11.1
1 tablespoon	0.5	14	vegetable oil	7.4
½ cup	4	113	water, at room temperature	59.25
1 egg white, whisked with 1 tablespoon water, for egg white wash (optional)				
Poppy seeds, sesame seeds, paprika, cumin seeds, caraway seeds, or kosher salt for topping				
TOTAL				180.45

1   In a mixing bowl, stir together the flour, salt, yeast, honey or sugar, oil, and just enough water to bring everything together into a ball. You may not need the full ½ cup water (4 ounces/113g), but be prepared to use it all if needed.

2   Sprinkle some flour on the counter (or use the oil slick method, as described on page 59) and transfer the dough to the counter. Knead for about 6 minutes, or until the ingredients are

Lavash Crackers   **187**

· · ·

This same dough makes a nice pita bread: Roll out 6-ounce (170g) pieces of the finished dough into 8-inch (20cm) circles (slightly less than ¼ inch/6mm thick) and bake them in a 500°F (260°C) oven on a baking stone or on a sheet pan. Bake just until they inflate and form a pocket, about 2 to 4 minutes. Then, count to 10, and remove the breads from the oven with a peel or a spatula before they brown and crisp. When they cool (and slowly deflate), they can be cut in half and used for pocket sandwiches.

evenly distributed. The dough should pass the windowpane test (page 61) and register 77°F to 81°F (25°C to 27°C). The dough should be firmer than French bread dough but not quite as firm as bagel dough (what I call a medium-firm dough), satiny to the touch, not tacky, and supple enough to stretch when pulled. Lightly oil a bowl and transfer the dough to the bowl, rolling it around to coat it with oil. Cover the bowl with plastic wrap.

3   Ferment at room temperature for 1½ hours to 2 hours, or until the dough doubles in size. (You can instead retard the dough overnight in the refrigerator immediately after kneading.)

4   Mist the counter lightly with spray oil (or make a light oil slick) and transfer the dough to the counter. Press the dough into a square with your hand and dust the top of the dough lightly with flour or mist it with spray oil. Roll it out with a rolling pin into a paper-thin sheet about 15 by 12 inches (38 by 30cm). You may have to stop from time to time so that the gluten can relax. At these times, lift the dough from the counter, wave it a little, and then lay it back down. Cover it with a towel or plastic wrap while it relaxes. When it is the desired thinness, let the dough relax for 5 minutes. Line a sheet pan with baking parchment. Carefully lift the sheet of dough and lay it on the parchment. If it overlaps the edge of the pan, snip off the excess with scissors.

5   Preheat the oven to 350°F (177°C) with the oven rack on the middle shelf. Mist the top of the dough with water or brush with egg white wash and (A) sprinkle a covering of seeds or spices on the dough (such as alternating rows of poppy seeds, sesame seeds, paprika, cumin seeds, caraway seeds, kosher or pretzel salt, and so on). Be careful with spices; a little goes a long way. If you want precut crackers, (B) use a pizza cutter (rolling blade) and cut diamonds or rectangles in the dough. You do not need to separate the pieces, as they will snap apart after baking. If you want to make shards, bake the sheet of dough without cutting it first.

6   Bake for 15 to 20 minutes, or until the crackers begin to brown evenly across the top (the time will depend on how thinly and evenly you rolled the dough).

7   When the crackers are ready, remove the pan from the oven and let them cool in the pan for about 10 minutes. You can then snap them apart or snap off shards and serve.

Light Wheat Bread

Here, whole wheat flour accounts for 33 percent of the total flour, which is the most popular formula for making light wheat bread. The result is a loaf similar to the soft wheat breads purchased off store shelves. Of course, this is a poor compromise for whole grain purists, which is why I am also including a bread formula with 100 percent whole wheat (page 288). But there are times when you just want a tasty, soft, but not altogether white sandwich bread, and this versatile loaf fits the bill.

Makes one 2-pound (907g) loaf

MEASURE	OUNCES	GRAMS	INGREDIENTS	%
2½ cups	11.25	319	unbleached high-gluten or bread flour	62.5
1½ cups	6.75	191	whole wheat flour	37.5
1½ tablespoons	0.75	21	granulated sugar or honey	4.2
1½ teaspoons	0.38	11	salt	2.1
3 tablespoons	1	28	powdered milk (DMS)	5.6
1½ teaspoons	0.17	5	instant yeast	0.94
2 tablespoons	1	28	vegetable oil or unsalted butter, at room temperature	5.6
1½ cups	12	340	water, at room temperature	67
TOTAL				185.4

BREAD PROFILE
Enriched, standard dough; direct method; commercial yeast

. . .

DAYS TO MAKE: 1
10 to 15 minutes mixing; 4½ hours fermentation, shaping, and proofing; 45 to 60 minutes baking

. . .

COMMENTARY
This is one formula that is not greatly improved by the pre-ferment or sponge technique. Because it is made by the direct-dough method, though, this formula is especially good for bread machines.

1   Stir together the flours, sugar (if using), salt, powdered milk, and yeast in a 4-quart mixing bowl (or in the bowl of an electric mixer). Add the oil or butter, honey (if using), and water. Stir (or mix on low speed with the paddle attachment) for about 1 minute, or until the ingredients form a coarse ball. If there is still flour in the bottom of the bowl, dribble in additional water. The dough should feel soft and supple. It is better for it to be a little too soft than to be too stiff and tough.

2   Sprinkle high-gluten or whole wheat flour on the counter, transfer the dough to the counter, and begin kneading (or mix on medium speed with the dough hook). Add more flour if needed to make a firm but supple dough that is tacky but not sticky. Kneading should take about 6 minutes. The dough should pass the windowpane test (page 61) and register 77°F to 81°F (25°C to 27°C). Lightly oil a large bowl and transfer the dough to the bowl, rolling it around to coat it with oil. Cover the bowl with plastic wrap. Stretch and fold the dough (see page 59) after 30 minutes. Repeat after an additional 30 minutes (for a total of 2 stretch-and-fold cycles).

3   Ferment at room temperature for 1½ to 2 hours, or until the dough doubles in size.

4   Make a light oil slick (see page 59) on the counter. Remove the dough from the bowl, place it on the oil slick, and press the dough by hand into a rectangle about ¾ inch (2cm) thick, 6 inches wide, and 8 to 10 inches (20 to 25cm) long. Form it into a loaf, as shown on page 85. Place the loaf in a lightly oiled 8½ by 4½-inch (22 by 11.5cm) bread pan. Mist the top with spray oil and loosely cover with plastic wrap.

5   Proof at room temperature for about 1½ hours, or until the dough crests above the lip of the pan.

6   Preheat the oven to 350°F (177°C) with the oven rack on the middle shelf.

7   Place the bread pan on a sheet pan and bake for 30 minutes. Rotate the pan 180 degrees for even baking and continue baking for 15 to 30 minutes, depending on the oven. The finished loaf should register above 190°F (88°C) in the center, be golden brown on the top and the sides, and sound hollow when thumped on the bottom.

8   When the bread is finished baking, remove it immediately from the loaf pan and cool it on a rack for at least 1 hour, preferably for 2 hours, before slicing or serving.

Marbled Rye Bread

Either of these two formulas, light rye or dark rye, will make a delicious rye bread. But combined, you can weave them together to make the fabled marbled rye of childhood memories and Seinfeld fame. They are made by the direct-dough method as opposed to the sourdough method preferred for onion rye and deli rye. The ease of making these breads, their soft texture, and their flexibility for braiding and blending make them a favorite of my students.

BREAD PROFILE
Enriched, standard dough; direct method; commercial yeast

• • •

DAYS TO MAKE: 1
10 to 15 minutes mixing; 3 hours fermentation, shaping, and proofing; 30 to 60 minutes baking

• • •

COMMENTARY
The most important principle when combining two or more bread doughs into one loaf is that they must have a similar texture and rising time. This is to ensure that the texture of each color is the same and that each dough bakes in the same time frame.

• • •

Bakers generally use clear flour when making rye bread (see page 28). This formula works fine with regular bread flour or high-gluten flour, but by all means use clear flour if you have access to it.

White rye flour has been sifted twice to remove the bran and germ. However, rye flour, even when sifted, retains an off-white color that distinguishes it from flour milled from wheat berries. Other versions of rye flour include whole rye flour (milled from the whole rye berry just like whole wheat flour), dark rye (which is milled from the outer endosperm of the rye berry and is thus coarser and full of pigments), pumpernickel rye (which is coarsely milled whole rye berries), and rye meal (which is even more coarsely milled, but can vary in coarseness from mill to mill). Dark rye flour is useful in some breads, especially German-style rye, but it tends to make a much heavier loaf, not appropriate for the marbled rye of this formula.

For years, many bakeries have used vegetable shortening rather than oil for these rye formulas (and my original version of this bread used shortening as well), but vegetable oil does a fine job in this bread and has the advantage of not being a hydrogenated fat, which is being phased out of cooking and baking for health reasons.

Makes 2 to 4 marbled rye breads

MEASURE	OUNCES	GRAMS	INGREDIENTS	%
LIGHT RYE				
1½ cups	6	170	white (aka light) rye flour	30.8
3 cups	13.5	382	unbleached bread or clear flour	69.2
1½ teaspoons	0.38	11	salt	1.9
1¾ teaspoons	0.19	5.5	instant yeast	0.97
1½ teaspoons	0.17	5	caraway seeds (optional)	0.87
1 tablespoon	0.75	21	molasses	3.8
2 tablespoons	1	28	vegetable oil	5.1
1¼ cups plus 2 tablespoons	11	312	water, at room temperature	56.4
DARK RYE				
1½ cups	6	170	white (aka light) rye flour	30.8
3 cups	13.5	382	unbleached bread or clear flour	69.2
1½ teaspoons	0.38	11	salt	1.9
1¾ teaspoons	0.19	5.5	instant yeast	0.97
1½ teaspoons	0.17	5	caraway seeds (optional)	0.87
1 tablespoon (2 tablespoons if using cocoa or other powder)	0.5 (1 ounce if using cocoa or other powder)	14 (28g if using powder)	liquid caramel coloring (cocoa, carob, or coffee powder dissolved in 2 tablespoons/ 1 ounce/28g water)	2.6 (5.1 if using powder)
1 tablespoon	0.75	21	molasses	3.8
2 tablespoons	1	28	vegetable oil	5.1
1¼ cups plus 2 tablespoons	11	312	water, at room temperature	56.4
1 egg or egg white, whisked with 1 tablespoon water until frothy, for egg wash				
TOTAL				169 for light rye, 171.6 for dark rye if using caramel coloring, 174.1 if using powder

1   To make the light rye, stir together the flours, salt, yeast, and the caraway seeds, if using, in a 4-quart mixing bowl (or in the bowl of an electric mixer). Add the molasses, oil, and 1¼ cups (10 ounces/284g) of the water. Mix until the dough gathers all the loose flour and forms a ball (or mix for about 1 minute on low speed with the paddle attachment), adding the additional 2 tablespoons water (1 ounce/28g) only if needed. Sprinkle a little flour on the counter (or use the oil slick method, as described on page 59), transfer the dough to the counter, and begin to knead (or mix on medium-low speed with the dough hook). Knead for 4 to 6 minutes (or 4 minutes by machine), adding sprinkles of flour, if necessary. The dough should feel supple and pliable, a little tacky but not sticky. Lightly oil a large bowl and transfer the dough to the bowl, rolling it to coat it with oil. Cover the bowl with plastic wrap.

2   To make the dark rye, stir together the flours, salt, yeast, the caraway seeds, if using, and the cocoa, carob, or coffee powder, if using, in a 4-quart mixing bowl (or in the bowl of an electric mixer). Add the molasses, oil, 1¼ cups (10 ounces/284g) of the water, and the liquid caramel coloring, if using. Mix until the dough gathers all the loose flour and forms a ball (or mix for about 1 minute on low speed with the paddle attachment), adding the additional 2 tablespoons water (1 ounce/28g) only if needed. Sprinkle a little flour on the counter (or use the oil slick method), transfer the dough to the counter, and begin to knead (or mix on medium-low speed with the dough hook). Knead for 4 to 6 minutes (or 4 minutes by machine), adding sprinkles of flour, if necessary. The dough should feel supple and pliable, a little tacky but not sticky. Lightly oil a large bowl and transfer the dough to the bowl, rolling it to coat it with oil. Cover the bowl with plastic wrap.

3   Ferment both doughs at room temperature for approximately 1½ hours, or until each dough doubles in size.

4   Turn each of the doughs onto a lightly floured or oiled counter and divide and shape them according to one of the methods shown on page 194.

5   Mist the loaves with spray oil and cover loosely with plastic wrap. Proof at room temperature for 1 to 1½ hours, or until the loaves nearly double in size. (Most ovens do not hold 2 sheet pans at once, so if you are using sheet pans, put 1 pan in the refrigerator instead of immediately proofing the dough. The dough can then be proofed and baked as much as 2 days later.)

6   Preheat the oven to 350°F (177°C) with the oven rack on the middle shelf. Brush the loaves evenly but gently with the egg wash.

7   Bake for approximately 30 to 60 minutes (the timing will vary depending on the oven and on whether you are making freestanding loaves on sheet pans or loaf pans (which take longer) and also the size of the loaves). You may need to rotate the pan(s) 180 degrees after 15 minutes for even baking. The internal temperature of the bread should be 190°F (88°C), and the loaves should make a hollow sound when thumped on the bottom.

8   When the loaves have finished baking, remove them immediately from the pans (if using) and let cool on a rack for at least 1 hour, preferably 2 hours, before slicing or serving.

. . .

Caramel coloring is basically burnt sugar and is available in liquid form in some markets and from bakery suppliers. When making dark rye bread with caramel coloring, you may need to hold back an equal amount of water to ensure that the final textures of the light and dark doughs match. Cocoa, instant coffee, or carob powder can be substituted, but they lend a bitter flavor to the dough that some people don't like (though I do). Because they are dry, I advise adding them with the flour and other dry ingredients rather than with the liquid ingredients, but you may need to add an extra tablespoon of water, or as needed, to match the texture of the light rye dough.

. . .

Rye breads should always be mixed for a shorter time than wheat breads because the pentosan gums in the rye interfere with gluten development (rye has a different protein profile than wheat, with glutelin replacing glutenin). Once the dough gums up, no amount of additional flour will make it feel less gummy.

. . .

If the gumminess does begin to kick in, finish mixing and proceed anyway, handling the dough with a little flour on your hands to protect against sticking.

*SHAPING MARBLED RYE LOAVES

(A) Cut each dough into 12 equal-size pieces. Separate the pieces into 2 piles, with an equal number of dark and light pieces in each. (B) Form each of the piles into a solid mass of dough and then (C) shape each into a *bâtard* (page 77). You can bake the loaves freestanding (recommended) or (D) in oiled 8½ by 4½-inch (22 by 11.5cm) loaf pans. For freestanding loaves, prepare 2 sheet pans by lining each pan with baking parchment. Place a shaped loaf across the length of a pan, using 1 pan for each loaf.

*SHAPING BULL'S-EYES OR SPIRAL LOAVES

Divide each dough into 4 equal-size pieces. (A) Roll out each piece with a rolling pin into an oblong about 5 inches (13cm) wide and 8 inches (20cm) long. For spirals, take a light rye piece and lay a dark rye piece on top, then add a light rye piece, then one more dark rye piece. (B) Roll this stack up into a *bâtard* and seal the bottom. Repeat with the remaining dough to make a total of 2 loaves. Place the loaves across the width of 2 baking parchment–lined sheet pans or in 2 oiled 8½ by 4½-inch (22 by 11.5cm) loaf pans. For bull's-eyes, roll up a dark rye piece into a *bâtard* about 8 inches (20cm) long. (C) Take a light rye piece and wrap it around the *bâtard* and seal the bottom. Repeat with the remaining dough to make a total of 4 small loaves. Place the loaves on 2 baking parchment–lined sheet pans.

For braided marbled rye, divide each dough into 4 equal-size pieces. Roll out each piece into a strand 10 to 12 inches (25 to 30cm) in length, thicker in the middle and slightly tapered toward the ends. Braid 2 light and 2 dark pieces together using the 4-braid method shown on page 90. Place the loaves widthwise on 2 baking parchment–lined sheet pans or in 2 greased 8½ by 4½-inch (22 by 11.5cm) loaf pans.

Multigrain Bread Extraordinaire

I am always exploring the multigrain genre in a never-ending quest for better and better ways to deliver nutritious bread in a delicious package. Adapting some of the advanced concepts we've discussed, such as the soaker technique (see page 55), to activate enzymes and break out natural sugars seems a natural progression. This is a variation of perhaps my best-known bread, *struan*, the flavor of which, in the original version, I thought impossible to top. This version preserves that flavor and opens up possibilities for grain variations not possible with the direct-dough technique of the original *struan*, as described in *Brother Juniper's Bread Book* and *Bread Upon the Waters*. Substituting, for instance, millet, quinoa, amaranth, or buckwheat for the corn or oats (or simply adding them to the blend) can be accomplished with the soaker method without precooking those grains. You can even use sprouted versions of those grains in the blend.

I say this with the confidence born of hundreds of customer testimonials: this bread and its variations make the best toast in the world. Because it is sweetened with both honey and brown sugar, it caramelizes quickly, both while baking and especially when toasting. The many grains hold onto moisture so that, while the slices crisp up when toasted, they also retain a moist sweetness. The flavors marry extremely well with mayonnaise-based sandwich fillings, such as egg salad, tuna salad, chicken salad, and BLTs. I nearly always top the loaves with poppy seeds because they add a complementary appearance and taste and look more attractive than, say, sesame seeds, though some people prefer sesame (you can also omit the seeds altogether). The dough can be formed into rolls and freestanding loaves for specific applications, but I believe that the most perfect use of this bread is either for sandwiches or toast (or even better, toasted sandwiches).

BREAD PROFILE
Enriched, standard dough; indirect method; commercial yeast

• • •

DAYS TO MAKE: 2
DAY 1: 5 minutes soaker

DAY 2: 10 to 15 minutes mixing; 3½ to 4 hours stretch and fold, fermentation, shaping, and proofing; 20 to 60 minutes baking

• • •

COMMENTARY
If you do not have wheat or oat bran on hand, you can sift whole wheat flour through a fine sieve and extract the bran. The flour that sifts through can be used in rye breads or in *pain de campagne* (or it can be stirred back into the whole wheat flour).

(continued)

This formula uses such a small amount of cooked rice that it's hardly worth cooking it just for the bread (unless you are making a larger batch of bread than this version). I suggest making brown rice for a meal and holding some back for special uses like this bread. You can keep it refrigerated for up to 4 days (any longer and it develops enzyme characteristics detrimental to the dough development) or you can freeze it in small packets for use over the next 6 months. You can also substitute cooked white or wild rice, but brown rice blends in the best.

• • •

You can leave out the buttermilk or milk altogether and replace it with an equal amount of water. The bread will be slightly chewier and lighter in appearance without milk, as the milk not only tenderizes and enriches the dough, but also adds a small amount of lactose sugar that helps caramelize the crust. Any nondairy milk, such as hemp, soy, rice, almond, or the like will also work.

Makes one 2-pound (907g) loaf or 6 to 12 rolls

MEASURE	OUNCES	GRAMS	INGREDIENTS	%
SOAKER				
3 tablespoons	1	28	coarse-grind cornmeal (also packaged as "polenta"), millet, quinoa, or amaranth	50
3 tablespoons	0.75	21	rolled oats or wheat, buckwheat, or triticale flakes	37.5
2 tablespoons	0.25	7	wheat or oat bran	12.5
¼ cup	2	57	water, at room temperature	100
DOUGH				
3 cups	13.5	382	unbleached high-gluten or bread flour	100
3 tablespoons	1.5	42.5	brown sugar	11.1
1½ teaspoons	0.38	11	salt	2.8
1 tablespoon	0.33	9.5	instant yeast	2.4
Use all	4	113	soaker	29.5
3 tablespoons	1	28	cooked brown rice	7.4
1½ tablespoons	1	28	honey	7.4
½ cup	4	113	buttermilk, or any kind of milk or nondairy milk	29.6
¾ cup	6	170	water, at room temperature	44.4
1 egg white, whisked with 1 tablespoon water, for egg white wash (optional)				
About 1 tablespoon poppy seeds, for garnish (optional)				
TOTAL				234.6

TOTAL DOUGH FORMULA AND %

	OUNCES	GRAMS	INGREDIENTS	%
	13.5	382	high-gluten or bread flour	100
	1	28	cornmeal	7.3
	0.75	21	rolled oats (or other)	5.5
	0.25	7	wheat or oat bran	1.8
	1	28	cooked brown rice	7.3
	0.38	11	salt	2.9
	1.5	42.5	brown sugar	11.1
	0.33	9.5	instant yeast	2.5
	1	28	honey	7.3
	8	227	water	59.4
	4	113	buttermilk	29.6
TOTAL				234.7

1   On the day before making the bread, make the soaker. In a small bowl, combine the cornmeal, oats, and bran (or any alternative grains) with the water. The water will just cover the grains, hydrating them slightly. Cover the bowl with plastic wrap and leave it at room temperature overnight to initiate enzyme action (if it is a very warm day, refrigerate the soaker before going to bed).

2   The next day, to make the dough, stir together the flour, brown sugar, salt, and yeast in a 4-quart mixing bowl (or in the bowl of an electric mixer). Add the soaker, cooked rice, honey, buttermilk, and ½ cup (4 ounces/113g) of the water. Stir (or mix on low speed with the paddle attachment). Add more of the water if any of the flour remains separate. You should have a coarse, slightly sticky ball of dough.

3   Sprinkle flour on the counter (or use the oil slick method, as described on page 59), transfer the dough to the counter, and begin to knead (or mix on medium speed with the dough hook). Knead (or mix) for about 8 minutes, sprinkling in flour or water, if needed, to make a dough that is soft and pliable, tacky but not sticky. The individual ingredients will homogenize into the greater dough, disappearing to an extent, and the dough will smooth out and become slightly shiny, supple, and tacky but not sticky. (If you are using an electric mixer, knead the dough by hand for a minute or two at the end.) The dough should pass the windowpane test (page 61) and register 77°F to 81°F (25°C to 27°C). Lightly oil a bowl and transfer the dough to the bowl, rolling it around to coat it with oil. Cover the bowl with plastic wrap. After 30 minutes, stretch and fold the dough (see page 59) and return it to the oiled bowl. If the dough feels too wet or sticky, work in more flour during the stretch and fold to firm it up.

4   Ferment at room temperature for 1½ to 2 hours, or until the dough doubles in size.

5   Remove the dough from the bowl and press it by hand into a rectangle about ¾ inch (2cm) thick, 6 inches (15cm) wide, and 8 to 10 inches (20 to 25cm) long. Form it into a loaf, as shown on page 85, or into rolls or any desired shape. Place the loaf into a lightly oiled 9 by 5-inch (23 by 13cm) loaf pan or onto a sheet pan lined with baking parchment if making a freestanding loaf. If making rolls, place on a parchment-lined sheet pan. Brush the top of the dough with egg wash (or mist the top of the dough with water) and sprinkle on the poppy seeds. Mist again, this time with spray oil, and loosely cover the dough with plastic wrap or a towel.

6   Proof at room temperature for approximately 1½ hours, or until the dough nearly doubles in size. If you are using a loaf pan, the dough should crest fully above the lip of the pan, doming about 1 inch (2.5cm) above it at the center.

7   Preheat the oven to 350°F (177°C) with the oven rack on the middle shelf.

8   Bake for about 20 minutes. Small rolls probably will be finished at this point. For everything else, rotate the pan 180 degrees and continue baking for another 15 minutes for a freestanding loaf and 20 to 40 minutes for a loaf-pan bread. The bread should register at least 185°F to 195 °F (85°C to 91°C) in the center, be golden brown, and make a hollow sound when thumped on the bottom.

9   When the loaf is finished baking, remove it immediately from the pan and let cool on a rack for at least 1 hour, preferably 2 hours, before slicing or serving (rolls will be cool enough to serve within 20 minutes).

Pain à l'Ancienne

When this book was published 15 years ago, it included the following observation: "The technique by which this bread is made has tremendous implications for the baking industry and for both professional and home bakers." Since that time, this has proven to be true in many ways. The unique delayed-fermentation method, which depends on cold water, releases flavors trapped in flour in a way different from the more traditional twelve-stage method. The final product has a natural sweetness and nutlike character that is distinct from breads made with exactly the same ingredients but fermented by the standard method, even with large percentages of pre-ferment. Also, because the dough is as wet as rustic ciabatta-style dough, it can be used in many ways, from baguettes, as Philippe Gosselin does in Paris, to ciabatta, pugliese, *stirato*, *pain rustique*, and even pizza and focaccia. Overnight, or delayed fermentation, breads have swept the bread-baking community, and it all began here (at least in published form) with this method. The implications have borne much fruit.

This bread shows us another way to manipulate time, and thus outcomes, by manipulating temperature. The cold mixing and fermentation cycles delay the activation of the yeast until after the amylase enzymes have begun their work of breaking out sugar from the starch. When the dough is brought to room temperature and the yeast wakes up and begins feasting, it feeds on sugars that weren't available the day before. Because the yeast has converted less of the released sugar to alcohol and carbon dioxide, a reserve of sugar remains in the fermented dough to flavor it and caramelize the crust during the baking cycle. I used to believe that this delayed-fermentation method wouldn't work for every dough (especially those that are enriched with sugar and other flavor-infusing ingredients), but I have since discovered that it can be adapted to nearly every kind of dough (as shown in my subsequent book *Artisan Breads Everyday*). When used properly, it evokes the fullness of flavor from the wheat beyond any other fermentation method I've encountered. As a bonus, and despite all the intimidating science, this version of *pain à l'ancienne,* which is based on, but different from, the Gosselin method (and also slightly different from the version that first appeared in the original *Bread Baker's Apprentice*), is actually one of the easiest doughs in this book to make.

Without question, this is the dough that continues to get the most attention from my students at Johnson & Wales and around the country in my daylong workshops for home bakers. It is not just the flavor of the bread that excites them, though without it, the concept would be interesting but moot. It is that this bread signifies the never-ending expansion into new frontiers of bread making, of realizing that there are still areas of exploration not previously

BREAD PROFILE
Lean, rustic dough; direct method; commercial yeast

. . .

DAYS TO MAKE: 2
DAY 1: 30 minutes mixing and stretch and folds.

DAY 2: 2 to 3 hours fermentation, shaping, and panning; 15 to 30 minutes baking

. . .

COMMENTARY
This dough also makes great oil-free pizza dough or focaccia. Refer to the variations that follow and then the formulas for Pizza Napoletana (page 217) and Focaccia (page 165).

. . .

This dough is very sticky, like ciabatta dough, so it is best made in an electric mixer or a food processor (page 57). If you opt to mix by hand, use the method described on page 58.

One of the testers of this recipe, Jill Myers, suggested using sharp scissors, instead of a knife or razor, to score the bread. This is a great idea, as the wet dough is difficult to slit in the normal manner. If you are using this method, try to get a long angle with the shears and make a long cut rather than short snips.

. . .

You can also make up to 9 thinner, lighter mini baguettes, similar to what the French call a *ficelle*, or even 12 to 15 smaller bread-stick-like strips, which bake up in about 10 to 15 minutes.

charted by even the professional community. We are learning that as we more fully understand the bread-baking process, we are still in the early discovery stage of what is possible. As in any facet of life, this is an exciting place to find oneself, like standing at the end of the world, facing the words that so often showed up on ancient maps, "Unknown Kingdoms Be Here."

Makes 6 baguettes, 6 to 8 pizzas, or one 17 by 12-inch (43 by 30cm) focaccia

MEASURE	OUNCES	GRAMS	INGREDIENTS	%
6 cups	27	765.5	unbleached bread flour	100
2¼ teaspoons	0.56	16	salt	2
1¾ teaspoons	0.19	5.25	instant yeast	0.7
2½ cups plus 3 tablespoons	21.5	609.5	water, cool (55°F/13°C)	79.6
Bread or semolina or cornmeal for dusting				
TOTAL				182.3

1   Combine the flour, salt, yeast, and water in the bowl of an electric mixer with the paddle attachment and mix for 1 minute on low speed (or mix by hand with a large spoon in a large mixing bowl). Switch to medium-low speed and mix for 2 additional minutes. The dough should be sticky on the bottom of the bowl but it should release from the sides of the bowl. If not, sprinkle in a small amount of flour until this occurs (or dribble in water if the dough seems too stiff and clears the bottom as well as the sides of the bowl). Make an oil slick on the counter (see page 59) and transfer the dough to the counter with an oiled bowl scraper and oiled or wet hands. Stretch and fold the dough (see page 59) to form a ball. Lightly oil a large bowl and cover the dough with the bowl. After 5 minutes, perform another stretch and fold and cover the dough again. Repeat this two more times at 5-minute intervals. After each stretch and fold, the dough will become a little firmer and less sticky but will still remain sticky, like a ciabatta dough. After the final stretch and fold, place the dough in the oiled bowl and mist the top of the dough with spray oil. Cover the bowl with plastic wrap.

2   Immediately place the bowl in the refrigerator and retard overnight.

3   The next day, check the dough to see if it has risen in the refrigerator. It will probably be partially risen but not doubled in size (the amount of rise will depend on how cold the refrigerator is and how often the door was opened). Leave the bowl of dough out at room temperature for 2 to 3 hours (or longer if necessary) to allow the dough to wake up, lose its chill, and continue fermenting. It should double from its original pre-refrigerated size.

4   When the dough is ready, liberally sprinkle the counter with bread flour (about ½ cup/2.25 ounces/ 64g). Gently transfer the dough to the floured counter with a plastic dough scraper that has been dipped in cold water or rubbed with oil, oiling your hands as well to keep the dough from sticking to them. Try to degas the dough as little as possible as you transfer it. If the dough is

very wet, sprinkle more flour over the top as well as under it. Dry your hands thoroughly and then dip them in flour. Roll the dough gently in the sprinkled flour to coat it thoroughly, simultaneously stretching it into an oblong about 8 inches (20cm) long and 6 inches (15cm) wide. If it is too sticky to handle, continue sprinkling flour over it. Dip a metal pastry scraper into cool water to keep it from sticking to the dough, and cut the dough in half widthwise by pressing the pastry scraper down through the dough until it severs it, then dipping it again in the water and repeating this action until you have cut down the full length of the dough. (Do not use this blade as a saw; use it as a pincer, pinching the dough cleanly with each cut.) Let the dough relax for 5 minutes.

5   Prepare the oven for hearth baking as shown on page 97, making sure to have an empty steam pan in place. Preheat the oven to 500°F (260°C) or to 550°F (290°C) if your oven goes this high. Cover the back of two 17 by 12-inch sheet pans with baking parchment, mist the paper lightly with spray oil, and dust with flour or cornmeal. Proceed with shaping as shown on page 202.

Like all rustic doughs, this one requires lots of extra flour, both on your hands and on the counter, in order to handle it.

6   Score the dough strips as for baguettes (page 96), slashing the tops with 3 diagonal cuts (or see Commentary for scissors method). Because the dough is sticky, you may have to dip the razor blade or serrated knife in water before each cut. You can also omit the cuts if the dough isn't cooperating.

7   Take 1 pan to the preheated oven and carefully slide the dough, parchment and all, onto the baking stone (depending on the direction of the stone, you can choose to slide the dough and parchment off the side of the sheet pan instead of off the end), or bake directly on the sheet pan. Make sure the pieces aren't touching (you can reach in and straighten the parchment or the dough strips if need be). Pour 1 cup hot water into the steam pan and close the door. After 30 seconds, spray the oven walls with water and close the door. Repeat twice more at 30-second intervals. After the final spray, lower the oven setting to 475°F (245°C) and continue baking. Meanwhile, dust the other pan of strips with flour, mist with spray oil, and slip into a food-grade plastic bag or cover with a towel or plastic wrap. If you don't plan to bake these strips within 1 hour, refrigerate the pan and bake later or the next day, straight from the fridge. If you'd like to bake them as rustic, ciabatta-style breads, leave them at room temperature for 1 to 2 hours and then bake. As the loaves proof, they will resemble and perform like ciabatta.

8   The bread should begin to turn golden brown within 8 or 9 minutes. If the loaves are baking unevenly at this point, rotate them 180 degrees. Continue baking 10 to 15 minutes more, or until the bread is a rich golden brown and the internal temperature registers at least 200°F to 205°F (93°C to 96°C).

9   Transfer the hot breads to a rack to cool. They should feel very light, almost airy, and will cool in about 20 minutes. While this batch is cooling, you can bake the remaining loaves, remembering to remove the parchment from the oven and turn the oven up to 500°F (260°C) or higher before baking the second round.

*SHAPING PAIN À L'ANCIENNE BAGUETTES

(A) Take 1 of the dough pieces and repeat the cutting action, but this time cut off 3 equal-sized lengths. Then do the same with the remaining half. This should give you 6 lengths. (B) Flour your hands and carefully lift 1 of the dough strips and transfer it to a parchment-lined pan, gently easing it out to the length of the pan or to the length of your baking stone. If it springs back, let it rest for 5 minutes and then gently pull it out again. Place 3 strips on the pan and then prepare another pan and repeat with the remaining strips. (Note: Some people prefer to lay the cut strips on the pan without stretching them, for more uniform loaves.)

GRACE NOTES

PAIN À L'ANCIENNE PIZZA

Heavily flour the counter and gently transfer the fully fermented dough from the bowl to the counter with a plastic dough scraper that has been dipped in cold water, dipping your hands as well to keep the dough from sticking to you. Divide the dough by continually dipping the pastry scraper into water and cutting the dough into 6 to 8 equal pieces. Gently round the pieces into balls, being careful not to degas them any more than necessary. Line a sheet pan with baking parchment and spray the paper lightly with oil. Place the floured dough balls on the parchment. Mist them with spray oil and place the pan into a food-grade plastic bag or loosely cover with plastic wrap and return the pan to the refrigerator, unless you plan to make the pizzas immediately. These pizza dough balls will keep for up to 3 days in the refrigerator. (You can also put them into the freezer in individual zipper bags, where they will keep for up to 3 months.) Remove the desired number of dough balls from the refrigerator 2 hours before shaping and baking your pizza and proceed with step 4 on page 221. (Note: If using frozen dough, transfer it to the refrigerator the day before and then treat it like refrigerated dough the following day.)

PAIN À L'ANCIENNE FOCACCIA

Line a 17 by 12-inch (43 by 30-cm) sheet pan with baking parchment. With floured hands, take the fully fermented dough from the bowl and proceed with shaping instructions on page 168. Ferment at room temperature for 2 to 3 hours, or until the dough rises and fills the pan, rising to about 1 inch (2.5cm) thick. Proceed with the baking instructions for focaccia.

Pain de Campagne (Country French Bread)

This is the perfect dough for creative shaping, and the one used throughout France for many types of breads sold under various local names. The dough is similar to regular French baguette dough, but it includes a small percentage of whole grain, either whole wheat, pumpernickel-grind or white rye, or even cornmeal. This additional grain gives the bread more character and grain flavor and contributes to the brownish-gold, country-style crust that distinguishes it from white flour French bread (also sometimes called "city bread"). Most important, this is the dough, as I learned it from Professor Raymond Calvel, that opened my thinking to the use of large percentages of pre-ferment.

On pages 79 to 81 and 83 you will see a number of shapes you can make from this dough. The most famous are the *fendu, épi, couronne,* and *auvergnat.* There are many others that you may also have seen. As always, though, the first emphasis must be on the quality of the dough. There is nothing more disappointing to a bread lover than to see a lot of work go into a shaping technique for a dough that does not deliver world-class flavor and texture. This particular dough never disappoints.

Makes 3 loaves of various shapes or numerous rolls

MEASURE	OUNCES	GRAMS	INGREDIENTS	%
3 cups	16	454	*pâte fermentée* (page 111)	168.4
1¾ cups	8	227	unbleached bread flour	84.2
⅓ cup	1.5	42.5	whole wheat, white (aka light) rye, or pumpernickel-grind flour	15.8
¾ teaspoon	0.19	5.5	salt	2
1 teaspoon	0.11	3	instant yeast	1.2
¾ cup plus 2 tablespoons	7	198	water, lukewarm (90°F to 100°F/32°C to 38°C)	73.7
All-purpose or bread flour, semolina, or cornmeal for dusting				
TOTAL				345.3

BREAD PROFILE
Lean, standard dough; indirect method; commercial yeast

. . .

DAYS TO MAKE: 2
DAY 1: 1¼ hours *pâte fermentée*

DAY 2: 1 hour to de-chill *pâte fermentée;* 12 to 15 minutes mixing; 3½ hours fermentation, shaping, and proofing; 25 to 35 minutes baking

. . .

COMMENTARY
The amount of whole grain used in this dough can vary from region to region, but typically it amounts to somewhere between 10 and 20 percent of the total flour. Feel free to adjust the relationship of white to whole grain as you play with this formula.

. . .

As with the baguette on page 174, this formula utilizes a full batch of dough as the pre-ferment for the final dough, effectively doubling the amount. Because the baker's formula is based on the relationship of each ingredient (in this case, *pâte fermentée*) to total flour weight, the percentage of pre-ferment amounts to 168 percent against the combined weight of bread flour and whole wheat or rye flour. It is this huge amount of pre-ferment that makes the bread perform so well in a home kitchen.

TOTAL DOUGH FORMULA AND %

	OUNCES	GRAMS	INGREDIENTS	%
	18 ounces	510	bread flour	92.3
	1.5	42.5	whole wheat or rye flour	7.7
	0.39	11.5	salt	2
	0.17	5	instant yeast	0.9
	13	368	water	72.2
TOTAL				175.2

1   Remove the *pâte fermentée* from the refrigerator 1 hour before making the dough. Cut it into about 10 small pieces with a pastry scraper or serrated knife. Cover with a towel or plastic wrap and let sit for 1 hour to take off the chill.

2   Stir together the flours, salt, yeast, and *pâte fermentée* pieces in a 4-quart mixing bowl (or in the bowl of an electric mixer). Add the water, stirring until everything comes together and makes a coarse ball (or mix on low speed with the dough hook for about 2 minutes). Add a few drops of additional water, if needed, to gather any loose flour into the ball. The dough should be soft and pliable.

3   Sprinkle flour on the counter (or use the oil slick method, as described on page 59), transfer the dough to the counter, and begin to knead (or mix on medium speed with the dough hook). Knead (or mix) for approximately 6 minutes, sprinkling in bread flour if needed to make a soft, pliable dough. It should be tacky or even slightly sticky. The dough should pass the windowpane test (page 61) and register 77°F to 81°F (25°C to 27°C). Lightly oil a large bowl and transfer the dough to the bowl, rolling it around to coat it with oil. Cover the bowl with plastic wrap.

4   After 30 minutes, stretch and fold the dough (see page 59), return it to the oiled bowl, and cover the bowl. Repeat the stretch and fold again after another 30 minutes. The dough will firm up slightly after each stretch and fold. Re-cover the bowl and ferment the dough at room temperature for approximately 1½ hours, or until the dough doubles in size. If the dough doubles in size more quickly, fold it lightly to degas it and let it rise again, covered, until it doubles from the original size.

5   Sprinkle a small amount of flour on the counter (or make an oil slick) and gently remove the dough from the bowl, being careful to degas it as little as possible. Divide the dough into 3 or more pieces by cutting it with a pastry scraper or serrated knife, again trying to avoid degassing any more than necessary. Shape the dough as shown on pages 76 to 91, depending on what shape you desire (rolls, baguette, *bâtard, couronne, épi, fendu,* or *auvergnat*). Line 2 sheet pans with baking parchment, sprinkle the parchment with semolina, flour, or cornmeal, and transfer the dough to the pans (or use the *couche* method described on page 33). Mist the dough with spray oil and loosely cover with plastic wrap, a food-grade plastic bag, or a towel.

Pain de Campagne, a traditional artisan loaf, can be shaped in many ways. Clockwise from center top: *tressé* (braid), pieces from an *épi* wreath, *épi*, *tabatière*, and *casquette* (a variation of *auvergnat*). In the center, an example of a baked *couronne bordelaise* before it is torn into rolls.

6　Proof for about 1 hour, or until the pieces are approximately 1½ times their original size.

7　Prepare the oven for hearth baking as described on page 97, making sure to have an empty steam pan in place. Preheat the oven to 500°F (260°C). If you are making *épis,* you can make the scissors cuts shown on page 80.

8　*Épis* can be baked directly on the sheet pans. For other shapes, generously dust a peel or the back of a sheet pan with flour or cornmeal and very gently transfer the dough pieces to the peel or pan. Slide the dough onto the baking stone (or bake directly on the sheet pan). Pour 1 cup of hot water into the steam pan and close the door. After 30 seconds, spray the oven walls with water and close the door. Repeat twice more at 30-second intervals. After the final spray, lower the oven setting to 450°F (232°C) and continue baking for 10 minutes. Check the loaves and, if necessary, rotate them 180 degrees for even baking. Continue to bake for 10 to 15 minutes longer for baguettes and *fendus,* less for rolls. The breads should be a rich golden brown all around and register 200°F to 205°F (93°C to 96°C) in the center. The loaves should sound hollow when thumped on the bottom.

9　Transfer the bread to a rack (off the sheet pan if used) and let cool for at least 40 minutes before slicing or serving (rolls will cool in about 15 to 20 minutes).

Pane Siciliano

This is one of the breakthrough breads that taught me the value of combining large portions of pre-ferment with overnight cold fermentation. Semolina is the gritty, sandy flour milled from durum wheat. (Durum is the strain of wheat most closely identified with pasta.) It is a hard, high-protein wheat, but it is not high in gluten. The golden color is mainly due to a high proportion of beta-carotene and other pigments, which also contributes both aroma and flavor. You can substitute a finer grind of this flour, called fancy durum (sometimes labeled "extra fancy durum"). When it is labeled "fancy durum," the flour is milled to the consistency of regular bread flour. This is the grind used in pasta and also used in the 100 percent durum bread called pugliese (page 233).

This version of *pane siciliano* consists of 40 percent semolina and 60 percent high-gluten or bread flour. The finished loaf has a beautiful blistered crust, not too crackly, and a crumb with large, irregular holes, open to the same degree as good French or Italian bread. The sweetness and nutty quality of the semolina and the complementary flavor of the sesame-seed garnish make this one of my absolute favorite breads.

BREAD PROFILE
Enriched, standard dough; indirect method; commercial yeast

• • •

DAYS TO MAKE: 3
DAY 1: 1¼ hours *pâte fermentée*

DAY 2: 1 hour to de-chill *pâte fermentée;* 12 to 15 minutes mixing; 3 hours fermentation, shaping, and panning

DAY 3: 0 to 2 hours proofing; 30 to 35 minutes baking

• • •

COMMENTARY
This dough can be used for many purposes beyond the traditional S-shaped loaf. It is a good dough for pizza (it makes enough for six 8-ounce/227g pizza crusts) or for small rolls of any shape, and it is great for breadsticks.

• • •

The bread can, in theory, be baked on the same day that it is shaped, but the difference in flavor and texture (and those "birds-eye" blisters) is dramatic if it is held overnight in the refrigerator (retarding method), as advised in the instructions. The overnight step makes this a 3-day process, though the final day is usually only baking the bread. Those who tested this recipe say the results are worth the delayed gratification.

Makes 3 loaves

MEASURE	OUNCES	GRAMS	INGREDIENTS	%
3 cups	16	454	*pâte fermentée* (page 111)	100
1¾ cups	8	227	unbleached high-gluten or bread flour	50
1¾ cups	8	227	semolina	50
1¼ teaspoons	0.31	9	salt	1.9
1¼ teaspoons	0.14	4	instant yeast	0.9
2 tablespoons	1	28	olive oil	6.3
1 tablespoon	0.75	21	honey	4.7
1½ cups	12		water, lukewarm (90°F to 100°F/32°C to 38°C)	75
1 egg white whisked with 1 tablespoon water, for egg white wash (optional)				
Sesame seeds, white or black, for garnish				
TOTAL				288.8

	OUNCES	GRAMS	INGREDIENTS	%
	18	511	bread flour	69.2
	8	227	semolina	30.8
	0.51	14	salt	1.9
	0.14	5.5	instant yeast	0.7
	1	28	olive oil	3.8
	0.75	21	honey	2.8
	18	510	water	69.1
TOTAL				178.3

1   Remove the *pâte fermentée* from the refrigerator 1 hour before making the dough to take off the chill. Cut it into about 10 small pieces with a pastry scraper or serrated knife. Cover with a towel or plastic wrap and let sit for 1 hour to take off the chill.

2   Stir together the flours, salt, and yeast in a 4-quart mixing bowl (or in the bowl of an electric mixer). Add the *pâte fermentée* pieces, oil, honey, and 1¼ cups (10 ounces/284g) water. Stir with a large spoon until the dough forms a ball (or mix on low speed with the dough hook). If the dough seems too stiff, dribble in water, 1 teaspoon at a time, until all the flour is gathered and the dough feels soft and pliable. If the dough seems sticky, don't worry; you can adjust the flour while kneading or mixing.

3   Sprinkle bread flour on the counter (or use the oil slick method, as described on page 59), transfer the dough to the counter, and knead (or mix on medium-low speed with the dough hook). Add flour as needed, sprinkling in a small amount at a time to make a smooth dough that is tacky but not sticky (it can be slightly sticky) and has the same pliability and suppleness as French bread dough. Knead or mix for about 6 minutes. The dough should pass the windowpane test (page 61) and register 77°F to 81°F (25°C to 27°C). Form the dough into a ball, lightly oil a large bowl, and transfer the dough to the bowl, rolling it to coat it with oil. Cover the bowl with plastic wrap.

4   After 30 minutes, stretch and fold the dough (see page 59), return the dough to the oiled bowl, and re-cover the bowl. Repeat the stretch and fold after another 30 minutes and return the dough to the bowl. Mist the dough with spray oil and re-cover the bowl with plastic wrap. Ferment at room temperature for about 2 hours, or until the dough doubles in size.

5   Gently divide the dough into 3 equal pieces on a lightly oiled counter. Shape as for baguettes (page 78), extending each piece to about 24 inches (61cm) in length and taking care to degas the dough as little as possible. Then, working from each end simultaneously, coil the dough toward the center, forming an S shape (see page 210). Line a sheet pan with baking parchment and sprinkle some semolina on the paper. Place each loaf on the pan (or set up 1 loaf each on

individual pans). Mist the loaves with water (or brush with the egg white wash) and sprinkle sesame seeds on the top of each loaf. Then mist the tops with spray oil and place the pan(s) in a food-grade plastic bag or loosely cover with plastic wrap.

6   Place the pan(s) in the refrigerator overnight.

7   The next day, remove the pan(s) from the refrigerator and determine whether the loaves have risen enough to bake or if they need additional proofing time. Gently poke the dough. If it springs back quickly, leave the pan(s) at room temperature, still covered, for a couple of hours, or until the dough wakes up and rises more. It should stay dimpled when poked, and the loaves should be nearly twice as large as when first shaped.

8   Prepare the oven for hearth baking (as described on page 97), making sure to put an empty steam pan in place. You do not need a baking stone. Preheat the oven to 500°F (260°C) with the oven rack on the middle shelf.

9   Uncover the bread dough and place the pan(s) in the oven. Pour 1 cup hot water into the steam pan and close the door. After 30 seconds, spray the oven walls with water and close the door. Repeat twice more at 30-second intervals. After the final spray, lower the oven setting to 450°F (232°C) and bake for about 15 minutes. If the loaves are touching, gently separate them. Rotate the pan(s) 180 degrees for even baking and continue baking for 10 to 15 minutes longer, or until the loaves are a rich golden brown all over. If there are still light or white sections of the dough, extend the baking time for a few extra minutes to maximize color and flavor. The internal temperature of the bread should register 200°F to 205°F (93°C to 96°C)

10 Remove the pan from the oven and transfer the loaves to a rack. Let cool for at least 45 minutes before serving. One way to slice this bread is to cut it lengthwise down the middle. Lay the cut side on the cutting board to stabilize the loaf and then slice into ¾-inch (2cm) thick slices across the width, either straight down or on a slight diagonal.

Panettone

Panettone is a traditional, rich Christmas bread originating, according to most sources, in Milan. There are many folktales about its origins, the most popular being that it was created a few hundred years ago by a humble baker named Tony to woo his beloved, the daughter of a rich merchant. More importantly, he had to win over the father to the idea of his daughter marrying a baker, so he pulled out all the stops, filling his bread with the baker's equivalent of the gifts of the wise men: butter, brandied dried and candied fruits, nuts, and sugar. The merchant was so impressed that he not only gave his daughter in marriage but also set Tony up with his own bakery in Milan with the promise that he would continue to make his bread, *pane Tony*.

For many years the standard panettone found in most bakeries and cookbooks has been one made with commercial yeast, a good but not great rendition. The best and most traditional versions are made by wild-yeast fermentation, sometimes augmented by a small amount of commercial yeast. A few years ago, one of the largest panettone bakeries in Italy changed its formula from commercial yeast back to wild yeast, returning to the more traditional method that had all but been abandoned. The bakers discovered that not only does the bread have a longer shelf life due to the increased acidity, but it also outsold the commercial-yeast version. That change added up to a huge increase in profits and, more important, to happier customers. I've noticed in recent years that this return to wild-yeast fermentation is on the rise.

The following formula will produce a long-keeping loaf that could easily become a perennial favorite at holiday time. It is more time-consuming to produce, but that's the price of world-class quality. You can also make a perfectly good panettone variation by following the Stollen formula on page 268, shaping it in the round panettone style.

(continued)

BREAD PROFILE
Rich, standard dough; indirect method; mixed leavening method

• • •

DAYS TO MAKE: 2
DAY 1: 5 minutes mixing; 4 hours fermentation

DAY 2: 12 to 15 minutes mixing; 4 to 6 hours fermentation, shaping, and proofing; 25 minutes to 1½ hours baking

• • •

COMMENTARY
The formula calls for candied fruit, but many people prefer using dried fruit, such as dried cranberries, apricots, and apples. Feel free to make a substitution if you prefer.

• • •

SAF makes a gold-labeled yeast that is osmotolerant (see page 63), which means it performs well in acidic and extra-sweet doughs. It is now available to home bakers but is not required. Regular instant yeast will also work, but it may take longer to wake up and perform, as the sugar and acid in the dough tends to shock it. For this reason, I have added a step I came up with while testing recipes for *Artisan Breads Everyday*, to dissolve the instant yeast in warm water first, which seems to allow it to perform more like osmotolerant yeast.

You are free to experiment with your liquor and extract choices. Some people prefer to use orange liqueur, for instance, or regular or flavored brandy (like cherry schnapps), whiskey, or rum. Extracts, such as almond, orange, or lemon, are also alcohol based, but the flavors are highly concentrated, so in some respects you will get more bang for your buck.

• • •

I prefer to use a blend of liquor and extracts, but you can double the amount of extract and eliminate the liquor. Fiori di Sicilia, a wonderful blend of extracts and floral oils that is ideal in this bread, is available through *The Baker's Catalogue* (see Resources, page 314) as well as other sources.

• • •

It is now possible to buy professional panettone baking papers (pictured on page 215) at kitchenware stores or through mail-order catalogs (see Resources, page 314). Like muffin-cup papers, they are decorative enough to leave the baked loaves in them. They come in many sizes, and, although they do not require oiling, I always mist them with spray oil for better release. If you bake your panettone in standard round pans or muffin tins, consult the photographs on page 215 for readying the pans for baking.

Makes 2 large or many small loaves

MEASURE	OUNCES	GRAMS	INGREDIENTS	%
WILD YEAST SPONGE				
1 cup	7	198	barm (mother starter, page 241)	156
1 cup	8	227	milk or milk substitute such as almond milk, lukewarm (90°F to 100°F/32°C to 38°C)	178
1 cup	4.5	128	unbleached all-purpose or bread flour	100
TOTAL				434
FRUIT BLEND				
1 cup	6	170	golden raisins	35.2
1 cup	6	170	candied fruit blend (see Commentary)	35.3
½ cup	4	113	brandy, rum, or whiskey	23.5
1 tablespoon	0.5	14	orange or lemon extract	2.95
1 tablespoon	0.5	14	vanilla extract or Fiori di Sicilia (see Commentary)	2.95
TOTAL				100
DOUGH				
3 cups	13.5	383	unbleached all-purpose or bread flour	100
3 tablespoons	1.5	42.5	granulated sugar	11.1
¾ teaspoon	0.19	5.5	salt	1.4
Use all	19.5	553	wild-yeast sponge	144.3
1 large	0.65	19	egg yolk	4.8
1 large	1.65	47	egg, at room temperature and slightly beaten	12.2
1 tablespoon	0.33	9.5	instant yeast (see Commentary)	2.4
6 tablespoons	3	85	water, lukewarm (90°F to 100°F/32°C to 38°C)	22.2
½ cup	4	113	unsalted butter, at room temperature	29.6
Use all	17	482	soaked fruit blend	126
1 cup	5	142	blanched almonds, slivered or chopped	37
TOTAL				491

TOTAL DOUGH FORMULA AND %

OUNCES	GRAMS	INGREDIENTS	%
21	610	bread or all purpose flour	100
0.19	5.5	salt	0.9
1.5	42.5	sugar	7
6	170	dried fruit	9.8
6	170	candied fruit	9.8
5	142	slivered or chopped almonds	23.3
0.33	9.5	instant yeast	1.55
1.65	47	eggs	7.7
0.65	19	egg yolk	3.1
8	227	milk	37.2
4	113	butter	18.5
4	113	brandy, rum, or other liquor	18.5
1	28	extracts	4.6
6.5	184	water	30.2
TOTAL			272.15

1   The day before making the bread, make the wild-yeast sponge. Stir together the barm, milk or milk substitute, and flour in a mixing bowl just long enough to hydrate all the flour and to make a sponge. Cover the bowl with plastic wrap and ferment at room temperature for approximately 4 hours, or until the sponge begins to foam and bubble, then put it in the refrigerator overnight.

2   While waiting for the sponge to ferment, assemble the fruit blend. Mix together the raisins and candied fruit in a bowl, add the liquor and extracts, and toss to mix. Cover the bowl and let it sit out overnight to allow the fruit to absorb the liquid fully.

3   The next day, remove the wild-yeast sponge from the refrigerator 1 hour before making the dough to take off the chill.

4   To make the dough, stir together the flour, sugar, and salt in a 4-quart mixing bowl (or in the bowl of an electric mixer). Add the sponge, egg yolk, and egg to the flour mixture. Stir the instant yeast in the lukewarm water to dissolve it and then add it to the bowl. Stir (or mix on low speed with the paddle attachment) for 1 to 2 minutes, or until the ingredients form a coarse but soft, supple ball. Stop mixing and allow the dough to rest for 20 minutes to let the gluten begin to develop. If using a mixer, switch to the dough hook. Add the softened butter and the soaked fruit mixture and continue stirring or mixing on low speed until the ingredients are evenly distributed.

5   Sprinkle flour on the counter (or use the oil slick method, as described on page 59), transfer the dough to the counter, and begin to knead (or mix on low speed with the dough hook). Knead (or mix) the dough gently for 2 to 4 minutes, or until it is soft and supple but not overly sticky (it can be very tacky). Add flour if necessary to allow you to knead without the dough sticking to your hands. You will probably have to sprinkle small amounts of flour continually as you knead to keep the dough from covering your hands, or you can oil your hands. While kneading, gradually work in the almonds until they too are evenly distributed. The entire process, after the resting period, should take about 6 minutes. The dough must be soft and supple, tacky but not sticky. It should pass the windowpane test (page 61) and register 77°F to 81°F (25°C to 27°C). Lightly oil a bowl and transfer the dough to the bowl, rolling it around to coat it with oil. Cover the bowl with plastic wrap.

6   Ferment the dough at room temperature for 2 to 4 hours. It will rise very slowly and should increase to only about 1½ times its original size.

7   If you are not using professional panettone papers, prepare pans as shown opposite.

8   Divide the dough into the desired sizes. If you are making two 2-pound loaves, divide the dough in half and round the pieces into 2 *boules*, as shown on page 76. Place them into the baking papers or into prepared pans 6 inches (15cm) in diameter. Press the dough down slightly to spread it into the papers or pans. The dough should reach halfway up the forms. Mist the dough with spray oil and loosely cover the pans with plastic wrap. If you are making mini panettones, use individual-size baking papers or grease muffin pans and fill each cup half full. (You will not need to make parchment collars or bottoms for the muffin pans.) For large and small loaves alike, proof the dough at room temperature for approximately 2 hours, or until it nearly doubles and has risen just to the height of the papers or pans.

9   Preheat the oven to 325°F (163°C) with the oven rack on the shelf in the lower third of the oven.

10 Bake large loaves for up to 1½ hours, depending on the oven; bake mini loaves for 25 to 35 minutes. The top of the dough may get very dark before the center reaches 185°F (85°C). If so, cover the tops with aluminum foil or a sheet of baking parchment. The finished breads should sound hollow when thumped on the bottom, be golden brown all around, and register at least 185°F (85°C) in the center. If using baking papers, you may leave the bread in the paper while it cools; if using pans, remove the breads from the pans. In both cases, let the breads cool completely on racks before serving, at least 2 hours.

11 These breads keep best if wrapped in aluminum foil once they have cooled completely. They can be stored at room temperature for as long as 2 weeks. (Some people keep them longer, but I think they lose quality beyond this point.) You can also freeze them for up to 3 months to save for special occasions.

✲ PREPARING PANETTONE PANS

Use the bottom of the round pan to trace a circle on baking parchment. **(A, B)** Cut out the circle and place it in the bottom of the pan. **(C)** You can also make a parchment collar to ensure easy removal after baking. Note: If using muffin pans, there's no need to use parchment lining.

GRACE NOTE

HOLIDAY BREAD BRÛLÉ

This is a great way to turn holiday bread into a simple but impressive dessert. It is essentially a fancy bread pudding with a broiled sugar top.

I first made it at Philippe Chin's restaurant, Philippe on Locust, for Philadelphia's the Book & the Cook Festival in March 2000. Pastry chef Michael Vandergeest added some creative serving accompaniments—fresh raspberries with a few drizzles of chocolate sauce and raspberry sorbet—to make this an elegant presentation. The sorbet lent a nice flavor contrast to the rich bread pudding brûlé. Here's how to make it.

Bake a full batch of either Panettone or Stollen (page 268) in 8 to 12 small rounds (I baked them in muffin cups at Philippe's, using about 3 ounces/85g dough for each). After baking, cut off the tops and scoop out the insides, collecting the scooped dough for the pudding. Set the hollowed shells and tops aside and cover with plastic wrap.

To make a custard base, combine 1½ cups milk or heavy cream; 1 cup granulated sugar; ½ teaspoon salt; 3 large eggs; 1 tablespoon vanilla extract; 1 tablespoon orange, lemon, or almond extract; and ¼ cup rum or brandy (optional) and whisk until a smooth batter forms.

Pour the batter over the scooped bread pieces. Spread this mixture into an oiled 6-inch (15cm) square baking pan or 1-quart casserole dish and place this dish in another, larger ovenproof dish or pan. Place the double pan in a preheated 325°F (163°C) oven and pour enough hot water into the outer pan to reach to the height of the bread filling in the smaller pan. Bake for approximately 1 hour, or until the bread pudding is above 180°F (82°C) in the center. Carefully remove the pans from the oven and then remove the smaller pan from the larger and let cool at room temperature for 30 minutes. Cover the pudding with plastic wrap and let cool in the refrigerator for another hour (or overnight).

Fill the hollowed bread shells with the bread pudding, sprinkle granulated sugar over the top (you can also use coarse AA sugar or sanding sugar if you have some on hand), and lightly mist the sugar with water. Place under a preheated broiler for about 3 minutes, or until the sugar melts and caramelizes. (If you have a small kitchen torch, you can caramelize the tops individually with the torch.) Lean the top of the shell against the side of the loaf or arrange in another decorative manner. Serve as is or with sorbet and berries.

Pizza Napoletana

BREAD PROFILE
Lean or enriched, rustic
dough; flat; direct method;
commercial yeast

• • •

DAYS TO MAKE: 2
DAY 1: 8 to 12 minutes mixing; 5 to 10 minutes dividing
and rounding

DAY 2: 2 hours resting; 10 to
25 minutes per pizza shaping;
5 to 8 minutes baking

Note: I wrote the recipe introduction that follows 3 years before I wrote *American Pie: My Search for the Perfect Pizza,* a book project that gave me the opportunity to travel the world uncovering the secrets of many great pizza makers. I'm pleased to say that all the subsequent research only proved the points made here; this formula works and, other than a few new instruction tweaks, I still believe this dough was and is as good as it gets. So, I'm leaving the introduction pretty much as it originally appeared.

Pizza is the perfect food, or so I'm so often told. When I moved to Providence, Rhode Island, I'd heard that there was great pizza to be had, so I asked everyone I met to recommend his or her favorite place. They all seemed to have a different style that they preferred, not unlike the diversity I've found in similar explorations into barbecue and chili. There is Sicilian thick-crusted pizza and thin New York style (the kind where the nose of the slice has to be flipped back into the center of the slice to keep all the cheese from running off). At least two-dozen franchise pizza shops exist within a three-mile radius of my home, some with pre-baked shells, others with house-made crust. There are double-decker pizzas, cheese-in-the-crust pizzas, and a very popular twice-baked crust, recently dubbed Argentinian pizza in some regions, but here it is mysteriously and incorrectly referred to as Neapolitan.

The best pizza I've had in recent years was in Phoenix at Pizzeria Bianco, a small restaurant run by Chris Bianco and his friends and family. Chris grows his own basil and lettuce behind the restaurant, makes his own mozzarella cheese, and hand-mixes his pizza dough in large batches (I mean really hand-mixes, on a bench and by hand). It is wet dough, like ciabatta, and sits for hours slowly fermenting. His is the closest I've had to pizza made in the style of Naples: simple, thin crusted, and baked fast and crisp. Pizzeria Bianco serves only about six kinds of pizza, a house salad, house-made Italian bread (from the pizza dough), and three or so desserts made by Chris's mom. They can't keep up with the business, and getting a seat in the pizzeria is like winning the lottery.

Naples is the birthplace of what we today call pizza. Genoa has its focaccia, Tuscany its *schiacciata,* and Sicily its *sfincione,* but true Neapolitan pizza is the perfect expression of the perfect food. Every other style may also be crust and topping, but life would be better if only this superior version were allowed to call itself pizza. More to the point, it is possible to make a great pizza at home even if your oven cannot reach the heat levels used by the very best pizzerias that burn hardwood or bituminous coal and reach between 800°F and 1,200°F (427°C to 650°C)!

The keys to shaping pizza dough are flouring your hands and using your fists (rather than fingertips) in the toss. Jennifer is getting the hang of it!

Jeffrey Steingarten wrote a wonderful piece in the August 2000 issue of *Vogue* in which he told of trying dozens of ways to generate enough heat to replicate a pizza oven in his home. He nearly burned down his house in the process. Unfortunately, most home ovens will not go beyond 550°F (290°C), if that, but the following dough will produce an amazing pizza even at that relatively low heat.

It has long been my contention that it is the crust, not the toppings, that make a pizza memorable. I've seen some expensive, wonderful ingredients wasted on bad crust, or, even more often, a decent dough ruined in an oven that was not hot enough to bake it properly. For many years, cookbooks have instructed to bake at about 350°F (177°C) or maybe at 425°F (218°C). Rarely do you see instructions that suggest cranking the oven to its fullest capacity, but that's what you have to do to make a great pizza at home.

The single biggest flaw in most pizza dough recipes is the failure to instruct the maker to allow the dough to rest overnight in the refrigerator (or at least for a long time). This gives the enzymes time to go to work, pulling out subtle flavor trapped in the starch. The long rest also relaxes the gluten, allowing you to shape the dough easily, minimizing the elastic springiness that so often forces you to squeeze out all the gas.

Lately, there's been a controversy regarding what type of flour to use. Unbleached is a given. It simply delivers more flavor and aroma. For the past few years the trend has been toward high-gluten or bread flour because it promotes oven spring and holds together better during handling (this is called dough "tolerance"). The trend now is to suggest all-purpose flour because it is more tender, that is, less hard (the hardness of flour is based on the amount of protein it contains). It makes sense that softer flour will have a softer chew, but it also makes the dough more prone to tear or rip when you toss it or roll it out.

The formula that follows will work with either type of flour, but I recommend adding olive oil to the high-gluten dough to tenderize it. (True Neapolitan dough is made without oil—it's actually a requirement—but Italian flour is, by nature, more slack and tender but very extensible and easy to form.) I find that high-gluten flour, despite its springy elasticity, is easier to work with as long as you give it plenty of rest. If you are using all-purpose flour, you can leave out the oil. As is so often said when there is more than one way to make something, try it both ways and decide for yourself which flour you prefer. My guess is, as with pizza in general, for every ten people who make the dough, there will be eleven opinions.

(continued)

COMMENTARY
This formula utilizes the *pain à l'ancienne* delayed-fermentation technique as discussed on page 199, but this version has a small amount of olive oil to tenderize the dough. The oil can be left out, if desired, which also conforms to the strictest guidelines of authentic Neapolitan pizza. I use the full amount of oil when making the dough with high-gluten flour, only half the amount of oil when using bread flour, and no oil when using all-purpose flour, but these are all individual choices. All these variations make the best pizza dough I have ever had or made. Using the delayed-fermentation method accomplishes all the flavor objectives of *poolish* and *biga* methods, and the small amount of yeast is just enough to leaven the dough without eating up all the sugar during fermentation. The result is a naturally sweet, thin, golden crust that crisps on the bottom and the edges but retains enough moisture to taste creamy in the mouth. Some of you may notice that in this version (and also in the *pain à l'ancienne* on page 199) the water temperature is a little higher than in the versions in the original *Bread Baker's Apprentice*, which allows for a little more flavor and gas development during the overnight fermentation. If you have had success with the original version, feel free to stick with that, or try this version, which also increases the hydration slightly, to see if you like it better.

Baking pizza at a low temperature ruins the crust because it takes so long to brown it that all the moisture evaporates, leaving a cardboard-dry shell behind. The key to great pizza is an extremely hot oven and baking surface. The balancing act between browning the crust and melting the cheese is one of the great culinary dramas, and if the two actions converge at exactly the same moment, you will have a memorable experience. The thinner you can stretch the dough without tearing it, and the more evenly you stretch it, the more likely that this baking convergence will occur.

This dough can also be used to make focaccia and any rustic bread.

Makes six 6-ounce (170g) pizza crusts

MEASURE	OUNCES	GRAMS	INGREDIENTS	%
4½ cups	20.25	574	unbleached high-gluten, bread, or all-purpose flour	100
1¾ teaspoons	0.44	12.5	Salt	2.2
1 teaspoon	0.11	3	instant yeast	0.54
¼ cup	2	57	olive or vegetable oil (optional; mainly if using high-gluten flour, see Commentary)	9.9 (or less)
1¾ cups plus 1 tablespoon	14.5	411	water, cool (about 55°F/13°C)	71.6
All-purpose or bread flour, semolina, or cornmeal for dusting				
TOTAL				184.2

1 Stir together the flour, salt, and yeast in a 4-quart mixing bowl (or in the bowl of an electric mixer). With a large metal spoon, stir in the oil (if using) and cool water until all the flour is absorbed (or mix on low speed with the paddle attachment). If you are mixing by hand, repeatedly dip one of your hands or the metal spoon into cold water and use it, much like a dough hook, to work the dough vigorously into a smooth mass while rotating the bowl in a circular motion with the other hand (see page 58). Reverse the circular motion a few times to develop the gluten further. Do this for 1 to 2 minutes, or until the dough forms a coarse ball and the ingredients are evenly distributed. Let the dough rest for 5 minutes to hydrate, then continue mixing by hand or, if you are using an electric mixer, switch to the dough hook and mix on medium speed for approximately 2 to 3 minutes, or as long as it takes to create a smooth, slightly sticky dough. The dough should clear the sides of the bowl but stick to the bottom of the bowl. If the dough is too wet and doesn't come off the sides of the bowl, sprinkle in some more flour just until it clears the sides. If it clears the bottom of the bowl, dribble in a teaspoon or two of cold water. The finished dough will be springy, elastic, and sticky, not just tacky, and register 60°F to 65°F (16°C to 18°C).

2 Sprinkle flour on the counter and transfer the dough to the counter (or use the oil slick method, as described on page 59). Stretch and fold the dough (see page 59) and form it into a ball. Prepare a sheet pan by lining it with baking parchment (or a silicone baking mat) and misting the parchment with spray oil (or lightly oil the parchment). Using a metal dough scraper, cut the dough into 6 equal pieces (or larger if you are comfortable shaping large pizzas). You can dip the scraper into the water between cuts (or rub it with oil) to keep the dough from sticking to it. Sprinkle flour over the dough. Make sure your hands are dry and then flour them. Lift each piece and gently round it into a ball. If the dough sticks to your hands, dip your hands into the flour again. Transfer the dough balls to the sheet pan. Mist the dough generously with spray oil and slip the pan into a food-grade plastic bag. (Note: you can also put the whole dough into an oiled bowl, cover it with plastic wrap, and refrigerate it overnight, dividing it into dough balls 2 hours before making the pizzas).

3   Put the pan into the refrigerator overnight to rest the dough, or keep for up to 3 days. (Note: If you want to save some of the dough for future baking, you can store the dough balls in a zippered freezer bag. Dip each dough ball into a bowl that has a few tablespoons of oil in it, rolling the dough in the oil, and then put each ball into a separate bag. Place the bags in the freezer for up to 3 months. Transfer them to the refrigerator the day before you plan to make pizza.)

4   On the day you plan to make the pizza, remove the desired number of dough balls from the refrigerator 2 hours before making the pizza. Dust the counter with flour, and then mist the counter with spray oil. Place the dough balls on top of the floured counter and sprinkle them with flour; dust your hands with flour. Gently press the dough into flat disks about ½ inch (13mm) thick and 5 inches (13cm) in diameter. Sprinkle the dough with flour, mist it again with spray oil, and cover the dough loosely with plastic wrap or a food-grade plastic bag. Let rest for 2 hours.

5   At least 45 minutes before making the pizza, place a baking stone either on the floor of the oven (for gas ovens) or on a rack in the lower third of the oven (the placement of the stone will depend on the particular oven). Preheat the oven as hot as possible, up to 800°F (427°C)—most home ovens will go only to 500°F (260°C) or maybe 550°F (288°C), but some will go higher. If your oven has convection, use it without the usual reduction in temperature used in breads. If you do not have a baking stone, you can use the back of a sheet pan.

6   Generously dust a peel or the back of a sheet pan with semolina or cornmeal. Make the pizzas one at a time. Dip your hands, including the backs of your hands and knuckles, in flour and lift 1 piece of dough by getting under it with a pastry scraper. Very gently lay the dough across your fists and carefully stretch it by bouncing the dough in a circular motion on your hands, carefully giving it a little stretch with your thumbs, on the edges only, with each bounce. If it begins to stick to your hands, lay it down on the floured counter, flour your hands again, and then continue shaping it. Once the dough has expanded outward, move to a full toss as shown on page 218, if you want to try it. If you have trouble tossing the dough, or if the dough keeps springing back, let it rest for 5 to 20 minutes so the gluten can relax and try again. You can also resort to using a rolling pin, though this isn't as effective as the back of the hand or toss method for creating a puffy *cornicione* (border or edge).

7   When the dough is stretched out to your satisfaction (about 9 inches/23cm in diameter for a 6-ounce/170g piece of dough, or up to 11 inches/28 cm for an 8-ounce/227g piece), lay it on the peel or pan, making sure there is enough semolina, flour, or cornmeal to allow it to slide. Lightly top it with sauce and then with your other toppings, remembering that the best pizzas are topped with a less-is-more philosophy. The American "kitchen sink" approach is counter-productive, as it makes the crust more difficult to bake and soggy. Usually no more than 3 or 4 toppings, including sauce and cheese, are sufficient (see page 222 for ideas).

. . .

It is perfectly acceptable to add a small amount (about 10 percent) of whole wheat or rye flour to the dough, substituting it for an equal amount of the white flour. This gives the pizza a more rustic quality, kind of a peasant-style crust. If so, you might try also adding an additional tablespoon or so of water.

. . .

I originally used water that I had chilled in the refrigerator to 40°F (4°C), which is the usual temperature for refrigerators. But now I float some ice cubes in a beaker of tap water long enough to chill the water to at least 55°F (13°C), then measure out what I need.

8 Slide the topped pizza onto the preheated stone (or bake directly on the sheet pan) and close the door. Wait for 2 minutes, then take a peek. If it needs to be rotated 180 degrees for even baking, do so. The pizza should take 5 to 8 minutes to bake. If the top gets done before the bottom, you will need to move the stone to a lower shelf before the next round. If the bottom crisps before the cheese caramelizes, you will need to raise the stone for subsequent bakes.

9 Remove the pizza from the oven and transfer it to a cutting board. Wait for 2 to 3 minutes before slicing and serving to allow the cheese to set slightly.

GRACE NOTE

SOME POINTERS FOR MAKING A BETTER PIZZA

Your sauce should not be too thick, as it will thicken in the hot oven. You do not need a lot of sauce, and you do not even need red sauce at all. Pesto, white or brown sauce, and cheese without sauce are viable options. Fresh clams tossed in garlic oil and spices (as made justifiably famous at Frank Pepé's Pizzeria in New Haven, Connecticut) is an amazing combination, topped with a sprinkle of dry aged cheese like romano or Parmesan. Less is more—but make the less truly more by using quality ingredients.

In general, I prefer a blend of 3 cheeses. One is a fresh hard cheese (not boxed or pregrated), such as romano, Asiago, Parmesan, or Sonoma dry Jack. The second is a good "melter," such as

mozzarella, Monterey Jack, Fontina, provolone, or Gruyère. The third can be any favorite, including some version of blue cheese or Cheddar. I grate or shred them with 1 part hard cheese to 2 parts "melter" and 1 part optional. Then I mix in a few teaspoons of a variety of dried or fresh herbs and spices, such as basil, oregano, thyme, *herbes de Provence*, black pepper, and granulated or fresh garlic. This blend gives the cheese a more interesting appearance and boosts the herbal flavor of the sauce.

The dough does not need a preformed "lip," but one inevitably occurs because the edge is usually thicker than the center and it doesn't have any sauce to hold it down. Do not try to build up the edge by crimping—you want it to bubble up on its own and create a light, airy crumb.

Poolish Baguettes

Bernard Ganachaud, in the early 1960s, made the *poolish* baguette the first legitimate alternative to the 60-2-2 baguette of the Parisian masses. When he retired 30 years later, his *la flûte Gana* was a licensed commodity, and bakers who paid for the right to make it were allowed to charge an extra franc above the government-controlled price. In the Coupe du Monde bread competition, the *poolish* baguette is now the standard that all countries must replicate. In my visits to the *boulangeries* of Paris, the *poolish* baguette made at the original Boulangerie Ganachaud was the second best baguette I ever had, with the first being the *pain à l'ancienne* of Philippe Gosselin. (I have since discovered many other great baguettes but, remember, I wrote this introduction back in 2002.) Ganachaud has a special medium-extraction flour (with his name prominently displayed on the bags, naturally) from which the bakery makes his baguettes, and there isn't any flour quite like it in America available at supermarkets for home bakers (though King Arthur and other mail-order operations now offer high- and medium-extraction flours for the home baker). It is slightly higher in ash content and bran than regular bread flour, more like clear flour (see page 28). The closest I've come to replicating that flour is described below and it makes a wonderful baguette, perhaps as good as can be done outside of the magical environment of Paris and without true Ganachaud-endorsed flour. Some people prefer it to the Gosselin baguette. See what you think.

BREAD PROFILE
Lean, standard dough; indirect method; commercial yeast

. . .

DAYS TO MAKE: 2
DAY 1: 3 to 4 hours *poolish*

DAY 2: 1 hour to de-chill *poolish;* 12 to 15 minutes mixing; 6 hours stretch and fold, fermentation, shaping, and proofing; 15 to 25 minutes baking

. . .

COMMENTARY
This formula, in the original *Bread Baker's Apprentice,* called for 8 ounces (227g) sifted whole wheat flour, but many people don't have sieves fine enough to filter out the bran (what we're trying to do is approximate the grade of flour known as high-extraction flour). So I have modified this formula to this new version, which is easier and just as good as the original.

Makes 3 small baguettes

MEASURE	OUNCES	GRAMS	INGREDIENTS	%
1 cup	7	198	*poolish* (page 112)	41.2
3½ tablespoons	1	28	whole wheat flour, sifted (or high-extraction or French type 65 flour)	6
3½ cups	16	218	unbleached bread flour	94
1½ teaspoons	0.37	10.5	salt	2.2
¾ teaspoon	0.08	2.25	instant yeast	0.47
1¼ cups	10	284	water, lukewarm (90°F to 100°F/32°C to 38°C)	58.8
All-purpose or bread flour, semolina, or cornmeal for dusting				
TOTAL				202.7

	OUNCES	GRAMS	INGREDIENTS	%
	19.4	550	bread flour	95.1
	1	28	whole wheat flour	4.9
	0.37	10.5	salt	1.8
	0.11	3	instant yeast	0.5
	13.6	386	water	67
TOTAL				169.3

1   Remove the *poolish* from the refrigerator 1 hour before making the dough to take off the chill.

2   Stir together the flours, salt, and yeast in a 4-quart mixing bowl (or in the bowl of an electric mixer). Add the *poolish* and all but 2 tablespoons of the water, and stir with a large spoon (or mix on low speed with the paddle attachment) until the ingredients form a ball, about 1 to 2 minutes. Add the remaining water or more flour as needed to create a dough that is soft but not sticky.

3   Sprinkle bread flour on the counter (or use the oil slick method, as described on page 59), transfer the dough to the counter, and begin to knead (or mix on medium speed with the dough hook). Knead or mix for about 6 minutes by machine), sprinkling in more bread flour if needed. The dough should be soft and pliable, tacky but not sticky. It should pass the windowpane test (page 61) and register 77°F to 81°F (25°C to 27°C). Lightly oil a large bowl and transfer the dough to the bowl, rolling it around to coat it with oil. Cover the bowl with plastic wrap. After 30 minutes, stretch and fold the dough (see page 59), return it to the bowl, and cover the bowl. Repeat again after another 30 minutes and return to the covered bowl.

4   Ferment at room temperature for approximately 2 hours, or until the dough nearly doubles in size. Remove the dough and stretch and fold it again. Return the dough to the bowl and cover it again.

5   Ferment for an additional 2 hours at room temperature; the dough should double in size.

6   Lightly sprinkle flour on the counter (or make an oil slick) and gently transfer the dough to the counter. Divide it into 3 equal pieces with a pastry scraper or serrated knife, being careful to degas it as little as possible. Shape the pieces into baguettes, as shown on page 78, and prepare them for proofing as described on page 33, using either the *couche* technique or parchment dusted with semolina, flour, or cornmeal.

7   Proof the baguettes at room temperature for 50 to 60 minutes, or until they grow to about 1½ times their original size and are still slightly springy to the touch.

8 Prepare your oven for hearth baking as described on page 97, making sure to have an empty steam pan in place. Preheat the oven to 500°F (260°C). Score the baguettes as shown on page 95.

9 Generously dust a peel or the back of a sheet pan with semolina, flour, or cornmeal and very gently transfer the dough pieces to the peel or pan. Transfer the baguettes to the baking stone (or bake directly on the sheet pan). Pour 1 cup hot water into the steam pan and close the door. After 30 seconds, spray the oven walls with water and close the door. Repeat twice more at 30-second intervals. After the final spray, lower the oven setting to 450°F (232°C) and bake for 10 minutes. Check the bread at this point and rotate 180 degrees, if necessary, for even baking. Continue baking for 8 to 12 minutes, or until the loaves are a rich golden brown and register at least 205°F (96°C) in the center. If they seem to be getting too dark before reaching this temperature, reduce the oven to 350°F (177°C), or turn it off, and bake for an additional 5 to 10 minutes.

10 Remove the bread from the oven and let cool on a rack for at least 40 minutes before slicing or serving.

• • •

It's always easiest to make the *poolish* the day before (or up to 3 days in advance) and then pull it out of the refrigerator an hour before you need it. However, you can also make it the same day as the final dough, as long as you make it about 8 hours in advance to give it plenty of time to bubble up and ferment.

• • •

It never hurts to add some old dough, *pâte fermentée*, if you have any hanging around from previous projects, in addition to the *poolish* (no other adjustments are necessary since *pâte fermentée* is a complete formula unto itself). I've added up to 50 percent (in this recipe that would equal about 8 ounces) and found that it reduces fermentation time by about 20 percent without any loss in flavor. In fact, some people like it even better than with *poolish* alone.

Portuguese Sweet Bread

BREAD PROFILE
Enriched, standard dough;
indirect method; commercial
yeast

• • •

DAYS TO MAKE: 1
1 to 1½ hours sponge;
15 minutes mixing; 5 to
7 hours fermentation, shaping, and proofing; 50 to
60 minutes baking

• • •

COMMENTARY
In addition to sandwiches and
snack bread, one of the great
uses for Portuguese sweet
bread is French toast. It is very
addictive. It also is ideal for
bread pudding.

• • •

Osmotolerant yeast, such as
SAF Gold (page 63), is a special strain of yeast designed
for sweet doughs like this
one, but it is not always
easy to find. The recipe will
work with regular instant
yeast, but if you can find it,
the osmotolerant yeast will
probably ferment the dough
more quickly. In the sponge
method, I call for dissolving
the instant yeast in water
before it is added to the flour,
a step not usually required.
Here, however, it helps regular
instant yeast perform more
like osmotolerant instant
yeast.

When I moved back to the East Coast in 1999, to Providence, Rhode Island, I found myself in the center of the Portuguese sweet bread universe. When I lived in California, I knew it as Hawaiian bread, but upon closer reading of the label, I learned that even the Hawaiians give credit to the Portuguese for this big, soft, sweet, round pillow of a loaf.

One man I know from Los Angeles who summers on Nantucket told me he was in love with the sandwiches made on this bread from a small shop on the island. He was the first person I met with the same passion for this bread that many people feel toward rustic and wild-yeast breads of the artisan movement. When I began teaching at Johnson & Wales University, I found that each of my classes included at least one student who shared my friend's passion for this sweet bread. Each of these students vowed to improve upon the general formula, and the version that follows is a result of the many tweaks the students who grew up with the real deal gave to the original version in an effort to make it conform to their childhood memories.

The most distinctive aspect of this bread, besides the softness and the shape, is the flavor imparted by the powdered milk (we call it DMS, for Dried Milk Solids). I have tried making versions with whole milk and buttermilk, but once you get the taste of the powdered-milk version in your mind, no other taste will do.

Makes two 1-pound (453g) loaves

MEASURE	OUNCES	GRAMS	INGREDIENTS	%
SPONGE				
½ cup	2.25	64	unbleached bread flour	14.3
1 tablespoon	0.5	14	granulated sugar	3.2
2¼ teaspoons	0.25	7	instant yeast (or osmotolerant yeast; see Commentary)	1.6
½ cup	4	113	water, at room temperature	25.4
DOUGH				
6 tablespoons	3	85	granulated sugar	19
1 teaspoon	0.25	7	salt	1.6
¼ cup	1.25	35	powdered milk (DMS)	7.9
2 tablespoons	1	28	unsalted butter, at room temperature	6.3
2 tablespoons	1	28	vegetable oil	6.3

2 large	3.3	93.5	eggs	21
1 teaspoon	0.17	5	lemon extract	1.1
1 teaspoon	0.17	5	orange extract	1.1
1 teaspoon	0.17	5	vanilla extract	1.1
3 cups	13.5	382	unbleached bread flour	85.7
¼ cup plus 2 tablespoons	3	85	water, at room temperature	19

EGG WASH

1 egg, whisked with 1 teaspoon water until frothy, for egg wash

TOTAL 214.6

1   To make the sponge, stir together the flour and sugar in a bowl. In a separate bowl, dissolve and stir the yeast into the water, then stir in the flour and sugar mixture, stirring until all the ingredients are hydrated and a smooth batter forms. Cover the bowl with plastic wrap and ferment at room temperature for 1 to 1½ hours, or until the sponge gets foamy and seems on the verge of collapse.

2   To make the dough, combine the sugar, salt, powdered milk, butter, and oil in a 4-quart mixing bowl (or the bowl of an electric mixer). Cream together with a sturdy spoon (or the paddle attachment) until smooth, then mix in the eggs and the extracts. Knead by hand (or switch to the dough hook) and mix in the sponge and the flour. Add the water, as needed, to make a very soft dough. The finished dough should be very supple and soft, easy to knead, tacky but not wet or sticky. It will take 10 to 12 minutes, with the mixer or by hand, to achieve this consistency. (Dough with high amounts of fat and sugar usually takes longer to knead because the gluten requires more time to set up.) The finished dough should pass the windowpane test (page 61) and register 77°F to 81°F (25°C to 27°C). Lightly oil a large bowl and transfer the dough to the bowl, rolling it around to coat it with oil. Cover the bowl with plastic wrap.

3   Ferment at room temperature for approximately 2 to 3 hours, or until the dough doubles in size.

4   Remove the dough from the bowl and divide it into 2 equal pieces. Form each of the pieces into a *boule*, as shown on page 76. Lightly oil two 9-inch (23cm) pie pans and place 1 *boule*, seam side down, in each pan. Mist the dough with spray oil and loosely cover the pans with plastic wrap.

5   Proof at room temperature for 2 to 3 hours, or until the dough fills the pans fully, doubling in size and overlapping the edges slightly. (If you only want to bake 1 loaf, you can retard the second loaf in the refrigerator for 1 day, although it will take 4 to 5 hours to proof after it comes out of the refrigerator.)

6 Very gently brush the loaves with the egg wash. Preheat the oven to 350°F (177°C) with the oven rack on the middle shelf.

7 Bake the loaves for 50 to 60 minutes, or until they register 190°F (88°C) in the center. After 30 minutes, check the loaves and rotate 180 degrees, if necessary, for even baking. Because of the high amount of sugar, the dough will brown very quickly, but don't be fooled into thinking it is done. Each loaf will get darker as the center gradually catches up with the outside, but it will not burn. The final color will be a rich mahogany brown.

8 Remove the bread from the pie pans and place on a rack to cool. The bread will soften as it cools, resulting in a very soft, pillowy loaf. Allow the bread to cool for at least 1½ hours before slicing or serving.

Potato Rosemary Bread

Rosemary has become a popular herb as culinary interest has grown and many of us have discovered how easy it is to cultivate it in our kitchen or backyard. It also has been overused, or used with a heavy hand in some instances, so I always advise restraint with rosemary: a little goes a long way.

The Italians call this bread *panmarino*, and it is to them that we owe thanks for this interesting concept. This bread is a good one for answering the question, what do I do with these leftover mashed potatoes? The potato starch softens the dough and gives the bread a pleasing tenderness, while the dough delivers other complex flavors from the *biga* and rosemary infusion.

Makes two 1-pound (453g) loaves or 18 dinner rolls

MEASURE	OUNCES	GRAMS	INGREDIENTS	%
1¼ cups	7	198	*biga* (page 113)	50
3 cups plus 2 tablespoons	14	397	unbleached high-gluten or bread flour	100
1½ teaspoons	0.38	11	salt	2.7
¼ teaspoon	0.03	0.85	black pepper, coarsely ground (optional)	0.21
1¼ teaspoons	0.14	4	instant yeast	1
1 cup	6	170	mashed potatoes	42.9
1 tablespoon	0.5	14	olive oil	3.6
2 tablespoons	0.25	7	coarsely chopped fresh rosemary	1.8
¾ cup plus 2 tablespoons	7	198	water, at room temperature (or warm if potatoes are cold)	53.6
4 tablespoons	1	28	coarsely chopped roasted garlic (optional)	7.1
Semolina or cornmeal for dusting				
Olive oil for brushing on top				
TOTAL				262.9

(continued)

BREAD PROFILE

Enriched, standard dough; indirect method; commercial yeast

. . .

DAYS TO MAKE: 2
DAY 1: 2½ to 4 hours *biga*

DAY 2: 1 hour to de-chill *biga*; 12 minutes mixing; 4 to 5 hours stretch and fold, fermentation, shaping, and proofing; 20 to 45 minutes baking

. . .

COMMENTARY

You can garnish this bread attractively by embossing a sprig of fresh rosemary in the top of the loaf. Mist the dough with water just after the final shaping and lay the sprig flat so that it adheres fully. Don't leave any of the needles hanging in the air, as they will burn during the baking stage without the protection of the dough.

. . .

Also, use oven- or pan-roasted garlic, not fresh or uncooked garlic, as the enzymes in raw garlic can adversely affect the gluten development of the dough. If you ever use fresh garlic in a dough, it should be added only during the final shaping stage.

TOTAL DOUGH FORMULA AND %

	OUNCES	GRAMS	INGREDIENTS	%
	18.25	517	high-gluten or bread flour	100
	0.38	11	salt	2.1
	0.14	4	instant yeast	0.8
	0.03	1	black pepper	0.2
	0.25	7	rosemary	1.4
	1	28	roasted garlic	5.4
	6	170	mashed potatoes	33
	10.25	291	water	56.3
	0.5	28	olive oil	5.4
TOTAL				204.6

1   Remove the *biga* from the refrigerator 1 hour before you plan to make the bread. Cut it into about 10 small pieces with a pastry scraper or serrated knife. Cover with a towel or plastic wrap and let sit for 1 hour to take off the chill.

2   Stir together the flour, salt, black pepper, and yeast in a 4-quart mixing bowl (or in the bowl of an electric mixer). Add the *biga* pieces, mashed potatoes, oil, rosemary, and ¾ cup plus 2 tablespoons water. Stir with a large spoon (or mix on low speed with the paddle attachment) for 1 minute, or until the ingredients form a ball. Add more water, if necessary, or more flour, if the dough is too sticky.

3   Sprinkle flour on the counter, transfer the dough to the counter, and begin to knead (or mix on medium speed with the dough hook). Knead or mix for approximately 6 minutes, adding more flour if needed, until the dough is soft and supple, tacky but not sticky. It should pass the windowpane test (page 61) and register 77°F to 81°F (25°C to 27°C). Flatten the dough and spread the roasted garlic over the top. Gather the dough into a ball and knead it by hand for 1 minute (you will probably have to dust it with flour first to absorb the moisture from the garlic). Lightly oil a large bowl and transfer the dough to the bowl, rolling it around to coat it with oil. Cover the bowl with plastic wrap. After 20 minutes, stretch and fold the dough (see page 59) and return it to the covered bowl. Repeat two more times at 20-minute intervals, each time returning the dough to the covered bowl.

4   Ferment at room temperature for approximately 2 hours, or until the dough doubles in size.

5   Remove the dough from the bowl and divide it into 2 equal pieces for loaves, or 18 equal pieces (about 2 ounces each) for dinner rolls. Shape each of the larger pieces into a *boule*, as shown on page 76, or shape the smaller pieces into rolls, as shown on page 86. Line a sheet pan with baking parchment (use 2 pans for rolls) and dust lightly with semolina or cornmeal. Place the dough on the parchment, separating the pieces so that they will not touch even after they rise. Mist the dough with spray oil and cover loosely with plastic wrap.

6   Proof at room temperature for 1 to 2 hours (depending on the size of the pieces), or until the dough doubles in size.

7   Preheat the oven to 400°F (204°C) with the oven rack on the middle shelf. Remove the plastic from the dough and lightly brush the breads or rolls with olive oil. You do not need to score these breads, but you can if you prefer (see page 95).

8   Place the pan(s) in the oven. Bake the loaves for 20 minutes and then rotate the pan 180 degrees for even baking. The loaves will take 35 to 45 minutes total to bake. Bake the rolls for 10 minutes, rotate the pans, and then bake for 10 minutes longer. The loaves and rolls will be a rich golden brown all around, and the internal temperature should register at least 195°F (91°C). The loaves should make a hollow sound when thumped on the bottom. If the loaves or rolls are fully colored but seem too soft, turn off the oven and let them bake for an additional 5 to 10 minutes to firm up.

9   Remove the finished loaves or rolls from the oven and let cool on a rack for at least 1 hour for loaves and 20 minutes for rolls before serving.

Pugliese

Pugliese refers to the southeastern Italian region of Puglia, but the variations on loaves with this name are endless. Many of the versions I've seen in the United States are similar to ciabatta—sometimes they actually are ciabatta but are called pugliese just to differentiate them from the competition. What is the same is that both of these breads, along with many others, fall into the category of rustic breads, which we define as hydration in excess of 65 percent, usually approaching 80 percent. In Italy, where the flour is naturally more extensible than the very elastic North American flour that we use, there is no need to overhydrate. But here we need to pump more water into the dough in order to stretch the gluten strands, giving the loaves their distinctive big-hole structure and delicious nutlike flavor.

One distinction between ciabatta, which is said to have originated in the Lake Como region of Lombardy (northern Italy), and pugliese is that pugliese breads are usually baked in rounds rather than in the slipper shape of ciabatta. *Pain rustique*, the French version of a rustic bread, is also slightly elongated, but it is more of a *bâtard* or rectangle than a slipper shape. Those, along with the *pain à l'ancienne* baguette (page 199) and the very elongated *stirato* and stubby *pain rustique* (pictured on page 142, made from the ciabatta dough), are all rustic breads, each with its own shape and ingredient makeup. An important distinction of the true pugliese bread, and one not always seen in American versions, is the use of golden durum flour, finely milled and packaged as fancy or extra fancy durum flour. Fancy durum is milled from the same strain of durum wheat as the sandy semolina flour that is sprinkled underneath hearth loaves and used in *pane siciliano* (page 207), but it is milled more finely.

There are bakeries in Puglia that make this bread with 100 percent fancy durum flour and some that use a blend of durum and regular bread flours. In the following formula, I suggest a blend, but feel free to play around with the proportions, moving even into a 100 percent durum version when you feel adventurous. The challenge for anyone tackling this bread is getting comfortable with wet dough. Once you do, you will find it difficult to resist the desire to make rustic bread all the time; the softness and pliability of the dough give it a wonderful feeling in the hand. Combined with the flavor enhancement of long fermentation, this formula brings forth a loaf that is so dramatic, so delicious, and so much fun to make that it will forever change your opinion of what constitutes great bread.

(continued)

BREAD PROFILE

Lean, rustic dough; indirect method; commercial yeast

. . .

DAYS TO MAKE: 2

DAY 1: 2½ to 4 hours *biga*

DAY 2: 1 hour to de-chill *biga*; 9 to 10 minutes mixing; 5 to 5½ hours stretch and fold, fermentation, shaping, and proofing; 20 to 30 minutes baking

. . .

COMMENTARY

If you do not have fancy durum flour, you can substitute semolina, but use only one-third as much as the formula calls for and replace the rest with an equal amount of either unbleached high-gluten or bread flour. You can also make this without any durum or semolina by using only high-gluten or bread flour.

. . .

This dough is yeasted and also boosted by a *biga* preferment, but you can make a wild-yeast, mixed-method version by replacing the *biga* with an equal amount of firm sourdough starter (page 245).

Makes two 1-pound (453g) loaves

MEASURE	OUNCES	GRAMS	INGREDIENTS	%
2 cups	10.8	306	*biga* (page 113)	105
2¼ cups	10	284	fancy or extra fancy durum flour and unbleached bread flour, in any combination (such as a 50-50 blend)	100
1½ teaspoons	0.38	11	salt	3.8
1 teaspoon	0.11	3	instant yeast	1.1
¼ cup	2	57	mashed potatoes (optional)	20
1 cup to 1 cup plus 2 tablespoons	8 to 9	227 to 255	water, lukewarm (90°F to 100°F/32°C to 38°C)	80 to 90
Semolina or cornmeal for dusting				
TOTAL				309.9 to 314.9

TOTAL DOUGH FORMULA AND %

	OUNCES	GRAMS	INGREDIENTS	%
	6.6	187	bread flour	40
	10	284	durum flour/bread flour blend (50-50 or your choice)	60
	0.38	11	salt	2.5
	0.12	4	instant yeast	0.85
	2	57	mashed potatoes	12
	12.7	360	water	76.4
TOTAL				191.75

1   Remove the *biga* from the refrigerator 1 hour before making the dough. Cut it into about 10 small pieces with a pastry scraper or serrated knife. Cover with a towel or plastic wrap and let sit for 1 hour to take off the chill.

2   Stir together the flour, salt, and yeast in a 4-quart mixing bowl (or in the bowl of an electric mixer). Add the *biga* pieces, mashed potatoes, and 1 cup (227g) of water. (If you are using all bread flour instead of durum, start with ¾ cup plus 2 tablespoons/198g water.) Using a large metal spoon (or on low speed with the paddle attachment), mix until the ingredients form a wet, sticky ball. If there is still some loose flour, add additional water as needed and continue to mix.

Because it is so wet, this dough is well-suited to mixing in a food processor. Follow the food processor instructions on page 57.

Mashed potato shows up as an ingredient in some versions of pugliese. A small amount adds a nice flavor and tenderizes the bread because of the potato starch. In this formula, it is an optional ingredient; if you use it, you may have to increase the flour to compensate for the added moisture. Be sure to use mashed potatoes that have already been seasoned with salt, such as those left over from dinner.

The amount of water in the final dough largely determined by the particular type and brand of flour you choose. Durum flour, in any form, tends to absorb more water than bread flour, so use the amount of water listed only as a guideline and starting point. Be prepared to adjust as the dough demands.

This dough also makes exceptional pizza dough or focaccia. See pages 168 and 221 for instructions on shaping it for these applications.

3   If you are mixing by hand, repeatedly dip one of your hands or the metal spoon into cold water and use it, much like a dough hook, to work the dough vigorously into a smooth mass while rotating the bowl in a circular motion with the other hand (see page 58). Reverse the circular motion a few times to develop the gluten further. Do this for about 5 minutes, or until the dough is smooth and the ingredients are evenly distributed. If you are using an electric mixer, switch to the dough hook and mix on medium speed for 4 to 5 minutes, or for as long as it takes to create a smooth, sticky dough. The dough should clear the sides of the bowl but stick to the bottom of the bowl. If the dough is still very sticky against the sides of the bowl, sprinkle in a little more flour (either type) until it clears the sides. Don't be alarmed if the dough seems very sticky. The wetter it is, the better the final bread will be.

4   Sprinkle enough bread flour on the counter to make a bed about 8 inches (20cm) square (or use the oil slick method, as described on page 59). Using a scraper or spatula dipped in water, transfer the dough to the bed of flour (or the oil slick) and proceed with the stretch-and-fold method shown on page 59. Mist the top of the dough with spray oil and loosely cover with plastic wrap or a food-grade plastic bag.

5   Let rest for 30 minutes. Repeat the stretch-and-fold method, mist again with spray oil, and re-cover. Let the dough rest another 30 minutes. (Each time you repeat this process, the dough will become stronger, more elastic, and less sticky.)

6   Lightly oil a large mixing bowl. For the third time, repeat the stretch-and-fold technique. With a spatula dipped in water, transfer the dough to the bowl. Cover the bowl with plastic wrap and ferment the dough at room temperature for 2 hours, undisturbed.

7   Generously dust the counter with flour. Uncover the dough and, using your hands and a bowl scraper dipped in flour, transfer the dough to the counter, taking care not to degas the dough any more than necessary. With a metal pastry scraper that has been dipped into flour, or a serrated knife dusted with flour, divide the dough into 2 equal pieces. Again dipping your hands into flour, gently shape the dough pieces into 2 *boules*, as shown on page 76. Let them relax, seam side down, on the counter for a few minutes while you prepare the proofing bowls.

8   Prepare 2 proofing bowls as shown on page 35, making sure to coat with spray oil and generously dust the entire surface of the cloth with flour. Gently transfer each dough portion, seam side up, to a bowl. If the seam opens up, pinch it closed. Mist the top of the dough with spray oil and cover the bowls with the flaps of the cloth.

9   Proof at room temperature for 1 to 1½ hours, or until the dough has expanded to about 1½ times its original size.

10   Prepare the oven for hearth baking as described on page 97, making sure to have an empty steam pan in place. Preheat the oven to 500°F (260°C).

11   Generously dust a peel or the back of a sheet pan with semolina or cornmeal. Gently transfer the dough to the peel or pan by carefully turning each bowl over onto the peel or pan, lifting off the bowl, and then carefully peeling off the cloth. The dough will spread out on the peel

or pan. With a sharp razor blade or French *lame* (page 96), score the loaves with a pound (#) sign, though you can also leave the loaves unscored. Transfer the dough to the baking stone (or bake on the sheet pan). Pour 1 cup hot water into the steam pan and close the door. After 30 seconds, spray the oven walls with water and close the door again. Repeat twice more at 30-second intervals. After the final spray, lower the oven setting to 450°F (232°C) and bake for 15 minutes. Check the loaves at this point and rotate 180 degrees, if necessary, for even baking. Continue baking for 5 to 15 minutes, or until the breads are a deep golden brown and register about 205°F (96°C) in the center.

12 Remove the loaves from the oven and transfer them to a rack. The crusts will soften somewhat as they cool. Allow the loaves to cool for at least 40 minutes before slicing or serving.

GRACE NOTE

BRUSCHETTA

Along with *grissini* (breadsticks), bruschetta, or sliced, toasted, and topped bread, has become a worldwide food trend. Bruschetta is yet another great Italian variation of pizza—that is, crust with topping. So much has been written about how to make so-called authentic bruschetta that I will add only a few comments to the canon.

You can use almost any kind of bread, but the best bread to use is rustic bread, like ciabatta or pugliese, with big holes and an easy-to-crisp texture. Slice it medium-thin, brush it with olive oil (garlic infused, if you like, or use garlic butter), and toast it under a broiler or in a sauté pan over medium-high heat until crisp. Then top it with your favorite topping, the most popular being fresh chopped tomatoes tossed with chopped fresh basil, extra virgin olive oil, coarse salt, and pepper. Another option is to simply rub a bread slice with a clove of garlic and then toast it.

You can return the topped slices to the broiler if you want to melt cheese or heat up the topping.

There are no rules governing toppings except one: flavor rules! Smoked eggplant purée is a topping that we love at home. To make it, buy 3 or 4 large eggplants and fire up a charcoal grill (this will not work as well on a gas grill, since you need the intense heat of hot coals). When the coals turn white, lay the whole eggplants on the grill 3 to 4 inches (8 to 10cm) above the coals. Turn them every 10 minutes, grilling until the outsides are charred and the insides are a soft mush. This will take 40 to 60 minutes. It is important to grill the eggplants until they become very mushy. Transfer them to a brown paper bag and close the bag to let them steam. When the eggplants are cool enough to handle, after 20 to 30 minutes, cut them open. Working with one at a time, scoop the soft interior eggplant flesh into a bowl. Discard the charred skin, the hard core, and any large seed sacs. Season the flesh with fresh lemon juice (about 2 tablespoons per eggplant), extra virgin olive oil (about 1 tablespoon per eggplant), and coarse salt to taste (start with ½ teaspoon per eggplant and increase from there). Purée this mixture in a food processor, adjusting the salt and lemon juice to taste. Black pepper or cayenne pepper can be added to taste, as can oven- or pan-roasted garlic. This makes a very smoky, lively dip, perfect for spreading on bruschetta and serving either room temperature or warm.

NOTE: Some people with gas stoves smoke the eggplants by turning them at 3-minute intervals over a gas burner, resting the eggplant against the grate as it chars. This is a messy but viable alternative to grilling over hot coals.

SOURDOUGH BREAD
AND VARIATIONS

COMMENTARY
Before embarking on the wild-yeast adventure, be sure to review the discussion on pages 67 to 69.

• • •

If you want to make a pure rye starter for 100 percent rye bread (rather than convert a regular starter as shown in most of the following rye-bread formulas), you can substitute whole rye or white (aka light) rye flour wherever the steps call for high-gluten or bread flour.

• • •

You can also make this seed culture with wheat flour alone, replacing the rye of Day 1 with unbleached bread or high-gluten flour. I find that the rye adds a more complex flavor and sort of jump-starts the process, but in the end, the seed culture will develop regardless of the flour you use.

What we call sourdough bread should more correctly be called wild-yeast bread, as it is natural wild yeast that leavens the loaf and not all wild-yeast breads taste sour. More important, as explained in the fermentation section on page 68, it is not the wild yeast that makes the bread sour, but the acids produced by the various bacteria that inhabit the dough. These acids lower the pH level of the dough, creating a wake of flavors in the process, most notably the distinctive sourness we associate with sourdough bread. This is the microbial world, quite active beyond our sight, constantly changing the medium, the bread dough, in which the organisms live.

There are dozens of valid methods for making wild-yeast breads, and every bakery has its own system. Some use a six-build system in which the starter is fed on a very specific schedule at precise times with precise temperatures, building (also called elaborating) the dough into larger and larger volumes until the last "build" serves as the starter for the final dough. These various builds, or elaborations, affect both flavor and structure. Some bakeries use only a simple two-build system, using a large portion (25 to 35 percent) of the previous batch of final dough as the starter for the next batch. Some systems use a wet-sponge *poolish*-like starter, others use a firm *biga*-like starter, and still others use a combination of the two. Many systems employ a combination of wild yeast and commercial yeast (called "spiking the dough") to create a hybrid loaf that is flavorful but faster rising and not too sour. Some bakeries use different systems for different breads (firm starter for one, sponge starter for another, spiked method for yet another), while other bakeries use a single master system and apply it to all of their breads. In other words, no single rule governs how to make a wild-yeast bread. I teach my students to first learn one system well and then feel free to learn as many systems as they want until they find the one that suits them best.

The wonderful artisan-style bakeries that now grace so many communities have introduced some beautiful and delicious versions of wild-yeast breads. They include multigrain variations; breads made with flavorful supplementary ingredients, such as roasted garlic, onions, potatoes, rosemary, and other herbs; and also wild-yeast rustic loaves made from wet dough (such as the wild-yeast pugliese variation mentioned on page 233). When we examine the art and science behind these loaves, we discover that each is made by the baker's chosen system and by his or her creative choice of ingredient variation. Again, each system involves choices: percentage of starter to use, method of starter, fermentation times and temperature, supplementary ingredients and design, and different blends of flours.

The following master system, like the one in my earlier book, *Crust & Crumb*, utilizes a three-build method. This system, however, uses a smaller percentage of wild-yeast starter and allows for greater variation in application. I still use both systems when I bake and teach. I love the chewy texture and flavor complexity of the *Crust & Crumb* sourdough (after all, I won a national bread competition with it), but I also appreciate the flexibility of the new system.

I would be remiss if I did not also say that if you already follow a system, whether self-taught or learned from another of the many excellent baking books available, you can apply the same principles to that system as you do to this one. In other words, you can be creative. A particular system of builds will produce subtle flavor or texture distinctions that differ from those of another system, but both systems, assuming they follow sound bread-baking science, will produce wonderful bread. In most instances, my starter in someone else's system should work as well as theirs and vice versa. It is the thesis of this book that once armed with the empowerment tools of bread baking—knowledge and information—you should be able to navigate the infinite options available to you. The broad strokes of the following formula can be used to make an unlimited number of recipe variations. The finer strokes of these variations will be addressed at the end of the formula.

My favorite sourdough variation is a walnut bread with blue cheese (see page 247).

Bear in mind that this system is designed for home baking and takes into consideration that home bakers do not have a crew to whom they can pass on feeding schedules. Very few people, for instance, have climate-controlled proof boxes that produce consistent results day after day. We fly without such a safety net (and so do many professional artisan bakers, by choice), but we still have the power to manipulate time and temperature to create amazing bread. The use of refrigeration is a modern invention not available to the great bakers of previous centuries. They did their manipulations by scrupulous attention to feeding cycles. Cold fermentation gives us a wider berth and a greater margin of error, and allows us to call our shots regarding when to take the next step in the twelve-stage process of bread making.

. . .

If you do not have pineapple juice or want to try using only water, use filtered or spring water. You can also substitute orange juice or even diluted lemon juice. The starter may or may not stay on the predicted feeding schedule, depending on the presence or absence of leuconostoc bacteria and other similar bacteria in your flour. Roughly 30 to 40 percent of starters end up with the leuconostoc problem, depending on the growing conditions in the wheat and rye fields that year. However, if you aerate, stir, or knead the starter a couple of times each day, the starter will eventually overcome any leuconostoc, even if you have not used pineapple juice.

. . .

Opinions are divided as to whether the pineapple juice is really necessary after Stage 1. It probably is not, but it won't hurt to use it during Stage 2 and may, in some instances, serve as insurance against the appearance of leuconostoc bacteria.

The following method will work with either organic or commercial flour and produces a mother starter, what I fondly call the barm, in 5 to 10 days, depending on the weather and location.

I updated my original seed culture to account for a strain of leuconostoc bacteria—and perhaps other bacteria as well—that hinders many starters but generates lots of carbon dioxide in the early stage of a seed culture starter, making it falsely seem that the wild-yeast cells are growing rapidly. I learned from a group of dedicated home bakers (all contributors to the King Arthur Flour Baker's Circle website) that the action of these bacteria can be counterbalanced by using pineapple juice or other acidic liquids on the first day or two. Of course, you can make this starter without the pineapple juice, as has been done for centuries; the acidic juice merely moves the process along more rapidly.

Seed Culture

MEASURE	OUNCES	GRAMS	INGREDIENTS	%
STAGE ONE (DAY 1)				
1 cup	4.25	120.5	coarse whole wheat or whole rye (or pumpernickel-grind) flour	100
½ cup	4	113	unsweetened pineapple juice (from a can) or orange juice, at room temperature	94
STAGE TWO (DAY 2)				
½ cup	2.25	64	unbleached high-gluten or bread flour	100
¼ cup	2	57	water or unsweetened pineapple juice, at room temperature	89
STAGE THREE (DAY 3 AND UP)				
1 cup	4.5	128	unbleached high-gluten or bread flour	100
½ cup	4	113	water, at room temperature	94
TOTAL				n/a

Stage One (Day 1): Mix the flour and juice together in a bowl until they form a wet, sticky dough or sponge. Be sure that all the flour is hydrated. Press this dough into a 4-cup (945ml) measuring beaker and place a piece of tape on the beaker to mark the top of the dough. Cover the beaker with plastic wrap and leave it at room temperature for 24 hours.

Stage Two (Day 2): The dough should not have risen much, if at all, during this time. In a mixing bowl, combine the Day 2 ingredients with the Day 1 sponge, mixing with your hand or a spoon until all the ingredients are evenly distributed to form a new sponge. This sponge will be even softer and wetter than the Day 1 sponge because of the switch to white flour (you can substitute whole wheat or whole rye flour if you prefer to make a 100 percent whole-grain starter). Return this to the beaker, pressing it down, and replace the old tape with a new piece of tape to mark the spot. Cover with plastic wrap and ferment for 24 hours at room temperature. Do not be put off by the strong aroma of the dough; it will eventually brighten. Even if there is fermentation activity, this does not always indicate wild-yeast activity. It is more likely bacterial fermentation masquerading as yeast activity, and the seed culture may go dormant for a few days as you enter Stage Three.

Stage Three (Day 3 and up): Check to see if there has been a rise or other activity in the dough. There may be some fermentation but not a lot, perhaps some bubbling or even up to a 50 percent rise. Regardless, discard half of the starter (or give it to a friend to cultivate) and mix the remaining half with the Day 3 ingredients to make a sticky sponge-like dough. Again, return it to the beaker and press it down. Reapply tape to the beaker to mark the top of the dough, cover, and ferment for 24 to 48 hours. If no observable rise has occurred after the first 24 hours, mix the dough again for a few seconds in a clean bowl, return it to the beaker, cover, and let it sit for another 24 hours. If there is still little or no rise or bubbling, repeat the mixing every 12 hours for up to 4 more days (Day 8), or until the dough shows signs of fermentation (bubbling) and growth to approximately 1½ times its original size, or even up to twice its size. This will usually occur sooner than Day 8 but not always, especially during cooler weather. Your seed culture is now ready to be turned into a barm, or mother starter. (Note: The mixing every 12 hours prevents molds from settling on the surface of the dough while the wild yeast and bacteria are growing in the dough. If the dough hasn't activated by Day 8, don't give up on it. Just keep stirring every 12 hours until it activates, even if it takes a few more days. It will happen.)

The full flavor of the barm will not develop until it has been refreshed 2 or 3 times over a 2-week period, during which time the organisms indigenous to your region will gradually take charge of it. (This is why a starter made from a seed culture imported from Egypt or Russia will, over time, produce bread that tastes like a starter made locally from scratch.) When the barm reaches its peak flavor, you will be able to maintain that flavor with periodic refreshments. However, you can begin using the barm as soon as it ripens. The leavening power will be strong from the first, since the wild yeast ferments the barm at a faster pace than the bacteria produce their flavorful acids.

Barm (Mother Starter)

Makes approximately 4 cups (1¾ pounds/794g) barm

MEASURE	OUNCES	GRAMS	INGREDIENTS	%
2 cups	9	255	unbleached high-gluten or bread flour	100
1 cup plus 2 tablespoons	9	255	water, at room temperature	100
1 cup	7	198	seed culture (page 240)	78
TOTAL				278

Stir together the flour, water, and seed culture in a mixing bowl (you can discard the remaining seed culture or give it to a friend to build into his or her own barm, or refrigerate it for up to 5 days as backup in case you need it). Make sure the seed culture is evenly distributed and all the flour is hydrated. It will be a wet, sticky sponge similar to a *poolish* (page 112). Note: If you prefer to work with a firmer mother starter, you can reduce the water to 4 to 5 ounces (113g to 142g) and knead by hand or mix in an electric mixer with the dough hook.

Transfer this sponge to a clean plastic, glass, or ceramic storage container that is twice as large as the barm is. When transferring it to the container, repeatedly dip your hand, spatula, or bowl scraper in water to keep the barm from sticking to it. Cover the container with a lid or plastic wrap and ferment at room temperature for 6 to 8 hours, until the barm is bubbly. The plastic wrap or plastic lid will swell like a balloon. When this happens, lift the lid or plastic wrap to let the gas escape (try not to breathe it as it escapes, as the carbonic gas mixed with ethanol fumes will knock you across the room!). Replace the cover and refrigerate the barm overnight, where it will slowly continue fermenting and growing while it also goes dormant. It will be ready to use the next day and will remain potent for 3 to 5 days. After that, or if you use more than half, you will need to refresh it as described next.

REFRESHING THE BARM

- The standard refreshment for barm is at least to double it. You can also quadruple it, however, as the organisms in the barm are capable of feeding on a large refreshment, up to 5 times the weight of the barm in new flour, and converting it into fresh starter. I double the barm at each feeding if I want a very sour bread, but I triple, quadruple, or even quintuple it when I want a less sour flavor. Remember, it takes longer for the bacteria than the yeast to work, so while a larger feeding dilutes both the bacterial and the wild-yeast communities, the yeast bounces back faster than the bacteria, creating a strong, but less acidic, leavening sponge. But by the second or third day in the refrigerator, the bacterial fermentation does catch up, and the sponge becomes quite acidic and sour (with a pH level of about 3.5). (Note: for those who don't think their starter is sour enough, you can add up to 1 ounce/28g of granulated sugar to it when you refresh it, which will promote the growth of more sour-producing bacteria. But only use this trick after first testing your unsugared starter in a bread or two.)

- It is important to understand what happens when you refresh the barm. After 4 to 7 days, the acids and protease enzymes in a barm that has not been refreshed break down the gluten, turning what was at first a strong, stringy sponge into a protein-weak, potato-soup–like consistency. There are still plenty of live organisms to leaven and flavor bread, but they will make a flaccid dough. For this reason, it is advisable to feed your barm 3 days or sooner before you plan to use it in a bread (ideally, the day before). If you have a lot of barm but haven't fed it for a while, discard all but 1 cup (7 ounces/198g) and refresh that cup with 3½ cups flour (16 ounces/454g) and 2 cups (16 ounces/454g) water (use less water if keeping a firm mother starter), stirring until all the flour is hydrated.

- If you have been using and feeding your barm regularly, you do not necessarily have to discard any. However, what you do not want to do is, for example, use 1 cup barm from your supply to make some bread, then refresh the remaining barm with only 1 cup flour and some water. You must always at least double the remaining barm. You can do this by either throwing out or giving away some barm before you refresh it, or by using up more of it before refreshing it (remember, you have a 3-to-5-day window before you need to feed it again).

- If you do not plan to use the barm for a while, do not throw any away until you plan to refresh it again, and follow the guidance given (see Commentary) to refrigerate or freeze it in a tightly sealed container. Since you do not want to freeze a glass or ceramic container, you should transfer the barm to a zippered freezer bag that has been misted with spray oil, or use a plastic container (allow enough room for expansion and gas development).

- Use high-gluten flour, if possible, for the refreshments (except in the case of a rye barm), as it has more gluten than bread flour and can thus better withstand the acid and enzymatic degradation. However, bread flour will also work, especially because high-gluten flour is hard for home bakers to find.

- You can refresh in two ways. One is to weigh the amount of barm you plan to refresh and the other is to eyeball it. I use both methods and find that as long as you stay in the doubling to quadrupling ballpark, you will have no problem keeping your mother starter strong, active, and clean tasting. By clean tasting I mean that no off-flavors develop, such as a musty or cheesy flavor caused by overfermenting at warm temperatures or by leaving it out too long. This allows unwelcome bacteria to join the party or for the yeast to create too much alcohol, resulting in what we think of as a too yeasty flavor. The yeasty flavor is a combination of alcohol and glutathione, an unpleasant-tasting amino acid released by yeast as it dies.

. . .

If you want to save the barm but do not plan to make bread for a while, you can refrigerate it for at least 2 months in an airtight container and then refresh it by discarding all but 1 cup (or even ½ cup) and building up from there. Or, you can freeze the barm for up to 6 months and then defrost it in the refrigerator 3 days before you need it. When it has thawed enough to use (the next day), discard all but ½ cup and refresh as described at left. Then refresh again the next day, building back to 4 to 6 cups barm, depending on your need. The following day you will have a strong, ready-to-use barm. Of course, you still have 1 or 2 more days of dough building to accomplish, as described in the formulas.

- The weighing method is simple: weigh the barm and calculate how much flour and water it will take to double, triple, or quadruple the weight (the easiest way is to figure equal parts water and flour). Thus, if you plan to refresh a 1 pound (16 ounces/454g) barm, you can build it to 2 pounds (32 ounces/908g) by adding 8 ounces (227g) each of flour (1¾ cups) and water (1 cup); or you can quadruple it by adding 1½ pounds (680g) each of flour (5¼ cups) and water (3 cups). The larger the refreshment ratio, the longer the fermentation time, usually 4 to 8 hours, depending on the size of the refreshment and how cold the barm was when you started. If you are using a cold barm just out of the refrigerator, warm the water up to about 90°F (32°C) to compensate and to hasten the onset of fermentation. Never let the starter actually be warm, however. It is best for the organisms we want to cultivate, the lactic- and acetic-producing bacteria, if the starter ferments slowly, between 65°F and 75°F (18°C and 24°C), or at room temperature.

- When the starter is bubbly and foamy, put it in the refrigerator overnight before using it. Technically, though, you could begin using it as soon as it foams up, but I wait for the overnight development because I believe it gives the bread a more complex flavor. Either way, with a ripe and ready barm, you are ready to move on to the next build.

The barm, or mother starter (back), is a wet sponge similar to a *poolish*, while the firm starter, or *levain*, is about the same teture as a *biga* or French bread dough.

Basic Sourdough Bread
(aka San Francisco Sourdough)

Makes two 1½-pound (680g) loaves

Note: The amount of water in this starter will depend on how firm or wet you keep your barm mother starter. Adjust the water, as needed, according to the instructions.

MEASURE	OUNCES	GRAMS	INGREDIENTS	%
FIRM STARTER (DAY 1)				
⅔ cup	4	113	barm (mother starter), page 241	88.3
1 cup	4.5	128	unbleached bread flour	100
2 to 4 tablespoons	1 to 2	28 to 57	water	22 to 44
TOTAL				210.3 to 232.3
FINAL DOUGH (DAY 2)				
4½ cups	20.25	574	unbleached bread flour or other flour combination (see page 246)	100
2 teaspoons	0.5	14	salt	2.44
Use all	9.5 ounces (approx.)	269 (approx.)	firm starter	47
1¾ cups	14	397	water, lukewarm (90°F to 100°F/32°C to 38°C)	69
All-purpose or bread flour, semolina, or cornmeal for dusting				
TOTAL				218.4

TOTAL DOUGH FORMULA AND %

	OUNCES	GRAMS	INGREDIENTS	%
	25	709	bread flour	100
	0.44	12.5	salt	1.9
			(instant yeast, see Grace Note, page 246)	
	18.75	532	water	68.25
TOTAL				170.15

Lean, standard dough; indirect method; wild yeast

• • •

DAYS TO MAKE: 2 OR 3
DAY 1: 5 hours firm starter

DAY 2: 1 hour to de-chill firm starter; 15 to 17 minutes mixing; 5 to 8 hours stretch and fold, fermentation, shaping, and proofing; 25 to 35 minutes baking (day 2 or 3)

• • •

COMMENTARY
This dough is made with a three-build method: barm to firm starter (also called, in some bakeries, the *levain* or *chef*) to final dough. As noted earlier, this process could go on to four, five, or six builds, but by using cold fermentation (retarding), we develop maximum flavor without all the intermediate builds.

• • •

Feel free to veer from this method and modify either the technique or the ingredients as you see fit. Consult the Grace Note for a number of options, but only your imagination limits the full range of possibilities.

1   Day 1: To make the firm starter, remove the barm from the refrigerator 1 hour before you plan to make the firm starter and measure the barm. To measure it, dip a ⅔-cup measuring cup into a bowl of water, then scoop the cup into the barm, filling it (the wet cup will ensure the barm slides out easily). Or weigh the barm in a bowl on a scale. Transfer the measured barm to a small bowl, cover with a towel or plastic wrap, and allow it to warm up for 1 hour.

2   Add the flour to the bowl and mix the barm and the flour together, adding only enough additional water to allow you to knead the mixture into a small ball that has about the same texture as French bread dough (the amount of water will depend on whether you keep a wet or firm barm). You do not need to work this very long, just until all the flour is hydrated and the barm is evenly distributed. Lightly oil a small bowl or mist the inside of a plastic bag with spray oil, and place the starter in the bowl or bag, turning to coat it with oil. Cover the bowl or seal the bag.

GRACE NOTE

VARIATIONS OF SOUR-DOUGH INGREDIENTS AND METHODS

Some bakers prefer to work exclusively with firm starters, keeping even the mother starter in a firm state. Professional bakers like this because they can throw the firm piece easily into a mixer for either refreshing or elaborating. It is less messy than working with big batches of wet sponge. One of my baking friends, Keith Giusto of Central Milling in Petaluma, keeps his mother starter as a very dry, firm dough, like bagel dough. This makes it not only easy to transport and handle (assuming you have a mixer capable of handling such stiff dough) but also ensures a more sour bread, for those who like it extra sour. Acetic

bacteria prefer the denser, less-aerated environment of the firm starter; lactic bacteria prefer the wetter sponge of the barm method. Home bakers, I find, prefer keeping a wet sponge (barm), as it is easy to refresh and keep track of it in small batches. However, if you prefer to use the firm starter system, simply reduce the water weight to 50 to 60 percent of the flour weight when you refresh your mother starter and then make your elaborations.

It is also perfectly acceptable to make your final dough directly from the barm (as long as it has been refreshed within the past 3 days). You will have to diminish the water in the final dough to compensate for the wetness of the barm, but otherwise you can proceed with an equal amount of barm for firm starter.

To spike the dough with commercial yeast, which guarantees a 1½- to 2-hour first fermentation and a 1- to 1½-hour final proofing (and a less sour flavor), add up to 1½ teaspoons instant yeast (0.17 ounce/5g) to the final dough.

You can substitute other types of flour, including whole wheat flour, for some or all of the high-gluten or bread flour. A classic French *pain au levain* includes about 10 percent whole wheat or whole rye flour (or a combination of each— about ½ cup/2.5 ounces/64g total).

You can make a *meteil* rye bread (less than 50 percent rye flour), or a *seigle* rye bread (more than 50 percent rye flour), by substituting the desired amount of rye flour, either white rye or a blend of white and whole rye or pumpernickel

3 Ferment at room temperature for 4 to 6 hours, or until the starter has at least doubled in size. If necessary, give it additional time, checking every hour or so. Then, put it into the refrigerator overnight.

4 Day 2: To make the final dough, remove the firm starter from the refrigerator 1 hour before making the dough. Cut it into about 10 small pieces with a pastry scraper or serrated knife. Mist with spray oil, cover with a towel or plastic wrap, and let sit for 1 hour to take off the chill.

5 Stir together the flour and salt in a 4-quart mixing bowl (or in the bowl of an electric mixer). Add the starter pieces and water. Stir with a large metal spoon (or mix on low speed with the dough hook) to bring everything together into a ball.

grind. This can be done either in the final dough or in the firm starter (or you can use a rye barm; see the formula for 100% Sourdough Rye Bread on page 253).

You can add roasted garlic; lightly toasted walnuts, sunflower seeds, pecans, or other nuts and seeds of your choice; raisins and other dried fruits; or cheese. The standard amount is about 40 percent of the final flour weight. It is best to add these ingredients during the final 2 minutes of mixing to protect against breaking them up too small. My all-time favorite is a blue cheese and walnut bread with 25 percent toasted walnuts and 15 to 20 percent crumbled blue cheese (firm, not creamy), adding the walnuts during the last 2 minutes of kneading and carefully folding in the blue cheese by hand at the end of kneading during the stretch and fold process. You can do this by flattening the dough and sprinkling

one-third of the cheese over the top, then rolling it up and repeating this two more times until all the cheese is incorporated. If you are using salty cheese, such as blue, feta, or Parmesan, reduce the salt in the formula by 25 percent (to 1½ teaspoons). Incidentally, the oil from the walnuts will turn the dough a burgundy color and the delicious flavor of the walnuts will permeate the entire loaf.

Cooked potatoes can be used to tenderize and flavor the dough. Use a ratio of 25 percent potatoes to flour in the final build.

Fresh herbs can be used to taste. Hand roll them into the dough as you would blue cheese. Dried herbs and spices, such as *herbes de Provence*, cumin, and oregano, can also be used, but with a gentle touch, as these flavors can easily dominate.

It is just as valid to make rustic, wet-dough breads with wild-yeast starters as it is to use commercial yeast and yeast pre-ferments, or to use the mixed, or spiked, method. Substitute an equal amount of barm (this is a perfect time to build the dough directly from barm) for the *poolish*. You can add commercial yeast (or not) during the final dough stage, bearing in mind that spiking it with yeast will allow you to make the bread on the same schedule as already written in the instructions.

If you make pure wild-yeast rustic bread (no commercial yeast at all), you will have to give the dough a 3- to 4-hour bulk fermentation and a 1½-hour final proofing. You can make any of the rustic variations, from ciabatta to pugliese to focaccia, with this dough.

6   Sprinkle the counter with flour (or use the oil slick method, as described on page 59), transfer the dough to the counter, and knead by hand for 8 to 10 minutes (or mix with the dough hook on medium-low speed for 4 minutes, allow the dough to rest for 5 to 10 minutes, and then mix for 2 to 4 additional minutes). Adjust the water or flour as needed. The dough should be firm but supple and tacky, like French bread dough. It should pass the windowpane test (page 61) and register 77°F to 81°F (25°C to 27°C). Lightly oil a large bowl and transfer the dough to the bowl, rolling it around to coat it with oil. Cover the bowl with plastic wrap. After 20 minutes, stretch and fold the dough (see page 59) and return it to the covered bowl. Repeat two more times at 20-minute intervals, each time returning the dough to the covered bowl.

7   Ferment at room temperature for 3 to 4 hours, or until the dough has nearly doubled in size.

8   Gently remove the dough from the bowl and divide it into 2 equal pieces (about 22 ounces/624g each), being careful to degas the dough as little as possible. Gently shape the dough into *boules*, *bâtards*, or baguettes, as shown on pages 76 to 91.

9   Proof the dough in *bannetons* or proofing bowls, on *couches*, or on parchment-lined sheet pans that have been dusted with semolina or cornmeal (see pages 32 to 35). Regardless of the method, mist the exposed part of the dough with spray oil and loosely cover the dough with a towel or plastic wrap, or slip the pans into a food-grade plastic bag. At this point you can either proof the loaves for 2 to 4 hours, or until they have risen to about 1½ times in size or retard overnight in the refrigerator. If retarding them, remove them from the refrigerator approximately 4 hours before you plan to bake them to allow them to proof.

10   Prepare the oven for hearth baking as described on page 97, making sure to have a steam pan in place. Preheat the oven to 500°F (260°C). Carefully remove the towel or plastic wrap from the dough, or slip the pan from the bag, 10 minutes before baking.

11   Generously dust a peel or the back of a sheet pan with flour, semolina, or cornmeal and gently transfer the dough to the peel or pan, carefully removing the cloth liner from the top of the dough for dough proofed in a bowl. (If the dough was proofed on a sheet pan, it can be baked directly on that pan.) Score the dough as shown on page 96. Slide the dough onto the baking stone (or bake directly on the sheet pan). Pour 1 cup hot water into the steam pan and close the door. After 30 seconds, spray the oven walls with water and close the door. Repeat twice more at 30-second intervals. After the final spray, lower the oven setting to 450°F (232°C) and bake for 13 minutes. Rotate the loaves 180 degrees, if necessary, for even baking and continue baking for another 12 to 22 minutes, or until the loaves are done. They should register 205°F (96°C) in the center, be a rich golden brown all over, and sound hollow when thumped on the bottom.

12   Transfer the finished loaves to a rack and let cool for at least 45 minutes before slicing or serving.

New York Deli Rye

I grew up on two definitive deli sandwiches: roast beef, chicken fat (schmaltz), and onion; and corned beef, coleslaw, and Russian dressing. Both sandwiches had to be served on onion rye to complete the experience. At least twice a month, our family would head out to Murray's Deli, Hymie's Deli, or the Chuckwagon on City Line Avenue (the delis are still there, but the Chuckwagon is long gone), and the big decision for me was which of the two sandwiches I should order. I never tired of either, and years later, after emerging from a long vegetarian period, the first meat dish I sought out was a corned beef, coleslaw, and Russian dressing sandwich on onion rye. These days I limit my intake of corned beef, and, sadly, of schmaltz, but I still chronically yearn for those sandwiches. However, I do continue to enjoy onion rye whenever I can get my hands on some, often making it myself.

BREAD PROFILE
Enriched, standard dough; indirect method; mixed leavening method

• • •

DAYS TO MAKE: 2
DAY 1: 3 to 4 hours rye sponge starter

DAY 2: 1 hour to de-chill starter; 6 minutes mixing; approximately 5 hours stretch and fold, fermentation, shaping, and proofing; 50 to 60 minutes baking

• • •

COMMENTARY
The best rye breads are made with a mix of wild-yeast starter and commercial yeast. The use of the starter is what makes them so flavorful and also improves the structure of the dough, as the acidity controls excessive enzyme activity that can cause a rye bread to become gummy. The addition of onions is optional; the bread is excellent with or without them, but I think the onions are integral to that true deli taste of memory. Most bakeries use dried onions, but I prefer using lightly sautéed fresh onions.

Slices of New York Deli Rye (front and right) and Pumpernickel Bread (back).

Some people have never had rye bread without caraway seeds and as a result think that rye tastes like caraway. The caraway seeds are also optional here, and I suggest making this bread with and without them to determine which you prefer. Buttermilk tastes better than milk in this bread, but if you don't have any on hand, feel free to substitute whole or low-fat milk, or simply replace the milk with water.

You can make these loaves into what is called deli corn rye by proceeding as directed and then misting the shaped loaves with water and rolling the tops (or the entire loaf) in medium-grind or polenta-grind cornmeal. This gives the loaves a great corn crunch!

Makes two 2-pound (907g) or three 1½-pound (680g) sandwich loaves

MEASURE	OUNCES	GRAMS	INGREDIENTS	%
RYE SPONGE STARTER (DAY 1)				
1 cup	7	198	barm (mother starter, page 241)	154.7
1 cup	4.5	128	white (aka light) rye flour	100
½ cup	4	113	water, lukewarm (90°F to 100°F/32°C to 38°C)	88.3
2 medium	12	340	yellow or white onions, diced	266
2 tablespoons	1	28	vegetable oil	22
FINAL DOUGH (DAY 2)				
3½ cups	16	454	unbleached high-gluten, bread, or clear flour	78
1 cup	4.5	128	white (aka light) rye flour	22
2 tablespoons packed	1	28	brown sugar	4.9
2¼ teaspoons	0.56	16	salt	2.7
2 teaspoons	0.22	6	instant yeast	1
2 teaspoons	0.22	6	caraway seeds (optional)	1
2 tablespoons	1	28	vegetable oil	4.9
1 cup	8	227	buttermilk or milk, lukewarm (90°F to 100°F/32°C to 38°C)	39
½ cup	4	113	water, or as needed, at room temperature	19.5
Bread or high-gluten flour, semolina, or cornmeal for dusting				
1 egg white, whisked with 1 teaspoon water until frothy, for egg white wash (optional)				
TOTAL				173

TOTAL DOUGH FORMULA AND %

OUNCES	GRAMS	INGREDIENTS	%
19.5	553	high-gluten or clear flour	68.5
9	255	rye flour	31.5
12	340	onions	42
2	56	vegetable oil	7
0.56	16	salt	2
1	28	brown sugar	3.5
0.22	6	instant yeast	0.7
0.22	6	caraway seeds (optional)	(0.7)
7.5	212	water	26
8	227	buttermilk	28
TOTAL			209.2 (209.9)

1   Day 1: Make the starter a day ahead. Mix together the barm, rye flour, and water in a small bowl until the ingredients are evenly distributed and a sponge-like dough forms. Cover with plastic wrap and set it aside. Using a skillet, very lightly sauté the onions in the oil over medium heat just until they sweat. Transfer the onions to a bowl and let cool until warm (make sure they are not hot). Stir the warm onions into the starter, re-cover with plastic wrap, and ferment the starter at room temperature until it bubbles and foams, 3 to 6 hours. Refrigerate overnight.

2   Day 2: The next day, remove the starter from the refrigerator 1 hour before making the dough to take off the chill.

3   To make the dough, stir together the flours, brown sugar, salt, yeast, and caraway seeds (if using) in a 4-quart mixing bowl (or in the bowl of an electric mixer). Add the rye sponge starter (with the onions), oil, and buttermilk or milk. Stir with a large metal spoon until the mixture forms a ball (or mix on low speed with the dough hook or paddle attachment), adding only as much water as it takes to bring everything together into a soft, not sticky mass. Let this sit for 5 minutes so the gluten can begin to develop.

4   Sprinkle high-gluten or bread flour on the counter, transfer the dough to the counter, and begin kneading the dough (or mix on medium-low speed with the dough hook). Add only as much flour as needed to make a firm, slightly tacky dough. Try to complete the kneading in less than 6 minutes (4 to 5 minutes by machine) to prevent the dough from getting gummy. The dough should pass the windowpane test (page 61) and register 77°F to 81°F (25°C to 27°C). Lightly oil a large bowl and transfer the dough to the bowl, rolling it around to coat it with oil. Cover

the bowl with plastic wrap. After 20 minutes, stretch and fold the dough (see page 59) and return it to the covered bowl. Repeat three more times at 20-minute intervals, each time returning the dough to the covered bowl (80 minutes total for stretch and folds).

5   Ferment at room temperature for 1½ to 2 hours, or until the dough doubles in size.

6   Remove the dough from the bowl and divide it into 2 or 3 equal pieces (they will weigh about 30 ounces for larger loaves and 20 ounces for smaller loaves). Shape them into sandwich loaves (see page 85) or *bâtards* for freestanding loaves (see page 77). If you are baking them in loaf pans, lightly oil the pans (8½ by 4½-inch (22 by 11.5cm) pans for small loaves; 9 by 5-inch (23 by 13cm) pans for larger loaves). If you are baking them freestanding, line 1 or 2 sheet pans with baking parchment and dust with flour, semolina, or cornmeal. Transfer the shaped dough to the pans and mist the tops with spray oil.

7   Proof at room temperature for approximately 1½ hours, or until they have grown 1½ times in size. The dough in the loaf pans should dome about 1 inch above the lip of the pans.

8   Preheat the oven to 350°F (177°C) for loaf-pan breads or 400°F (204°C) for freestanding loaves, with the oven rack on the middle shelf. Brush freestanding loaves with the egg wash. You can score freestanding loaves as shown on page 77, but this is optional. The egg wash is optional for loaf-pan breads. Place the loaf pans on a sheet pan before putting them into the oven (this protects the bottoms of the breads).

9   Bake the loaves for 20 minutes, rotate the pans 180 degrees for even baking, and continue to bake for 15 to 40 minutes, depending on the size and shape. The internal temperature should register 185°F to 195°F (85°C to 91°C) in the center. The loaves should be golden brown all over and make a hollow sound when thumped on the bottom.

10   Remove the loaves from the pans and let cool for at least 1 hour before slicing or serving.

100% Sourdough Rye Bread

There are many ways to make rye bread, but very few versions contain 100 percent rye flour. Rye has so little of its unique type of gluten (6 to 8 percent) that it is hard to develop the structure and lift necessary for a decent crumb without the addition of a fair amount of high-gluten wheat flour or pure vital wheat gluten. Many people love dense rye bread, however, and many others eat it because they can tolerate the gluten of this bread but not the gluten in wheat breads.

A lot of drama goes on inside a sourdough rye bread. Rye flour is high in natural sugars and dextrins and contains pentosan, a gum protein that causes the dough to become gummy if it is mixed as long as wheat breads. Also, the wild-yeast starter creates an acidic environment that slows down the enzymatic release of sugar during the baking cycle (sometimes referred to as "starch attack") but, at the same time, allows for the proper amount of sugars to emerge from the grain during the fermentation cycle. If properly mixed and fermented, the result is a sweet, creamy, yet chewy texture quite unlike that of any other bread.

Makes two 1-pound (453g) loaves

MEASURE	OUNCES	GRAMS	INGREDIENTS	%
FIRM RYE STARTER (DAY 1)				
½ cup	3.5	99	barm (mother starter, page 241) or rye barm (see Commentary)	77.8
1 cup	4.5	128	white (aka light) rye flour	100
About ¼ cup	2	57	water, at room temperature	44.5
TOTAL				222.3
SOAKER (DAY 1)				
½ cup	2	57	coarse whole rye flour (or pumpernickel-grind) or rye chops (cracked rye)	100
½ cup	4	113	water, at room temperature	200
TOTAL				300

BREAD PROFILE
Lean, standard dough; indirect method; wild yeast

• • •

DAYS TO MAKE: 2
(or 3 if using overnight method)

DAY 1: 4 to 6 hours firm rye starter and soaker

DAY 2: 1 hour to de-chill starter; 6 minutes mixing; 7 hours stretch and fold, fermentation, shaping, and proofing; 25 to 35 minutes baking

• • •

COMMENTARY
The bread is best when made with a variety of grinds, from fine white (light) rye to coarse whole rye, pumpernickel-grind, or even rye chops (cracked rye kernels). This version uses a blend and also utilizes the soaker method to condition the grain and develop enzyme activity.

If you make rye bread regularly, you can keep a rye barm (mother starter) on hand in addition to your regular barm. Otherwise, you can use your regular barm starter and turn it into a rye starter, but it will contain a proportion of wheat. To make a pure rye-only starter, consult the Commentary on page 238.

• • •

Allow 3 days to make this bread (or start early on the second day to bake it around dinnertime). Because it is low in gluten, the bread will have a fairly tight crumb, not large and irregular as with standard hearth breads. The dough is slightly softer than French bread but not as wet as *ciabatta* and other rustic doughs. This added hydration provides some physical leavening (steam) in support of the biological (wild-yeast) leavening provided by the starter. The result is a relatively dense loaf with a long shelf life.

FINAL DOUGH (DAY 2)

Use all	10	284	firm rye starter	74.3
Use all	6	170	soaker	44.5
3 cups	13.5	382	white (aka light) rye flour	100
1½ teaspoons	0.38	11	salt	2.9
2 tablespoons	0.5	14	caraway or other seeds (optional)	3.7
¾ cup	6	170	water, lukewarm (90°F to 100°F/32°C to 38°C)	44.5

White or coarse whole rye, semolina, or cornmeal for dusting

TOTAL				269.9

TOTAL DOUGH FORMULA AND %

	OUNCES	GRAMS	INGREDIENTS	%
	1.75	50	high-gluten or bread flour	8
	18	510	white (light) rye	83
	2	57	coarse rye	9
	0.38	11	salt	1.8
	0.5	14	caraway (optional)	(2.3) optional
	13.75	390	water	63.2
TOTAL				165 (167.2)

1 Day 1: The day before making the dough, make the rye starter and soaker. For the starter, mix together the barm and rye flour in a bowl, adding only enough water to form a ball. It should be firm and a little tacky but not sticky or sponge-like. Work quickly. It is not necessary to develop the gluten, only to hydrate all the flour and form a dough that is shaggy but firm. Lightly oil a bowl and transfer the starter to the bowl, rolling it around to coat it lightly with the oil. Cover the bowl with plastic wrap.

2 Ferment at room temperature for 4 to 6 hours or longer, or until the dough doubles in size (it will become softer and stickier as it rises). Refrigerate overnight.

3 Also on the day before making the final dough, make the soaker. Combine the coarse rye flour and water in a bowl. Cover the bowl with plastic wrap and let it sit at room temperature overnight.

4 Day 2: The following day, remove the rye starter from the refrigerator 1 hour before making the dough. Cut the starter into about 10 small pieces with a pastry scraper or serrated knife. Mist with spray oil, cover the pieces with a towel or plastic wrap, and let sit for 1 hour to take off the chill.

5   To make the final dough, stir together the white rye flour, salt, and seeds in a 4-quart mixing bowl (or in the bowl of an electric mixer). Add the soaker and the starter pieces. With a large metal spoon, stir in enough lukewarm water to bring everything together to form a ball (or mix on low speed with the paddle attachment). Add more water if necessary.

6   Sprinkle white or whole rye flour on the counter and transfer the dough to the counter. Sprinkle the dough with more rye flour and gently knead the dough until all the pieces of starter are assimilated into the dough and the dough forms a very tacky ball (or mix on medium speed with the dough hook). This will take 5 to 6 minutes by hand (4 to 5 minutes by machine). Add flour as needed (or small amounts of water if the dough is tight). Let the dough rest on the counter for 5 minutes, and then give it a few more folds to complete the kneading. It should register 77°F to 81°F (25°C to 27°C). This dough cannot be stretched for the windowpane test because of its low gluten content. Lightly oil a large bowl and transfer the dough to the bowl, rolling it around to coat it with oil. Cover the bowl with plastic wrap. After 20 minutes, stretch and fold the dough (see page 59) and return it to the covered bowl. Repeat two more times at 20-minute intervals, each time returning the dough to the covered bowl.

7   Ferment for approximately 3 to 4 hours, or until the dough nearly doubles in size.

8   Sprinkle white or whole rye flour on the counter (or use the oil slick method, as described on page 59) and transfer the dough to the counter, being careful to degas it as little as possible. Divide the dough into 2 equal pieces and gently shape them into *bâtards*, as shown on page 77. Line a sheet pan with baking parchment and sprinkle the parchment with white or coarse whole rye, semolina, or cornmeal. Place the loaves on the pan at least 4 inches (10cm) apart. Mist the dough with spray oil and cover loosely with plastic wrap.

9   Either proof the dough for 2 hours at room temperature or slip the entire pan into a food-grade plastic bag and immediately refrigerate overnight. If you held the dough overnight, remove the pan from the refrigerator and proof the dough at room temperature for 4 hours, or until it is about 1½ times its original size. It will spread sideways as well as upward.

10   Prepare the oven for hearth baking as described on page 97, making sure to have a steam pan in place. Preheat the oven to 500°F (260°C). Remove the pan from the bag or lift off the plastic and let the dough sit exposed for 5 minutes; then score it as shown on page 96.

11   Slide the parchment and dough onto the back of a sheet pan or onto a peel and then transfer it to the stone (or bake the dough on the sheet pan on which it was rising). Pour 1 cup hot water into the steam pan and close the door. After 30 seconds, mist the oven walls with water and close the door. Repeat twice more at 30-second intervals. After the final spray, lower the oven setting to 425°F (218°C) and bake for 15 minutes. Rotate the loaves 180 degrees, if necessary, for even baking and continue baking for another 15 to 25 minutes, or until done. The internal temperature should register approximately 200°F (93°C) and the crust should be hard and somewhat coarse (it will soften as the bread cools).

12   Transfer the breads to a rack and let cool for at least 1 hour before slicing or serving.

• • •

This same formula can also be used for making spelt bread, another wheat relative that is lower in gluten (mainly it is lower in gliadin, which is the offensive half of gluten to those with sensitivities). Just substitute spelt flour for all or part of the rye and follow the same directions.

• • •

As always with rye breads, the use of caraway, anise, or other seeds is optional. This bread is delicious with or without them.

Poilâne-Style Miche

BREAD PROFILE
Lean, standard dough; indirect method; wild yeast

• • •

DAYS TO MAKE: 2
DAY 1: 4 to 6 hours firm starter

DAY 2: 1 hour to de-chill starter; 15 minutes mixing; 6 to 8 hours stretch and fold, fermentation, shaping, and proofing; 55 to 65 minutes baking

The most well-known bread baker in the world, until his death in a helicopter accident in 2002, was probably Lionel Poilâne, whose *boulangerie* in Paris's Latin Quarter (now run by his daughter Apollonia) makes only a few products. The most famous is a round, 2-kilo, naturally fermented (wild-yeast) country bread that he called a *miche* but that everyone else calls *pain Poilâne*. When I met Lionel in 1996, his system (described on pages 16 to 18) was simple: each baker, Poilâne's personally trained apprentice, was (and still is) responsible from start to finish for his loaves. This entails mixing and baking as well as stacking his own firewood and stoking his own fire. Poilâne taught his apprentices to bake by feel as much as by formula, so there is no thermostat in the oven. The baker must determine when the oven is ready by holding his hand in the oven or tossing in a piece of paper to see how long it takes to turn to parchment and then burn. Poilâne critiqued a loaf from each batch daily to keep abreast of the work of his men, since there were nearly twenty bakers in his stable at that time, most working outside of Paris at his *manufacture* in Bièvres.

The key to the Poilâne Boulangerie method is comprehending the craftsmanship of handwork, including understanding the fermentation process and commitment to the finest ingredients. The Poilâne flour is organically grown and is sifted to a partial whole wheat, an 85 to 90 percent extraction rate (this means that much, but not all, of the bran is still in the flour). The finished bread is somewhat dense and very chewy, its flavors changing in the mouth with each chew, and it keeps for about a week at room temperature.

Bread pilgrims still come from all over the world to buy a Poilâne loaf (this includes those who visit Lionel's brother Max, who makes similar loaves at his own bakeries scattered around Paris). When I visited Boulangerie Poilâne on rue du Cherche-Midi, I noticed some very attractive gift boxes, complete with cutting board and knife. Apparently, many visitors buy these and have them shipped to family and friends. It speaks volumes that one man can become so iconic because of a commitment to his craft. Of course, it's fitting that in France this craft is bread baking.

The following version of the Poilâne-style *miche* utilizes a long fermentation and a three-build system (the barm counts as the first build). It makes creative use of common kitchen bowls to replicate the difficult to find *banneton* proofing baskets of Poilâne's operation. As always with baking, necessity is the mother of invention, and a home kitchen can always be modified to imitate, on a small scale, a commercial bakery.

Makes 1 large country miche (large *boule*), or 2 or 3 smaller *boules*

MEASURE	OUNCES	GRAMS	INGREDIENTS	%
FIRM STARTER				
1 cup	7	198	barm (mother starter, page 241)	77.7
2 cups	9	255	sifted medium-grind whole wheat flour, 50-50 blend (see commentary), or high-extraction flour	100
About ½ cup	4	113	water, at room temperature	44.3
TOTAL				222
FINAL DOUGH				
7 cups	32	907	sifted medium-grind whole wheat flour, 50-50 blend (see commentary), or high-extraction flour	100
3¼ teaspoons	0.81	23	salt (or 2 tablespoons coarse sea salt)	2.5
Use all	20	566	firm starter	62.4
2 to 2¾ cups	16 to 22	510 to 624	water, lukewarm (90°F to 100°F/32°C to 38°C)	56 to 69
Bread flour, semolina, or cornmeal for dusting				
TOTAL				220.0 to 233.9

TOTAL DOUGH FORMULA AND %

POILÂNE-STYLE MICHE

	OUNCES	GRAMS	INGREDIENTS	%
	35.5	1006	sifted whole wheat, high extraction, or flour blend	100
	0.81	23	salt	2.3
	27.5	780	water	77.5
TOTAL				179.8

COMMENTARY
You can sift medium-grain whole wheat flour to approximate the high-extraction whole wheat flour of the Poilâne *miche*. Choose a flour, preferably hard spring or winter wheat, or one with a bread flour gluten specification of 11.5 to 13 percent. Pass it through a sieve or sifter. It is better not to use regular (fine-grind) whole wheat flour, as most of the bran passes right through the sieve. With the medium-grind flour, the smaller particles of bran and germ will sift through, but the largest pieces will remain in the sieve. These sifted bran particles can be used for multigrain breads or as add-ins to country breads made from white flour. Another option is to make a 50-50 blend of half whole wheat flour and half bread flour (or one-third whole wheat and two-thirds bread flour, your choice) wherever the instructions call for sifted whole wheat flour. (Note: it is now also possible to order high-extraction flour from mail-order companies like King Arthur Flour, Central Milling, and others. It is sometimes referred to as Type 85 flour.)

1   The day before making the bread, make the firm starter. In a 4-quart mixing bowl, use a large metal spoon to mix together the barm, flour, and enough water to form a firm ball. Sprinkle flour on the counter and transfer the dough to the counter. Knead for about 3 minutes, or until all the flour is hydrated and the ingredients are evenly distributed. Lightly oil a bowl, place the ball of dough in the bowl, and roll it around to coat it with oil. Cover the bowl with plastic wrap.

Poilâne insisted on using gray Normandy sea salt in his bread, as he felt it made a crucial difference. If you can get a hold of such salt, try it. But if not, proceed with any salt, by weight. Remember, the coarser the salt, the less it will weigh per teaspoon, so 1 teaspoon table salt is equal to almost 2 teaspoons coarse sea salt or kosher salt.

• • •

Many of the people who tested this formula commented that the full-size *miche* was too heavy to handle easily in their home ovens. Feel free to divide this dough into 2 or even 3 smaller loaves—perhaps we should call them *petits pains Poilâne*— and reduce the baking time but not the temperature. Smaller batch sizes can be mixed in a home mixer.

• • •

According to M. Poilâne, this bread tastes best on the second or third day after it's baked. I prefer it about 3 hours after it comes out of the oven. Such is taste. . . .

2 Ferment at room temperature for 4 to 8 hours, or until the dough doubles in size. Refrigerate overnight.

3 Remove the starter from the refrigerator 1 hour before making the dough. Cut the starter into about 12 small pieces with a pastry scraper or serrated knife. Cover with a towel or plastic wrap and let sit for 1 hour to take off the chill.

4 This dough is too large for most home mixers, so knead it by hand. In a large mixing bowl, stir together the flour, salt, and starter pieces. Using a large metal spoon, stir in at least 2 to 2¼ cups (16 to 18 ounces/454 to 510g) of the water, or enough to bring together all of the ingredients into a soft ball. As you mix, adjust the flour and water as needed.

5 Sprinkle flour on the counter and transfer the dough to the counter. Knead the dough for about 10 minutes, continuing to adjust the flour and water to form a supple, tacky but not sticky dough. All of the ingredients should be evenly distributed. The dough should pass the windowpane test (page 61) and register 77°F to 81°F (25°C to 27°C). Lightly oil a large bowl and transfer the dough to the bowl, rolling it around to coat it with oil. Cover the bowl with plastic wrap. After 20 minutes, stretch and fold the dough (see page 59) and return it to the covered bowl. Repeat two more times at 20-minute intervals, each time returning the dough to the covered bowl.

6 Ferment at room temperature for approximately 3 to 4 hours, or until the dough nearly doubles in size.

7   Transfer the dough to the counter and gently form it into a large *boule*, as shown on page 76. Proof the dough in a *banneton* or prepare a proofing bowl large enough to hold the dough when it rises to nearly double in size, as shown on page 35. Place the dough, seam side up, in the *banneton* or bowl and mist the exposed part of the dough with spray oil. Cover with a cloth or plastic wrap.

8   Proof at room temperature for 2 to 3 hours, or until the dough grows 1½ times in size, or retard overnight in the refrigerator. If you are retarding the dough, remove the dough from the refrigerator 4 hours before you plan to bake it.

9   Prepare the oven for hearth baking as described on page 97, making sure to have an empty steam pan in place. Preheat the oven to 500°F (260°C). Carefully remove the top layer of cloth or plastic wrap from the dough 10 minutes before baking.

10 Generously dust a peel or the back of a sheet pan with flour, semolina, or cornmeal. Gently turn out the dough onto the peel or pan, carefully lifting the cloth liner off the dough, if using. Score the dough with a large square or pound (#) sign, as shown below. Slide the dough onto the baking stone (or bake directly on the sheet pan). Pour 1 cup hot water into the steam pan and close the door. Immediately lower the oven setting to 450°F (232°C). After 25 minutes, rotate the loaf 180 degrees and lower the oven setting to 425°F (218°C). Continue to bake for another 30 to 40 minutes, or until the dough registers 200°F (93°C) in the center. The bread should be deeply browned. If the bottom seems to be getting too dark before the loaf reaches the desired temperature, place an inverted sheet pan under the bread to protect the bottom. Likewise, if the top gets too dark, tent a piece of aluminum foil over the loaf to shield it from the heat.

11 Transfer the bread to a rack and let cool for at least 2 hours before slicing or serving. Store the bread in a brown paper bag. It should be good for 5 to 7 days.

Scoring *pain Poilâne.*

Pumpernickel Bread

BREAD PROFILE
Enriched, standard dough;
indirect method; mixed leavening method

• • •

DAYS TO MAKE: 2
DAY 1: 4 to 5 hours rye starter

DAY 2: 1 hour to de-chill
starter; 6 minutes mixing;
4½ hours stretch and fold,
fermentation, shaping, and
proofing; 30 to 70 minutes
baking

• • •

COMMENTARY
This version uses a mixed-
method combination of wild-
yeast starter and commercial
yeast. The starter serves as
both a pre-ferment and a
soaker, improving the flavor
enormously, while the commercial yeast gives a reliable
final rise and diminishes the
sour characteristics. If you
prefer extra-sour bread, you
can leave out the instant yeast
and treat the dough as the
sourdough bread described on
pages 245 to 248, remem-
bering to factor in the longer
fermentation cycles.

For 20 years I have been fascinated by, and have experimented with, rye breads in their many manifestations, but pumpernickel has always impressed me as the definitive rye (maybe it's just that it has the best name). There are countless versions of pumpernickel bread. Many Americans think the name simply refers to a dark rye, made dark by the addition of caramel coloring. What the name really refers to is a loaf made with coarsely ground whole grain rye flour, the distinguishing characteristic of this particular type of rye bread. Some versions, though not the one that follows, are extremely dense, what I call cocktail or Bavarian rye, which needs to be sliced very thin. People who love this dense rye really do passionately love it, but it has a relatively small (though growing) following in the United States. In some eastern European villages, this bread was, and still is, made by adding the bread crumbs from previously baked loaves to the new dough. This gives the bread a wonderful texture. You can make the following formula with or without bread crumbs, but it's a great way to use up dried-out leftover slices from the last loaf.

Makes two 1-pound (453g) loaves

MEASURE	OUNCES	GRAMS	INGREDIENTS	%
RYE STARTER (DAY 1)				
1 cup	7	198	barm (mother starter, page 241)	165
1 cup	4.25	120	coarse whole rye or pumpernickel-grind flour	100
¾ cup	6	170	water, at room temperature	141.7
TOTAL				406.1
FINAL DOUGH (DAY 2)				
2 cups	9	255	unbleached high-gluten, clear, or bread flour	100
2 tablespoons	1	28	brown sugar	11
1 tablespoon, or	0.5	14	cocoa, carob, or instant coffee powder	5.5
1 teaspoon liquid caramel coloring	0.25	7	1 teaspoon liquid caramel coloring	2.3
1½ teaspoons	0.38	11	salt	4.3
1¼ teaspoons	0.14	4	instant yeast	1.6
Use all	17.25	488	rye starter	191.4
¾ to 1 cup	4	113	dry or fresh bread crumbs, preferably from rye bread (optional)	44.3
2 tablespoons	1	28	vegetable oil	11
About ¼ cup	2	57	water, at room temperature	22.3
Coarse rye, semolina, or cornmeal for dusting, if making freestanding loaves				
TOTAL				393.7

TOTAL DOUGH FORMULA AND %

	OUNCES	GRAMS	INGREDIENTS	%
	12.5	354	high-gluten, clear, or bread flour	75
	4.25	120	coarse rye flour	25
	0.38	11	salt	2.3
	1	28	brown sugar	5.9
	0.14	4	instant yeast	0.8
	0.5 ounce (0.25 ounce)	14 (7)	cocoa, carob or instant coffee (or caramel coloring)	1 (0.5)
	1	28	vegetable oil	5.9
	4	112	bread crumbs	23.6
	11.5	326	water	68.8
	TOTAL			208.3 (208.05)

• • •

The rye flour is turned into a rye starter in order to acidify the rye flour. This not only activates enzymes for flavor but also makes the rye more digestible. Although not all rye breads are made this way, as a general rule, rye bread is always improved by using an acidic starter even when the final leavening push is provided by commercial yeast.

• • •

Cocoa is a traditional coloring agent for this bread, but you can also use one of the alternatives given, or you can leave out the coloring agent altogether.

1   Day 1: The day before making the bread, make the starter. Mix together the barm, rye flour, and water in a bowl. It will make a wet, pasty sponge. Cover the bowl with plastic wrap and ferment at room temperature for 4 to 8 hours, or until the sponge becomes bubbly and foamy. Immediately put it in the refrigerator overnight.

2   Day 2: Remove the rye starter from the refrigerator about 1 hour before making the dough to take off the chill.

3   To make the dough, stir together the flour, sugar, cocoa (or other powder or liquid flavoring), salt, and yeast in a 4-quart mixing bowl (or in the bowl of an electric mixer). Add the rye starter, bread crumbs, and oil and stir until the ingredients form a ball (or mix on low speed with the paddle attachment). Add water if the dough ball doesn't pick up all the flour or more bread flour if the dough seems too wet.

4   Sprinkle flour on the counter and transfer the dough to the counter. Knead the dough for about 6 minutes (or mix on low speed with the dough hook for 4 to 5 minutes). Add flour as needed to make a smooth, pliable dough. It should be tacky but not sticky. (Note: Rye bread will become gummy if you mix it too long, so try to make all your adjustments early in the mixing process and minimize the mixing or kneading time.) The dough should pass the windowpane test (page 61) and register 77°F to 81°F (25°C to 27°C). Lightly oil a large bowl and transfer the dough to the bowl, rolling it around to coat it with oil. Cover the bowl with plastic wrap. After 20 minutes, stretch and fold the dough (see page 59) and return it to the covered bowl. Repeat two more times at 20-minute intervals, each time returning the dough to the covered bowl.

5   Ferment at room temperature for 2 hours, or until the dough nearly doubles in size.

6   Sprinkle a small amount of flour on the counter and transfer the dough to the counter, taking care to degas it as little as possible. Divide the dough into 2 equal pieces and shape them into either *boules* or *bâtards* for freestanding loaves (see pages 76 and 77) or into sandwich loaves (see page 85). Line a large sheet pan with baking parchment and sprinkle with rye or semolina or cornmeal, or lightly oil two 8½ by 4½-inch (22 by 11.5cm) bread pans. Transfer the dough to the pan(s), mist the dough with spray oil, and loosely cover with plastic wrap or a towel.

7   Proof at room temperature for approximately 1½ hours, or until the dough crests 1 inch (2.5cm) above the lip of the bread pans at the center for sandwich loaves, or rises to 1½ times its original size for freestanding loaves.

8   If you are making freestanding loaves, prepare the oven for hearth baking as described on page 97, making sure to have an empty steam pan in place. Preheat the oven to 450°F (232°C). Score the loaves as shown on page 96. If you are making loaf-pan breads, preheat the oven to 350°F (177°C) with the oven rack on the middle shelf. Place the loaf pans on a sheet pan.

9   If you are baking freestanding loaves, transfer the dough to the baking stone (or bake directly on the sheet pan). Pour 1 cup hot water into the steam pan and close the door. After 30 seconds, open the door, spray the oven walls with water, and close the door. Repeat twice more at 30-second intervals. After the final spray, lower the oven setting to 400F° (200°C) and continue baking for another 15 to 30 minutes. Check the breads, rotating them 180 degrees, if necessary, for even baking. The finished loaves should register 200°F (93°C) in the center and sound hollow when thumped on the bottom. If you are baking in loaf pans, transfer the sheet pan with the loaf pans to the oven. Bake for about 20 minutes, then rotate the sheet pan 180 degrees for even baking. Continue baking for another 20 to 30 minutes, or until the loaves register 190°F to 195°F (88°C to 91°C) in the center and sound hollow when thumped on the bottom.

10 Remove the finished loaves from the pans and let cool on a rack for at least 1 hour before slicing or serving.

Sunflower Seed Rye

BREAD PROFILE
Lean, standard dough; indirect method; mixed leavening method

• • •

DAYS TO MAKE: 2
DAY 1: 4 to 5 hours soaker and firm starter

DAY 2: 1 hour to de-chill firm starter; 6 minutes mixing; 3½ to 4 hours stretch and fold, fermentation, shaping, and proofing; 25 to 35 minutes baking

• • •

COMMENTARY
You can substitute barm for the firm starter, but remember to cut back on the water in the final dough.

I love anything with sunflower seeds, and this bread is loaded with them. The seeds are nutritious, taste good, and are "loyal" (that is, they leave a long, nutty finish that fills the mouth so that you enjoy the bread long after you eat it). This is a variation of a formula developed by Craig Ponsford and the Coupe du Monde team in 1995. This new version utilizes a firm wild-yeast starter instead of *pâte fermentée*. The dough requires the starter, commercial yeast, and a soaker, so it entails a commitment, but the results are so memorable that it is well worth the effort.

Makes two 1-pound (453g) loaves

MEASURE	OUNCES	GRAMS	INGREDIENTS	%
SOAKER (DAY 1)				
1⅓ cups	5.65	160	coarse whole rye or pumpernickel-grind flour or rye meal	100
¾ cup	6	170	water, at room temperature	106.25
TOTAL				206.25
DOUGH (DAY 2)				
1 cup	5.5	156	firm starter (page 245, Basic Sourdough Bread)	61
2 cups	9	255	unbleached high-gluten or bread flour	100
1½ teaspoons	0.38	11	salt	4.3
1¼ teaspoons	0.14	4	instant yeast	1.6
Use all	11.65	330	soaker	129.4
½ to ¾ cup	4 to 6	113 to 170	water, lukewarm (90°F to 100°F/32°C to 38°C)	44 to 66.7
½ cup	2	57	toasted sunflower seeds	22.2
High-gluten or bread flour, semolina, or cornmeal for dusting				
TOTAL				362.5 to 385.2

TOTAL DOUGH FORMULA AND %

	OUNCES	GRAMS	INGREDIENTS	%
	12.25	347	high-gluten or bread flour	68.5
	5.65	160	coarse rye flour	31.5
	0.38	11	salt	2.2
	0.11	4	instant yeast	0.8
	2	57	sunflower seeds	11.2
	14.25	404	water	80
TOTAL				194.2

1 Day 1: The day before making the bread, make the soaker by stirring together the coarse rye flour and water in a small bowl. The rye will soak up the water quickly, but it will all hydrate. Cover the bowl with plastic wrap and leave it out overnight at room temperature.

2 Also the day before baking (or up to 3 days before), make a firm starter, following the instructions in Basic Sourdough Bread but making only half the recipe.

3 Day 2: The next day, remove the starter from the refrigerator 1 hour before making the dough. Sprinkle a little flour on the counter and transfer the starter to the counter. Cut it into 8 to 10 pieces with a pastry scraper or serrated knife. Mist with spray oil, cover with a towel or plastic wrap, and let sit for 1 hour to take off the chill.

4 To make the dough, stir together the high-gluten or bread flour, salt, and yeast in a 4-quart mixing bowl (or in the bowl of an electric mixer). Add the soaker and starter pieces and then slowly add the water, stirring with a large metal spoon as you do (or mixing on low speed with the dough hook), until the ingredients form a soft ball.

5 Sprinkle flour on the counter, transfer the dough to the counter, and knead the dough (or mix on medium speed with the dough hook), sprinkling on bread flour (not rye flour) as needed until the dough feels soft and supple, tacky but not sticky. Try to accomplish this within 4 minutes, by hand or machine, to avoid overmixing (rye flour gets gummy if mixed too long). Add the sunflower seeds by gradually working them into the dough within the next 2 minutes. Total mixing time should not exceed 6 to 7 minutes, if possible. The dough should pass the windowpane test (page 61) and register 77°F to 81°F (25°C to 27°C). If it is not up to 77°F (25°C), it will take longer to ferment, but do not continue mixing. Lightly oil a large bowl and transfer the dough to the bowl, rolling it in the bowl to coat it with oil. Cover the bowl with plastic wrap. After 30 minutes, transfer the dough to a lightly oiled counter and stretch and fold it (see page 59), then return it to the covered bowl. Repeat this stretch and fold after an additional 30 minutes, again returning the dough to the covered bowl.

6 Ferment the dough at room temperature for 1½ hours, or until it doubles in size.

7   Sprinkle flour on the counter and gently transfer the dough to the counter, taking care to minimize degassing of the dough. Divide the dough into 2 equal pieces and gently form them into *boules*, as shown on page 76. Let them rest on the counter for 5 minutes, then shape them into a *couronne*, as shown on page 79. Transfer the dough to a sheet pan that has been lined with baking parchment and misted with spray oil, or use the *couche* method shown on pages 33 to 34. Mist the dough with spray oil and cover loosely with plastic wrap or a towel.

8   Proof the dough at room temperature for 1 to 1½ hours, or until it increases to about 1½ times its original size.

9   Prepare the oven for hearth baking as described on page 97, making sure to have an empty steam pan in place. Preheat the oven to 500°F (260°C).

10   Generously dust a peel or the back of a sheet pan with flour or cornmeal and gently transfer the dough to the peel or pan. Slide the dough onto the baking stone (or bake directly on the sheet pan). Pour 1 cup hot water into the steam pan and close the door. After 30 seconds, open the door, spray the walls with water, and close the door. Repeat twice more at 30-second intervals and then lower the oven setting to 450°F (232°C) and bake for 10 minutes. Check the breads, rotating them 180 degrees, if necessary, for even baking. Lower the oven setting to 425°F (218°C) and continue baking until the loaves are golden brown and register at least 200°F (93°C) in the center. This should take 15 to 25 minutes longer.

11   Remove the loaves from the oven and let cool on a rack for at least 1 hour before slicing or serving.

Stollen

BREAD PROFILE
Rich, standard dough; indirect method; commercial yeast

. . .

DAYS TO PREPARE: 2
DAY 1: Soak the fruit

DAY 2: 1 hour sponge; 20 minutes mixing; 2 hours fermentation, shaping, and proofing; 50 to 70 minutes baking

When you look at recipes for European holiday breads like panettone, stollen, *tsoureki,* and *christopsomo,* it seems as if they are all related, often sharing similar ingredients and proportions of fat and sugar. The main differences among these breads are usually in their shaping and in their history and symbolism. But heaven help any of us if we propose that thought to someone who grew up with any of those breads. I once made stollen, panettone, and *kulich* (Russian Easter bread) from a recipe for multipurpose holiday bread for a group of chefs and explained my theory of their similarities. Later, one of the American chefs told me I had offended some of the Germans who grew up on stollen and who were adamant that stollen is nothing like panettone. So I will resist the temptation to call this formula a multipurpose holiday bread (though I have made many types of holiday breads from it) and instead limit it to its application as Dresden stollen.

Dresden is considered the spiritual home of this traditional Christmas bread. The bread symbolizes the blanket of the baby Jesus, and the colored fruits represent the gifts of the Magi. As in nearly every festival bread, the story aspect of this loaf is culturally important, for it is a way parents teach their children about their heritage. When such a story is accompanied by the flavor memory of a particular food, you have a tool much more powerful than didactic or pedagogical teaching. I'm convinced this must be the reason I offended those Germans that day when I implied that a stollen was like a panettone. Perhaps in taste and ingredients, yes, but never in association.

(continued)

Stollen, heavily dusted with powdered sugar, with a panettone variation from the same dough in the background.

COMMENTARY

This version (and there are hundreds of authentic versions of stollen) is particularly good because it not only tastes great, but it also can be made in a reasonable amount of time, about 4 hours from start to finish (not counting the overnight soaking of the fruit mixture). This is because of the strong sponge that leavens the rather heavy dough at a brisk pace. Of course, if you want to do it right, soak the fruit a few days ahead of time in the brandy, rum, or schnapps, adding ¼ to ½ cup (2 to 4 ounces/57 to 227g) more liquor than the instructions indicate. This improves the flavor and preserves the bread for weeks. Here's how to do it: Two days before making this bread, soak the raisins and candied fruit in the brandy, rum, or schnapps and the orange or lemon extract, tossing the fruit a few times a day until the liquid is absorbed. If you'd prefer not to use alcohol, you can double the amount of extract and add ½ cup (4 ounces/113g) water. You can also simply add the fruit, without the alcohol, to the final dough and add the extract directly to the dough.

MEASURE	OUNCES	GRAMS	INGREDIENTS	%
DAY 1: FRUIT BLEND				
1 cup	6	170	golden raisins, plus additional for sprinkling on the final dough	n/a
1 cup	6	170	candied fruit mix, plus additional for sprinkling on the final dough	n/a
½ cup	4	113	brandy, rum, or schnapps	n/a
1 tablespoon	0.5	14	orange or lemon extract	n/a
TOTAL	16.5	467		n/a
DAY 2: SPONGE				
½ cup	4	113	whole milk	32.5
½ cup	2.25	64	unbleached all-purpose flour	18.4
4 teaspoons	0.44	12.5	instant yeast	3.6
DOUGH				
2¼ cups	10	284	unbleached all-purpose flour	81.6
1 tablespoon	0.5	14	sugar	4
¾ teaspoon	0.19	5.5	salt	1.58
1 teaspoon	0.11	3	grated orange zest (optional)	0.85
1 teaspoon	0.11	3	grated lemon zest (optional)	0.85
1 teaspoon	0.25	7	ground cinnamon	2
1 large	1.65	47	egg	13.5
5 tablespoons	2.5	71	unsalted butter, at room temperature	20.4
About ¼ cup	2	57	water, at room temperature	16.4
Use all	16.5	476	fruit blend	134.2
½ cup	2	57	slivered blanched almonds (or marzipan, see Commentary)	n/a
Vegetable oil or melted unsalted butter for coating				n/a
Powdered sugar for coating				n/a
TOTAL				329.9

TOTAL DOUGH FORMULA AND %

	OUNCES	GRAMS	INGREDIENTS	%
	12.25	348	all purpose flour	100
	0.19	5.5	salt	1.6
	0.5	14	sugar	4
	0.25	7	cinnamon	2
	0.44	12.5	instant yeast	3.6
	0.22	6	orange and lemon zest	1.7
	6	170	raisins	49
	6	170	candied fruit	49
	18.75	532	water	16.4
	4	113	milk	32.5
	2.5	71	butter	20
	1.65	47	egg	13.5
	4	113	brandy or liquor	32.5
	0.5	14	lemon or orange extract	4
TOTAL				329.8

A German friend, chef Heinz Lauer, told me he prefers to let his stollen dry out for a few days or even weeks before eating it. He cuts off thin, hard slices and dips them in wine or coffee, almost like biscotti. I tend to prefer it fresh from the oven.

• • •

Heinz also told me he prefers his stollen with a marzipan center. This is a common variation, and if you like this intensely flavored sweetened almond paste, as I do, you may replace the slivered almonds in the formula with a thick band of marzipan rolled into the center of the loaf.

• • •

You can substitute regular dried fruit, such as dried cranberries or apricots, for the candied fruit mix, if you prefer.

1 Day 1: Stir together the raisins, candied fruit mix, brandy, and orange extract. Cover and set aside at room temperature overnight.

2 Day 2: To make the sponge, warm the milk to about 100°F (38°C). Remove from the heat and whisk in the flour and yeast to make a pastelike batter. Cover with plastic wrap and ferment for 1 hour, or until the sponge is very foamy and ready to collapse when tapped.

3 To make the dough, stir together the flour, sugar, salt, orange and lemon zests, and cinnamon in a 4-quart mixing bowl (or in the bowl of an electric mixer). Then stir in (or mix in on low speed with the paddle attachment) the sponge, egg, butter, and enough water to form a soft, but not sticky, ball. This should take about 2 minutes. When the dough comes together, cover the bowl and let the dough rest for 10 minutes.

4 Add the fruit and mix it with your hands (or for a few seconds on low speed with the paddle attachment) to incorporate.

5 Sprinkle flour on the counter (or use the oil slick method, as described on page 59), transfer the dough to the counter, and begin kneading (or mixing on medium low speed with the dough hook) to distribute the fruit evenly, adding additional flour if needed. The dough should feel soft and satiny, tacky but not sticky. This should take about 4 to 6 minutes (4 minutes by machine). Lightly oil a large bowl and transfer the dough to the bowl, rolling it around to coat it with oil. Cover the bowl with plastic wrap.

⁎ SHAPING STOLLEN, METHOD 2

This shaping method results in more of a "blanket-in-the-manger" look. With your hands, form the dough into a thick rectangle that measures 8 by 4 inches (20 by 10cm), or 5 by 3 inches (13 by 8cm) for 2 smaller loaves, and dust it with flour. **(A)** Sprinkle the top with the slivered almonds and the extra fruit. **(B)** Take a small rolling pin and press down on the center of the rectangle and then roll the dough in the center only, leaving 1 inch (2.5cm) at both the top and the bottom edges as thick as the original rectangle. The new rectangle, with its thick top and bottom edges, should be 12 inches wide (30.5cm) by 6 inches (15cm) long (8 by 5 inches/20 by 13cm for 2 smaller loaves). The interior of the rectangle should be about ½ inch (13mm) thick. Using a pastry scraper, loosen the dough from the counter and then lift the top edge and bring it down and over the bottom edge, going just past the bottom edge. The thin inside part of the rectangle should remain behind the bottom edge.

(C) Turn the dough seam side up and tuck additional slivered almonds and fruit under the dough flap. **(D)** Fold the top edge back over the bottom edge and rest it on the thin center section. Tuck more almonds and fruit under the new fold. The dough should have a folded, layered look, with fruit and almonds peeking out both sides. Gently squeeze the loaf to press it together.

6 Ferment at room temperature for about 45 minutes. The dough will rise somewhat but will not double in size.

7 Sprinkle flour lightly on the counter (or make an oil slick) and transfer the dough to the counter. If you are making 2 loaves, divide the dough in half. Proceed in one of the following ways. Method 1: Roll out the dough into a 9 by 6-inch (23 by 15cm) rectangle (7 by 5-inch/ 18 by 13cm rectangle for 2 smaller loaves) rectangle for 2 smaller loaves) and sprinkle the slivered almonds and additional fruit (to taste) over the top (or add a generous bead of marzipan). Roll the dough up into a *bâtard*, as shown on page 77, sealing the crease by pinching the dough with the edge of your hand. Or use Method 2 (opposite).

8 Line a sheet pan with baking parchment. Transfer the stollen to the pan, curling the dough into a slight crescent as you set it on the pan. Mist the dough with spray oil and cover loosely with plastic wrap. Proof for approximately 1 to 2 hours at room temperature, or until the dough is 1½ times its original size.

9 Preheat the oven to 350°F (177°C) with the oven rack on the middle shelf.

10 Bake the stollen for 20 minutes. Rotate the pan 180 degrees for even baking and continue to bake for 20 to 50 minutes, depending on the size of the loaves. The bread will bake to a dark mahogany color, should register 190°F (88°C) in the center, and should sound hollow when thumped on the bottom.

11 Transfer the bread to a rack and brush the top with vegetable oil or melted butter while still hot. Using a sieve or sifter, immediately tap a layer of powdered sugar over the top of the bread. Wait for 1 minute and then tap another layer over the first. The bread should be coated generously with the powdered sugar. Let cool for at least 1 hour before serving. When completely cool, store in a plastic bag. Or leave out uncovered overnight to dry out slightly, German style.

Swedish Rye (Limpa)

BREAD PROFILE
Enriched, standard dough;
indirect method; commercial
yeast

• • •

DAYS TO MAKE: 2
DAY 1: 4 hours sponge

DAY 2: 1 hour to de-chill
sponge; 6 minutes mixing;
3½ hours fermentation,
shaping, and proofing;
35 to 50 minutes baking

• • •

COMMENTARY
By scoring this bread before
the final proofing, it takes on
a different look than when
scored just prior to baking,
as is customary for most
breads. The cuts fill in during
the rising period and spread
out. When the bread bakes,
it seems as if the cuts have
healed, leaving behind a
different shade of crust where
the cuts were made.

What makes this version of rye different from the more popular German and deli ryes is the use of licorice-flavored aniseeds and fennel seeds along with orange peel and a touch of cardamom. Nutritionists are now quantifying the therapeutic benefits of orange peel, licorice-flavored spices, and bitters as digestive aids that various traditional cultures have espoused for centuries. By making the bread with a combination of wild-yeast starter and commercial yeast, this formula creates an even more complexly flavored loaf than the more customary versions leavened only by commercial yeast. The lactic acid not only conditions the flour, predigesting it to an extent, but also gives it a longer shelf life and better flavor. Think of this bread as a baked version of anisette.

Makes two 1-pound (453g) loaves or one 2-pound (907g) loaf

MEASURE	OUNCES	GRAMS	INGREDIENTS	%
SPONGE (DAY 1)				
¾ cup plus 2 tablespoons	7	198	water, room temperature	139.4
2½ tablespoons	1.75	49.5	molasses	34.9
1 tablespoon or 1 teaspoon	0.33 0.17	9.5 5	dried orange peel orange oil	6.7 (3.5)
1 teaspoon	0.33	9.5	ground aniseeds	6.7
1 teaspoon	0.11	3	ground fennel seeds	2.1
1 teaspoon	0.11	3	ground cardamom	2.1
1 cup	7	198	barm (mother starter, page 241)	139.4
1 cup plus 2 tablespoons	5	142	white (light) rye flour	100
TOTAL	21.6	612		431.3
DOUGH (DAY 2)				
2½ cups	11.25	319	unbleached high-gluten, clear, or bread flour	100
2 teaspoons	0.22	6	instant yeast	1.9
1½ teaspoons	0.38	11	salt	3.4
4½ tablespoons	2.25	64	firmly packed brown sugar	n/a
Use all	21.6	612	day 1 sponge	192
2 tablespoons	1	28	vegetable oil	8.8
Unbleached high-gluten flour, semolina, or cornmeal				
1 egg white, whisked with 1 teaspoon water until frothy, for egg wash (optional)				
TOTAL				306.1

OUNCES	GRAMS	INGREDIENTS	%
14.74	418	high-gluten or bread flour	75
5	142	light rye flour	25
0.38	11	salt	2
0.33 or 0.17	9.5 5	dried orange peel or orange oil	1.8 (0.9)
0.33	9.5	ground anise seeds	1.8
0.11	3	ground fennel seeds	0.5
0.11	3	ground cardamom seeds	0.5
0.22	6	instant yeast	1
2.25	64	brown sugar	11.4
1	28	vegetable oil	5
1.75	49.5	molasses	8.8
10.5	297	water	53
TOTAL			185.35

1   Day 1: The day before making the bread, make the sponge. Combine the water, molasses, orange peel, aniseeds, fennel seeds, and cardamom in a saucepan. Bring the mixture to a boil and then turn off the heat. Let cool to lukewarm. Stir in the barm and rye flour until the flour is fully hydrated and evenly distributed. This should make a thick sponge. Cover with plastic wrap and ferment at room temperature for 4 to 6 hours, or until the mixture becomes foamy. Refrigerate overnight.

2   The next day, remove the sponge from the refrigerator 1 hour before making the bread dough to take off the chill.

3   To make the dough, in a 4-quart mixing bowl (or in the bowl of an electric mixer), stir together the flour, yeast, salt, and brown sugar. Add the sponge and the oil. Mix with a large metal spoon (or on low speed with the paddle attachment for 1 minute) until the dough forms a ball. Sprinkle flour on the counter, transfer the dough to the counter, and begin kneading (or mix on medium speed with the dough hook) for approximately 4 minutes. Adjust with additional high-gluten or bread (not rye) flour, if needed. The dough should be slightly tacky but not sticky. Do not overknead, as the rye flour will become gummy. The entire kneading or mixing process should be completed within 6 minutes. The dough should pass the windowpane test (page 61) and register 77°F to 81°F (25°C to 27°C). Lightly oil a large bowl and transfer the dough to the bowl, rolling it to coat it with oil. Cover the bowl with plastic wrap.

4   Ferment at room temperature for about 2 hours, or until the dough doubles in size.

5   Remove the dough from the bowl and knead for 1 minute to degas. Divide the dough into 2 equal pieces for 1-pound loaves or leave intact for one 2-pound loaf. Shape the dough into 1 or 2 sandwich loaves (page 85), or into 1 or 2 *bâtards* (page 77) for freestanding loaves. Lightly oil two 8½ by 4½-inch (22 by 11.5cm) pans or one 9 by 5-inch (23 by 13cm) pan; for freestanding loaves, line a large sheet pan with baking parchment and sprinkle with flour, semolina, or cornmeal. Transfer the shaped dough to the pan(s) and score the top(s) with 3 parallel slashes as shown on page 96. Mist bread(s) with spray oil and cover loosely with plastic wrap or a food-grade plastic bag.

6   Proof at room temperature for approximately 1½ hours, or until the dough crests 1 inch (2.5cm) above the lip of the loaf pan(s) at the center, or rises to 1½ times its original size for a freestanding loaf.

7   Preheat the oven to 350°F (177°C). For a freestanding loaf, brush the egg wash over the surface of the dough just prior to baking. This is optional for a loaf-pan bread.

8   Bake for 20 minutes, then rotate the pan(s) 180 degrees for even baking. Continue to bake for 15 to 30 minutes, depending on the size of the loaf. The bread should register 190°F (88°C) in the center, be a light golden brown, and make a hollow sound when thumped on the bottom. If the sides are still white or soft, return the pan(s) to the oven to finish.

9   When the bread is ready, immediately remove from the pan(s) and let cool upside down on a rack for at least 1 hour before slicing or serving.

Tuscan Bread

What makes Tuscan bread unique in the bread lexicon is that it is salt-free, which makes it wonderful for people on salt-restricted diets. Unfortunately, the lack of salt also makes it rather dull and flat tasting. Tuscans, no slouches when it comes to full-flavored food, remedy this by lavishing it with intensely flavored spreads, dips, and sauces, or eating it with flavorful dishes, such as garlic-and-olive-oil–infused white bean soup. A technique that is also unique to this bread is the use of a cooked flour paste, made the day before. This is different from a pre-ferment since there is no yeast added and the paste does not ferment, but the gelatinized starches release flavors and sweetness that gives this bread a distinct quality quite unlike any other bread. This is one of those underused techniques that offers great opportunity for exploration. Once you've mastered it in this bread, try applying it to some other doughs, like Vienna or Italian. It is yet another way to control flavor by manipulating time, temperature, and ingredients.

BREAD PROFILE
Enriched, standard dough; indirect method; commercial yeast

• • •

DAYS TO MAKE: 2
DAY 1: 15 minutes flour paste

DAY 2: 10 to 12 minutes mixing; 3½ hours fermentation, shaping, and proofing; 20 to 50 minutes baking

• • •

COMMENTARY
A variation of this bread can be made with a *biga* instead of the flour paste, and it comes out nicely as a salt-free Italian or French bread. I wouldn't call it true Tuscan bread, though, because it doesn't have that unique flavor brought about by the cooked flour.

• • •

Unlike most hearth breads where 1 cup of water is poured into a steam pan, this bread calls for a pan with 2 cups water to be preheated along with the oven. This extra water ensures a moist oven that yields a better shine on the crust.

Makes two 1-pound (453g) loaves

MEASURE	OUNCES	GRAMS	INGREDIENTS	%
FLOUR PASTE (DAY 1)				
1¾ cups	14	397	boiling water	156
2 cups	9	255	unbleached bread flour	100
TOTAL	23	652		256
DOUGH (DAY 2)				
2⅔ cups	12	340	unbleached bread flour	100
2½ teaspoons	0.28	8	instant yeast	2.3
Use all	23	652	flour paste	191.7
2 tablespoons	1	28	olive oil	8.3
About ½ cup	4	113	water, at room temperature	33.3
Bread flour, semolina, or cornmeal for dusting				
TOTAL				335.6

	OUNCES	GRAMS	INGREDIENTS	%
	21	595	bread flour	100
	0.28	8	instant yeast	1.3
	18	510	water	85.7
	1	28	olive oil	4.7
TOTAL				191.7

1   Make the paste 1 or 2 days before making the bread. Pour the boiling water over the flour in a mixing bowl and stir vigorously until the flour is hydrated and a roux-like thick smooth paste forms. Let cool, cover, and leave out overnight at room temperature. If not using the next day, refrigerate it instead of leaving it out.

2   The next day, make the dough. With a large metal spoon, stir together the flour and yeast in a 4-quart mixing bowl (or in the bowl of an electric mixer). Add the flour paste and olive oil and continue to stir (or mix on low speed with the paddle attachment), adding as much water as it takes to make a soft, supple ball. It's okay if the dough is a little sticky because you can add more flour while kneading.

3   Sprinkle flour on the counter (or use the oil slick method, as described on page 59), transfer the dough to the counter, and knead (or mix on medium speed with the dough hook) for 6 to 8 minutes. (You can let the dough rest after 4 minutes of mixing and resume 5 minutes later to make it easier on your hands or your machine). The dough should be supple and tacky but not sticky. Sprinkle in more flour if needed. The dough should pass the windowpane test (page 61) and register 77°F to 81°F (25°C to 27°C). Lightly oil a large bowl and transfer the dough to the bowl, rolling it around to coat it with oil. Cover the bowl with plastic wrap.

4   Ferment at room temperature for approximately 2 hours. If the dough doubles in size prior to that, knead it lightly to degas it (the "punch down") and return it to the bowl to continue fermenting until it doubles again or until a total of 2 hours has elapsed.

5   Line a sheet pan with baking parchment and lightly sprinkle with flour, cornmeal, or semolina. Gently divide the dough into 2 equal pieces (they should weigh about 18 ounces/510g each), being careful to minimize degassing the dough. With a light touch to protect the internal gas, form the dough into *boules*, as shown on page 76. If you plan to bake the loaves as rounds, transfer the dough to the prepared sheet pan. If you prefer oblong loaves, shape the dough rounds into *bâtards* (see page 77) after a 15-minute resting period, and then place them on the prepared pan. Mist the dough lightly with spray oil and cover loosely with plastic wrap.

6   Proof the dough at room temperature for 1 to 1½ hours, or until it nearly doubles in size. (You can also retard the dough by placing the covered pan in the refrigerator immediately after shaping and leave it overnight. The dough should be nearly ready to bake when you pull it out of the refrigerator. If not, leave out at room temperature for a couple of hours.)

7   Prepare the oven for hearth baking as described on page 97, making sure to have a steam pan in place. Pour 2 cups water into the steam pan. Preheat the oven to 500°F (260°C). Just prior to baking, mist the loaves with water and dust lightly with bread flour by tapping some through a sieve held over the loaves or by flinging the flour across the surface of the dough. Score the breads as shown on page 96.

8   Slide the breads directly onto the baking stone, parchment and all, or place the sheet pan on the middle rack of the oven. After 30 seconds, open the door, spray the oven walls with water, and close the door. Repeat twice more at 30-second intervals and then lower the oven setting to 450°F (232°C) and bake for 10 minutes. Remove the steam pan 10 minutes after loading the oven (if water remains in the pan, be careful not to splash yourself), rotate the loaves 180 degrees for even baking, and continue baking for 10 to 20 minutes longer, or until the loaves turn a rich golden color and register over 200°F (93°C) in the center (a single 2-pound loaf will take up to 50 minutes to bake). If the crust is getting too dark and the inside has not reached above 200°F (93°C), place an aluminum foil tent over the loaves and continue baking until the desired temperature is reached.

9   Transfer the loaves to a rack and let cool for at least 1 hour before slicing or serving.

Vienna Bread

BREAD PROFILE
Enriched, standard dough;
indirect method; commercial
yeast

• • •

DAYS TO MAKE: 2
DAY 1: 1¼ hours *pâte
fermentée*

DAY 2: 1 hour to de-chill *pâte
fermentée;* 10 to 12 minutes
mixing; 4 to 4½ hours stretch
and fold, fermentation, shaping, and proofing; 20 to
35 minutes baking

• • •

COMMENTARY
This version of Vienna
dough is improved by the
pre-ferment method that
I've been touting throughout
this book. You will rarely
find another version made in
quite this same way, as most
Vienna bread formulas are
made by the direct-dough
method. But the use of more
than 100 percent pre-ferment
adds so much character to
the bread that I'll never turn
back. Vienna rolls made from
this dough are a huge hit
at Johnson & Wales, where
students eagerly line up
whenever we make them for
their final sandwich project.

With all the emphasis on French and Italian rustic breads these days, it is easy to overlook the fact that the real center of the bread and pastry universe for hundreds of years was Vienna. Most of the great French breads that we love today, including baguettes, croissants, and even puff pastry, came to France a couple hundred years ago via the Austro-Hungarian empire, where they found a hungry audience willing to support these Austrian (which included Polish) bakers. Nowadays, the main distinction in American (and even European) bakeries among French, Italian, and Vienna breads is the presence of a few enrichments in the latter. A little added sugar and malt causes the crust to brown faster, and a small amount of butter, oil, or fat tenderizes the dough by coating and "shortening" the gluten strands. The shape, as with all culturally based bread, is determined by the baker based on function, but we usually think of modern Vienna bread as typically 12 inches (30.5cm) long and weighing 1 pound. It is often scored down the middle to make a nice "ear," but does not have quite as hard a crust or as open a crumb as French bread. This dough makes exceptional *pistolets* (like torpedo rolls), similar to the hoagie rolls made from the Italian bread on page 178, and it can also be baked in loaf pans for excellent sandwich loaves. One of the best applications for this dough is to make Dutch crunch bread, as discussed on page 283.

Note: You will need to make the *pâte fermentée* a day or two ahead or earlier in the same day as the final dough, so plan accordingly (you can also save *pâte fermentée* dough or French bread dough in the freezer and use it as the *pâte fermentée* as long as you slowly thaw it in the refrigerator the day before using it).

Makes two 1-pound (453g) loaves or 9 to 12 pistolets

MEASURE	OUNCES	GRAMS	INGREDIENTS	%
2⅓ cups	13	369	*pâte fermentée* (page 111)	108.5
2⅔ cups	12	340	unbleached bread flour	100
1 tablespoon	0.5	14	granulated sugar	4.1
1 teaspoon, or	0.25	7	diastatic barley malt powder or	2
1 tablespoon	0.75	21	barley malt syrup	6.1
1 teaspoon	0.25	7	salt	2
1 teaspoon	0.11	3	instant yeast	0.9
1 large	1.65	47	egg, slightly beaten	13.8

1 tablespoon	0.5	14	unsalted butter, at room temperature or melted, or vegetable oil	4.1
¾ cup plus 2 tablespoons	7	198	water, lukewarm (90°F to 100°F/32°C to 38°C)	58.3
Bread flour, semolina, or cornmeal for dusting				
TOTAL				293.6 (297.7 if using malt powder)

TOTAL DOUGH FORMULA AND %

	OUNCES	GRAMS	INGREDIENTS	%
	19.75	560	bread flour	100
	0.5	14	granulated sugar	2.5
	0.25 (0.75)	7 (21)	diastatic barley malt powder or barley malt syrup	1.25 (3.75)
	0.4	11	salt	2
	0.14	4	instant yeast	0.7
	1.65	47	egg	8.4
	0.5	14	butter	2.5
	12.25	347	water	62
TOTAL				179.35 (181.5)

1   Remove the *pâte fermentée* from the refrigerator 1 hour before making the dough. Cut it into about 10 small pieces with a pastry scraper or serrated knife. Cover with a towel or plastic wrap and let sit for 1 hour to take off the chill.

2   Stir together the flour, sugar, malt powder (if using), salt, and yeast in a 4-quart mixing bowl (or in the bowl of an electric mixer). Add the *pâte fermentée* pieces, egg, butter, malt syrup (if using), and ¾ cup (6 ounces/170g) of the water. Stir together with a large metal spoon (or mix on low speed with the paddle attachment) until the ingredients form a ball. If not all the flour is absorbed, add the remaining 2 tablespoons (1 ounce/28g) water, or as much as is necessary to make the dough soft and supple, not firm and stiff.

3   Sprinkle flour on the counter and transfer the dough to the counter. Knead or mix on medium speed with the dough hook for 6 minutes, adding flour if needed to make a firm but supple dough, slightly tacky but not sticky. The dough should pass the windowpane test (page 61) and register 77°F to 81°F (25°C to 27°C). Lightly oil a bowl and transfer the dough to the bowl, rolling it around to coat it with oil. Cover the bowl with plastic wrap. After 20 minutes, stretch and fold the dough (see page 59) and return it to the covered bowl. Repeat two more times at 20-minute intervals, again returning the dough to the covered bowl.

4 Ferment at room temperature for 2 hours. If the dough doubles in size before then, remove it from the bowl and knead for a few seconds to degas it (the "punch down") and then return it to the bowl to continue fermenting until 2 hours have elapsed or until the dough doubles in size again.

5 Remove the dough from the bowl and divide it into 2 equal pieces for loaves, or into 9 to 12 smaller pieces (3 to 4 ounces (85 to 113g) each) for *pistolets*. Shape larger pieces into *boules* (see page 76) or smaller pieces into rolls (see page 86). Mist the dough lightly with spray oil, cover with a towel or plastic wrap, and let the dough rest for 20 minutes.

6 Shape the larger pieces into *bâtards* (page 77) or the smaller pieces into *pistolets* (page 84). Line a sheet pan with baking parchment, dust with flour or cornmeal, and transfer the dough to the pan. Mist the dough lightly with spray oil and cover the pan loosely with plastic.

7 Proof at room temperature for 1 to 1½ hours, or until the loaves or rolls have risen to approximately 1¾ times their original size.

8 Prepare the oven for hearth baking as described on page 97, making sure to have an empty steam pan in place. Preheat the oven to 450°F (232°C). Just prior to baking, mist the loaves or rolls with water and dust lightly with bread flour by tapping some through a sieve or by flinging the flour across the surface of the dough. Score the loaves or rolls down the center as shown on page 96, or leave the rolls uncut.

Vienna Bread is the perfect loaf for a Dutch-crunch topping.

9   Slide the loaves directly onto the baking stone, parchment and all, or place the sheet pan with the loaves or rolls in the oven. Pour 1 cup hot water into the steam pan and close the oven door. After 30 seconds, open the door, spray the oven walls with water, and close the door. Repeat twice more at 30-second intervals. After the final spray, lower the oven setting to 400°F (204°C) and bake for 10 minutes. Rotate the breads 180 degrees, if necessary, for even baking and continue baking until they are a medium golden brown and register at least 200°F (93°C) in the center. This should take anywhere from 5 additional minutes for rolls to 20 minutes for loaves.

10 Remove the loaves or rolls from the oven and transfer them to a rack. Let cool for at least 45 minutes before slicing or serving.

GRACE NOTE

DUTCH CRUNCH OR MOTTLED BREAD

Dutch crunch is one of many names given to bread made with a special mottled topping. It doesn't refer to any particular dough formula, as the crunch topping can be spread on pretty much any type of bread. But if you grew up with a certain brand of Dutch crunch, you may associate it with particular styles of bread, like a chewy white bread or a light wheat loaf. Dutch bakers were among the many northern European bread makers who popularized this style of garnishing loaves, and the method caught on quickly in certain regions of America when it was first introduced. I find that Austrian-style bread, with its slightly enriched but chewy texture, is particularly suited to this treatment, which is a slurry paste made with rice flour, sugar, yeast, oil, salt, and water. However, feel free to use it on any type of sandwich dough or enriched breads (but not on lean French bread dough, with its hard crust).

The paste is brushed on the dough either right before the final proofing stage or just before the bread goes into the oven. (If you brush it on before proofing, the separation and mottling is greater and more dramatic; brushing it on just before baking results in a more even coating.) The paste is fermented by the yeast, and it grows while the dough grows. But because the rice flour has very little gluten to hold it together, it spreads apart and then gelatinizes and caramelizes when the bread is baked. This leaves a mottled, slightly sweet, crunchy coating on the bread that kids find especially mesmerizing. You can use the topping on loaf-pan bread as well as on freestanding loaves.

Rice flour is available at most natural foods markets. You can use either white or brown rice flour or even Cream of Rice cereal. Alternatives would be fine cornmeal, cornstarch, potato starch, semolina, or cake flour (it is low in gluten), but they each deliver a different flavor and texture. Rice flour or Cream of Rice cereal is the most common choice because it is, well, perfect for the job.

TOPPING
1 tablespoon bread flour
¾ cup rice flour
¾ teaspoon instant yeast
2 teaspoons granulated sugar
¼ teaspoon salt
2 teaspoons vegetable oil
6 to 8 tablespoons water

To make the topping, whisk together all of the ingredients to make a paste. If the mixture seems too thin to spread without running off the top of the dough, add more rice flour. It should be thick enough to spread with a brush, but not so thick that it sits like a lump of mud. This makes enough for 2 to 4 loaves.

White Bread: Three Multipurpose Variations

BREAD PROFILE
Enriched, standard dough; direct or indirect method; commercial yeast

• • •

DAYS TO MAKE: 1
1 hour sponge (Variation 3 only); 8 to 10 minutes mixing; 3½ to 4 hours fermentation, shaping, and proofing; 15 to 45 minutes baking

• • •

COMMENTARY
This is one type of bread that does not greatly improve from a pre-ferment or sponge because so much of the flavor comes from external, rather than internal, factors. Although it can be made by the sponge method, as Variation 3 demonstrates, the fast action and the amount of yeast and enrichments ensure that this is a fast-moving dough the flavor of which is largely a result of enrichments, not fermentation. For this reason, it is one of the easiest breads to make, whether made by the direct method or the indirect method. It is quite delicious and functional in its many applications regardless of the method followed. All the variations make excellent soft dinner rolls or hot dog or hamburger buns.

White bread is known under many names, including pullman, milk dough, *pain de mie* (bread of the crumb), and just plain old white bread. It has many uses, including dinner and knotted rolls, sandwich bread, burger buns, and hot dog buns. This style of dough is often referred to as milk dough because in most versions, the hydration is primarily from fresh milk (or powdered milk and water). These white breads fall into the category of enriched breads, as they are made with the most frequently used natural dough conditioners: fat (butter or oil), sugar, and milk. These cause the crust to caramelize quickly and, when fermented correctly, give the finished bread a light-as-air quality with a very soft texture. The internal temperature needs only reach just above 180°F (82°C) for rolls and 185°F to 190°F (85°C to 88°C) for loaves. Because of the enrichments, it is best to bake full-size loaves at 350°F (177°C) and small rolls at 400°F (204°C), but never at 450°F (232°C) as you would with lean hearth breads.

The three variations that follow give you some flexibility regarding ingredients. You may substitute powdered milk (DMS) for the liquid milk and vice versa, and you can also substitute in equal measure low-fat milk, buttermilk, or skim milk for the whole milk (and also nondairy milks such as soy, rice, or almond milk). Making these substitutions will affect the final outcome slightly in both flavor and texture, so try making the breads with the variations and see which version you prefer (I tend to be a buttermilk guy). You can also freely substitute margarine, shortening, or even liquid oil for the butter. Again, the type of fat you use will affect flavor and texture, but they all tenderize the bread. Shortening, which has been phased out by many bakeries due to its trans-fat nature (or replaced with non-trans-fat versions), gives the softest texture; butter, the best flavor.

Variation 1

Makes two 1-pound loaves (453g), 18 dinner rolls, or 12 burger or hot dog buns

MEASURE	OUNCES	GRAMS	INGREDIENTS	%
4½ cups	21.5	610	unbleached bread flour	100
1½ teaspoons	0.38	11	salt	1.8
¼ cup	1.33	38	powdered milk (DMS)	6.2
3¼ tablespoons	1.66	47	sugar	7.7
2 teaspoons	0.22	6	instant yeast	1
1 large	1.65	47	egg, slightly beaten, at room temperature	7.7
3¼ tablespoons	1.65	47	unsalted butter or margarine, melted or at room temperature, or vegetable oil	7.7
1½ cups plus 2 tablespoons	13	369	water, at room temperature	60.5
1 egg, whisked with 1 teaspoon water until frothy, for egg wash (optional)				
Sesame or poppy seeds for garnish (optional)				
TOTAL				183.9

1   Mix together the flour, salt, powdered milk, sugar, and yeast in a 4-quart mixing bowl (or in the bowl of an electric mixer). Pour in the egg, butter, and 1½ cups plus 1 tablespoon (12.5 ounces/354.5g) water and mix with a large metal spoon (or on low speed with the paddle attachment) until all the flour is absorbed and the dough forms a ball. If the dough seems very stiff and dry, trickle in more water until the dough is soft and supple.

2   Sprinkle flour on the counter, transfer the dough to the counter, and begin kneading (or mix on medium speed with the dough hook), adding more flour, if necessary, to create a dough that is soft, supple, and tacky but not sticky. Continue kneading (or mixing) for 5 to 7 minutes. (In the electric mixer, the dough should clear the sides of the bowl but stick ever so slightly to the bottom.) The dough should pass the windowpane test (page 61) and register approximately 81°F (27 °C). Lightly oil a large bowl and transfer the dough to the bowl, rolling it to coat it with oil. Cover the bowl with plastic wrap.

3   Ferment at room temperature for 1½ to 2 hours, or until the dough doubles in size.

4   Remove the fermented dough from the bowl and divide it in half for sandwich loaves, into eighteen 2-ounce (57g) pieces for dinner rolls, or twelve 3-ounce (85g) pieces for burger or hot dog buns. Shape the pieces into *boules* (page 76) for loaves or tight rounds (page 86) for dinner rolls or buns. Mist the dough lightly with spray oil and cover with a towel or plastic wrap. Allow to rest for about 20 minutes.

5   For loaves, shape as shown on page 85. Lightly oil two 8½ by 4½-inch (22 by 11.5cm) loaf pans and place the loaves in the pans. For rolls and buns, line 2 sheet pans with baking parchment. Rolls require no further shaping. For hamburger buns, gently press down on the rolls to form the desired shape. For hot dog buns, shape as shown on page 84, though without tapering the ends. Transfer the rolls or buns to the sheet pans.

6   Mist the top of the dough with spray oil and loosely cover with plastic wrap or a towel. Proof the dough at room temperature for 1 to 1½ hours, or until it nearly doubles in size.

7   Preheat the oven to 350°F (177°C) for loaves or 400°F (204°C) for roll and buns, with the oven rack on the middle shelf. Brush the rolls or buns with the egg wash and garnish with poppy or sesame seeds. Sandwich loaves can also be washed and garnished, or score them down the center and rub a little vegetable oil into the slit.

8   Bake the rolls or buns for approximately 15 minutes, or until they are golden brown and register just above 180°F (82°C) in the center. Bake the loaves for 35 to 45 minutes, rotating the pans 180 degrees halfway through for even baking, if needed. The tops should be golden brown and the sides, when removed from the pans, should also be golden. The internal temperature of the loaves should be close to 190°F (88°C), and the loaves should sound hollow when thumped on the bottom.

9   When the loaves have finished baking, immediately remove them from the pans and let cool on a rack for at least 1 hour before slicing or serving. Rolls should cool on a rack for at least 15 minutes before serving.

Variation 2

Makes two 1-pound (453g) loaves, 18 dinner rolls, or 12 burger or hot dog buns

MEASURE	OUNCES	GRAMS	INGREDIENTS	%
4¼ cups	19	539	unbleached bread flour	100
1½ teaspoons	0.38	11	salt	2
3 tablespoons	1.5	42.5	sugar	7.9
2 teaspoons	0.22	6	instant yeast	1.1
1 large	1.65	47	egg, slightly beaten, at room temperature	8.7
4 tablespoons	2	57	unsalted butter, margarine, or vegetable oil, at room temperature	10.6
1½ cups	12	340	buttermilk or whole milk, at room temperature	63
TOTAL				193.3

Proceed as directed for Variation 1, substituting the buttermilk or whole milk for the water. Add more buttermilk (or milk) or flour, as needed, while mixing.

Variation 3

Makes two 1-pound (453g) loaves, 18 dinner rolls, or 12 burger or hot dog buns

MEASURE	OUNCES	GRAMS	INGREDIENTS	%
SPONGE				
2½ cups	11.25	319	unbleached bread flour	60
2 teaspoons	0.22	6	instant yeast	1.1
1¼ cups	12	340	whole milk, lukewarm (90°F to 100°F/ 32°C to 38°C)	64
DOUGH				
1⅔ cups	7.5	213	unbleached bread flour	40
1½ teaspoons	0.38	11	salt	2
3 tablespoons	1.5	42.5	sugar	8
1 large	0.66	19	egg yolk, slightly beaten, at room temperature	3.6
¼ cup	2	57	unsalted butter, margarine, or vegetable oil, at room temperature	10.7
TOTAL				184.4

1   To make the sponge, mix together the flour and yeast in a 4-quart mixing bowl. Stir in the milk until all the flour is hydrated. Cover the bowl with plastic wrap and ferment at room temperature for 45 to 60 minutes, or until the sponge becomes aerated and frothy and swells noticeably.

2   To make the dough, add the flour, salt, and sugar to the sponge. Then add the egg yolk and butter or other fat. Proceed with step 1 of Variation 1 from this point on, noting that both the first and the second fermentation cycles should be 5 to 10 minutes faster than in the direct-dough method of Variation 1.

Whole Wheat Bread

BREAD PROFILE
Enriched, standard dough;
indirect method; commercial
yeast

• • •

DAYS TO MAKE: 2
DAY 1: 2 to 4 hours soaker
and *poolish*

DAY 2: 1 hour to de-chill
poolish; 15 minutes mixing;
3½ hours fermentation, shaping, and proofing; 45 to
60 minutes baking

• • •

COMMENTARY
Coarse flour weighs slightly
less per cup than regular-
grind flour because it doesn't
pack as tightly and contains
more air. This explains why
the coarse flour is only
4.25 ounces (120.5g) while
the regular whole wheat flour
used in the rest of the formula
weighs 4.5 ounces (128g) per
cup. If you don't have coarse-
grind whole wheat flour, you
can use regular grind at the
same weight (but slightly less
than 1 cup).

• • •

The bread will develop a more
open crumb if the flour is
high in protein. The strongest
flour comes from hard spring
wheat, which can often be
found at natural food markets
that offer a variety of flours
(see also Resources, page
314). You can also substitute
regular whole wheat flour
from the supermarket.

There are some terrific baking books that focus on 100 percent whole grain bread, and this style of bread has a fanatically loyal (and growing) following. I began my bread journey over 40 years ago as a devotee of organic whole grain bread, mainly for philosophical and health reasons. Although I've branched out to explore the entire bread kingdom and its infinite per-mutations, I still have a soft spot for what we used to call "pure bread" (or "real bread"). In fact, once again, I try to eat only whole grain breads (except when I have to grade a student's baguette and ciabatta) just on general principles, and have written two books that focus on 100 percent whole grain breads. (*Peter Reinhart's Whole Grain Breads*, which came out about 5 years after *The Bread Baker's Apprentice*, builds on the method that follows.)

The challenge a baker faces in making such breads is extracting the best of the grain flavor while overcoming some of the grassy and bitter tones of the bran and germ. Another chal-lenge is attaining a crumb network that opens up to provide both flavor and texture.

The best way to evoke flavor, as we show in many of the formulas, is to give the grain enzymes enough time to break out sugars trapped in their starches. One way to do this when working with whole grains is to use a large amount of pre-ferment, such as a *poolish* or soaker. In this version, both methods are used. A soaker is especially effective when coarse grains are part of the formula, and it also leaves open the option of substituting other grains, such as corn or oats, in place of the wheat to vary the texture of the finished loaf. Using a *poolish* to extend fermentation time contributes more flavor by developing acidity, balancing out the grassy flavor of the bran and germ in the process.

Makes two 1-pound (453g) loaves

MEASURE	OUNCES	GRAMS	INGREDIENTS	%
SOAKER (DAY 1)				
1 cup	4.25	120.5	coarse whole wheat flour or other coarse-grind whole grains (oats, corn, barley, rye)	100
¾ cup	6	170	water, at room temperature	141.2
TOTAL				242.2
WHOLE WHEAT POOLISH (DAY 1)				
1½ cups	6.75	191	high-protein whole wheat flour	100
¼ teaspoon	0.03	0.8	instant yeast	0.4
¾ cup	6	170	water, at room temperature	89
TOTAL				189.4
DOUGH (DAY TWO)				
2 cups	9	255	high-protein whole wheat flour	100
1⅓ teaspoons	0.33	9.5	salt	3.7
1 teaspoon	0.11	3	instant yeast	1.2
Use all	12.78	362	*poolish*	142
Use all	10.25	390.5	soaker	153
2 tablespoons	1.5	42.5	honey	16.7
1 tablespoon	0.5	14	vegetable oil (optional)	5.5
1 large	1.65	47	egg, slightly beaten (optional)	18.4

2 tablespoons sesame seeds, poppy seeds, quick rolled oats, or wheat bran for garnish (optional)

1 egg white, whisked with 1 tablespoon water, for egg white wash (optional)

TOTAL				440.5

TOTAL DOUGH FORMULA AND %

	OUNCES	GRAMS	INGREDIENTS	%
	20	567	whole wheat flour	100
	0.33	9.5	salt	1.7
	0.14	4	instant yeast	0.7
	0.5	14	vegetable oil	2.5
	1.5	42.5	honey	7.5
	1.65	47	egg	8.3
	12	340	water	60
TOTAL				180.7

The use of oil and/or egg is offered as an option to tenderize the bread and to help with the rise and cell structure. If you use either of them, you will probably need to add additional flour during the final mixing. Let the dough determine how much flour to add, as you knead it to a firm, slightly tacky consistency. Another way to tenderize the dough is to use milk or buttermilk instead of water when making the *poolish*.

1   The day before making the bread, make the soaker and the *poolish*. For the soaker, stir together the coarse whole wheat flour and the water in a bowl, cover the bowl with plastic wrap, and leave it at room temperature until the next day. For the *poolish*, mix together the whole wheat flour and yeast and then stir in the water to make a thick paste. Stir only until all the flour is hydrated; then cover the bowl with plastic wrap and allow to ferment at room temperature for 2 to 4 hours, or until it just begins to bubble. Then put the *poolish* in the refrigerator overnight.

2   The next day, remove the *poolish* from the refrigerator 1 hour before making the dough to take off the chill. Stir together the whole wheat flour, salt, and yeast in a 4-quart mixing bowl (or in the bowl of an electric mixer). Add the *poolish*, soaker, honey, and the oil and egg, if using, and stir with a large metal spoon (or mix on low speed with the paddle attachment for 1 minute) until the dough forms a ball, adding more water or flour if needed.

3   Sprinkle whole wheat flour on the counter, transfer the dough to the counter, and knead (or mix on medium speed with the dough hook) until the dough forms a firm, supple dough, adding flour, if needed. This will take approximately 10 to 12 minutes (or slightly less time by machine). The dough should be tacky but not sticky. It should pass the windowpane test (page 61) and register 77°F to 81°F (25°C to 27°C). Lightly oil a large bowl and transfer the dough to the bowl, rolling it around to coat it with oil. Cover the bowl with plastic wrap.

4   Ferment at room temperature for approximately 2 hours, or until the dough doubles in size.

5   Divide the dough into 2 equal pieces (they should weigh about 18 ounces/510g each). Shape them into sandwich loaves, as shown on page 85. Lightly oil two 8½ by 4½-inch (22 by 11.5cm) loaf pans and place the loaves in the pans. Mist the tops with spray oil and loosely cover with plastic wrap.

6   Proof at room temperature for about 1½ hours, or until the dough nearly doubles in size and is cresting above the lip of the pans.

7   Preheat the oven to 350°F (177°C) with the oven rack in the middle of the oven. Just before baking, you may choose to garnish the loaves by brushing the tops with egg white wash and sprinkling on sesame seeds or other garnish.

8   Bake the loaves for about 30 minutes and then rotate them 180 degrees, if necessary, for even baking. Continue baking for 15 to 30 minutes longer. The finished bread should register between 185°F and 190°F (85°C to 88°C) in the center and should sound hollow when thumped on the bottom. The loaves should be golden brown all around and firm on the sides as well as on the top and bottom. If they are soft and squishy on the sides, return them to the pans and continue baking until done.

9   When the loaves have finished baking, immediately remove them from the pans and let cool on a rack for at least 1 hour, preferably 2 hours, before slicing or serving.

Between the time I wrote the original *Bread Baker's Apprentice* and this anniversary edition, I have continued to learn new things about bread, much of which is contained in my five subsequent books. Even in this volume, I've slipped in some newer techniques or steps not in the original, such as additional stretch-and-fold steps and longer fermentation cycles. So, as a thank you to all of you who are now in possession of this new edition (both new and former *BBA* owners), I have included three never-before-published formulas that draw on my more recent discoveries. If you like them, I refer you to my later books for more like them and for additional background information.

Sprouted Wheat and Brown Rice Bread

One of the most exciting developments in the bread world is the discovery that sprouted whole grain flour makes extraordinary bread. In my 2014 book, *Bread Revolution*, I introduced readers to the details, benefits, and joys of baking with sprouted wheat and other sprouted grain flours and provided numerous formulas. Since that time, interest in sprouted grains has continued to grow, as has interest in other types of whole grain and multigrain breads, including the use of cooked grains as a major ingredient in the dough. I've been incorporating cooked brown rice and other cooked grains—wild rice, steel-cut oats, bulgur, grits—in my breads ever since my first *struan* bread, introduced in *Brother Juniper's Bread Book* in 1991 (and the flagship loaf of Brother Juniper's Bakery before that). But in more recent times, porridge-style breads, like those made at Chad Robertson's Tartine Bakery in San Francisco (and now other bakeries as well), have moved the dial on what's possible with this method. When I followed Chad Robertson's lead in using 50 percent (by weight) cooked grains in my doughs, the results were spectacular. So I've brought that method together with sprouted whole wheat flour (which is now, in my opinion, the most delicious and nutritious flour for whole grain breads and is becoming readily available at most markets) to create what I think of as the ultimate whole grain porridge bread. This version uses cooked brown rice; I like to use cooked sprouted brown rice, which, at the time of writing, is only available through mail order from To Your Health (see Resources, page 314). Regular brown rice (or any other

BREAD PROFILE
Lean dough; direct method; commercial yeast

. . .

DAYS TO MAKE: 1
8 minutes mixing; 4 hours stretch and fold, fermentation, shaping, and proofing; 30 to 60 minutes baking

. . .

COMMENTARY
If you want a taller, more open-holed loaf, here are two options: Add vital wheat gluten to the dough at a ratio of 3 percent against the flour weight (in this version, you would need to add 0.5 ounce/14g or about 1½ tablespoons). Or, replace half the sprouted wheat flour (8 ounces/227g) with an equal amount of unbleached bread flour. This produces a loaf similar to a high extraction bread, such as the Poilâne Miche on page 256.

cooked grain) works just fine, however. The biggest advantage of using sprouted whole wheat flour is that the sprouting process replaces the need for long fermentation or pre-ferments, as the full potential of flavor (and nutrients) trapped in the grain is released during the sprouting and milling process, making this a very easy bread to make.

Makes one large 2-pound (907g) or two 1-pound (453g) sandwich or hearth loaves

MEASURE	OUNCES	GRAMS	INGREDIENTS	%
About 1½ cups	8	227	cooked brown rice or other whole grain, such as grits, buckwheat, barley, steel-cut oats, millet, or bulgur	50
3¾ cups	16	454	sprouted whole wheat flour	100
1⅓ teaspoons	0.35	10	salt	2.2
2 teaspoons	0.22	6	instant yeast	1.4
1½ cups	12	340	water, lukewarm (90°F to 100°F/32°C to 38°C)	75
All-purpose or bread flour, Semolina, or cornmeal for dusting				
TOTAL				228.6

1   A day or two before making the bread, cook the rice or other grain (see below for cooking instructions, or use leftover cooked grain from a meal). Let cool and then cover and refrigerate until needed.

2   Stir together the flour, salt, and yeast in a 4-quart mixing bowl (or in the bowl of an electric mixer). Add the cooked grain and water and stir until the flour is hydrated and a coarse, wet dough forms (or mix on low speed with the paddle attachment for about 1 minute). Do not add more flour, as the dough will thicken while it rests. Let the dough rest in the bowl, uncovered, for 5 minutes. Then, using a large metal spoon and dipping it in water as needed to prevent sticking, stir (or mix on medium-low speed with the paddle) for 1 to 2 minutes. The dough should firm up slightly but still be very soft and sticky (similar to ciabatta dough). Add flour or water only if necessary to achieve that texture; the dough will firm up during the next phase.

3   Prepare an oil slick on the counter, as described on page 59. Using a bowl scraper dipped in water or oil, transfer the dough to the oiled surface. With wet or oiled hands, stretch and fold the dough and then form it into a ball. Place it in a lightly oiled bowl, roll it around the bowl to coat it with oil, and cover the bowl with plastic wrap. After 20 minutes, with wet or oiled hands, return the dough to the oiled surface and stretch and fold the dough (see page 59). The dough will firm up slightly but still be soft and somewhat sticky. Return the dough to the covered bowl (or cover it with the bowl). Repeat the stretch-and-fold technique two more times at

20-minute intervals. The dough should feel stronger and less sticky after each stretch and fold and have a springy or bouncy quality when patted. Return the dough to the oiled bowl, mist the top with spray oil, and cover the bowl with plastic wrap.

4   Ferment at room temperature for approximately 1½ hours, or until the dough nearly doubles in size.

5   Using an oiled bowl scraper, gently transfer the dough to a floured or oiled work surface. If making 1 large loaf, shape the dough with floured or oiled hands into a *boule* or *bâtard* (see pages 76 and 77). Alternatively, divide them into the desired-size pieces for loaf pans or smaller freestanding hearth breads. Shape them into sandwich loaves (see page 85) or *boules* or *bâtards* for freestanding loaves. If you are baking them in loaf pans, lightly oil the pans (8½ by 4½-inch/22 by 11.5cm pans for 1-pound/453g loaves; 9 by 5-inch/23 by 13cm pans for 2-pound/907g loaves). If you are baking them freestanding, line 1 or 2 sheet pans with baking parchment and dust with flour, semolina, or cornmeal. Transfer the shaped dough to the pan(s), mist the tops with spray oil, and cover the dough loosely with plastic wrap. (Note: you may also use prepared *bannetons* for hearth loaves. See page 32.)

6   Proof at room temperature for approximately 45 to 90 minutes, or until the dough has grown 1½ times in size.

7   Prepare the oven for hearth baking as described on page 97, making sure to have an empty steam pan in place, and preheat to 450°F (232°C). For loaf-pan breads, preheat the oven to 375°F (190°C) with the oven rack on the middle shelf (no steam pan is needed for loaf-pan breads).

8   Score the freestanding bread(s) as desired (see page 96). Generously dust a peel or the back of a sheet pan with flour, semolina, or cornmeal and very gently transfer the freestanding loaves to the peel or pan. Transfer the loaves to the baking stone (or bake directly on the sheet pan). Pour 1 cup hot water into the steam pan and close the door. After 30 seconds, spray the oven walls with water and close the door. Repeat twice more at 30-second intervals. After the final spray, lower the oven setting to 425°F (218°C) and bake for 20 minutes. Check the bread at this point and rotate 180 degrees, if necessary, for even baking. Continue to bake for 20 to 30 minutes, longer, depending on the size. If baking loaf-pan breads, place them on the middle oven rack and bake for 45 to 55 minutes, rotating them after the first 20 minutes for even baking. The finished loaves should be a rich golden brown on all sides and sound hollow when thumped on the bottom. The internal temperature of the bread should be 200°F (93°C) for hearth bread and 190°F (88°C) for loaf-pan bread.

9   Remove the bread(s) from the oven, and remove the loaves from the pans, if using. Let cool on a rack for at least 45 minutes before slicing or serving. The crust will tend to soften as the bread cools but can be recrisped by returning the bread to a hot oven (450°F/232°C) for about 5 minutes.

Sprouted Whole Wheat Onion and Poppy Seed Bialys

BREAD PROFILE
Slightly enriched dough (honey); direct method; commercial yeast

• • •

DAYS TO MAKE: 1
8 minutes mixing; 4 hours stretch and fold, fermentation, shaping, and proofing; 10 to 18 minutes baking

• • •

COMMENTARY
Secrets of a Jewish Baker author George Greenstein suggests dusting the top of the filling with a sprinkle of rye flour, which will stabilize the filling and hold it in place. It's a nice tip, though strictly optional.

Bialys (properly called *bialystoker kuchen*) are the underappreciated stepbrothers of the bagel, though they are far from underappreciated by anyone who knows them. They have their own glorious history, which you can read about in books like *The Bialy Eaters* by Mimi Sheraton, *Inside the Jewish Bakery* by Stanley Ginsberg and Norman Berg, or the wonderful *Secrets of a Jewish Baker* by George Greenstein. But for me they are about rekindling childhood memories and about an amazing flavor explosion of bread and filling, whether onion, poppy seed (or better yet, onion and poppy, as this recipe shows), cheese, or some concoction of your own. A bialy dimple replaces the bagel hole and becomes the platform for the filling, and unlike bagels, bialys are not boiled, just baked. They can be made using the bagel dough formula on page 125, or, as I prefer, with a slightly softer, 100 percent whole grain dough that uses sprouted whole wheat flour, like the recipe that follows.

Makes 8 to 10 bialys

MEASURE	OUNCES	GRAMS	INGREDIENTS	%
DOUGH				
4¼ cups	18	510	sprouted whole wheat flour	100
1¼ teaspoons	0.33	9.5	salt	1.85
1¼ teaspoons	0.14	4	instant yeast	0.8
4½ teaspoons	1	28	honey	5.6
1¾ cups plus 1 tablespoon	15	425	water	83.3
TOTAL				191.55

ONION-POPPY SEED FILLING

2 tablespoons (1 ounce/28g) vegetable oil

2 medium-size (16 ounces/454g) yellow onions, finely chopped or minced

½ teaspoon (0.13 ounce/3.5g) salt

2 tablespoons (0.5 ounce/14g) poppy seeds

⅛ teaspoon (0.04 ounce/1g) ground black pepper, or to taste

1   To make the dough, stir together the flour, salt, and yeast in a 4-quart mixing bowl (or in the bowl of an electric mixer). Add the honey and water and stir until the flour is hydrated and a coarse, wet dough forms (or mix on low speed with the paddle attachment for about 1 minute). Don't add more flour, as the dough will thicken while it rests. Let the dough rest in the bowl, uncovered, for 5 minutes. Then, using a large metal spoon and dipping it in water as needed to prevent sticking, stir (or mix on medium-low speed) for 1 to 2 minutes. The dough should firm slightly but still be soft and slightly sticky (similar to baguette dough). Add flour or water only if necessary to achieve that texture; the dough will firm up during the next phase.

2   Prepare an oil slick on the counter, as described on page 59. Using a bowl scraper dipped in water or oil, transfer the dough to the oiled surface. With wet or oiled hands, stretch and fold the dough, form it into a ball, place it in a lightly oiled bowl, roll it around the bowl to coat it with oil, and cover the bowl with plastic wrap. After 20 minutes, with wet or oiled hands, return the dough to the oiled surface and stretch and fold the dough (see page 59). The dough will firm up slightly but still be soft and somewhat sticky. Return the dough to the covered bowl (or cover it with the bowl). Repeat the stretch-and-fold technique two more times at 20-minute intervals. The dough should feel stronger and less sticky after each stretch and fold and have a springy or bouncy quality when patted. Return the dough to the oiled bowl, mist the top with spray oil, and cover the bowl with plastic wrap.

3   Ferment at room temperature for 1 to 1½ hours, or until the dough nearly doubles in size.

4   Line a sheet pan with baking parchment or a silicone baking mat and mist it lightly with spray oil. Using an oiled bowl scraper, gently transfer the dough to an oiled work surface. Divide the dough into 8 to 10 equal-size pieces (about 3 ounces/85g each for smaller bialys and about 4 ounces/113g for larger bialys). Form each piece into a tight round, as if making dinner rolls (see page 86) or small *boules* (see page 76) and lay them out evenly spaced on the prepared pan. Mist the tops of the dough balls with spray oil and cover the pan loosely with plastic wrap.

5   Proof at room temperature for 1 to 1½ hours, or until the dough doubles in size.

6   While the dough is proofing, prepare the filling. Heat the oil in a skillet over medium heat. Add the onions and salt and sauté for 1 minute. Reduce the heat to medium-low and gently stir every minute or so, until the onions begin to soften and turn a light golden brown. This should take 5 to 10 minutes. Remove from the heat and stir in the poppy seeds and pepper. Spread the onions out on a sheet pan to cool completely while the dough balls continue to rise. (Note: The filling can be prepared up to 1 week in advance and kept in a covered container in the refrigerator.)

7   Preheat the oven to 500°F (260°C) with oven racks on the upper shelves. Line a second sheet pan with baking parchment or a silicone baking mat and mist with spray oil.

8   When the dough balls have doubled in size, dip your fingertips into a bowl of water and use them to dimple each dough ball into a flat disk, widening it to about 4 inches (10cm) in diameter but retaining a thick outer ring about a ½ inch (13mm) wide (like the *cornicione* of a pizza). The center can be pressed down until very thin—even paper-thin. Divide the shaped pieces between the 2 prepared pans. Dividing the filling evenly among all the shaped pieces, place a spoonful of the filling into the center of each piece and spread it over the flattened section. Bake both pans in the oven on the upper racks for about 5 minutes. Switch the pans between the racks and rotate them 180 degrees, so that they bake evenly. Bake for 5 to 10 minutes longer, or until the bialys are a rich golden brown. (If you prefer to bake only 1 pan at a time, cover the second pan with plastic wrap and refrigerate it.)

9   Remove the pans from the oven and let the bialys cool for at least 5 minutes before serving. (Note: for shinier bialies, brush the surface of the baked bialies with a little vegetable oil or melted butter as soon as they come out of the oven.)

Beyond Ultimate Cinnamon and Sticky Buns

One of the most popular recipes in *Peter Reinhart's Artisan Breads Everyday* (*ABE* for short) is for chocolate cinnamon *babka*, a luscious rich dough rolled around a filling of semisweet chocolate, butter, and cinnamon sugar and then baked into a loaf. The dough is so delicious that I started thinking about other things I could make with it. Since the ingredients are very similar to those of brioche (butter, egg yolks, milk, and sugar), I consider it a member of the brioche family, much like *Kugelhopf*, *baba au rhum*, and Easter *kulich*. When I was on the road demonstrating various doughs from *ABE*, I often made cinnamon buns and sticky buns with the traditional white sweet dough recipe in the book, and *babka* with the richer, more golden *babka* dough. One time a student asked what would happen if we made the cinnamon buns and sticky buns using the *babka* dough instead. So, of course, we decided to try it out, and all I can say is that if it wasn't true before, it certainly is now: they are called sticky buns because they truly stick to your buns! But, oh, is it worth it!

This is a 2-day process because the dough is too fragile to roll out and fill while still at room temperature. By holding it overnight in the refrigerator, the dough firms up, making it easy to roll out on a lightly oiled counter and fill with cinnamon sugar. At this point, the dough can be finished off as cinnamon buns, baked on a sheet pan, and glazed after they come out of the oven, or they can be baked in a caramel glaze in a cake pan for a superdecadent sticky bun to end all sticky buns. You can refer to the cinnamon bun and sticky bun instructions on page 150 for the glazes, but I've also added two other new glazes here, which can be used on the other buns, as well. These are not for the faint of heart, and I advise a gym membership and regular workouts for anyone who eats them. But, hey, it's kind of fun to push the envelope from time to time.

(continued)

BREAD PROFILE
Enriched, standard dough; direct method; commercial yeast

• • •

DAYS TO MAKE: 2
DAY 1: 5 to 8 minutes, mixing; overnight cold fermentation

DAY 2: 2 hours shaping, panning, and proofing. 20 to 25 minutes baking

• • •

COMMENTARY
This dough is made in a different manner than most of the doughs in this book, in that the instant yeast is added to the warm milk and the soft dough firms up during the overnight cold fermentation. It won't rise very much during the final proofing stage but has a strong oven spring, nearly doubling size during the bake. It is best eaten while still warm, but can also be warmed up in the oven at any time to restore it to it's freshly baked softness.

Makes 8 to 12 buns

MEASURE	OUNCES	GRAMS	INGREDIENTS	%
2 tablespoons	0.67	19	instant yeast	4.5
¾ cup	6	170	whole or low-fat milk, lukewarm (90°F to 100°F/32°C to 38°C)	40
6 tablespoons	3	85	unsalted butter, at room temperature	20
2 tablespoons	1	28	melted vegetable oil	6.7
6 tablespoons	3	85	granulated sugar	20
1 teaspoon	0.25	7	vanilla extract	1.7
5 large	3	85	egg yolks	20
3¼ cups	15	425	unbleached all-purpose flour	100
Scant 1 teaspoon or 1½ teaspoons	0.21 0.21	6 6	salt kosher salt	1.4
2 tablespoons	1	28	unsalted butter, melted, for brushing	
½ cup	4	113	cinnamon sugar (6½ tablespoons granulated sugar mixed with 1½ tablespoons ground cinnamon)	
TOTAL				214.3
White Fondant Glaze for Cinnamon Buns (page 153) or Cream Cheese Glaze, for cinnamon buns (page 300)				
Caramel Glaze for Sticky Buns (page 153), Honey-Almond Glaze (page 301), or Old-Fashioned Caramel Glaze for Sticky Buns (page 301)				
½ to ¾ cup walnuts or pecans, for sticky buns (optional)				
½ to ¾ cup raisins, dried cranberries or cherries, or other dried fruit, for sticky buns (optional)				

1 In a small bowl, sprinkle the yeast in the lukewarm milk. Stir the mixture with a spoon or whisk to dissolve the yeast. Set aside for about 5 minutes before mixing it into the dough.

2 Place the butter, oil, and sugar in the bowl of an electric mixer fitted with the paddle attachment and cream together on medium speed until smooth (or use a large metal spoon and mixing bowl and do it by hand). In a small bowl, lightly whisk together the vanilla and egg yolks to break up the yolks. Add the egg yolk–vanilla mixture to the butter-sugar mixture in four installments, beating on medium speed (or vigorously by hand) after each addition until incorporated, and before adding the next addition. When all the egg yolks are incorporated, increase the mixer speed to medium-high and continue mixing for another 2 minutes, or until the mixture is fluffy, stopping to scrape down sides of the bowl with a spatula or bowl scraper once or twice, if needed (or beat vigorously by hand). Turn off the mixer and add the flour, salt, and yeast mixture. On low speed, mix for 2 to 3 minutes, or until a soft, slightly sticky dough forms (you may have to switch to the dough hook if your mixer struggles with the paddle attachment; if mixing by hand, use a strong spoon or your hands).

3 Sprinkle flour on the counter (or use the oil slick method, as described on page 59). Use a plastic bowl scraper to transfer the dough to the work surface. Knead the dough by hand for an additional 2 minutes, adding more flour, only if needed, to make the dough pliable but still tacky. The dough should be a beautiful golden color and feel soft and supple, "like a baby's bottom." Form the dough into a ball and place it into a lightly oiled bowl, rolling it around to coat it with oil. Cover the bowl with plastic wrap and place in the refrigerator overnight (or for up to a maximum of 3 days). The dough will rise somewhat but will not double in size (if it rises significantly in less time, you can degas it and return it to the refrigerator). During this interval, prepare your cinnamon sugar and chosen glaze and set it aside or refrigerate.

4 On the day of the bake, remove the dough from the refrigerator about 1 hour before you plan to bake but begin rolling out and shaping the dough immediately, while the dough is still cold and firm. Melt the butter for brushing. Mist the counter with spray oil, or create a light oil slick, and transfer the chilled dough to it. Using a rolling pin, gently roll out the dough into a 16- to 18-inch (41 to 46cm) square ¼ to ⅓ inch (6 to 8.5mm) thick. Brush the melted butter over the surface and then sprinkle the cinnamon sugar evenly over the surface, leaving a ¼-inch (6mm) border uncovered around the full perimeter. Roll up the dough like a jelly roll (or like a carpet), forming a log, and place it, seam side down, on the counter. Using your palms and firm but gentle pressure, roll the log to extend its length a few more inches, preferably to between 20 and 24 inches (51 to 61cm). Cut the log crosswise into 8 to 12 spiral buns, each about 2 inches (5cm) thick.

5 If making cinnamon buns, line 2 sheet pans with baking parchment or silicone baking mats and place the buns, face up (spiral side up), on the sheet pans, spacing them about 2 inches (5cm) apart. Preheat the oven to 325°F (163°C) with the oven racks on the middle shelves. Proof the buns at room temperature while the oven heats up; the cold dough will not rise now, but it will rise dramatically after you place the pans in the oven. Bake the buns for 10 minutes. Rotate the pans and continue baking for 5 to 15 minutes longer, or until the buns are a rich golden brown. When the buns are ready, remove the pan(s) from the oven and let cool in the pan for 5 to 10 minutes. If using the fondant glaze, drizzle it over the warm buns. If using the cream cheese glaze, spread it on the buns with an offset spatula or icing spreader. You can serve these immediately after glazing or let them cool on the pan or on cooling racks for the glaze to firm up or set.

6 If making sticky buns, mist 3 round 9-inch (23cm) cake pans with spray oil and then coat the bottoms with a ¼-inch (6mm) thick layer of the caramel or honey almond glaze or a ⅓-inch (8.5mm) thick layer of the old-fashioned caramel glaze. (You may not need all the glaze; the leftover will keep in a covered container in the refrigerator for about 2 weeks.) Sprinkle the nuts or dried fruit over the glaze (the addition is optional but highly advised for flavor). Place 4 buns, nicest spiral side face down, in each pan, spacing them about 1 inch (2.5cm) apart. The buns will rise and spread while baking, filling the pans. Preheat the oven to 325°F (163° C) with a rack in the lower third of the oven (so the glaze gets plenty of bottom heat). Set up a second rack on the lowest level. Bake the buns as soon as the oven is ready, rotating the pans every 10 minutes for even baking. They should take 25 to 35 minutes. The glaze will melt, bubble, and caramelize, and the visible dough will be a dark golden brown. If the glaze begins to bubble over the rim of any pan, place a sheet pan on the lowest oven rack to catch the drips. But do not put the second pan in the oven unless the glaze bubbles over, as the direct bottom heat is important during the first part of the bake. To see how the buns are doing, lift a bun with a metal spatula or pair of tongs; the underside should be a light caramel brown, not white. The glaze itself should turn a rich amber or golden brown, and all the sugar should have melted to become caramel. If the glaze is still grainy and not richly caramelized, place a sheet of aluminum foil over the top of the buns and keep baking until the glaze becomes smooth and caramelized.

7   When the buns are ready, remove the pans from the oven and let the buns cool for 3 to 5 minutes to allow the caramel to begin to firm up. Invert a plate over the top of a pan, flip the pan and plate together, place on the counter, and lift off the pan. Be careful, as the glaze will still be very hot. Use a rubber spatula to carefully scoop any run-off glaze or any glaze remaining in the pan over the buns. Repeat with the remaining pans. Wait for at least 15 minutes before serving.

Sticky Bun Slurry

1 cup granulated sugar

1 cup light brown sugar

8 ounces (2 sticks) unsalted butter at soft room temperature, or melted

¼ cup light corn syrup

¼ teaspoon salt (⅓ teaspoon if coarse kosher salt)

½ teaspoon lemon or orange extract (optional)

Cream the sugar and butter together with the paddle attachment, or with a large spoon, until the butter is smooth and incorporated. Add the remaining ingredients and mix with the paddle attachment (or in a food processor) on medium speed for about 2 minutes. Increase to medium high and continue mixing until the slurry becomes fluffy, about 1 to 2 additional minutes. This will keep in the refrigerator for at least 2 weeks.

Cream Cheese Glaze

4 ounces (113g) cream cheese, at room temperature

4 tablespoons unsalted butter, melted

1 cup powdered sugar, sifted

1 teaspoon vanilla extract

¼ teaspoon lemon or orange extract (or 1 teaspoon fresh lemon juice or orange liqueur)

Pinch of salt

Using an electric mixer fitted with the paddle attachment, cream together the cream cheese, butter, and powdered sugar on low speed until well mixed (or use a mixing bowl and a large spoon and cream by hand). Add the extracts and salt and beat on medium speed until a smooth paste forms. Increase the speed to medium-high for about 20 seconds to fluff up the glaze (or beat vigorously by hand). Use as directed in the recipe.

Honey Almond Glaze

1 cup honey

1 cup unsalted butter at soft room temperature or melted

¼ tsp salt (⅓ teaspoon kosher salt)

Using an electric mixer fitted with the paddle attachment, cream together the honey, butter, and salt on medium-high speed until smooth (or use a mixing bowl and a large spoon and cream by hand). Use as directed in the recipe, but top with slivered or coarsely chopped almonds in place of the walnuts, pecans, or dried fruit.

Old-Fashioned Caramel Glaze

⅔ cup granulated sugar

⅔ cup firmly packed light brown sugar

⅔ cup heavy cream

1 tablespoon unsalted butter at soft room temperature or melted

1 tablespoon light corn syrup

Using an electric mixer fitted with the paddle attachment, cream together the sugars, cream, butter, and corn syrup on medium speed until smooth (or use a mixing bowl and a large spoon and cream by hand). Use as directed in the recipe.

WOOD-FIRED BAKING IN BENNETT VALLEY

The following was written in the year 2000, and the recipes refer to the breads Tim Decker made then, before he and his wife, Crystal, moved the operation to Roan Mountain, Tennessee, a few years later. I have not been to Smokey Mountain Bakers, their new Tennessee bakery, but I have heard that, in addition to their great breads and pastries, Tim and Crystal are now also making amazing pizzas.

Maggie Glezer's wonderful book, *Artisan Baking Across America,* profiles some of the finest bakeries in the United States, along with many of their distinctive breads. Maggie is someone with whom I love talking bread. Unfortunately, she wrote her book before Bennett Valley Bread and Pastry opened in the spring of 2000 and was thus unable to feature them. Crystal makes the award-winning pastries and Tim, who used to be my head baker at Brother Juniper's Bakery in Santa Rosa, creates and bakes all the breads. Tim's breads won fifteen double-gold medals at the prestigious Sonoma County Harvest Fair, including the sweepstakes award for best in show—and that was just a few months after the shop opened! The last person to do as well was Craig Ponsford of Artisan Bakers, who then went on to win the world championship of bread at the 1995 Coupe du Monde de la Boulangerie.

Tim is a true bread fanatic and purist, nurturing his doughs from start to finish with almost the same degree of love as if they were his children (and his real kids sometimes help at the bakery, knowing how important the loaves are to their dad). He plays his wood-fired oven the way he plays his electric guitar (he was in a heavy metal and blues band when we first met)— that is, with intensity, pushing it to its limits. In the middle of each night, he builds a wood fire from local oak on the deck of the oven and waits for it to burn down to ashes, which he then sweeps out. At that point the oven is up to about 650°F (343°C) and is ready to receive the first of many doughs. The oven will bake each round of strategically chosen bread as it gradually cools over the next eight to twelve hours; the pizzas, focaccia, and hard crusty breads going first, while the softer, more enriched doughs are saved for the later, cooler cycles. At the time

◄ *Épis* emerge from the hot deck with a rich, deep golden brown crust. We affectionately refer to this dark color as "European bake" to distinguish it from the American style of light crust.

of writing, Tim held the national record for consecutive bakes from a single firing: sixteen. I asked him who keeps track of such arcane statistics, and he assured me that there is a network of fire and oven freaks out there who take these things seriously. Tim is able to sustain the heat from a single firing because of a unique insulation system he devised to supplement the original system that the late, great oven master Alan Scott, founder of Oven Crafters, designed. This makes it possible for Tim to bake all day (and night) without having to build a new fire on the deck. Other wood-fired oven bakers are now coming to see Tim, even though he's the new guy on the block, for tips on how to insulate their ovens for better heat retention.

Tim and Crystal's story is significant because it is a good example of the kind of passion fueling the bread revolution. Bread baking is a difficult career and one that does not lead to riches, except in rare cases. You do it because it brings about other kinds of satisfaction and rewards and because it makes people happy.

Hearth baking begins by firing the oven with hardwood, in this instance, oak.

A wood-fired deck radiates enough heat to bake bread as long as eight hours after the initial firing.

I had the good fortune of watching Tim grow both as a baker and in his love for the well-crafted loaf. He first learned the craft while making bread at Lotus Bakery, an organic, whole grain bakery in Santa Rosa owned by Lynn and Jim Dow, also friends of mine. (It is important to convey that the bread bakers of Sonoma County have achieved that collegial fellowship born of friendly competitiveness. Everyone knows one another and helps out when someone is short of ingredients or needs equipment help, and there is a free flow of shared ideas and respect for one another's style and products. As a result, many of the local bakers are friends as well as competitors, and this friendship is also fostered on a wider scale by the Bread Bakers Guild of America, of which many of the local bakers are members.)

Tim came to Brother Juniper's for the next stage in his bread-baking evolution and spent 7 years perfecting my breads, all the while nurturing his own budding vision. After I sold Brother Juniper's, he went to work at another award-winning shop, the Village Bakery in Sebastopol, just outside of Santa Rosa. There, Tim was able to focus more on wild-yeast breads and dive fully into starters and pre-ferments, while also adding to his skills by participating in training seminars and networking with other bakers. Crystal went to work at the Village Bakery as the pastry chef, so they were finally able to work together in the same bakeshop. It was there they realized that their true dream was to have a bakery of their own, one in which they could have total control of the systems and formulas to produce breads and pastries the way they wanted them to be, according to their own vision.

So, having served their long apprenticeship and fully knowing what they were getting into, they resurrected a defunct bakeshop in a Santa Rosa neighborhood called Bennett Valley, built a wood-fired oven to supplement the existing, creaky, revolving-reel oven, and plunged into business. The bakery was discovered almost immediately by the savvy foodies of Sonoma County. Then, because they couldn't keep up with the demand for their products, they faced the same problem that Lionel Poilâne faced (and solved) in Paris: how to grow their business but stay true to their artisan vision. It's an age-old quandary: how to make an honest living without compromising the quality of your work. Knowing Tim and Crystal and the integrity that they embody, and their love of the work they do together, I expected they would come up with some very creative solutions. As we went to press with the original edition of this book, Tim was discussing the possibility of building a second wood-fired oven at his original training ground, Lotus Bakery, where Jim and Lynn Dow were willing to help the Deckers

expand their baking capacity to meet the growing demand. Since then, of course, they simply transplanted their vision to Tennessee and have, once again, drawn a large following.

This is a classic feel-good story. It makes me proud to see one of my apprentice protégés go beyond where I could go when I was an active baker, taking the handoff, so to speak, not just from me but from a lineage of others who were also giving and taking handoffs. Tim and Crystal Decker personify the craftsperson tradition at its finest—a transmission of knowledge from hand to hand, knowledge building upon knowledge. Their story exemplifies what I am trying to accomplish with this book, this transmission. I hope that you, each and every reader, will take the handoff of this vision and run with it. Take all that has gone before and find your own baking voice, and build your bread your way.

As a fitting epilogue and a parting gift, here are two of Bennett Valley Bread and Pastry's most popular breads, created and handed off to you, the next generation, by Tim Decker.

Tim, his long-handled peel, and his oven.

Potato, Cheddar, and Chive Torpedoes

Makes two 1½-pound (680g) loaves

MEASURE	OUNCES	GRAMS	INGREDIENTS	%
1 large or 2 small	8	227	potatoes, unpeeled, coarsely chopped, boiled in 3 cups water until soft, and cooled	44.5
½ to 1 cup	4 to 8	113 to 227	potato water, lukewarm (90°F to 100°F/32°C to 38°C)	22 to 44.4
1½ cups	10.5	298	barm (mother starter, page 241, refreshed within 24 hours)	58.4
4 cups	18	510	unbleached bread flour	100
2 teaspoons	0.22	6	instant yeast	1.2
2 teaspoons	0.5	14	salt	2.9
¼ to ½ cup	1	28	chopped fresh chives	5.5
6 thin slices	about 4	about 113	sharp Cheddar cheese	22.2
Bread flour, semolina, or cornmeal for dusting				
TOTAL				256 to 279.1

TOTAL DOUGH FORMULA AND %

	OUNCES	GRAMS	INGREDIENTS	%
	23	659	bread flour	100
	8	227	potatoes	34.5
	0.22	6	instant yeast	0.9
	0.5	14	salt	2.1
	5.25	149	water (in barm)	22.6
	4 to 8	113 to 227	potato water	17 to 34
	1	28	chives	4.2
	4	113	Cheddar cheese	17
TOTAL				198.3 to 215.3

BREAD PROFILE
Enriched, standard dough; indirect method; mixed leavening method

• • •

DAYS TO MAKE: 1 (WITH BARM)
1 hour to prepare potatoes and de-chill barm; 45 minutes mixing; 4 hours stretch and fold, fermentation, shaping, and proofing; 35 to 40 minutes baking.

• • •

COMMENTARY
These are mixed-method (wild yeast spiked with commercial yeast) *bâtards*. They pucker open with a *grigne* of crispy Cheddar cheese, followed by a beautiful soft cheese spiral highlighted with bits of green chives. Notice that the bread is made with a wet-sponge starter (the barm), but it can also be made with a firm starter, in which case you will need about ½ cup (4 ounces/113g) more water or potato water. The potato water, by the way, adds minerals and dissolved potato starch and sugars that greatly enhance the flavor and soften the dough.

1   Prepare the potatoes in advance, allowing time for the potatoes and the cooking water to cool to lukewarm. Set these aside until needed. Pull the measured amount of barm out of the refrigerator 1 hour before making the bread to take off the chill.

2   With a large metal spoon, stir together the barm, half of the flour, the yeast, cooked potatoes, and ½ cup (4 ounces/113g) of the potato water in a 4-quart mixing bowl (or in the bowl of an electric mixer using the paddle attachment) to form a coarse, wet dough. Let this sit uncovered for 30 minutes.

3 Add the rest of the flour and the salt and stir together (or mix on low speed with the dough hook) for a minute or two, or until the ingredients form a ball, adding as much as you need of the remaining water.

4 Sprinkle flour on the counter, transfer the dough to the counter, and knead the dough for 4 to 6 minutes (or mix on medium-low speed with the dough hook for 4 minutes), adding flour or water if needed, until the dough is very tacky but not sticky. Add the chives and continue kneading (or mixing) until they are evenly distributed, 1 to 2 minutes. (In the mixer, the dough should clear the sides of the bowl as well as the bottom of the bowl.) The dough should pass the windowpane test (page 61), remain very tacky but not sticky, and register 77°F to 81°F (25°C to 27°C). Lightly oil a large bowl and transfer the dough to the bowl, rolling it to coat it with oil. Cover the bowl with plastic wrap. After 20 minutes, stretch and fold the dough (see page 59) and return it to the covered bowl. Repeat two more times at 20-minute intervals, again returning the dough to the covered bowl.

5 Ferment at room temperature for about 1½ hours, or until the dough doubles in size.

6 Transfer the dough to the counter and cut it into 2 equal pieces. Press each piece into a rectangle about 6 inches (15cm) wide and 8 inches (20cm) long. Lay 3 slices of cheese on each rectangle, covering the surface but leaving a ½-inch (13mm) border uncovered around the edges. Tightly roll up the dough, from bottom to top, jelly-roll style, creating a spiral with the cheese. Seal the ends of the rolled dough, which should look like a log, into points by rolling them more forcefully with your hands. This will give the dough a torpedo look, plump in the center and tapered at the ends. As you roll down on the ends, be sure to squeeze out any trapped air pockets to avoid separation of the layers. Seal the bottom seam closed with the edge of your hand, as shown on page 85.

7 Line a sheet pan with baking parchment, mist the parchment lightly with spray oil, and then dust the parchment with flour or cornmeal. Lay the 2 loaves across the width of the pan, mist the tops lightly with spray oil, and cover them loosely with plastic wrap or a towel.

8 Proof at room temperature for approximately 1 hour, or until the dough nearly doubles in size.

9 Prepare the oven for hearth baking as described on page 97, making sure to have an empty steam pan in place. Preheat the oven to 500°F (260°C). Score the top of each loaf with 2 diagonal slashes (as shown on page 96), making sure to cut through to the first layer of cheese.

10 Generously dust a peel or the back of a sheet pan with flour or cornmeal and very gently transfer the loaves, with or without the parchment, to the peel or pan. Slide the loaves onto the baking stone or bake the loaves directly on the pan. Pour 1 cup hot water into the steam pan and shut the door. After 30 seconds, spray the oven walls with water and close the door again. Repeat twice more at 30-second intervals. After the final spray, lower the oven setting to 450°F (232°C) and bake for 35 to 40 minutes. After 15 minutes, rotate the loaves 180 degrees, if necessary, for even baking. The loaves should register 200°F (93°C) in the center, be nicely browned all over, and sound hollow when thumped on the bottom. The cheese will bubble out of the cuts, crisp up, and also brown.

11 Transfer the finished loaves to a rack and let cool for at least 45 minutes before slicing or serving.

Roasted Onion and Asiago Miche

Makes 2 large rounds

Note: This dough is too large for most home mixers (other than a Magic Mill), so it is best to make it by hand.

BREAD PROFILE
Enriched, semirustic dough; indirect method; mixed leavening method

• • •

DAYS TO MAKE: 3
DAY 1: 8 hours sponge

DAY 2: 1 hour to de-chill sponge and prepare onions; 15 minutes mixing; 3 to 4 hours stretch and fold, fermentation and shaping

DAY 3: 2½ hours proofing and final shaping; 35 to 50 minutes baking

• • •

COMMENTARY
This bread takes 3 days to make from start to finish, though the amount of time actually spent on the dough is not that long. *Mise en place*, as always, is vitally important. Having everything prepared in advance, such as the onions and cheese, will save you from unnecessary stress. Please read the instructions thoroughly before starting, and plan out your steps accordingly.

MEASURE	OUNCES	GRAMS	INGREDIENTS	%
SPONGE (DAY 1)				
¼ cup	2	57	barm (mother starter, page 241)	17.9
1 cup	8	227	water, at room temperature	71.2
2½ cups	11.25	319	unbleached bread flour	100
TOTAL				189.1
ROASTED ONION (DAY 1)				
1 large or 2 small	8.5	241	yellow or white onions	n/a
1 tablespoon	0.5	14	olive oil	n/a
pinch, or to taste			coarsely ground black pepper	n/a
¼ teaspoon	0.06	1.75	salt	n/a
DOUGH (DAYS 2 AND 3)				
7 cups	32	907	unbleached bread flour	100
2¼ teaspoons	0.25	7	instant yeast	0.8
2¼ cups	18	510	water, lukewarm (90°F to 100°F/32°C to 38°C)	56.2
Use all	n/a	n/a	sponge	56.2
4 teaspoons	1	28	salt	3
3 tablespoons	1.5	42.5	olive oil	4.7
3 cups	16	454	shredded or grated Asiago cheese (or substitute freshly grated Parmesan, romano, or dry Monterey Jack)	50
½ cup	2	57	coarsely chopped fresh chives	6.3
½ cup	2	57	coarsely chopped scallions	6.3
Use all			roasted onions	26.7
Bread flour, semolina, or cornmeal for dusting				
TOTAL				254

TOTAL DOUGH FORMULA AND %

	OUNCES	GRAMS	INGREDIENTS	%
	44.25	1,254 (1.25kg)	bread flour	100
	8	227	roasted onion	18.1
	0.25	7	instant yeast	0.55
	1	28	salt	2.2
	2	57	chives	4.5
	2	57	scallions	4.5
	16	454	asiago cheese	36
	27	765	water	61
	2	57	olive oil	4.5
TOTAL				231.35

This dough is made from a sticky starter that, in turn, is built from a small amount of barm (mother starter). This is a large, round, dimpled loaf with lots of big holes in the crumb between the dimples. It calls for oven-roasted onion, which is cooked in a very hot oven and can be done a day or two in advance (or substitute sautéed onions).

1   Day 1: One day before making the dough and 2 days before baking the bread, make the sponge. Stir together the barm, water, and flour in a bowl until the flour is completely hydrated and the mixture forms a sticky dough. Cover the bowl with plastic wrap and ferment at room temperature for 8 hours, or until the sponge is very bubbly. If it is a cool day and the sponge is fermenting slowly, you can leave it out overnight. Otherwise, put it in the refrigerator when it foams and is bubbly.

2   Day 1: To roast the onion, preheat the oven to 500°F (260°C) and line a sheet pan with baking parchment. Coarsely chop the onion and toss the pieces in a bowl with the olive oil. Spread the onion on the sheet pan. Sprinkle the pepper and salt over the onion. Roast the onion, stirring every 3 to 5 minutes, until the pieces turn golden brown or even begin to char slightly. This will take 15 to 20 minutes (or sauté them in the oil in a hot skillet; it will take about the same amount of time). Remove the onion from the pan and set aside to cool, then refrigerate until needed.

3   Day 2: Remove the sponge from the refrigerator about 1 hour before making the dough to take off the chill.

4   To make the dough, stir together the flour and yeast in a large mixing bowl (or in the bowl of a large electric mixer such as a Magic Mill or 12- or 20-quart Hobart) with a large metal spoon. Add the water and the sponge and stir until all the ingredients are evenly distributed and the dough forms a coarse ball (or mix on low speed with the dough hook). Let sit for 5 minutes, then add the salt and olive oil and stir (or mix) to distribute. Add half of the grated cheese and all of the chives and scallions. Stir (or mix on low speed) for a few seconds to distribute evenly.

5   Sprinkle flour on the counter and transfer the dough to the counter. Knead the dough (or mix on medium-low speed with the dough hook) for 2 to 4 minutes, or until all the ingredients

are evenly distributed, adding additional flour as needed to make a soft, tacky, but not sticky dough. The dough should pass the windowpane test (page 61), register about 74°F (23°C), and be very supple. Lightly oil a large bowl and transfer the dough to the bowl, rolling it to coat it with oil. Cover the bowl with plastic wrap. After 20 minutes, stretch and fold the dough (see page 59) and return it to the covered bowl. Repeat two more times at 20-minute intervals, each time returning the dough to the covered bowl.

6   Ferment at room temperature for 2 to 3 hours, or until the dough nearly doubles in size.

7   Line 2 sheet pans with baking parchment, mist with spray oil, and dust with flour, semolina, or cornmeal. Dust the counter with flour and transfer the dough to the counter, taking care not to degas the dough. Divide the dough into 2 equal pieces and gently shape them into large *boules*, as shown on page 76. Place a round of dough on each pan. Mist the dough with spray oil and slip each pan into a large food-grade plastic bag or cover loosely with plastic wrap.

8   Place the pans in the refrigerator overnight.

9   Day 3: Remove each pan from the refrigerator 2 hours before you plan to bake (you can hold them in the refrigerator for up to 3 days, baking each pan on a different day, if you wish). Proof the dough for approximately 2 hours at room temperature.

10 Prepare the oven for hearth baking as described on page 97, making sure to have an empty steam pan in place. Preheat the oven to 500°F (260°C). Brush the top of the dough with olive oil and, using your fingertips, make dimples all over the dough, pressing almost to the bottom of the loaf and creating a series of ridges and pockets all over the surface. Sprinkle the remaining cheese evenly over the top of each loaf. Divide the roasted onion pieces into 2 portions and evenly distribute them over the top of the cheese. Let the dough rest for 15 to 30 minutes.

11 Generously dust a peel or the back of a sheet pan with flour, semolina, or cornmeal and very gently transfer the loaves, with or without parchment, to the peel or pan. Slide the loaves onto the baking stone (or bake the loaves directly on the pan). Pour 1 cup hot water into the steam pan and close the door. After 30 seconds, open the door, spray the walls of the oven with water, and close the door. Repeat twice more at 30-second intervals. After the final spray, lower the oven setting to 450°F (232°C) and bake for 20 minutes. Rotate the bread 180 degrees, if necessary, for even baking and continue baking for 15 to 20 minutes. The bread should be golden brown and the cheese melted and brown. The internal temperature of the bread should exceed 195°F (91°C), and the loaf should make a hollow sound when thumped on the bottom. If the cheese seems too brown, but you still need more baking time, cover the top with aluminum foil or a piece of baking parchment to gain a few more baking minutes. You can also turn off the oven and let the residual heat continue baking the bread for an additional 10 minutes (again, covering the tops to protect the cheese from burning).

12 Transfer the finished bread to a rack and let cool for at least 1 hour before slicing or serving.

FINES
5¢ PER DAY
FOR
OVERDUE BOOKS

Roasted Onion and Asiago Miche

RESOURCES

In the years since the publication of the original *The Bread Baker's Apprentice*, the landscape of baking resources has not only grown dramatically but also continues to evolve. Back then, the Internet had just begun, and it took much longer to access anything on the information superhighway. Nowadays, nearly everything we need is just a click away, so I will focus here on just a handful of links and a modest selection of books, fully aware that any list would be out of date before this book hits store shelves. To keep up with what's going on, I advise you to go online to The Bread Baker's Guild of America and to the wealth of bread blogs and other bread sites and to visit bookstores to see what new bread books are available.

BOOKS

I think the most interesting recent development in bread books is in the literary (aka creative nonfiction) genre, where books about the journey, whether in pursuit of baking techniques, authentic traditions, or socially relevant issues such as sustainability, have taken center stage. Here are my current top favorites on an ever-changing list of titles.

Bread, Wine, and Chocolate: The Slow Loss of Foods We Love, by Simran Sethi (New York: HarperOne, 2015)

Cooked: A Natural History of Transformation, by Michael Pollan (New York: Penguin Books, 2014)

From the Wood-Fired Oven: New and Traditional Techniques for Cooking and Baking with Fire, by Richard Miscovich (White River Junction: Vermont: Chelsea Green, 2013)

Grain of Truth: The Real Case For and Against Wheat and Gluten, by Stephen Yafa (New York: Hudson Street Press, 2015)

In Search of the Perfect Loaf: A Home Baker's Odyssey, by Samuel Fromartz (New York: Penguin Books, 2014)

The New Bread Basket: How the New Crop of Grain Growers, Plant Breeders, Millers, Maltsters, Bakers, Brewers, and Local Food Activists Are Redefining Our Daily Loaf, by Amy Halloran (White River Junction, Vermont: Chelsea Green, 2015)

White Bread: A Social History of the Store-Bought Loaf, by Aaron Bobrow-Strain (Boston: Beacon Press, 2012)

Wood-Fired Cooking: Techniques and Recipes for the Grill, Backyard Oven, Fireplace, and Campfire, by Mary Karlin (Berkeley: Ten Speed Press, 2009)

I also highly advise seeking out books by Chad Robertson, Jeffrey Hamelman, Michael Kalanty, Ciril Hitz, Ken Forkish, and Michel Suas, among many other terrific bread authors and educators.

WEBSITES

In the previous edition, I listed a number of flour mills and schools. But, because this list changes almost daily, I suggest that if you are looking for local mills—and I do encourage you to support them—an Internet search is the best way to locate them. That said, I do want to give a shout-out to Carolina Ground, my home state's incarnation of a mill using locally grown grains (carolina-ground.com), and to the wonderful Maine Grains, in Skowhegan, Maine (mainegrains.com). I cite these two operations only because I know them personally and love what they are doing. But I also know there are dozens of similar mills out there, so seek them out.

The following list includes just some of the sites that I have found most useful. Many more quality sites exist, of course. The best way for you to stay current on these constantly changing resources is to attend some of the many regularly held festivals and classes or to join The Bread Baker's Guild of America (which, despite the name, has a growing international membership) or any local organizations that support artisan values.

American Institute of Baking (aibonline.org) For serious technical baking.

Bread Festivals The **Asheville Bread Festival** (ashevillebreadfestival.com), the **Kneading Conference** (kneadingconference.com), and **The Grain Gathering** (thebreadlab.wsu.edu/the-grain-gathering/) offer wonderful opportunities to take classes and to meet leaders in the artisan bread movement. There are similar gatherings in the United Kingdom, such as **The Real Bread Festival** (readlbreadfestival.com), so check them out wherever you live. I call them fantasy camps for serious bread-heads.

Central Milling (centralmilling.com) One of my favorite flour companies, Central Milling is a leading go-to source for organic and specialty flours.

Craftsy (craftsy.com) This site offers online video courses on nearly every subject, including some excellent courses on bread (full disclosure: three courses by me but also by Richard Miscovich, Jeffrey Hamelman, Michael Kalanty, and others). I consider Craftsy a true bargain and the future of online video education.

King Arthur Flour (kingarthurflour.com) A veritable one-stop shop, King Arthur offers classes led by Jeffrey Hamelman and other guest instructors and a website that provides networking, access to tools,

wide-ranging baking information, and all kinds of specialty ingredients.

Lindley Mills (lindleymills.com) One of the leaders of the sprouted and organic flour movement, North Carolina–based Lindley is my source for locally milled sprouted flour.

Northwest Sourdough (northwestsourdough.com) A terrific website for all things sourdough, including recipes and techniques.

Pizza Quest (pizzaquest.com) A shameless plug for a site dedicated to my ongoing search for the perfect pizza. Labeled "a journey of self-discovery through pizza," it features interesting videos, interviews with pizza luminaries, guest columns, recipes, and more.

Proof Box (brodandtaylor.com/folding-proofer/) A pretty cool tool and a lot cheaper than a commercial proof box.

San Francisco Baking Institute (sfbi.com) Great weeklong hands-on classes on many aspects of artisan baking.

Sur la Table (surlatable.com) A great resource for tools and for introductory classes. There used to be only a few bricks-and-mortar locations, but now they are popping up everywhere.

The Baking Steel (bakingsteel.com) The next level beyond baking stones.

The Bread Bakers Guild of America (bbga.org) The single most important resource for serious artisan bakers. The guild provides weekend hands-on master classes throughout the year, as well as access to its full

repository of formulas, technical papers, and training sessions from the past twenty years of the artisan bread movement.

To Your Health Sprouted Flour (healthyflour.com) The largest selection of organically grown sprouted grains and flours. The sprouted cornmeal makes the best corn bread ever.

Whole Grains Council (wholegrainscouncil.org) Leading the education and marketing dialogue for all things related to whole grains.

Finally, a shout-out to all of the culinary schools, including the many community colleges that have developed fine artisan bread programs. We teachers all know that you cannot fully train an apprentice baker in a program that lasts just a few short weeks, but we can give that baker a great start and some important mentoring. The number and quality of culinary educators has grown considerably since the first edition of this book, and I'm proud to be associated with all of these dedicated teachers. What we instructors have learned is that our product is no longer our breads but rather the bakers whom we train. Our success is reflected in the achievements of our students, and just as we have been the resources for them, we look forward to seeing how they become the resources for those who follow after them.

If you have any questions regarding the information or recipes in this book, email me at peter@breadfrontier.com.

Split bread. *See Fendu*
Sponge
  definition of, 55
  regular, 54
  See also Poolish; Starters
Spray oil, 37
Sprouted wheat
  and brown rice bread,
    291–93
  onion and poppy seed
    bialys, 294–96
Stages of bread production
  overview, 49
  stage 1: *mise en place,*
    50–51
  stage 2: mixing, 52–61
  stage 3: primary
    fermentation, 61–70
  stage 4: punching down
    (degassing), 70–72
  stage 5: dividing, 72
  stage 6: rounding, 72–73
  stage 7: benching, 73–74
  stage 8: shaping and
    panning, 74–91
  stage 9: proofing, 92–94
  stage 10: baking, 95–102
  stage 11: cooling, 102–3
  stage 12: storing and
    eating, 103–7
Standard doughs, 44, 46
Starches
  broken down into sugars,
    62, 65–67, 106
  gelatinizing, 98, 99–100,
    102, 106
  left in crumb, 106
Starters
  feeding, 69
  refrigerating or freezing, 69
  rye, 254, 261
  various systems for
    building, 239–42
  See also Barm
Steam, 97–99
Steingarten, Jeffrey, 21, 219
Sticky buns, 150–53
  beyond ultimate, 297–301
  caramel glaze for, 153
  formula, 151–53
  profile, 150
  shaping, 152

time estimates, 150
Stiff doughs, 44, 46
Stirato, 142, 233
Stollen, 268–73
  formula, 270–71, 273
  history of, 268
  holiday bread brûlée
    from, 216
  profile, 268
  shaping, 272
  time estimates, 268
Storing
  barm, 243
  bread, 103–5
  sourdough starter, 69
  whole-wheat flour, 30
  yeast, 31, 64
Straight dough method. *See*
  Direct doughs
Stretch-and-fold technique,
  59, 146
Stromboli, 165
Struan, 195
Suas, Michel, 314
Sugar
  caramelizing, 100–101
  cinnamon, 154
  fermentation and, 62,
    65–67
  weight and volume of, 26
Summer Loaf Festival, 7, 23
Sunflower seed rye, 264–67
  formula, 264, 266–67
  profile, 264
  time estimates, 264
Swedish rye *(limpa),* 274–76
  formula, 274–76
  profile, 274
  time estimates, 274

T

Tabatière (pouch), 83
Tartine Bakery, 291
Tassajara Bakery, 8
Thermometers, 32
Thorne, John, 23
Thumbprint sweet rolls, 150
Tolerance, 73–74
Torpedo roll, 84
Torpedo shape. *See Bâtard*
Total flour weight (TFW),
  39, 40, 41

Total percentage (TP), 40
Training programs, 315
Tsoureki. See Lambropsomo
Tuscan bread, 277–79
  formula, 277–79
  profile, 277
  time estimates, 277
240 factor, 53

U

Umami, 8, 106
Unbleached flour
  preferability of, 29–30
  weight and volume of, 26
Unyeasted doughs, 45

V

Vandergeest, Michael, 216
Vassilopita, 117
Vienna bread, 280–83
  formula, 280–83
  profile, 280
  time estimates, 280
Vienna rolls. *See* Kaiser rolls
Village Bakery, 305
Vinegar washes, 94

W

Walnuts
  beyond ultimate sticky
    buns, 297–301
  bread, cinnamon raisin,
    154–55
  celebration bread,
    cranberry-, 160–62
  christopsomos, 117,
    119–20
  in sourdough breads,
    239, 247
Washes, 94
Water
  absorption of, by dough,
    60, 61
  in the baker's math-
    formula system, 40
  bottled vs. tap, 31
  temperature, 53
  in washes, 94
  weight and volume of,
    26–27
Webbing, 70
Websites, 314–15

Weights, 25–27, 50–51.
  See also Baker's math-
    formula system
Wheat
  berries, 27
  gluten in, 27–28, 60
  strains of, 27–28, 207
  See also Flour; Sprouted
    wheat; Whole wheat
    flour
White breads, 284–87
  formulas, 285–87
  names for, 284
  profile, 284
  pullman, 42–43
  time estimates, 284
White rye flour, 192
Whole wheat bread, 288–90
  formula, 289–90
  profile, 288
  time estimates, 288
Whole wheat flour
  sprouted, 291–92
  storing, 30
  weight and volume of, 26
Wild mushroom
  ciabatta, 148
Windowpane test, 60, 61
Wood-fired baking, 17,
  303–6

Y

Yeast
  fermentation and, 64–70
  minimizing use of, 30, 54,
    64–65
  storing, 31
  types of, 30–31,
    63–64, 211
  weight and volume of, 26
  wild, 67–70

Copyright © 2016 by Peter Reinhart
Photographs copyright © 2001 by Ron Manville

All rights reserved.
Published in the United States by Ten Speed Press, an imprint of the Crown Publishing Group,
a division of Penguin Random House LLC, New York.
www.crownpublishing.com
www.tenspeed.com

Ten Speed Press and the Ten Speed Press colophon are registered trademarks of
Penguin Random House LLC.

Originally published in somewhat different form as *The Bread Baker's Apprentice* in 2001.

The bagel recipe (page 121) originally appeared in *Fine Cooking* (Feb./Mar. 2001); the corn bread and the
cranberry-walnut bread recipes (pages 157 and 160) originally appeared in *Bon Appétit* (Nov. 1999).
The wheat diagram on page 27 is used with permission from the Wheat Foods Council.

All photographs are by Ron Manville with the exception of those noted here: photos on page 4 and
pages 304–306 by Aaron Wehner; photo on end sheet by Yoko Shimada, taken at Union Square Tokyo.

Library of Congress Cataloging-in-Publication Data
Names: Reinhart, Peter, author.
Title: The bread baker's apprentice : mastering the art of extraordinary bread / by Peter Reinhart ;
    photography by Ron Manville.
Description: 15th anniversary edition. First revised edition | Berkeley : Ten Speed Press, [2016] |
    Includes index.
Identifiers: LCCN 2016015576
Subjects: LCSH: Bread.
Classification: LCC TX769 .R4147 2016 | DDC 641.81/5—dc23 LC record available at
    https://lccn.loc.gov/2016015576

Hardcover ISBN: 978-1-60774-865-6
eBook ISBN: 978-1-60774-866-3

Printed in China

Design by Debbie Berne
Jacket design by Chloe Rawlins
Jacket photographs by Ron Manville

10 9 8 7 6 5 4 3 2 1

First Revised Edition